Unmasking Catholicism

Mary Ann's hard work and research helped to clear my mind...I thank her for being faithful to her calling. Her commitment has helped the healing of my soul.

—Esther Ruth
A former Catholic

The questions that this book asks, and its researched conclusions, should cause us all to wake up and understand what we believe, and why we believe it...If you are a seeker of truth, I challenge you to read this book, investigate its conclusions, and decide for yourself the ultimate truth of what you read. I encourage you to delve into each topic for yourself and make a decision based on knowledge, not ignorance.

As a former Catholic, as well as a former member of a religious order, I have a great love for all those sincere and gentle people who, with great faithfulness, have been ardent lovers of the Catholic Church. I am so sorry to have to say that no institution or tradition can replace the truth of the words of our Risen Savior. Each of us has the responsibility to seek His truth, lest we drift away because of our own carelessness.

—Margaret K. Ward
A former Roman Catholic Nun

Today's ecumenical movement has drawn many Protestants and Catholics together under the belief of sharing a common faith, but underlying this movement is a lack of familiarity with the history and official doctrines of the Roman Catholic Church...Many Catholic teachings remain out of view for the average church-goer and mass-attendee. Unmasking Catholicism uncovers and documents a great deal of this information, and presents it in easy-to-understand language.

—Jeff Lawlor
An Evangelical who married a Catholic

Unmasking Catholicism is a well-documented, historical summary of significant "behind-the-scenes" facts that urge the reader to evaluate and further explore. Consistent invitations to check out the sources are made easy, by providing the specific Internet site addresses for referenced articles. Manuscript references, and excellent websites for additional personal study, are also provided. Both Catholics and non-Catholics will be encouraged to examine previously held presuppositions, and to consider the serious issues that are presented, according to God's standards. In itself, the book is not meant to be exhaustive, but a starting point, stimulating examination of any one, or all, of the topics addressed. It is not weighted down with technical details, but divided into sections that are clear and concise. Appendix C presents an easy-to-use Glossary. Difficult information, that needs to be known, is offered in a gracious manner that personally challenges the reader to think critically, in order to responsibly examine and respond to the truth that is presented.

—Mary C. Hertel
A former Roman Catholic Nun

In plain-speaking, simple-to-read language, Mary Ann Collins clarifies the complex issues surrounding the "hot" topics of the day in regard to Roman Catholic apologetics. In doing so, she has provided the Evangelical community with a work that exposes the errors of Roman Catholicism and acts as a wake-up call to those entertaining the notion of abandoning the true gospel of Jesus Christ for the aberrant gospel of Rome.

—Dr. Eric Svendsen, Director
New Testament Research Ministries

Mary Ann has written with passion and compassion, and a real desire to tell the truth and honor God…The gentle approach to proclaiming the truth is in contrast to the harshness of the truths themselves.

—Bob Hellyer
An Evangelical with Catholic friends

Too often, we read apologetic books that serve up the author's opinion. Not so here. Mary Ann Collins is graciously hard-hitting in exposing Roman Catholicism's false doctrines. She also gives an enormous amount of references for you to read for yourself. Anyone with a heart for reaching Catholics should read this from cover to cover.

—Stan Weber
A former Catholic

Unmasking Catholicism

Unmasking Catholicism

What Hides Behind the Modern Public Image?

Mary Ann Collins
A Former Catholic Nun

iUniverse, Inc.
New York Lincoln Shanghai

Unmasking Catholicism
What Hides Behind the Modern Public Image?

All Rights Reserved © 2004 by Mary Ann Collins

No part of this book may be reproduced or transmitted in any form or by any means, graphic, electronic, or mechanical, including photocopying, recording, taping, or by any information storage retrieval system, without the written permission of the publisher.

iUniverse, Inc.

For information address:
iUniverse, Inc.
2021 Pine Lake Road, Suite 100
Lincoln, NE 68512
www.iuniverse.com

Second edition, 2004

You have permission to quote from this book on condition that you do it accurately and fairly. You have permission to copy portions of this book for use in classes on religion.

ISBN: 0-595-31678-6 (Pbk)
ISBN: 0-595-66368-0 (Cloth)

Printed in the United States of America

To Jesus Christ

*Worthy is the Lamb that was slain
to receive power, and riches, and wisdom,
and strength, and honour, and glory, and blessing.*

(Revelation 5:12)

Contents

The Truth xi
Preface xiii
Communication Is Complicated xv
Foreword xvii
A Letter to the Reader xix
Personal Testimony xxi

Hiding
Chapter 1   Hiding Behind Words 3

Popes and Power
Chapter 2   Ecclesiastical Curses 9
Chapter 3   The Council of Trent 13
Chapter 4   Ecumenism 16
Chapter 5   Spiritual Coercion 19
Chapter 6   Hunting "Heretics" 23
Chapter 7   Was the Early Church Roman Catholic? 31
Chapter 8   Forged Documents and Papal Power 45
Chapter 9   The Popes 49
Chapter 10 Imperial Popes 54
Chapter 11 Undermining the Bible 57

Doctrine and Credentials
Chapter 12 New Age Catholicism 69
Chapter 13 False Credentials 85
Chapter 14 According to Tradition 93
Chapter 15 What Is Our Source of Authority? 95
Chapter 16 Faith Versus Works 114
Chapter 17 The Good Thief 118

Chapter 18	The Numbers Game	120
Chapter 19	Devotion to Mary	122
Chapter 20	What Is Idolatry?	136

Practical Problems

Chapter 21	Mandatory Celibacy	141
Chapter 22	Mind Control	144
Chapter 23	Serving Two Masters	150
Chapter 24	Canon Law and Religious Freedom	154
Chapter 25	The Presence of God	157
Chapter 26	Catholic Mysticism	160

The Spirit of Catholicism

Chapter 27	Mixing Paganism with Christianity	173
Chapter 28	Behind the Mask	175
Afterword		179

Appendixes

Appendix A	Eternal Life	185
Appendix B	For Former Catholics	189
Appendix C	Glossary	217
Appendix D	Pictures	243
Appendix E	Testimonies of Former Catholics	249
Appendix F	History and the Catholic Church	251
Appendix G	Doctrinal Issues	261
Appendix H	Books, Videos, and Websites	271

Bibliography and Notes

| Bibliography | 277 |
| Notes | 281 |

The Truth

The truth can stand on its own. That is because Jesus Christ is Truth Incarnate. He said, "I am the way, the truth, and the life". (John 14:6) And Jesus promised that the Holy Spirit would guide us into all truth. (John 16:13)

I started out as a secular humanist. (You can read about it in my Personal Testimony.) My first prayer was, "God, if You're out there, show me." And He did. (It was a gradual process.)

Because of that, I am confident that God will also reveal Himself, and His truth, to readers who ask Him to. Therefore, as you read my book, I encourage you to pray and ask God to show you the truth. Also, pray when you read the writings of other people. The Apostle Paul said:

> "…your faith should not stand in the wisdom of men, but in the power of God." (1 Corinthians 2:5)

I am asking God to show you and me what is true and what is not true. We all need that—all the time.

God is powerful enough to open our eyes when they need to be opened. And He is loving enough to want to do it. The crucial question is, what is more important to us—the truth, or staying in our comfort zone? If we really want the truth, then God will show it to us.

I encourage you to check out my sources for yourself and come to your own conclusions. That is because you and I are responsible for our own lives. We need to base our decisions on our own personal convictions, and not on what somebody else tells us.

Some day, you and I will stand before God, and our works will be tested by fire. The Bible says:

> "Every man's work shall be made manifest: for the day shall declare it, because it shall be revealed by fire; and the fire shall try every man's work of what sort it is. If any man's work abide which he hath built thereupon, he shall receive a reward. If any man's work shall be burned, he shall suffer loss: but he himself shall be saved; yet so as by fire." (1 Corinthians 3:13-15)

When you and I stand before God, we will not be able to give excuses based on what somebody else told us. God expects **us** to test everything. The Bible says:

> "Prove all things; hold fast that which is good." (1 Thessalonians 5:21)

According to "Strong's Concordance," the word "prove" means "to test." We have to test everything ourselves. We cannot depend on "experts" to do it for us. And we cannot hide behind "experts" when we stand before God.

The Bible promises that if we really want wisdom, and we ask God for it, then He will give it to us. The Apostle James says:

> "If any of you lack wisdom, let him ask of God, that giveth to all men liberally, and upbraideth not: and it shall be given him." (James 1:5)

So as you read, please ask God to give you wisdom, and to reveal His truth to you. And ask Him to reveal Himself to you, to help you understand His nature and His character.

May the Lord lead us all into a greater understanding of His truth.

Preface

In the early 1900s, a professional baseball team was accused of cheating. Unfortunately, the accusation proved to be true. A young fan met one of the team's players and, in tears, said: "Say it ain't so, Joe!"

I have often felt that way while doing research about the Catholic Church. But I continued to pursue the research in spite of it, because I wanted to know the truth.

The truth is precious, even when it is distressing. Our God is truth incarnate. (John 14:6; Romans 3:4) God promised that the truth would set us free. (John 8:32)

We all need God's truth. And we all need the strength and courage to live according to it. Keeping the long-range perspective of eternity helps.

Before you read this book, I'd like to share a poem with you.

Jesus, son of David, have mercy on me.

Light my path and guide my way.
Make me faithful, so I'll stay
Close to You throughout the day,
Devoted to You in every way.

Jesus, son of David, have mercy on me.

Open my eyes that I may see
The precious truth that You have for me.
Open my heart to love as You do.
Enable me to be faithful and true.

Jesus, son of David, have mercy on me.

Communication Is Complicated

Judging by some responses from readers, it seems that communication is more complicated than I realized. You can have one thing in mind, and write about it, and you think that you made your point clear. But then you discover that some of your readers thought you were saying something quite different from what you intended to communicate.

People think differently. Our minds work differently. We interpret what we read based on our knowledge and personal experience. If we aren't careful, we may make assumptions, or jump to conclusions.

Please don't read things into this book that I haven't said. For example, when I say that a person did something, all I am doing is describing actions that can be objectively verified. I am not attributing motives to people. I can't do that, because I don't know the people.

This book discusses the Inquisition. What the Inquisitors **did** was bad. However, only God is qualified to judge the **men** who did it. There is a difference between people and their actions. Sometimes people who do bad things are looking for God, but we would never recognize it because of their behavior. The Apostle Paul is an example. Before his conversion, he persecuted Christians to the death.

Another example is a man who interrogated prisoners and tortured them. One of his victims told him about Jesus Christ. (I believe that it may have been Pastor Richard Wurmbrand in Communist Romania. However, I'm not sure, because I read the story years ago.) The torturer became a Christian. It took a lot of courage to do that. He knew that he would probably be put in prison, where he would be at the mercy of men he had tortured.

According to the Bible, people can do bad things, but mistakenly think that they are doing good things. The Bible says:

> "There is a way which seemeth right unto a man, but the end thereof are the ways of death." (Proverbs 14:12)

> "…yea, the time cometh, that whosoever killeth you will think that he doeth God service." (John 16:2)

Only God is qualified to judge people. Our job is to love them. Jesus told us that we should even love our enemies. He said:

"But I say unto you, Love your enemies, bless them that curse you, do good to them that hate you, and pray for them which despitefully use you, and persecute you" (Matthew 5:44; also see Luke 6:27-28)

That is why one of the first articles I wrote was about forgiveness. Once we forgive people, then it becomes easier to love them.

The following story illustrates the complexities of communication. (I don't remember the source of the story.)

A farmer wanted to sell his horse, so he and his son took the horse to market. The farmer rode on the horse, and his son walked beside him. As they were going on their way, they met a man who said to the farmer: "What kind of a father are you, making your son walk while you ride?"

So the farmer got off the horse and let his son ride. As they continued on their way, they met a man who said to the son: "Don't you have any respect for your father? How can you ride while he is walking?"

So the farmer and his son both rode on the horse. Then they met a man who said: "What are you doing to your horse? You can't expect a horse to carry two full-grown men!"

So the farmer and his son got off of the horse and walked beside it. When they got to market, nobody wanted to buy the horse. The people said: "That horse can't be any good if you won't even ride it."

Foreword

Unmasking Catholicism is based on a lot of research. It deals with subjects that are often presented in a complex or academic fashion. I have tried to be simple and straightforward in my presentation, in order to be easily understood by people from a wide variety of backgrounds.

My first edition was 424 pages. That made it expensive. So I deleted some material and made some formatting changes in order to have a shorter, more economical book.

I have thoroughly documented the information in *Unmasking Catholicism*. In addition to using resource books, I have included references to numerous Internet articles. You can study these issues yourself and come to your own conclusions. Much of my information comes from Catholic books and websites. I have also drawn from my personal experience with Catholicism.

This book confronts some touchy issues. I have tried to do so with compassion and objectivity, but sometimes I have had to be blunt in order to make my point clear. Jesus told us to speak the truth in love. I have tried to do that.

I want to make it clear that my problem is with the Catholic **system**—not the people. I love the people. There are many Catholics who really love the Lord. I used to be one of them.

When I was a Catholic, I loved the Lord. I was sincere, devout, and zealous—and confused. My Catholic training and my devotional practices were in conflict with Scripture. However, I did not realize that there was a conflict. It took many long years for me to gradually understand that there was a problem.

Some Practical Issues

You have my permission to quote from *Unmasking Catholicism*, as long as you do it accurately and fairly. You may also copy portions of it to share with your friends, or to use in Bible studies or other classes.

I wanted to give you some good quotations from some papal encyclicals. However, I don't have permission to quote the material. So I paraphrased the information. You can read the encyclicals for yourself, because they are online, and I will tell you how to find them.

I created a website for *Unmasking Catholicism*. You can read the entire book online. You can also contact me through the website. I encourage you to tell your friends about it.

www.UnmaskingCatholicism.com

In quoting from *The Catholic Encyclopedia*, I have used the classic 1914 edition. This edition has two advantages. First, it is online, so you can read the articles for yourself. Second, it was written before the Second Vatican Council (1962-1965).

Following the Second Vatican Council, the Catholic Church placed a strong emphasis on ecumenism. It made many changes in its outward appearance, in order to be more palatable to Protestants. The 1914 edition of *The Catholic Encyclopedia* speaks openly and frankly about some things that more modern editions would probably avoid or water down.

My biography mentions that I left the convent when I was a novice. I never made vows. Some people have asked me why I refer to myself as a "former nun" when I never made vows. According to the 1914 edition of *The Catholic Encyclopedia*, if a novice has been accepted into a religious order (I was), and has been given a habit (I wore it), then he or she is a monk or a nun in the broad sense of the term.

You can buy *Unmasking Catholicism* online at Amazon.com and iUniverse.com. If you have a bookstore, you can get a discount at iUniverse. If your bookstore is online, tell them that you have a "dot-com" store so that you can get a better discount. In order to get the discount, you have to order the book by phone (877-823-9235).

This book gives Internet addresses for many online articles. In addition, there are some things that you can easily find for yourself. Please read the information at the beginning of the Notes. It tells you how to find papal encyclicals, articles from *The Catholic Encyclopedia*, and other helpful things. It also tells you how to locate information in the online edition of *The Catechism of the Catholic Church*. (Originally, I gave Internet addresses for these things, but that made the book too long, so I deleted them. I thought that you would rather search for them yourself than have to pay more money for the book.)

All Scripture quotations are from the King James Version of the Bible.

You can contact me by email (MaryAnnCollins@juno.com).

A Letter to the Reader

Dear Reader,

When I was a Catholic, my Catholic training made it difficult for me to understand who Jesus is and how much He loves me. I loved Jesus, but I was confused because of some of the things I had been taught. If you have the same problem, then I want to help remove some of that confusion, so that you can know Jesus better.

If you are not a Catholic, but you have Catholic friends or family members, then I want to help you understand them better.

If you are considering converting to Catholicism, then I want you to have a better understanding of what is involved. You need to make your own decision, based on your own personal convictions. But it would be good to be well informed before you decide.

In this book I will sometimes tell about people who did destructive things, or who said things that are not correct. I am not judging those people. Only God knows their hearts. I am just giving you some historical facts.

I believe that there are two kinds of people in this world—those who know Jesus Christ, and those who have the potential to know Him. We should love people in the first group because they are our brothers and sisters in Christ. And we should love people in the second group because they need to see the love of God in us and through us. It is the goodness of God that leads people to repentance. (Romans 2:4) When Christians are loving, it demonstrates God's goodness.

An example of this is Corrie ten Boom, a Dutch woman whose family hid Jews during the Second World War. A man betrayed her family and reported them to the Nazis. Corrie's father died in prison. Corrie and her sister Betsie were sent to a death camp. Betsie died there but Corrie survived. Corrie found out that the man who had betrayed her family was in prison and was scheduled to be executed. She wrote to that man. She told him that she forgave him, and she told him about Jesus. He wrote back to Corrie saying that if she could forgive him after what he had done, then he wanted to know her God.

I hope that this book will be a blessing to you. If you disagree with me, that's OK. We don't have to agree. But we should love and respect one another.

The Bible says that we need to test **everything** against Scripture. Therefore, as you read this book—or any other book—I encourage you to ask

God to give you His perspective about the things that you are reading. We all need to habitually seek God for His guidance.

I have a website with some Biblically-based articles whose purpose is to strengthen and encourage people. I wanted to include some of them in this book, because we live in stressful times, and we all need encouragement. However, that would have made the book too long. But you can read those articles online.

www.NewLifeWithChrist.com

May the Lord bless you and guide you. And may He give you a revelation of how much He loves you.

Mary Ann Collins
March 22, 2004

Personal Testimony

I was raised a secular humanist. When I went to college, I started investigating Catholicism. After two years of intense study, I became a Catholic.

I was zealous. I kept studying the lives of the saints and the teachings of various prominent Catholics. I often went to Mass several times a week, and sometimes every day. I transferred to a Catholic college in order to take classes in religion.

I entered the convent for several reasons. I wanted to be closer to God and to serve Him more wholeheartedly. I wanted to learn more about God and to spend my life being more intensely focused on Him. And I believed that God wanted me to be a nun.

The convent was not a healthy place, either spiritually or emotionally. Our self-imposed penances, and our other attempts to make ourselves more holy, actually encouraged self-righteousness. We were not allowed to have friendships, or to be close to any human being. We were supposed to be emotionally detached. We were taught to love people in a detached, impersonal way.

This is not Biblical. God said: "It is not good for man to be alone." He was referring to more than just marriage. The Bible encourages close relationships.

Our example of the perfect human being is Jesus. He was unmarried, but he was not at all emotionally detached. He wept publicly. His heart was "moved with compassion." He made many statements that showed strong emotions. He had special friends (Peter, James, and John) and a "best friend" (John).

I left the convent after two years, before making vows. I was still a novice, undergoing training and "spiritual formation" in preparation for making vows.

After I left the convent, I was frustrated with the local Catholic churches. I did not see strong faith or zeal for God. Some of the priests preached things that were so contrary to Scripture that they were acutely distressing to me.

My parents had become Christians. They were members of a Protestant church. I visited their church and discovered that I was hungry for the Bible-based teaching. For years, I attended two services on Sundays: early morning Mass, followed by the service at my parents' church.

Eventually, I left the Catholic Church and joined my parents' church. And I finally found the personal relationship with God that I had been looking for all of my life.

I used to be all tied up in rules, regulations, and rituals. But now I have found a wonderful, vibrant, personal relationship with the Creator of the universe, who loves me. And with Jesus Christ, who loves me so much that He died for me. And He has put a new song in my heart:

> *Your Word brings life to save my soul.*
> *Your Truth brings light to make me whole.*
>
> *Your perfect love casts out my fears,*
> *Comforts me, and dries my tears.*
> *I'm in the shadow of Your wings*
> *Where you teach my heart to sing.*
>
> *Safe and secure from all alarm,*
> *Your faithful love keeps me from harm.*
>
> *I will bless You all my days.*
> *You fill my heart with songs of praise.*

Hiding

Chapter 1

Hiding Behind Words

What happens if two people are talking, and they use the same vocabulary, but they have a different dictionary? What if the same word means quite different things to them?

They may think that they understand one another when, in reality, they have no idea of what the other person is thinking. They may think that they are in agreement about something when they actually disagree.

This can happen between Catholics and Protestants. For example, let's look at the word "grace." According to the Bible, salvation cannot be earned. The Apostle Paul said:

> "For by grace are ye saved through faith; and that not of yourselves: it is the gift of God: Not of works, lest any man should boast." (Ephesians 2:8-9)

[handwritten note: See James 1]

> "Not by works of righteousness which we have done, but according to his mercy he saved us…" (Titus 3:5)

However, according to Catholic doctrine, if people do good works, and they fulfill certain specified requirements, then they can **merit** a "divine reward" from God.[1] This is a doctrine of earning spiritual things by doing good works.

The liturgical ritual for baptizing infants includes a prayer asking God to give grace to the water in the baptismal font (the water that will be used to sprinkle the infant).[2] So for Catholics, "grace" is something that can be given to inanimate objects, such as water.

When I was a Catholic, this made sense to me, because I was used to accepting whatever the priest said without question. Now that I am a Protestant, and I have some understanding of Scripture, the idea is incomprehensible.

In the Bible, grace seems to be a simple thing. But somehow the Catholic Church makes it seem complicated and mystifying. The *Pocket Catholic Dictionary* has a complex, technical, three-paragraph definition of "grace" that ends by recommending that the reader also look at entries for actual grace, efficacious grace, habitual grace, justifying grace, sacramental grace, sanctifying grace, and sufficient grace. It also has entries for "baptismal graces" and "state of grace."[3]

Here is an example of how Protestants can think that they understand Catholicism, when they really don't.

A Catholic priest wrote to me saying that the Catholic Church teaches that we are saved by grace through faith in Jesus Christ. He failed to mention something. It teaches that we are saved by grace through faith in Jesus Christ—**PLUS** being baptized, going to Mass on Sundays, receiving communion at least once a year, going to confession at least once a year, believing the official doctrines of the Catholic Church, and dying in a state of grace. (In America, Mass on Saturdays can be substituted for Mass on Sundays.)

Until the Second Vatican Council (1962-1965), popes openly declared that there is no salvation apart from the Pope.[4] That involves more than faith in Jesus Christ.

Modern popes taught that salvation comes through Mary.[5] According to the *Catechism of the Catholic Church*, Mary has a "saving office" and her intercession brings us our salvation.[6] In 1993, Pope John Paul II said that Mary "obtains for us divine mercy."[7]

Words can cause confusion. For example, Catholic theologians speak of three degrees of homage, which have Latin words. *Latria* is the kind of worship that is due to God alone. *Dulia* is appropriate for honoring the saints. *Hyperdulia* is appropriate for honoring Mary. It is higher than *dulia*, but not *latria*. Because of these three words, Catholic theologians say that Catholics do not worship Mary.

However, in the real world, these theological distinctions don't work. Most Catholics have never heard of these words. Of those who have, how many know how to apply them in practical ways? Catholics are not taught how to engage in *hyperdulia* without crossing a line that results in actually practicing *latria* towards Mary without realizing it.

When I was a Catholic, sometimes people would ask me about praying to Mary and the saints. I used to say that I was just asking them to pray for me, like I would ask a friend. But there is a difference. When I talk to my friends, I am talking to people who are alive—not people who have died. The Bible tells us that we should not communicate with dead people, that we should not seek the dead on behalf of the living. (Isaiah 8:19; Deuteronomy 18:11-12)

So what I said was misleading. However, I didn't realize it at the time.

Some ways of using words can result in statements that are technically correct, but the result is misleading. Here is an example.

For centuries, the Catholic Church would not allow the Bible to be translated into English. It was only available in Latin.

A Catholic apologist told me that this made no difference, because the common people were illiterate. They were unable to read and write. They would not have been able to read the Bible even if it had been available in English.

However, during Mass, the priests read passages from Scripture **out loud**. Even people who can't read are able to understand what they hear. If the Scripture passages had been read in English, then the people would have understood them.

When the Bible was finally translated into English, it was kept in a church. All day long, men took turns reading the Bible out loud, while crowds of people listened.[8]

Practical Consequences of Misleading Vocabulary

I have an Evangelical friend who has seriously studied Catholicism. He had an urgent, practical need for the information, because he married a Catholic woman.

At the time that he married her, he believed that Catholicism was "just another valid form of Christianity." He attended Mass with his wife on Sundays. After a while, he began to feel that something was wrong. Then he started investigating Catholicism. This is what my friend Jeff has to say:

> "Today's ecumenical movement draws many Protestants and Roman Catholics together, because they believe that they share a common faith. The Protestants believe that there are outward differences, but the faith is the same. The Catholics believe that their faith is Biblical, and that Protestants are just separated brothers and sisters who need the Mother Church in order to experience the fullness of the faith. When you look into it, though, you'll find that the majority of Protestants and Catholics are unfamiliar with the history and official doctrines of the Roman Catholic Church, and, indeed, unfamiliar with the Bible. They prefer to get along with one another in matters of faith, rather than to investigate, understand, and contend for the Gospel of Christ, as laid out in the Bible, and to compare it with official Catholic doctrine. As a result, many Roman Catholic teachings remain out of view for the average church-goer and mass-attendee. Those who do earnestly investigate Catholicism, and compare it with the Bible, find that **some of the language appears to be the same, but the definitions, beliefs, applications, and perspectives behind this language are**

anything but the same. They also find a multitude of additional layers and dimensions to Roman Catholicism that they would never have imagined." (Jeff Lawlor, used by permission. Emphasis added.)

In Jeff's case, the situation worked out. His wife became an Evangelical Christian. Jeff and his wife are in agreement about how to raise children, where to go to church, and how to practice their religion in their home.

I have corresponded with many suffering Christians whose situation did not work out well. After they married a Catholic, they discovered that Catholicism is radically different from what they thought it was. Because of that, they are no longer able to attend Mass, or to instruct their children in the Catholic faith. They have discussed their problem with their Catholic spouse, but their spouse remains loyal to the Catholic Church. As a result, their home is full of conflict and confusion, and their children suffer because of it.

Because these people didn't understand the differences between Catholicism and Protestantism back when they were courting, they and their children are suffering today. Verbal confusion can result in serious practical consequences.

Popes and Power

Chapter 2

Ecclesiastical Curses

According to the 1914 edition of *The Catholic Encyclopedia*, there is a solemn, written ritual that enables the Pope to put ecclesiastical curses (anathemas) on people. The article in *The Catholic Encyclopedia* describes the ritual in detail, including extensive quotations from it. (You can read this article online.)[1]

In pronouncing the anathema, the Pope wears special vestments. He is assisted by twelve priests who hold lighted candles. Calling on the name of God, the Pope pronounces a solemn, ecclesiastical curse. He ends by pronouncing the "sentence" and declaring that the anathematized person is condemned to Hell with Satan. The priests reply: "*Fiat!*" (Let it be done!) and throw down their candles.

As we will see, the Catholic Church considers heresy (disagreement with Catholic doctrine) to be a crime. The Council of Trent declared that any person who disagrees with even one of its doctrinal statements is thereby automatically anathematized.

When the Pope pronounces an anathema, he is said to be passing sentence on a criminal.

The Catholic Encyclopedia says that the anathema ritual is deliberately calculated to terrify the "criminal" and cause him to repent (in other words, to unconditionally submit to the Catholic Church).

For those whose crime is heresy, repentance means renouncing everything that they have said or done that conflicts with Catholic doctrine. In other words, they have to renounce their own conscience and discernment, and the conclusions that they reached in their best efforts to understand Biblical principles. They are required to submit their minds and wills unconditionally to every official doctrinal declaration of the Catholic Church. As we will see, modern Canon Law says that this unquestioning submission of the mind and will is required.

The Catholic Encyclopedia states that a person's religious beliefs should not be subject to his or her "free private judgment." Because religious beliefs are important, and individuals can make mistakes, Rome says that religious beliefs should be determined by the Catholic Church, rather than by individuals. This attitude is consistent with the spirit behind anathematizing people. (You can read about this online.)[2]

The new *Code of Canon Law* was published by the authority of Pope John Paul II in 1983. It claims to be inspired by the Second Vatican Council (1962-1965) and to put its reforms into concrete form. According to Canon 752, whenever the Pope or the college of bishops makes a declaration concerning faith or morals, "the Christian faithful" are **required** to submit their intellect and will to it. Furthermore, they are required to avoid anything that disagrees with it. (The new *Code of Canon Law* is online. You can read this law for yourself.)[3]

So it is against Roman Catholic Canon Law for "the Christian faithful" to doubt or deny or dispute any Catholic doctrine. If something is against the law, then any person who does it commits a crime. In other words, he or she is a criminal. Canon Law has punishments for such criminals. It refers to these punishments as "a just penalty." This is a broad term that gives immense discretion to the person passing judgment. During the Inquisition and the Protestant Reformation, "just penalties" for disagreeing with Catholic doctrine included imprisonment, torture, confiscation of property, and being burned at the stake.

Enforcement

According to Canon 1311, The Catholic Church has the right to **coerce** "the Christian faithful" who do things contrary to Canon Law. Canon 1312 says that penal sanctions can include depriving people of spiritual goods (such as the sacraments) and temporal goods (things that people need for life on this earth). During the Protestant Reformation, the Catholic Church penalized Protestants by depriving them of their property, their freedom, and their life.[4]

In the case of John Hus, the Catholic Church did more than that. Hus was a Catholic priest who lived in the fifteenth century. He was burned at the stake for "heresy" because he believed the Bible more than he believed the Pope. Before Hus was burned, an archbishop and six bishops subjected him to a "ceremony of degradation." He was dressed in priest's vestments, and a chalice was put in his hands. (A chalice is a large goblet that is used for wine during Mass.) He was taken to the high altar, as if he was going to say Mass. Then the bishops took the chalice from him, and stripped him of his vestments, one piece at a time. Each time that they removed something, they pronounced a solemn curse over him. Then they placed an imitation of a bishop's miter on his head. It had three demons painted on it.

When the the archbishop and the bishops placed the mock miter on Hus' head, they said: "We commit your soul to the devil." Hus looked up to Heaven and said: "And I commit it to the most merciful Lord Jesus Christ." Hus began singing to the Lord. As the flames started to burn him, he kept on singing. You would expect that a man who was being burned alive would be screaming because of the pain. But Hus died singing.[5] (You can read about it online.)

The Catholic Church has never renounced its past practice of killing people that it considers to be heretics. On the contrary, the Office of the Inquisition still exists. It is part of the Roman Curia (the group of men who govern the Catholic Church). In 1965, its name was changed to The Congregation for the Doctrine of the Faith. It is headed by Cardinal Ratzinger. (This information is online.)[6]

On December 8, 1854, Pope Pius IX declared the dogma of the Immaculate Conception of Mary. This says that Mary was conceived without the influence of original sin (the sin resulting from the disobedience of Adam and Eve).

After defining the dogma, the Pope said that if any person "dares" to disagree with his declaration, then that person shipwrecks his or her faith, and is cut off from the Catholic Church. The Pope declared that such people are "condemned." He said that if any person says, or writes, or in any other way outwardly expresses the "errors" in his or her heart, then that person becomes subject to punishment. (Papal encyclicals are online. They are easy to find. The beginning of the Notes tells you how.)[7]

The Pope's reference to punishment is significant, because a man had been executed for heresy 28 years before this papal bull was issued. In 1826, a Spanish schoolmaster was hanged because he substituted the phrase "Praise be to God" in place of *"Ave Maria"* ("Hail Mary") during school prayers.[8]

On November 1, 1950, Pope Pius XII issued a papal bull defining the dogma of the Assumption of Mary. This says that Mary was taken bodily up into Heaven.

The Pope ended by saying that it is forbidden for any person to oppose his declaration, or to say anything contrary to it. He said that any person who attempts to do so will incur the wrath of God, and the wrath of the Apostles Peter and Paul.)[9]

Although this papal bull doesn't openly threaten punishment, it still implies the possibility of some form of punishment. The difference in tone between the encyclicals of 1854 and 1950 reflects the decrease in power of the Catholic Church. In 1854, a man had recently been executed for heresy. In 1950, the political power of the Catholic Church had decreased. By 1950, the kind of language that was used in the 1854 encyclical would not have created a good image.

Conclusion

The Roman Catholic Church believes that the Pope has the power and the authority to damn people to Hell. The anathema ritual demonstrates this belief.

Many Catholics deny this, saying that only God can condemn people to Hell. But look at the ritual of the anathema, as described in *The Catholic Encyclopedia*. And look at the following solemn declaration of excommunication, which was pronounced by Pope Innocent III:

"We excommunicate, anathematize, curse and damn him…" [10]

The anathema ritual and its wording are a demonstration that popes believed that they could consign people to Hell. The fear that the anathema produced is a demonstration that other people also believed it. So is the power that anathemas gave the popes over civil rulers. (See the chapter, "Spiritual Coercion.")

The anathema ritual is still on the books, so we must assume that modern popes still believe that they can do this. The ritual was formulated by Pope Zachary, who reigned from 741 to 752. He is a canonized saint. (This is online.)[11]

Chapter 3

The Council of Trent

The Council of Trent anathematized every Christian who disagrees with any detail of Catholic doctrine. These anathemas have never been canceled. An anathema means that the Catholic Church has placed someone under a solemn, ecclesiastical curse. (See the chapter, "Ecclesiastical Curses.")

The Council of Trent (1545-1564) was the Roman Catholic Church's response to the Protestant Reformation. It denounced every single doctrine that was proposed by the Protestant Reformers. It declared that any person who believes even one of these doctrines is "anathema" (anathematized by the Catholic Church).

It also defined Catholic doctrines, detail by detail, and declared that anybody who denies even one of these details is anathema. These doctrines include: the authority of the Pope, the practice of indulgences, veneration of Mary and the saints, the use of statues and other "sacred images," and the belief that Jesus Christ is literally and fully present (body, blood, soul, and divinity) in every crumb of consecrated bread and every drop of consecrated wine. So the Council of Trent anathematized all Protestants.

There are 125 anathemas. These are doctrinal declarations of the Council of Trent that are sandwiched between two statements. The opening statement is: "If any man…" The closing statement is: "…let him be anathema." The doctrinal statements and the anathemas are so interwoven that they cannot be separated.

I don't have permission to use quotations from the Council of Trent, so I will use a statement about a well-known children's book as an example. Applying the language of the Council of Trent to *Mother Goose Rhymes*, you could say: "If any man does not believe that the cow jumped over the moon, let him be anathema."

You can read the declarations of the Council of Trent for yourself. They were published as a book. It can be ordered through regular bookstores. You can also read it online. (The Notes give Internet addresses.)[1]

Official Modern Endorsement of the Council of Trent

The declarations and anathemas of the Council of Trent have never been revoked. On the contrary, the decrees of the Council of Trent are confirmed by both the Second Vatican Council (1962-1965) and the official *Catechism of the Catholic Church* (1992).

The documents of the Second Vatican Council cite the Council of Trent as an authority for doctrinal statements, both in the text and in the notes. The *Dogmatic Constitution on the Church* states that the Second Vatican Council "proposes again the decrees of" three previous councils, one of which is the Council of Trent.[2] The *Decree on the Training of Priests* says that the Second Vatican Council continued the work of the Council of Trent.[3] (You can read these documents online.)

When the Second Vatican Council began, Pope John XXIII said that he accepted what the Council of Trent declares about justification. (It declares that any person who believes that we are saved by faith alone is anathema.) He also confirmed all past anathemas against "false doctrine"—in other words, the Protestant doctrines that were condemned by the Council of Trent. Every Catholic clergyman who participated in the Council signed a document affirming the declarations of the Council of Trent. (This is online.)[4]

The *Catechism of the Catholic Church* was written for the purpose of summarizing the essential and basic teachings of the Roman Catholic Church. It was approved by Pope John Paul II in 1992. It has been published in many languages. The English translation was released in 1994. The *Catechism* has numbered paragraphs. Therefore, statements can be located in any language, and in any edition of the book.

The Council of Trent is mentioned in 75 paragraphs of the *Catechism of the Catholic Church*. It is always mentioned in a positive, authoritative way. Some paragraphs mention it two or three times. Paragraph 9 says that the Council of Trent was the origin of Catholic catechisms. The other 74 paragraphs that mention the Council of Trent cite it as an authoritative source that supports their doctrinal statements. (You can verify this online. The Note tells how.)[5]

The Anathemas of the Council of Trent Cannot Be Revoked

According to the *Catechism of the Catholic Church*, the Catholic doctrine of infallibility applies not only to the Pope, but also to Catholic Church Councils. This includes the Council of Trent. (Information about this is online.)[6]

As a result, the official statements of the Council of Trent are considered to be infallible. This means that they cannot be changed. Therefore, the anathemas of the Council of Trent cannot be revoked.

The Catholic Church may find it expedient not to call people's attention to these anathemas, but it cannot revoke them.

Both the Second Vatican Council and the *Catechism of the Catholic Church* confirm the decrees of the Council of Trent. These decrees contain the anathemas. So the anathemas are part of the doctrinal package, whether or not the Catholic Church chooses to talk about them.

Chapter 4
Ecumenism

There is a hidden agenda behind ecumenism. As we shall see, official Roman Catholic documents from the Second Vatican Council show that the purpose of ecumenism is to bring Protestants into the Roman Catholic Church.

Vatican II and Ecumenism

The Second Vatican Council (1962-1965) wrote 16 official documents. It also gave some groups of experts the task of working out the details of how to apply the principles and directives of the Council. These groups of men wrote official "post conciliar" documents to more fully elaborate what had been written by the Council. The conciliar and post conciliar documents are published together in a two-volume work.

The Council's *Decree on Ecumenism* states that ecumenical activity cannot result in changing any aspect of the Catholic faith. (You can read this online.)[1] This foundational principle is reflected in the post conciliar documents dealing with ecumenism.

For example, Post Conciliar Document No. 42 says that the purpose of ecumenism is to transform the thinking and behavior of Christians who are not Catholics, so that eventually all Christians will be united in one Church. It states that unity means being "in the Catholic Church." (This is online.)[2]

In other words, "unity" means that Protestants and Orthodox Christians will become Roman Catholics.

From the Vatican's perspective, the goal of ecumenism is to undo both the Protestant Reformation and the "Great Schism" (the separation of the Orthodox Christians from the Roman Catholic Church). Rome wants her "separated brethren" to come back under the authority of the Pope.

In order to make Catholicism more palatable for Protestants, the Catholic Church made some changes in appearance. The priest faced the people, instead of having his back to them. The Mass was said in the language of the people, instead of Latin. Statues became less prominent in Catholic churches.

Because of these changes, Protestants could feel more comfortable attending Mass. There no longer seemed to be a cultural gulf between Protestants and Catholics.

The fasting requirements were relaxed. Except for special days during Lent, Catholics were allowed to eat meat on Fridays. They could now eat with their Protestant friends on Fridays, without requiring special food (fish or a vegetarian meal). Removing this cultural gap got rid of a barrier between Catholics and Protestants, thereby encouraging ecumenism.

However, in spite of all these changes in surface appearance, official Catholic documents show that the Catholic Church really has not changed much.

There is an old saying, *semper eadem* ("always the same"). It means that Rome never changes. She may change her image for strategic reasons, but behind the scenes, she remains essentially the same.

The following chapters will show some of the areas in which the Catholic Church's new, public image is quite different from what is said in its official documents.

Inconsistency

The Council of Trent anathematized every Christian who disagrees with any detail of Catholic doctrine. These anathemas have never been canceled. (See the chapters, "Ecclesiastical Curses" and "The Council of Trent.")

The modern, ecumenical approach of reaching out in a friendly, respectful way to Protestants ("separated brethren") seems inconsistent with the anathemas of the Council of Trent.

In 1302, Pope Boniface VIII declared that no person can be saved unless he or she is subject to the Pope.[3] (Papal encyclicals are online. They are easy to find.)

In 1849, and again in 1863, Pope Pius IX declared that no person can be saved outside of the Roman Catholic Church.[4]

According to the Catholic doctrine of infallibility, these are infallible statements. (This is online.)[5] Therefore, they cannot be reversed.

Freedom of religion is opposed by modern Canon Law (1983). Canon 1366 says that parents are to be punished if they allow their children to instructed in, or baptized in, a "non-Catholic religion." (You can read this law online.)[6] The reference to baptism shows that this refers to Christians.

Protestants and Orthodox Christians are "non-Catholics." During the Protestant Reformation, Protestants were punished for their "non-Catholic religion." Penalties included imprisonment, torture, and being burned at the stake. (See the chapter, "Hunting 'Heretics.'")

The modern Catholic approach to ecumenism seems inconsistent with the doctrine that there is no salvation outside of the Roman Catholic Church. It also seems inconsistent with modern Canon Law.

The Pope Speaks

In his opening speech to the Second Vatican Council (1962), Pope John XXIII said that the Catholic Church has always opposed "errors" (disagreement with Catholic doctrine). He said that in the past, the Catholic Church often condemned "errors" with great severity, but now it "prefers" to use mercy rather than severity. The Pope said that the Catholic Church is presently dealing with "errors" by doctrinal debate rather than by "condemnations." (You can read his speech online.)[7]

Rome's present preference for a gentler approach to people who disagree with Catholic doctrine may explain the apparent discrepancy between the Council of Trent and ecumenism.

Conclusion

The Catholic Church is presently engaging in ecumenical dialog with Protestants, calling them "separated brethren" and speaking as if it respects their beliefs. But at the same time, behind the scenes, official Catholic documents declare that Protestants are damned to Hell because of their beliefs.

According to documents from the Second Vatican Council, the purpose of ecumenism is to get Protestants to become Catholics. This stragegy is working. Since 1993, over 480 Protestant pastors have converted to Catholicism. Hundreds more are seriously considering it. The rate of conversions per year is increasing.[8]

An entire Protestant church converted to Catholicism.[9] In addition, an Evangelical church seems to be heading in that direction. Their last retreat was led by a Catholic priest, and their pastor is going to that priest for "spiritual direction."[10]

Chapter 5

Spiritual Coercion

Pope Innocent III reigned from 1198 to 1216. He excommunicated Markward of Anweiler. In passing the sentence of excommunication, Innocent declared that he anathematized Markward, cursed him, and damned him to Hell.[1]

Innocent and other popes ruled over kings, emperors, and noblemen by using the "spiritual weapons" of excommunication and interdict. Excommunicated people are cut off from the Catholic Church and from the sacraments. Catholics who are placed under interdict remain members of the Catholic Church, but most of the sacraments are denied to them. (You can read this online.)[2]

These "weapons" were effective, because Roman Catholics believed that the Pope had the power to deprive them of the grace that they needed in order to get to Heaven. Catholics believed that the Catholic Church and the sacraments were necessary for salvation. Therefore, a sentence of excommunication was seen as being a sentence to Hell. It had a powerful impact on individuals and on entire nations.

I live in America. In our modern, western society, we are used to thinking independently. It is not unusual for Catholics to believe some Catholic doctrines, but to disbelieve (or just ignore) others. (According to Catholic doctrine, this approach is heretical—but most "cafeteria Catholics" probably don't realize that.) Therefore, it may be difficult for us to understand the terror caused by excommunication, and the power that this "spiritual weapon" gave to the popes.

In 1014, Pope Leo IX excommunicated the entire Orthodox Church. This means that, according to Catholic theology, every single Orthodox priest, nun, layman, and laywoman was damned to Hell unless he or she repented and submitted to the Catholic Pope. "Infallible" popes and "infallible" Catholic Church councils have declared that there is no salvation apart from the Roman Catholic Church. (Information is online.)[3]

In 1965, Pope Paul VI removed that excommunication. I'm grateful that he removed it. However, that does not change the fact that, for 951 years, every single Orthodox Christian lived and died under that curse.

Interdicts are applied to large groups of people, including entire nations. Baptism and the "last rites" (extreme unction) are allowed, but all other sacraments are forbidden. Church services and Christian burial are also forbidden. If the Pope is in conflict with a secular ruler, then he can put the ruler's subjects under interdict, in order to get them to put pressure on their ruler. It works. The ruler's Catholic subjects become desperate to get the interdict removed. They put pressure on their ruler, to get him to submit to the Pope, so that the Pope will remove the interdict.[4]

It works. But at what price? What happens to the innocent people who had nothing to do with the conflict between their ruler and the Pope? They are allowed to receive the "last rites," but that only works for people who know that they are dying. What about people who die suddenly and unexpectedly? Because of the interdict, they were not able to have a priest absolve them of their sins. According to Catholic doctrine, if they have committed a mortal sin, and they have not had that sin be absolved by a priest, then they will go to Hell.

So in effect, popes were willing to send people to Hell, in order to get political power over secular rulers. Whether or not they actually had the power to send people to Hell is beside the point. They thought that they had the power, and they were willing to use it.

Interdicts were used primarily during the Middle Ages. However, as we will see, the interdict was used as recently as 1962.

Pope Innocent III (1198-1216) used interdicts, and the threat of interdicts, 85 times, in order to force secular rulers to submit to him. He put entire nations unter interdict. He was so successful that kings declared that the Pope was their feudal lord. For example, King John of England became the vassal of the Pope and paid him an annual tribute. Innocent declared that the English *Magna Carta* was immoral. The Pope declared it to be null and void, and he excommunicated everyone who supported it. (You can read about this online.)[5] The *Magna Carta* established the principle that kings are not above the law. It was the beginning of democracy in England. It also influenced the men who wrote the Constitution of the United States.

Innocent III wore clothes covered with gold and jewels. He made kings and cardinals kiss his foot. (You can read about this online.)[6] In the encyclical, *Deliberatio*, Innocent declared that kings and princes were subject to him.[7] (Papal encyclicals are online. They are easy to find.)

Pope Boniface VIII reigned from 1294 to 1303. On November 18, 1302, he issued the encyclical, *Unam Sanctam*, in which he declared that the Pope has both spiritual and worldly power. Boniface declared that there is no salvation apart from submission to the Pope.[8]

One of the most famous incidents of excommunication occurred when Pope Gregory VII excommunicated the Holy Roman Emperor, Henry IV. In order to receive forgiveness from the Pope, and have the excommunication be removed, the Emperor had to spend three days repenting in front of the castle where the Pope was staying. It was bitter cold (January 1077). Henry spent most of his time kneeling in the ice and snow, weeping and pleading for forgiveness. When Pope Gregory finally allowed Emperor Henry to come into the castle, he publicly humiliated him. (This is online.)[9]

Pope Gregory VII declared that the Pope has the right to depose kings and emperors, to make laws, and to require secular rulers to kiss his foot. He said that nobody has the right to judge the Pope.[10]

Excommunication and interdicts are not ancient history. The authority, and the procedure for exercising it, exist today. Pope John Paul II issued a new edition of Roman Catholic Canon Law in 1983. (Canon Law is a collection of laws that govern the Catholic Church.) Canons 1331 and 1332 deal with punishments for people who have been excommunicated or placed under interdict. Canons 1364 to 1399 deal with penalties for "delicts" (offenses against Canon Law). These penalties include being excommunicated or placed under interdict. (You can read these laws online.)[11]

Coercing Voters in 1962

A modern example of spiritual coercion is the 1962 election in Malta (a small island in the Mediterranean Sea, near Sicily).

Dr. Mark F. Montebello is a Catholic priest from the Island of Malta. He wrote a series of three articles called, "Civil Rights in Malta's Post-Colonial Age." The third article describes how the Archbishop of Malta required Malta's Catholic priests to help him prevent Catholics from voting for Mintoff (the Labor Party candidate) in Malta's 1962 election.

According to Dr. Montebello, the Archbishop instructed the priests to use the sacrament of confession to coerce the consciences of Catholic voters. He ordered the priests to threaten people with eternal damnation. He also endorsed literature that contained "medieval intimidations" (the kind of spiritual coercion that was used during the Middle Ages). (You can read about this online.)[12]

The Catholic Church officially declared that it was a mortal sin to vote for Mintoff. Priests who failed to cooperate were silenced. Some of them were forced to leave Malta and become missionaries in foreign countries. (This information is online.)[13]

Maltese Catholics who voted for Mintoff were placed under interdict. It became a mortal sin to vote for Mintoff. Catholics who voted for Mintoff were banned from church life and from the sacraments. They were denied a Christian burial. Instead, they were buried in a section of the cemetery that was called "the rubbish dump," implying that the soul of the dead person was damned. A citizen of Malta recounts:

> "The Catholic Church used the pulpit, the confessional, the media and even public meetings in its vigorous campaign. I asked my father about his experience. When he went to confession, the priest asked him how he intended to vote in the general election and refused to give him absolution." (This quotation is from an online article.)[14]

The Catholic Church categorizes sins as either mortal sins (the most serious kind) or venial sins (which are considered to be less serious).[15] According to Catholic doctrine, if a person dies in a state of mortal sin, then he or she is damned to Hell.[16] In order for a mortal sin to be forgiven, a Catholic must go to confession and receive absolution from a priest.[17] However, if Catholics are under interdict, then they are not allowed to receive the sacraments, and therefore they cannot receive absolution for their sins. (This information is online. See Notes 15 to 17.)

So what happened to Maltese Catholics who voted for Mintoff? According to the Catholic Church, they committed a mortal sin when they voted for Mintoff. As a result of voting for Mintoff, they were placed under interdict. Therefore, they could not have that mortal sin be absolved by a Catholic priest. As a result, they probably died (or will die) in a state of mortal sin. According to Catholic doctrine, people who die in a state of mortal sin go to Hell.

There is one exception. Catholics who are under interdict are allowed to receive the "last rites." However, in order to do this, several things have to happen. They must be in imminent danger of dying, so that they qualify to receive the "last rites." In spite of being near death, they must be in good enough shape mentally and physically to be able to look for a priest (or to ask friends or family members to look for a priest). They must be able to find a priest who is willing to help them. And the priest must arrive in time to give them the "last rites" before they die. According to Catholic doctrine, this means the difference between spending eternity in Heaven or Hell.

Chapter 6

Hunting "Heretics"

Augustine lived from 354 to 430 A.D. He had a vision of an ideal society, with the Roman Catholic Church at its center, governing all aspects of human life. His ideal society required conformity in belief and practice. Augustine taught that it was right and necessary for the Catholic Church to **make** this happen, even if it meant coercing people to comply. This laid the theological foundation for persecuting "heretics" and for the Inquisition. (You can read about this online.)[1]

For over a thousand years, the Roman Catholic Church hunted down "heretics" and killed them. Some of these "heretics" were people with strange beliefs. However, as we shall see later, many of them were Bible-believing Christians.

Jesus predicted that true Christians would be rejected, persecuted, and killed. He told His disciples:

> "…yea, the time cometh, that whosoever killeth you will think that he doeth God service." (John 16:2)

For the Roman Catholic Church, "heresy" means to "obstinately" doubt or deny any official Catholic doctrine. This definition is given in Canon 751 of the *Code of Canon Law*, which is the body of laws used to govern the Catholic Church. (You can read this law online.)[2]

Doctrines that have often been disputed include the authority of the Pope, Purgatory, indulgences, the veneration of Mary and the saints, and transubstantiation (the doctrine that the body, blood, soul, and divinity of Jesus Christ are literally and fully present in every fragment of consecrated bread and every drop of consecrated wine).

Some Catholic doctrines conflict with the plain meaning of Scripture. As a result, people who read the Bible for themselves are likely to doubt or dispute those doctrines. One way of solving that problem is to prevent laymen from reading the Bible. The Catholic Church took that approach for hundreds of years.

Starting about 1080, there were many incidents where scholars wanted to translate the Bible into the language of the common people, but it was forbidden by the Pope, Church councils, or individual bishops.[3]

William Tyndale was burned as a "heretic," because he translated the Bible into English.[4] People were burned as "heretics" for owning or reading his translation. (You can read about this online.)[5]

For centuries, laymen were forbidden to possess the Scriptures in any language, including Latin. Reading the Bible was considered to be proof that someone was a heretic. Men and women were burned at the stake for reading the Bible in Latin.[6]

With the Protestant Reformation, the Bible was translated into English, German, and other languages. With the invention of the printing press, Bibles became so plentiful that they could no longer be suppressed. That is why people like us, who are not Latin scholars, are able to read the Bible today.

Christian "Heretics"

Who were some of the Christian "heretics" who were persecuted by the Roman Catholic Church? I would like you to meet the Waldensians.

When "heretics" were hunted, their writings were confiscated and burned. What we read about their beliefs was written by their enemies. As a result, it is often difficult to know what they really did believe.[7]

We do know what the Waldensians taught. Some of their writings survived.

In some ways, the Waldensians were similar to the Franciscans. Both groups taught the value of poverty and simplicity. They both had poor, humble, itinerant preachers, who were barefoot and wore humble peasant clothing.[8]

As we shall see, the Pope examined the Waldensians and found no heresy in them. However, another Pope reversed that decision.

Who were these courageous men and women who endured centuries of persecution for their faith?

The Waldensians

The Waldensians are also known as Waldenses or Vaudois. Dr. Bill Jackson made an in-depth study of them in his book, *The Noble Army of "Heretics."* He visited the valleys where the Waldensians lived and he studied their original documents.

One of the most famous Waldensians was Peter Waldo (1140-1218), a wealthy merchant of Lyons, France. He asked a priest how to live like Jesus Christ. The priest told Waldo about a conversation that Jesus had with a rich young ruler (Matthew 19:16-22). Jesus told the young man what to do, and Waldo guided his life by those words. Jesus said:

> "...If thou wilt be perfect, go and sell that thou hast, and give it to the poor, and thou shalt have treasure in heaven: and come and follow me." (Matthew 19:21)

Waldo made financial provision for his family, gave the rest of his money to the poor, memorized Scripture, and began preaching. Some scholars believe that Peter Waldo was the founder of the Waldensians. However, there is strong evidence that the Waldensians began long before Peter was born, and that Peter was given the surname Waldo because of his association with them. (You can read about the Waldensians online.)[9]

The Waldensians traveled in pairs, preaching the Gospel. They were humble people who believed in "apostolic poverty." They were barefoot, owning nothing, and they shared all things in common. Their teaching was orthodox, but they were considered to be a threat, because they set standards that made many members of the Catholic clergy look bad by comparison.[10]

The humility and voluntary poverty of the Waldensians were a striking contrast to the pride and luxury of the hierarchy of the Roman Catholic Church. A prime example of this was Pope Innocent III. He reigned from 1198 to 1216, which was during Waldo's lifetime. Innocent wore clothes covered with gold and jewels. He made kings and cardinals kiss his foot. (This is online.)[11] He said that the Pope is below God, but higher than the rest of mankind.[12]

Another example is Pope Boniface VIII, who reigned from 1294 to 1303. He said that he was Caesar, the Roman Emperor. His crown was covered with over 200 costly jewels.[13] Boniface declared that nobody could be saved unless he or she was subject to the Pope.[14]

Waldo's beliefs were founded on the Bible, especially the Gospels. He believed that there was no need to interpret the Bible, because it spoke clearly for itself. All that was needed was to make the whole of Scripture available to the people. Waldo was French, so he commissioned two priests to translate the Bible into French, starting with the Gospels. As soon as the first Gospel (Matthew) had been translated, Waldo applied it to his life and began preaching it to the people.[15]

In 1179, Pope Alexander III found no evidence of heresy among the Waldensians. However, because they were laymen, he ordered them not to preach unless they were requested to do so by a bishop.

The Archbishop of Lyons ordered Waldo to stop preaching. Waldo replied: "We ought to obey God rather than men." (Acts 5:29) He kept on preaching.

The Archbishop excommunicated him. Then, in 1184, Pope Lucius III excommunicated Waldo and his followers.[16]

In 1211, more than 80 Waldensians were burned at the stake for "heresy." This was followed by centuries of persecution. (This is online.)[17]

Because they were persecuted, the Waldensians went underground and spread to other countries, especially Italy, Switzerland, and Austria. The magnitude of their persecution is shown by the fact that in one year, in Italy alone, 9,000 Waldensians were killed, and another 12,000 were put into prison, where most of them died. In spite of this, somehow the itinerant Waldensian preachers were able to maintain links throughout Europe.[18]

In the sixteenth century, the Waldensians joined the Protestant Reformation. In 1848, the Italian government granted them emancipation. Finally, they were free from persecution (except for a brief period, when Mussolini persecuted them during World War II). In spite of everything, there are still Waldensian churches today. (Information is online.)[19]

The Inquisition

One of the things that was used to try to suppress the Waldensians and other "heretics" was the Inquisition. It began in 1180, four years before Waldo and the Waldensians were excommunicated by the Pope.

From 1180 to 1230, the Catholic Church enacted legislation (Canon Law) against heresy. It created a permanent tribunal, staffed by Dominican friars, which became known as the Inquisition.

The Inquisition used procedures that were banned in regular secular courts. It used anonymous informers. People were allowed to accuse their personal enemies.

When men and women were accused of heresy, they were not allowed to know who their accusers were, or what crime they were accused of. They were not allowed to have anybody defend them. The Inquisitors used torture to get accused people to "confess."

Once a person was accused, some kind of punishment was inevitable. If secular officials were reluctant to punish the victims, then the officials were accused of heresy, which meant that they also became victims of the system. In other words, they were blackmailed into doing the dirty work of the Inquisitors.[20]

If enough witnesses testified that a person was guilty, then he or she was presumed to be guilty. At that point, the accused person had to choose between confessing and renouncing his or her "errors," or being burned. If people confessed, then they would be sentenced, which often meant life imprisonment. However, they would be spared being burned at the stake.[21]

(If you want to know what "heretics" went through, read *Foxe's Book of Martyrs*. You can find it online by searching for the title.)

Because the Inquisitors themselves did not do the actual killing, Catholic apologists can say that the Inquisition didn't kill many people. That is technically correct, but it is misleading. The Inquisition was responsible for the deaths of those people.

If people wanted to confess, they had a problem. How do you confess to the correct crime if you don't know what you have been accused of? If you are unable to confess, because you don't know the charges, then how do you get the torture to stop? Under those circumstances, it is not surprising that people sometimes went insane. In 1808, Napoleon conquered Spain. His troops discovered a monastery with torture chambers that were full of prisoners, many of whom had gone insane.[22]

When secular rulers resisted the harsh methods of the Inquisition, popes pressured them by excommunicating the rulers and placing their subjects under interdict. (See the chapter, "Spiritual Coercion.") For example, King Edward II protested that torture was contrary to English law. Pope Clement V told the King that the law of the Roman Catholic Church was higher than the law of England. The Pope commanded the King to torture people. (You can read about this online.)[23]

The Pope gave orders to the King of England, and the King obeyed. The nation of England took a giant step backwards and started torturing people again.

The Inquisition was financed by confiscating the property of people who were condemned. It had to get people convicted in order to get the money that it needed for its operations. This was a strong motive for using torture to make people "confess."[24]

Even the grave was no protection from having property be confiscated. Corpses were dug up and dead people were convicted of heresy. This allowed the Inquisitors to take the property of the heirs of the dead "heretics."[25]

Sometimes people were convicted of heresy for reasons that are difficult to understand. In 1766, a French nobleman failed to take his hat off when a religious procession was going through the streets. It was raining at the time. That young man paid a heavy price for wanting to keep his head dry. He was convicted of blasphemy. He was sentenced to unusually severe torture. His hands were cut off. His tongue was ripped out with pincers. Then he was burned alive.[26]

The Inquisition published an Index of prohibited books. Catholics were threatened with damnation if they read one of these books. The Index included all Protestant Bibles and all books written by Protestant Reformers.

The list of forbidden books was kept current until 1966, when Pope Paul VI abolished it.[27]

Until 1966, Catholics were still threatened with damnation if they read a Protestant Bible. I corresponded with a former Catholic who had a King James Bible back in the days when he was still a Catholic. His priest ordered him to burn it. He obeyed the priest and burned the Bible.

In the eighteenth century, the Inquisition became less active due to lack of funds. Its last execution was in the early nineteenth century (1826).[28]

The Office of the Inquisition still exists. It is located in the Vatican. In 1965, its name was changed to The Congregation for the Doctrine of the Faith. It is headed by Cardinal Ratzinger. (This is online.)[29]

The Inquisition is an embarassment to the Catholic Church. As a result, some Catholic theologians have done creative things to try to justify it. For example, the article "Inquisition" in *The Catholic Encyclopedia* says that, according to the Law of Moses, heretics were to be tortured or killed.[30] That is not Biblical. People who tried to get the Israelites to worship "foreign gods" were stoned to death. Stoning was the normal method of execution in those days. Having a mob of people throw large rocks at a person would kill him quickly—it was not torture.

Worshiping "foreign gods" was not at all comparable to heresy. An example of "heresy" is Martin Luther, who said that we are saved by faith alone, instead of faith plus works. An example of worshiping "foreign gods" is abandoning Christianity in order to become a Hindu.

For the Israelites, an example of worshiping "foreign gods" would be to become a Baal worshiper. This involved burning children alive. The prophet Jeremiah said:

> "…they have forsaken me, and have estranged this place, and have burned incense in it unto other gods, whom neither they nor their fathers have known, nor the kings of Judah, and have **filled this place with the blood of innocents**: They have built also the high places of Baal, to **burn their sons with fire for burnt offerings unto Baal**…" (Jeremiah 19:4-5, emphasis added)

> "And they built the high places of Baal, which are in the valley of the son of Hinnom, **to cause their sons and their daughters to pass through the fire unto Molech**; which I commanded them not, neither came it into my mind, that

they should do this abomination, to cause Judah to sin." (Jeremiah 32:35, emphasis added)

The worship of other "foreign gods" also involved burning children alive. (See 2 Kings 17:31 and 2 Kings 23:10.) That is not at all comparable to "heretics" like William Tyndale who read the Bible and said that Christians are saved by faith alone.

In Old Testament times, Israelites were stoned to death if they burned their babies alive as sacrifices to pagan gods. In the Middle Ages, Christians were burned alive for believing the Bible.

Conclusion

There was a wide variety of Christian "heretics." On the one hand, there were the Waldensians, who were simple, humble people. They were just trying to live according to Biblical principles. But when told not to preach, they continued preaching.

On the other hand, there were people like Wycliffe, who said things that made the Pope angry. Wycliffe started out as a Catholic Reformer. He eventually became a Protestant. He taught that the government of England should remove morally corrupt churchmen and confiscate their property. He said that the Pope is the Antichrist. Wycliffe's followers (the Lollards) were severely persecuted. (Information is online.)[30]

Did Jesus and His disciples kill people for saying offensive things? They could have. Elijah called down fire on people. The Bible says:

> "And when his disciples James and John saw this, they said, Lord, wilt thou that we command fire to come down from heaven, and consume them, even as Elias [Elijah] did? But he turned, and rebuked them, and said, Ye know not what manner of spirit ye are of." (Luke 9:54-55)

There is a story about a man who asked a woman: "Would you sleep with me for a million dollars?" She replied: "Well, for a million dollars, I guess maybe I would." Then he said: "Would you sleep with me for five dollars?" She answered: "What kind of woman do you think I am?" And he replied: "We've already established that. Now we're haggling price."

A million dollars is a strong enticement. For the Pope to be publicly accused of being the Antichrist is a strong provocation. But no matter how great the enticement, or the provocation, some things are just plain wrong.

Killing "heretics" because of their religious convictions was never justifiable. If a "heretic" resisted, then the Inquisition required the local authorities to kill the person, thus murdering the person's body. If a "heretic" complied and acted against his or her conscience, then the Inquisition murdered the person's soul.[31]

Chapter 7

Was the Early Church Roman Catholic?

The Roman Catholic Church claims that the early Christians were all Roman Catholics and that (aside from the Orthodox Church) all Christians were Roman Catholics until the Protestant Reformation. It also claims that the Apostle Peter was the first Pope, ruling from Rome.

But do these claims stand up to the test of history? Or are they false credentials?

There is historical evidence that the Roman Catholic Church began with Emperor Constantine. Many Protestants believe that, throughout Church history, there have been many true Christians who were not Catholics, and these Christians were often killed by the Catholic Church. They also believe that Peter was just one of the apostles.

Constantine

On October 28, 312 A.D., the Roman Emperor Constantine met with Bishop Miltiades. (Catholics would later refer to him as Pope Miltiades, but at the time he was known as the Bishop of Rome.) Miltiades was assisted by Silvester, a Roman who spoke educated Latin and acted as interpreter.

The previous day, Constantine had seen a sign in the heavens: a cross in front of the sun. He heard a voice say that he would conquer in the sign that he had seen. Constantine painted crosses on the shields of his soldiers. They won an important battle. He believed that the victory was due to the power of the sign he had seen. He asked for two of the three nails that were used to crucify Jesus. One nail was made into a bit for his horse. Another nail was made a part of his crown, signifying that Constantine ruled the Roman Empire in the name of Jesus. He allowed Miltiades to keep the third nail.[1]

The fact that Constantine saw the cross and the sun together may explain why he worshiped the Roman sun god, while at the same time professing to be a Christian. After his "conversion," Constantine built a triumphal arch featuring the sun god (the "unconquered sun"). His coins featured the sun. Constantine made a statue of the sun god, with his own face on it, for his new city of Constantinople. He made Sunday (the day of the Roman sun god) into a day of rest when work was forbidden.[2]

Constantine declared that a mosaic of the sun god (riding in a chariot) represented Jesus. During Constantine's reign, many Christians followed the Emperor's example and incorporated worship of the sun god into their religion. They prayed kneeling towards the east (where the sun rises). They said that Jesus Christ drives his chariot across the sky (like the sun god). They had their worship services on Sunday, which honored the sun god. (Days of the week were named in honor of pagan gods.) They celebrated the birth of Jesus on December 25, the day when sun worshipers celebrated the birthday of the sun, following the winter solstice.[3]

Historians disagree as to whether or not Constantine actually became a Christian. His character certainly did not reflect the teachings of Jesus Christ. Constantine was vain, violent and superstitious. He worshiped the sun god. He had little respect for human life. He was known for wholesale slaughter during his military campaigns. He forced prisoners of war to fight for their lives against wild beasts. He had several family members (including his second wife) executed for questionable reasons. Constantine waited until he was dying before asking to be baptized. Historians disagree as to whether or not he actually was baptized.[4]

Constantine wanted to have a state church, with Christian clergy acting as civil servants. He called himself a bishop. He said that he was the interpreter of the Word of God. He claimed to be the voice that declares what is true and godly. According to historian Paul Johnson, Constantine saw himself as being an important agent of salvation, on a par with the apostles. Bishop Eusebius (Constantine's eulogist) relates that Constantine built the Church of the Apostles with the intention of having his own body be kept there along with the bodies of the apostles. Constantine's coffin was to be in the center (the place of honor), with six apostles on each side of him. He expected that devotions honoring the apostles would be performed in the church. Constantine expected to share the title and honor of the apostles.[5]

Constantine told Bishop Miltiades that he wanted to build two Christian basilicas, in honor of the Apostles Peter and Paul. He offered a large, magnificent palace for the use of Miltiades and his successors. Miltiades refused. He could not accept the idea of having Christianity be promoted by the Roman Empire.[6]

Constantine rode off to war. By the time that he returned in 314 A.D., Miltiades had died. Bishop Silvester was Miltiades' successor. Silvester was eager to have the Church be spread, using Roman roads, Roman wealth, Roman law, Roman power, and Roman military might. Constantine officially approved of Silvester as the successor of Miltiades. Then he had a coronation ceremony for Silvester and crowned him like a worldly prince. This was the first time that a bishop had ever been crowned.[7]

Before Constantine's "conversion," Christians were persecuted. Now, instead of facing persecution, Bishop Silvester lived in luxury. He had a beautiful palace, with the finest furniture and art. He wore silk brocade robes. He had servants to wait on him. Near his palace was a basilica that served as his cathedral. This luxurious building had seven altars made of gold, a canopy of solid silver above the main altar, and 50 chandeliers. The imperial mail system and transportation system were placed at Silvester's disposal. It was now possible to have worldwide church councils.[8]

Have you read the Book of Acts and the Epistles? If so, compare the Church, as portrayed there, with the Church of Bishop Silvester. Here is how the Apostle Paul described the kinds of things that he had to endure, as a leader in the early Church:

> "Of the Jews five times received I forty stripes save one. Thrice was I beaten with rods, once was I stoned, thrice I suffered shipwreck, a night and a day I have been in the deep; In journeyings often, in perils of waters, in perils of robbers, in perils by mine own countrymen, in perils by the heathen, in perils in the city, in perils in the wilderness, in perils in the sea, in perils among false brethren; In weariness and painfulness, in watchings often, in hunger and thirst, in fastings often, in cold and nakedness." (2 Corinthians 11:24-27)

After Constantine's "conversion," the Church was radically changed. Suddenly, being Christian resulted in power, prestige, and promotion (whereas previously it had resulted in persecution). Suddenly, by the Emperor's decree, Christianity became politically correct. As a result, ambitious people joined the Church for worldly reasons. The Bishop of Rome was supported by the military might, political power, and wealth of the Roman Emperor. Worldwide church councils were convened.

This was the birth of the Roman Catholic Church. It was created in the year 314 A.D. by Emperor Constantine and Bishop Silvester.

A Tale of Two Bishops

The degree of change that Constantine caused in the Church can be illustrated by looking at the lives of two Bishops of Rome. Let's go back in history to look at the life of Bishop Pontian, who died 76 years before Constantine's "conversion." Then we will compare Pontian's life with the life of Bishop Silvester.

The following information about Bishops Pontian and Silvester comes from Malachi Martin, *The Decline and Fall of the Roman Church* (G.P. Putnam's Sons, 1981), pages 19-38.

Pontian became the Bishop of Rome in the year 230 A.D. He was made bishop suddenly and unexpectedly, when his predecessor was arrested and killed by Roman authorities.

On September 27, 235 A.D., Emperor Maximinus decreed that all Christian leaders were to be arrested. Christian buildings were burned. Christian cemeteries were closed. The personal wealth of Christians was confiscated.

Bishop Pontian was arrested the same day. He was put in the Mamertine Prison, where he was tortured for 10 days. Then he was sent to work in the lead mines of Sardinia.

When prisoners arrived at Sardinia, their left eye was gouged out. A number was branded on their forehead. Iron rings were soldered around their ankles, linked together with a six-inch chain that hobbled them. A tight chain around their waist was fastened to their ankle-chain in such a way that they were permanently bent over.

The prisoners worked for 20 hours a day, with four one-hour breaks for sleep. They had one meal of bread and water per day. Most prisoners died within six to fourteen months from exhaustion, malnutrition, disease, beatings, infection, or violence. Some went insane or committed suicide.

Pontian only lasted four months. In January, 236 A.D., Pontian was killed. His body was thrown into the cesspool.

What happened to Pontian was not unusual. Many Christians were sent to the Sardinian lead mines, or persecuted in other ways. If a man accepted the position of being a Christian leader, he knew that his life from that time on was likely to be short and painful. There were 14 Bishops of Rome in the 79 years between Pontian and Silvester.

Then along came Constantine.

In the year 314 A.D., Emperor Constantine crowned Silvester as Bishop of Rome. Silvester lived in luxury, with servants waiting on him. Constantine confessed his sins to Silvester and asked for his advice. Silvester presided over worldwide Church councils. He had a splendid palace and a sumptuous cathedral. He had power, prestige, wealth, pomp, and the favor of the Emperor.

Silvester died in December, 336 A.D. He died peacefully, in a clean, comfortable bed, in the Roman Lateran Palace. He was surrounded by well-dressed bishops and attended by Roman guards. His body was dressed in ceremonial robes, put in an elegant casket, and carried through the streets of Rome in a solemn procession. He was buried with honor and ceremony, attended by leading members of Roman society.

It is understandable that many Christians would have preferred an officially approved status for the Church. But what was the result?

Before Constantine, the Church was a band of heroic men and women who were so committed to serve the Lord Jesus Christ that they would endure any hardship. After 314 A.D., the Church became infiltrated by opportunists who were seeking power and political advancement. Church leaders were no longer in danger of persecution. Rather, they enjoyed power, prestige, and luxury.

Did the Roman Empire surrender to Christianity? Or did Christianity prostitute itself in order to gain benefits from the Roman Empire?[9]

The temptation for an ungodly alliance with the Roman Empire was very great. But at what cost?

State Religion

In 380 A.D., Emperor Theodosius published an edict requiring that all Roman subjects profess the faith of the Bishop of Rome. Those who refused were considered to be "heretics." Jews, pagans, and "heretics" were subject to harsh punishments. In 390 A.D., Bishop Ambrose excommunicated Emperor Theodosius. In order to be restored to the Church, the Roman Emperor had to do penance for eight months. Theodosius complied. (Information is online.)[10]

It is amazing how much power the Roman Catholic Church gained in 76 years. Constantine promoted the Church by giving it special benefits, but Theodosius forced people to become Roman Catholics. He imposed harsh punishments on anybody who disagreed with the Bishop of Rome. Constantine asked for advice from Bishop Silvester, but Theodosius obeyed orders given by Bishop Ambrose.

Catholicism was now the state religion of the Roman Empire. The Roman Catholic Church, which was born under Emperor Constantine, had now become so powerful that a bishop could give orders to the Roman Emperor.

From Martyrs to "Heretic" Hunters

Emperor Constantine and Bishop Silvester created the Roman Catholic Church in 314 A.D. Forty years later, Augustine was born. He became a bishop and a "doctor of the Church." He lived from 354 to 430 A.D.

Augustine insisted that it was right and necessary to use force to bring about unity among Christians. He said that "heretics" should not just be expelled from the Church. Rather, they should be **compelled** to denounce their beliefs and conform to "orthodoxy," or else be destroyed. This became the basis for the Inquisition. It was used to justify killing "heretics" throughout the history of the Catholic Church.[11]

During the century following Constantine, the Roman Catholic Church went through an amazing transformation. Catholics became "heretic" hunters. They killed people who disagreed with them.

By the time of the Middle Ages, the Roman Catholic Church burned people at the stake for translating the Bible into the language of the common people. They even burned people for reading the Bible in Latin. (See the chapter, "Hunting 'Heretics.'")

The Book of Acts tells how the high priest and the Jewish leaders put the Apostles in prison. They wanted to kill them, because the Apostles told people about Jesus. Gamaliel, a respected rabbi, urged them not to persecute the Christians. He said:

> "And now I say unto you, Refrain from these men, and let them alone: for if this counsel or this work be of men, it will come to nought: But if it be of God, ye cannot overthrow it; lest haply ye be found even to fight against God." (Acts 5:38-39; see Acts 5:17-40)

Jim Jones was a religious leader who ordered his 900 followers to commit suicide. They obeyed him. Jones and his followers demonstrated that Gamaliel was right. They destroyed themselves. Their religious movement died with them.

The men who translated the Bible into the language of the common people also demonstrated that Gamaliel was right. The Catholic Church was unable to suppress the translation of the Bible. That is why people like us, who are not Latin scholars, are able to read the Bible today.

How does the persecution of "heretics" compare with the picture of Jesus that we see in the Gospels? Did Jesus try to force people to conform to His teachings?

With amazing patience, Jesus kept on teaching the crowds of people, healing the sick, and demonstrating the love and the power of God. When His disciples didn't understand His teachings, He explained them. (Luke 8:5-15) When the rich young man turned away from Jesus, He didn't rebuke him or threaten him. He let him go. (Matthew 19:16-22)

Many of Jesus' disciples left Him. Jesus asked the Twelve: "Will ye also go away?" (John 6:67) He didn't threaten them or rebuke them. He didn't try to force them to believe what He taught them. He left them free to believe or not believe, to stay or to leave.

Was Peter a Pope?

Peter did not describe himself as being a high and mighty Pope, with authority over the entire Church. Rather, he called himself "a servant." (2 Peter 1:1) According to *Strong's Concordance*, the word means, "a slave." Peter also referred to himself as a fellow "elder." (1 Peter 5:1)

Rather than claiming special authority for himself, Peter said that all believers are a "royal priesthood." He said:

> "But ye are a chosen generation, a royal priesthood, an holy nation, a peculiar people; that ye should shew forth the praises of him who hath called you out of darkness into his marvellous light" (1 Peter 2:9)

In the Book of Revelation, the Apostle John confirmed Peter's statement that all true believers are priests. (Revelation 1:5-6; 5:9-10; 20:6) (Catholic Bibles refer to the *Book of Revelation* as *The Apocalypse*.)

Peter (supposedly the first Pope) prohibited the attitudes and practices that have been prevalent in the papacy. He said that leaders must not act like lords (people with rank, power, and special privileges) and they must not seek wealth ("filthy lucre"). Peter described himself as being an elder, like the other elders. He said:

> "The elders which are among you I exhort, **who am also an elder**, and a witness of the sufferings of Christ, and also a partaker of the glory that shall be revealed: Feed the flock of God which is among you, taking the oversight thereof, not by constraint, but willingly; **not for filthy lucre**, but of a ready mind; **Neither as being lords over God's heritage**, but being ensamples to the flock." (1 Peter 5:1-3, emphasis added)

How does Peter, as portrayed in the Bible, compare with the Pope? Peter was a humble fisherman. The Pope is a monarch who sits on a throne. When he celebrates a Pontifical Mass, the Pope enters the sanctuary seated in a portable throne that is carried on the shoulders of uniformed men. As head of the Catholic Church, the Pope controls immense wealth, with widespread investments around the world. The wealth of the Vatican is amazing.[12]

Catholic theologians claim that Jesus built the Roman Catholic Church on the Apostle Peter. They base this on Matthew 16:18, where Jesus told Peter: "And I say unto thee, That thou are Peter, and upon this rock I will build my church; and the gates of hell shall not prevail against it."

Does the rock on which the church is built represent Peter, or does it represent Jesus Christ? Peter himself called Jesus the rock. He said:

> "If so be ye have tasted that the Lord is gracious. To whom coming, as unto a **living stone**, disallowed indeed of men, but chosen of God, and precious." (1 Peter 2:3-4, emphasis added)

The Apostle Paul also called Jesus the Rock. He said:

> "Moreover, brethren, I would not that ye should be ignorant, how that all our fathers were under the cloud, and all passed through the sea; And were all baptized unto Moses in the cloud and in the sea; And did all eat the same spiritual meat; And did all drink the same spiritual drink: for they drank of that spiritual Rock that followed them: and **that Rock was Christ**." (1 Corinthians 10:1-4, emphasis added)

Did Peter act like he was in charge of the early Church? The Book of Acts describes a controversy about whether or not gentile converts to Christianity should be required to be circumcised and to follow the Jewish dietary laws. Paul and Barnabas went to Jerusalem to confer with the apostles about it. (Acts 15:2-4) Peter and other people spoke. (Acts 15:7-13) Following a period of silence, James (not Peter) made the final decision in the matter. He called it a "sentence." According to *Strong's Concordance*, the word means a judicial sentence, a decree, or a judgment. The Bible says:

> "And after they had held their peace, **James answered**, saying, Men and brethren, hearken unto me...**Wherefore my sentence is**, that we trouble not them, which from among the Gentiles are turned to God: But that we write unto them, that they abstain from pollutions of idols, and from fornication, and from things strangled, and from blood." (Acts 15:13, 19-20, emphasis added)

This is the last mention of Peter in the Book of Acts. The Book of Acts is the history of the early Church up until a few years before Peter's death. If

Peter was "the first Pope," and the officially recognized head of the Church, would we not expect that the Biblical history of the early Church would have said more about him?

The Book of Acts says nothing about Peter being in authority over the whole Church. It shows no connection between Peter and Rome.

Acts 28:14-15 tells how Paul met with the "brethren" in Rome, but it makes no mention of Peter. As we shall see, when Paul met with Peter in Jerusalem, Peter was identified by name.

Acts 2:14 and Acts 8:14 say that Peter was in Jerusalem. Acts 9:36-43 says that Peter went to Joppa, which is near Jerusalem. In chapter 10 of the Book of Acts, Peter is still in Joppa. Acts 11:2 says that Peter returned to Jerusalem.

Joppa is about 30 miles from Jerusalem. If the Book of Acts records this much detail about Peter's visit to a nearby town, wouldn't it tell us if Peter went all the way to Rome? Particularly since it does tell us that Paul went to Rome.

Acts 15:1-20 tells how Paul and Barnabas went to Jerusalem to meet with the "apostles and elders" of Jerusalem. Peter is identified as being one of the apostles of Jerusalem. The Bible says:

> "And certain men which came down from Judaea taught the brethren, and said, Except ye be circumcised after the manner of Moses, ye cannot be saved. When therefore Paul and Barnabas had no small dissension and disputation with them, **they determined that Paul and Barnabas, and certain other of them, should go up to Jerusalem unto the apostles and elders about this question.** And being brought on their way by the church, they passed through Phenice and Samaria, declaring the conversion of the Gentiles: and they caused great joy unto all the brethren. **And when they were come to Jerusalem, they were received of the church, and of the apostles and elders**, and they declared all things that God had done with them. But there rose up certain of the sect of the Pharisees which believed, saying, That it was needful to circumcise them, and to command them to keep the law of Moses. **And the apostles and elders came together for to consider of this matter. And when there had been much disputing, Peter rose up, and said unto them,** Men and brethren, ye know how that a good while ago God made choice among us, that the Gentiles by my mouth should hear the word of the gospel, and believe." (Acts 15:1-7, emphasis added)

The Apostle Paul identified Peter as being an apostle in Jerusalem. He said:

> "Then after three years **I went up to Jerusalem to see Peter**, and abode with him fifteen days. But **other of the apostles** saw I none, save James the Lord's brother." (Galatians 1:18-19, emphasis added)

The Book of Romans was written by the Apostle Paul. He addressed it to **"all that be in Rome,** beloved of God, called to be saints…" (Romans 1:7, emphasis added) In Romans 16:1-15, Paul greeted 26 people by name. He never mentioned Peter. If Peter was the leader of the Church in Rome, then why didn't Paul mention him?

Paul wrote five letters from a Roman prison (Ephesians, Philippians, Colossians, 2 Timothy, and Philemon). He never mentioned Peter. The man who stayed with Paul in Rome, to help him and encourage him, was Luke—not Peter. (Colossians 4:14; 2 Timothy 4:11)

Paul only mentioned Peter in one of his epistles. In Galatians 1:18-19, Paul said that he went to Jerusalem to see Peter and James. In Galatians 2:8, Paul said that he preached to the gentiles and Peter preached to the Jews (the "circumcision").

In Galatians 2:11-15, Paul recounted how he publicly rebuked Peter, because Peter had become so intimidated by the Judaizers that he "walked not uprightly." Evidently, Paul's public correction of Peter did not cause a problem between them. Peter loved and respected Paul as a brother. He exhorted the Church to heed Paul's wisdom. Peter said:

> "And account that the longsuffering of our Lord is salvation; even as **our beloved brother Paul** also according to **the wisdom given unto** him hath written unto you; As also in all his epistles, speaking in them of these things…" (2 Peter 3:15-16, emphasis added)

Later in this book, you will read about some popes. Please compare their behavior, attitude, and demeanor with that of Peter. If you were Peter, would you want them to say that they represent you?

Legends and Traditions

I was taught that, when he was a boy, George Washington chopped down a cherry tree and confessed his transgression to his father. Parson

Weems' biography of George Washington is the source of that story. According to modern historians, the cherry tree event never happened. I was quite surprised to hear that, because I had never questioned the story.

Some people say that Parson Weems deliberately created the cherry tree legend some time between 1800 and 1809. But perhaps Parson Weems wasn't deliberately deceiving people. Perhaps he was simply passing on a story that he believed to be true. Either way, modern biographers of George Washington say that the cherry tree episode never really happened. (Information is online.)[13]

If we hear a story repeated often enough, then we tend to believe it. The idea of questioning it becomes almost unthinkable, because the story is so familiar and so widely accepted.

I believe that something similar has happened with the Catholic Church's stories about Peter. These traditions have been repeated so often that many people never question them. (See the chapter, "According to Tradition.")

The "Early Fathers"

Catholic apologists often quote the "Early Fathers" in support of Catholic doctrines, the papacy, and other Catholic claims. Who were these people?

There were many early Christian leaders, including priests, bishops, and scholars. There were a lot of these men. They had a wide variety of opinions on religious matters. Their theological differences were as widely varied as those of theologians from different denominations are today.[14]

So one person finds some Early Fathers to support one position, and another person finds some other Early Fathers to support the opposite position. But it's not a level playing field. Among all of those early Christian leaders, who decided which ones qualified to be called Early Fathers? The Catholic Church.

There is also the problem of knowing which documents are authentic. Some documents were forged. They were falsely attributed to Early Fathers, in order to give them credibility. In addition, some genuine documents were changed by forgers, in order to give credibility to papal claims of power and authority. Sometimes these altered documents wound up saying the opposite of what they had originally said. (See the chapter, "Forged Documents and Papal Power.")

Apostolic Succession

The Roman Catholic Church paints a picture of an orderly succession of popes, who faithfully followed in the footsteps of the Apostle Peter. However, according to Biblical standards, some of these men were not fit to rule a house church, let alone be bishops. (This is discussed in the chapter, "The Popes").

One example was Pope Benedict IX (1033-1045). He had sex with boys, women, and animals. He practiced witchcraft and Satanism. He gave orders for people to be murdered. He filled the Lateran Palace with prostitutes.[15]

In spite of all that, Catholic doctrine says that Benedict's decisions about theological matters were infallible. (This is online.)[16]

Infallibility

According to Roman Catholic doctrine, popes and Catholic church councils are infallible. This means that, whenever they make official declarations concerning matters of faith or morals, God supernaturally protects them from making errors. Infallibility applies to all Roman Catholic popes and church councils: past, present, and future. (This is online.)[17]

What happens if a pope or a Catholic church council makes an "infallible" declaration that directly contradicts the "infallible" declaration of another pope or church council?

Truth does not contradict truth. Therefore, if the "infallible" pronouncements of the popes and Catholic church councils really are infallible, they will never contradict other "infallible" pronouncements. So if there is even one contradiction, then the doctrine of infallibility cannot be correct.

The claim for papal infallibility does not stand up to the test of history. Pope Zosimus (417-418 A.D.) reversed the pronouncement of a previous pope. He also retracted a doctrinal pronouncement that he himself had previously made. Pope Honorious was condemned as a heretic by the Sixth Ecumenical Council (680-681 A.D.). (This means that Pope Honorious made doctrinal statements that are contrary to Roman Catholic doctrine.) He was also condemned as a heretic by Pope Leo II, as well as by every other pope until the eleventh century. So here we have "infallible" popes condemning another "infallible" pope as a heretic. In 1870, the First Vatican Council abolished some "infallible" papal decrees. It also abolished some decrees of two "infallible" Catholic Church councils.[18]

The doctrine of the Assumption of Mary states that Mary was taken bodily up to Heaven. This was officially declared to be a dogma of the Roman Catholic faith on November 1, 1950. Therefore, every Roman Catholic is required to believe this doctrine without questioning it. However, as we will see, the teaching of the Assumption of Mary originated with heretical writings that were officially condemned by the early Church.

In 495 A.D., Pope Gelasius declared that the doctrine of the Assumption of Mary is a heresy, and that people who teach it are heretics. In the sixth century, Pope Hormisdas declared that anyone teaching this doctrine is a heretic. Two "infallible" popes both declared that this doctrine is a heresy. Then, on November 1, 1950, Pope Pius XII (another "infallible" pope) declared that the same doctrine is official Roman Catholic dogma, which all Catholics are required to believe.[19]

So before November 1, 1950, any Catholic who believed in the Assumption of Mary was a heretic (because of "infallible" declarations of popes). But after November 1, 1950, any Catholic who failed to believe in the Assumption of Mary was a heretic (because of the "infallible" declaration of Pope Pius XII).

In 1864, Pope Pius IX "infallibly" declared that the idea that people have a right to freedom of conscience and freedom of worship is "insanity," "evil," "depraved," and "reprobate." He also declared that non-Catholics who live in Catholic countries should not be allowed to publicly practice their religion. In 1888, Pope Leo XIII "infallibly" declared that freedom of thought and freedom of worship are wrong.[20] (These encyclicals are online. They are easy to find.)

The Second Vatican Council (1962-1965) produced a document called *Declaration on Religious Liberty*. It states that all people have a right to freedom of religion.[21]

Now I certainly agree with the idea of freedom of religion. However, it totally contradicts the "infallible" declarations of Popes Pius IX and Leo XIII. It also contradicts the anathemas of the Council of Trent, the killing of "heretics," the Inquisition, the burning of people who translated the Bible into English, and the persecution of Protestants during the Protestant Reformation.

Freedom of religion also contradicts modern Canon Law (1983). Canon 1366 says that parents are to be punished if they allow their children to be baptized in a "non-Catholic religion" or taught to observe it. The reference to baptism shows that this means Christian religions that are not Roman Catholic. (You can read this law online.)[22]

Here the Catholic Church is on the horns of a dilemma. If it says that people have a right to freedom of religion, then it admits that it is not infallible. If it says that it is infallible, then it admits that it really does not believe that people have a right to freedom of religion.

The Catholic Church can claim infallibility, or it can claim that it has seen the error of its ways and it now supports freedom of religion. But it can't have it both ways.

Two Roman Catholic organizations have found contradictions between "infallible" doctrinal declarations of the Second Vatican Council and "infallible" doctrinal pronouncements of Pope Pius IX. Articles dealing with these contradictions are online.[23]

The conservative group (True Catholic) concludes that, therefore, the Second Vatican Council must not be legitimate. The liberal group (Women Priests) concludes that, therefore, Pope Pius IX taught "errors." Either way, there are contradictions between official doctrinal declarations of an "infallible" pope and an "infallible" church council.

True Catholic also claims that Pope John Paul II has taught 101 things that are contrary to "infallible" Catholic doctrines that were declared by "infallible" popes and church councils. They conclude that John Paul II is therefore a heretic. According to Canon Law, that would mean that he is not a valid pope. So they call him an antipope. (This is online.)[24]

If John Paul II is not a valid pope, then the papal chair has been vacant. In order to rectify this situation, True Catholic has elected a pope. On May 20, 1998, Pope Pius XIII was elected. (This is online.)[25]

So we now have two men who claim to be Pope: John Paul II and Pius XIII. It seems that having two men claim to be Pope at the same time is not confined to the Middle Ages. (This is discussed in the chapter, "The Popes".)

Conclusion

The Roman Catholic Church was created by Emperor Constantine and Bishop Silvester in the year 314 A.D.

Peter did not act like a Pope and he did not describe himself as having any special authority. In the Church meeting that is described in chapter 15 of the Book of Acts, James appears to be the person in authority. He makes the final decision. The Bible shows Peter as being in Jerusalem, not in Rome.

There are "infallible" doctrinal declarations that contradict one another. Therefore, the doctrine of infallibility is not valid.

The contradiction of "infallible" doctrines has caused some very conservative Catholics to believe that John Paul II is not a valid pope, and the Second Vatican Council was not a valid council. It has also caused some very liberal Catholics to believe that Pope Pius IX taught doctrinal errors.

Chapter 8
Forged Documents and Papal Power

What we now call popes were originally bishops of Rome (one bishop among brother bishops from other cities). Then they became popes, with power over the entire Catholic Church. Then they became so powerful that they were able to depose kings and emperors. They became so powerful that they were able to force kings use their secular might to enforce the Inquisition. In 1870, the Pope was declared to be infallible.

Hans Küng is a Catholic priest and a theologian. He was a theological consultant to the Second Vatican Council (1962-1965). However, in 1979, he was disciplined by the Vatican because he opposed the doctrine of papal infallibility. According to Küng, historical research shows that, starting as early as the fifth century, the popes "decisively extended their power with explicit forgeries."[1]

These forged documents were used to change people's perception of the history of the papacy and of the Catholic Church. They created false credentials and an illusion of antiquity. For example, if a Pope wanted to depose a king, he could cite a forged document that said that an early pope had done the same kind of thing. This would establish a false precedent to justify his actions.

One of the most famous forgeries is the *Pseudo-Isidorian Decretals*, which were written around 845 A.D. (They are also known as the *False Decretals*.) They consist of 115 documents that were supposedly written by early popes.[2]

The Catholic Encyclopedia admits that these are forgeries. It says that the purpose of these forged documents was to enable the Church to be independent of secular power, and to prevent the laity from ruling the Church.[3]

In other words, the purpose of the forgeries was to increase the power of the Pope and the Catholic Church.

In addition to documents that were total forgeries, many genuine documents were altered. Forged material was added to 125 genuine documents, in order to increase the power of the Pope. Many early documents were changed to say the opposite of what they had originally said.[4]

One of the forgeries is a letter that was falsely attributed to Saint Ambrose. It said that if a person does not agree with the Holy See (the Vatican), then he or she is a heretic. This is an example of how papal power was promoted by fraudulently claiming the authority of highly respected Early Fathers.[5]

Another famous forgery from the ninth century was *The Donation of Constantine*. It claimed that Emperor Constantine gave the western provinces of the Roman Empire to the Bishop of Rome. The Pope used it to claim authority in secular matters.[6]

When Greek Christians tried to discuss issues with the Church in Rome, the popes often used forged documents to back their claims. This happened so frequently that, for 700 years, the Greeks referred to Rome as "the home of forgeries."[7]

For three hundred years, the *Pseudo-Isidorian Decretals* and other forgeries were used by Roman Popes to claim authority over the Church in the East. The Patriarch of Constantinople rejected these false claims of primacy. This resulted in the separation of the Orthodox Church from the Roman Catholic Church.[8]

In the middle of the twelfth century, a monk named Gratian wrote the *Decretum*, which became the basis for Canon Law (the legal system for running the Roman Catholic Church). It contained numerous quotations from forged documents. Gratian drew many of his conclusions from those quotations. He quoted 324 passages that were supposedly written by popes of the first four centuries. Of those passages, only 11 are genuine. The other 313 quotations are forgeries.[9]

In the thirteenth century, Thomas Aquinas wrote the *Summa Theologica* and numerous other works. His writings are the foundation for scholastic theology. Aquinas used Gratian's *Decretum* for quotations from church fathers and early popes.[10] Aquinas also used forged documents that he thought were genuine.[11]

The importance of Thomas Aquinas' theology can be seen in the encyclical of Pope Pius X on the priesthood. In 1906, Pius said that, in their study of philosophy, theology, and Scripture, men studying for the priesthood should follow the directions given by the popes and the teaching of Thomas Aquinas.[12]

William Webster wrote the book, *The Church of Rome at the Bar of History*. He is a former Catholic. Webster has an online article called, "Forgeries and the Papacy: The Historical Influence and Use of Forgeries in Promotion of the Doctrine of the Papacy." It gives detailed information about the *Pseudo-Isidorian Decretals* and other forged documents, showing their influence on the power of the papacy, and on the theology of the Catholic Church.[13]

Four quotations from Webster's article are below. (They are used by permission.) Webster writes:

> "In the middle of the ninth century, a radical change began in the Western Church, that dramatically altered the Constitution of the Church, and laid the ground work for the full development of the papacy. The papacy could never have

emerged without a fundamental restructuring of the Constitution of the Church and of men's perceptions of the history of that Constitution. As long as the true facts of Church history were well known, it would serve as a buffer against any unlawful ambitions. However, in the 9th century, a literary forgery occurred that completely revolutionized the ancient government of the Church in the West. This forgery is known as the *Pseudo-Isidorian Decretals*, written around 845 A.D. The *Decretals* are a complete fabrication of Church history. They set forth precedents for the exercise of sovereign authority of the popes over the universal Church prior to the fourth century and make it appear that the popes had always exercised sovereign dominion and had ultimate authority even over Church Councils.

"...The historical facts reveal that the papacy was never a reality as far as the universal Church is concerned. There are many eminent Roman Catholic historians who have testified to that fact as well as to the importance of the forgeries, especially those of *Pseudo-Isidore*. One such historian is Johann Joseph Ignaz von Dollinger. He was the most renowned Roman Catholic historian of the last century, who taught Church history for 47 years as a Roman Catholic. [Webster quotes extensively from Dollinger.]

"...In addition to the *Pseudo Isidorian Decretals* there were other forgeries that were successfully used for the promotion of the doctrine of papal primacy. One famous instance is that of Thomas Aquinas. In 1264 A.D. Thomas authored a work entitled *Against the Errors of the Greeks*. This work deals with the issues of theological debate between the Greek and Roman Churches in that day on such subjects as the Trinity, the Procession of the Holy Spirit, Purgatory and the Papacy. In his defense of the papacy Thomas bases practically his entire argument on forged quotations of Church fathers...These spurious quotations had enormous influence on many Western theologians in succeeding centuries.

"...The authority claims of Roman Catholicism ultimately devolve upon the institution of the papacy. The papacy is the center and source from which all authority flows for Roman Catholicism. Rome has long claimed that this institution was established by Christ and has been in force in the Church from the very beginning. But the historical record gives a very different picture. This institution was promoted primarily through the falsification of historical fact through the extensive use of forgeries as Thomas Aquinas' apologetic for the papacy demonstrates. Forgery is its foundation."

There is a website with several articles about the Catholic Church's used of forged documents.[14] These forgeries were one of the causes of the "Great Schism" between the Roman Catholic Church and the Orthodox Church.[15]

Forged documents are the foundation of the power of the papacy. They also had a significant influence on Catholic theology and Canon Law.

Chapter 9

The Popes

The Roman Catholic Church paints a picture of an orderly chain of succession of popes who followed in the footsteps of the Apostle Peter. If even one of these men was not a valid Pope, then the chain is broken.

What does it take to be a valid Pope? What does the Bible say are the minimum requirements for Church leaders? In order to be a Pope or a cardinal, a man must first be a bishop. Therefore, a Pope must at least meet the Biblical requirements for being a bishop.

The Apostle Paul gave Timothy and Titus instructions regarding the necessary qualifications for bishops. He told them:

> "A bishop then must be **blameless**, the husband of one wife, vigilant, **sober**, of **good behaviour**, given to hospitality, apt to teach; **Not given to wine, no striker [not violent], not greedy of filthy lucre [money]**; but patient, **not a brawler, not covetous**; One that ruleth well his own house, having his children in subjection with all gravity; (For if a man know not how to rule his own house, how shall he take care of the church of God?) Not a novice, lest being lifted up with pride he fall into the condemnation of the devil. Moreover **he must have a good report of them that are without**; lest he fall into reproach and the snare of the devil." (1 Timothy 3:2-7, emphasis added)

> "For a bishop must be **blameless**, as the steward of God; **not selfwilled, not soon angry, not given to wine, no striker [not violent], not given to filthy lucre [money]**; But a lover of hospitality, a lover of good men, **sober, just, holy, temperate**; Holding fast the faithful word as he hath been taught, that he may be able by sound doctrine both to exhort and to convince the gainsayers." (Titus 1:7-9, emphasis added)

We are going to look at some popes and compare their lives with the Biblical qualifications for being a bishop. In the process, we will learn about some distressing things. However, we should not be surprised. Jesus told us that there would be tares among the wheat. (Matthew 13:24-30) He also warned us that there would be wolves among the sheep. (Matthew 7:15) So did the Apostle Paul. (Acts 20:29-30)

Every church has had its share of tares and wolves. However, the Catholic Church claims to have apostolic succession—an unbroken chain of valid popes that go all the way back to the Apostle Peter. My reason for telling you about these "wolf" popes is to demonstrate that some popes were not even valid bishops, let alone valid popes. And that breaks the "chain" of apostolic succession.

I apologize for putting you through this, but I can't adequately make my point without giving you this information. (You can read about these popes online.)

Pope Honorius reigned from 625 to 638 A.D. He was condemned as a heretic by the Sixth Ecumenical Council (680-681). He was also condemned as a heretic by Pope Leo II, as well as by every other pope until the eleventh century.[1]

In 769, Pope Stephen IV came to power with the help of an army that conquered the previous Pope. Stephen gave orders for his papal rival to be flogged, have his eyes cut out, have his kneecaps broken, and be imprisoned until he died. Then Pope Stephen sentenced a second man to die a slow, agonizing death, by having pieces of his body cut off every day until he finally died.[2]

Pope Leo V only reigned for one month (July 903). Cardinal Christopher put Leo in prison and became Pope. Then Christopher was put in prison by Cardinal Sergius. Sergius killed Leo and Christopher while they were in prison. He also killed every cardinal who had opposed him.[3]

Pope John XII reigned from 955 to 963. He was a violent man. He was so lustful that people of his day said that he turned the Lateran Palace into a house of prostitution. He drank toasts to the devil. When gambling, he invoked pagan gods and goddesses. He was killed by a jealous husband while in the act of committing adultery with the man's wife.[4]

In the tenth century, a wealthy Italian noblewoman named Marozia put nine popes into office in eight years. In order to do that, she also had to get rid of reigning popes. Two of them were strangled, one was suffocated, and four disappeared under mysterious circumstances. One of the popes was Marozia's son; he was fathered by a Pope.[5]

In 1003, Pope Silvester II was murdered by his successor, Pope John XVII. Seven months later, John was poisoned.[6]

Pope Benedict VIII reigned from 1012 to 1024. He bought the papacy with bribery. He kept a private force of "pope's men" who were known for torture, maiming, and murder.[7]

When Benedict VIII died, his brother seized power and became Pope John XIX. He had himself ordained a priest, consecrated as a bishop, and crowned as pope, all in the same day. John died under suspicious circumstances.[8]

Pope Benedict IX reigned from 1032 to 1044, in 1045, and from 1047 to 1048. He became Pope through bribery. He had sex with men, women and animals. He gave orders for people to be murdered. He also practiced witchcraft and Satanism. The citizens of Rome hated Benedict so much that, on two occasions, he had to flee from Rome. Benedict sold the papacy to Pope Gregory VI. As part of the deal, he continued to live in the Lateran Palace, with a generous income. Benedict filled the Lateran Palace with prostitutes.[9]

In 1298, Pope Boniface VIII ordered that every man, woman, child, and animal in the Italian town of Palestrina be slaughtered. He was known for torture, massacre, and ferocity.[10]

Pope Clement VI reigned from 1342 to 1352. He ordered the slaughter of an entire Italian town. He lived a life of luxury and extravagance. He openly admitted that he sold church offices and he used threats and bribery to gain power. Clement purchased a French palace, which became famous for its prostitutes.[11]

Pope Alexander VI reigned from 1492 to 1503. He was known for murder, bribery, and selling positions of authority in the Church. He was grossly licentious. On one occasion, he required 50 prostitutes to dance naked before him, and to engage in sexual acts for his entertainment. He had cardinals killed so that he could confiscate their property and sell their positions to ambitious men. He died of poison after having dinner with a cardinal. It was rumored that the cardinal suspected that Alexander would try to poison him, and he therefore switched wine goblets with the Pope.[12]

Pope Julius II reigned from 1503 to 1513. He became Pope through bribery. He was ruthless and violent. He had a reputation for lust, drunkenness, rages, deception, and nepotism.[13]

Pope Leo X reigned from 1513 to 1521. He put a statue of himself in Rome's Capitol, to be saluted by the public. He had statues of Greek gods and goddesses put in Rome.[14]

Pope Gregory VII reigned from 1073 to 1085. He required kings and emperors to kiss his foot. Gregory and his successors used forged documents in order to expand the power of the papacy. Some Roman Catholics tried to expose these forgeries, but they were excommunicated for it. However, the Orthodox Church kept records and wrote detailed information about the forgeries.[15] (See the chapter, "Forged Documents and Papal Power.")

Simony was rampant among clerics. It was commonplace for priests to pay money in order to become bishops and abbots. Pope Gregory VII said that he knew of more than 40 men who became Pope by means of bribery.[16]

Pope Innocent III reigned from 1198 to 1216. He said that the Pope is the ruler of the world and the father of princes and kings. He claimed that every priest and bishop must obey the Pope, even if the Pope commands something evil.

Pope Innocent wanted to get rid of the Albigensian "heretics" who lived in France. He forced the King of France to kill hundreds of thousands of French citizens. Albigensians and Catholics lived together in the same area in France. Pope Innocent commanded that every person in the region, including the Catholics, be killed. This was called the Albigensian Crusade, or the Albigensian Massacre. The Pope gave the Albigensian Crusaders a special indulgence that was supposed to guarantee that, if they died in battle, then their sins would be remitted, and they would go to Heaven.[17]

Would you want any of these men to be your pastor?

Sometimes two or more men would claim to be Pope at the same time. All of these claimants to the papacy had followers. Eventually, one contender would be declared to be Pope and the other would be declared to be an antipope. For centuries, Roman Catholic books differed as to which men they considered to be the genuine popes. However, today there is much more agreement about which men were popes and which men were antipopes. According to *The Catholic Encyclopedia*, there were 30 antipopes. (This online.)[18]

None of these men met the biblical requirements for being an ordinary bishop, let alone Pope. Therefore, they were not valid popes. There are so many breaks in the chain of apostolic succession that it is not a chain at all.

There is one Biblical qualification for being a bishop that most popes have not met. The Apostle Paul said:

> "A bishop then must be blameless, the **husband of one wife**...One that ruleth well his own house, **having his children in subjection** with all gravity; **(For if a man know not how to rule his own house, how shall he take care of the church of God?)**" (1 Timothy 3:2, 4-5, emphasis added)

Paul said that even deacons should be married men whose home lives demonstrated their ability to rule the Church. He instructed Timothy as follows:

> "Let the deacons be the **husbands of one wife, ruling their children** and their own houses well." (1 Timothy 3:12, emphasis added)

Pope Gregory VII wanted to increase the power of the papacy. For reasons of politics and power, he abolished clerical marriage. In 1074, he passed laws requiring that priests be celibate, and he got rid of married priests. (Information is online.)[19]

As a result, since 1074, no Pope has been able to meet the Apostle Paul's requirement for bishops.

Now I realize that some individuals (such as the Apostle Paul) are called to be celibate. I could understand a few exceptions to the rule. But for nearly a thousand years, not one Pope or cardinal or bishop has been able to meet Paul's qualifications for being a bishop.

Chapter 10

Imperial Popes

In the year 314 A.D., Pope Silvester was crowned by Emperor Constantine. (At the time, Silvester was known as the Bishop of Rome, but Catholics refer to him as Pope Silvester.) The Roman Emperor wanted to promote Christianity. The Pope wanted to have the favor of the Roman Emperor, instead of being persecuted. This alliance between Pope and Emperor created the Roman Catholic Church.

Constantine gave Pope Silvester a beautiful palace and a magnificent cathedral. Instead of being a humble bishop, Silvester lived like a Roman nobleman. He had wealth, power, prestige, and the favor of the Roman Emperor. The power and influence of the Roman Empire were at the Pope's disposal.[1]

Churchmen wore purple robes, reflecting the purple of Constantine's court. That was an external change. The most important change was an internal one. Under Pope Silvester, the internal structure of the Church took on the form and practice and pomp of the Roman Empire. Popes dressed and acted like Roman emperors, and they had the same imperial attitude. They lived in luxury and they wanted to rule over both Church and state.[2]

Imperial papacy reached its peak during the Middle Ages. Popes were rich and powerful, and they ruled over kings and emperors. A well known example is the public humiliation of the Holy Roman Emperor by Pope Gregory VII. (Information is online.)[3]

Gregory declared that the Pope has the right to depose kings and emperors, to make laws, and to require secular rulers to kiss his feet. He said that nobody has the right to judge the Pope. Gregory also declared that, because of the merits of Saint Peter, every duly elected Pope is a saint.[4] (Because of that, some people refer to him as the Pope who canonized himself.)

Pope Innocent III reigned from 1198 to 1216. He called himself the Ruler of the World. He wore a gold crown covered with jewels. He sat upon a purple throne. His clothes sparkled with gold and jewels. His horse was covered with scarlet. Kings and churchmen kissed his foot. The Inquisition persecuted people who disagreed with him. Innocent became the most powerful man in the world. (This is online.)[5]

Pope Boniface VIII reigned from 1294 to 1303. He said that he was Caesar, the Roman Emperor. His crown was covered with over 200 costly jewels (rubies, emeralds, sapphires, and large pearls).[6]

Boniface sought to further increase the Pope's power and authority. In his encyclical, *Unam Sanctam*, he said that the Catholic Church has authority over national governments. He also declared that salvation depends on being subject to the Pope.[7]

(The rest of the information in this chapter is available online. You can check it out for yourself, including looking at pictures. See the Notes.)

Purple dye used to be extremely expensive. The color was a symbol of wealth and power. Purple was worn by Roman emperors and by Roman Catholic popes. During the Middle Ages, wealthy popes used gems and purple stones in papal architecture. The purple came from porphyry (a stone that has crystals embedded in a purple groundmass).[8]

Pope Paul II reigned from 1464 to 1471. In 1464, the Pope introduced the use of scarlet as another symbol of wealth and power. He called it "Cardinal's Purple," because it was worn by his cardinals. Scarlet became a luxury dye during the Middle Ages. Catholic cardinals still wear scarlet.[9]

Pope Paul VI reigned from 1963 to 1978. He was the last Pope to wear the papal tiara. This is a triple crown, covered with jewels. (You can see pictures of it online.)[10]

The Pope is an absolute monarch in the Vatican. He sits on an ornate throne. (You can see pictures of it online.[11]

Cardinals are called "princes of the church." They are citizens of the Vatican, in addition to being citizens of their homelands.[12]

Popes, cardinals and bishops wear gold and jewels. They wear rings and crosses. The Pope has a special ring known as the "Ring of the Fisherman." He also has magnificent pontifical rings that he wears on special occasions. Cardinals have rings of sapphire and gold. They often have additional rings of their own choosing.[13]

Catholics kiss the Pope's ring. They also kiss the rings of cardinals and bishops. It is traditional to kneel when kissing the Pope's ring. On August 2, 2002, the President of Mexico kissed the Pope's ring. He bowed instead of kneeling, but even that caused a political controversy.[14]

On special occasions, the Pope, cardinals, and bishops wear gold miters and gold vestments.[15] Popes wear ermine (an expensive fur often worn by royalty). They have a special cape called a mozzetta that is trimmed with ermine.[16]

For solemn occasions, popes use a portable throne called a *sedia gestatoria*. It is a richly adorned chair that is covered with silk. Long rods go through gold-covered rings. The throne is carried by twelve uniformed footmen.

When the Pope celebrates solemn pontifical Mass in Saint Peter's Basilica, he arrives in state, preceded by a procession of cardinals, bishops, and prelates. The Pope is carried on the *sedia gestatoria*, with a canopy over him, and special fans made of white feathers on either side of him.[17]

Pope Pius XII reigned from 1939 to 1958. When Vatican officials came into his presence, they had to kneel while speaking with him, and leave the room walking backwards. When he telephoned Vatican officials, they had to drop to their knees with the phone in their hand and remain kneeling while they spoke to him. This was going on in 1958. That is less than 50 years ago.[18]

The Pope has a huge, luxurious palace. The Pontifical Palace, the Sistine Chapel, and Saint Peter's Basilica are filled with priceless paintings and statues. The architecture is rich and ornate. The ceiling of the Sistine Chapel was painted by Michelangelo. In addition, there are 22 Vatican museums that are full of art treasures. You can see pictures of all of these things online. Words are inadequate to convey the rich architectural complexity and the artistic elegance of the Pope's palace, chapel, and church. Their opulence defies description.[19]

Chapter 11

Undermining the Bible

The Roman Catholic Church claims that it gave us the Bible. However, as we shall see, this claim does not stand up to the test of history.

The Old Testament was written by God's inspired prophets, patriarchs, psalmists, judges and kings. It was faithfully copied and preserved by Jewish scribes. The Old Testament of modern Protestant Bibles contains the same books as the Hebrew Bible.

The New Testament was written by Christian apostles. None of them were Catholics, because there was no Roman Catholic Church at the time. This was over two centuries before Constantine's "conversion" and the formation of the Roman Catholic Church in 314 A.D. (See the chapter, "Was the Early Church Roman Catholic?")

The early Church did not have the New Testament as we know it. Rather, individuals and local congregations had portions of it. They would have one or more of the Gospels, some of the letters that Apostles had written, and perhaps the Book of Acts or the Book of Revelation.

Why weren't all of these books collected in one place? Look at what the books themselves say. Individual apostles wrote them for specific audiences. The Gospel of Luke and the Book of Acts were written for Theophilus. (Luke 1:3; Acts 1:1) Most of the Epistles were written to specific churches or to specific individuals. (Romans 1:7; 1 Corinthians 1:2; 2 Corinthians 1:1; Galatians 1:2; Ephesians 1:1; Philippians 1:1; Colossians 1:2; 1 Thessalonians 1:1; 2 Thessalonians 1:1; 1 Timothy 1:2; 2 Timothy 1:2; Titus 1:4; Philemon 1:1-2; 3 John 1:1)

The early Christians expected that Jesus would return for His Church at any moment. As a result, they didn't see the need for long-term planning for future generations. Furthermore, Christians were persecuted by the Romans. When your life is in constant danger, it is difficult to collect writings that are scattered all over the Roman Empire. So it took time to collect all of these writings, decide which ones were authoritative Scripture, and make complete sets of them.

By the time of Origen (185-254 A.D.), there was general agreement about most of the New Testament. However, there was disagreement as to whether the following six epistles should be part of the New Testament: Hebrews, James, 2

Peter, 2 John, 3 John, and Jude. This was 60 years before the "conversion" of Emperor Constantine and the formation of the Roman Catholic Church.[1]

The Council of Carthage was held in 397 A.D. By then, there was general agreement as to which books belonged in the New Testament. The Council made a list of these books. It described the books that had already been accepted as being authoritative Scripture. In other words, the Council of Carthage did not create the canon of the New Testament. Rather, it just described the canon that already existed.[2]

The Catholic Church did not give us the Bible. However, Catholic monks helped preserve the Bible by copying it.

As we will see, the Catholic Church kept the Bible in Latin. This prevented people from reading the Bible in their own language. Most people didn't know Latin. Therefore, they had to depend on priests to read the Bible for them and explain it to them. They were not able to check what the priests taught against Scripture.

The Catholic Church changed the Bible. In 1548, at the Council of Trent, it added the Apocrypha to the Bible. The apocryphal books contain passages that are used to justify some Catholic doctrines, such as praying for the dead. (The Apocrypha are discussed later in this chapter.)

Keeping the Bible in Latin

Under Roman rule, Latin became a universal language. So when the Bible was originally translated from Greek and Hebrew into Latin, that made it more available to people. However, with the collapse of the Roman empire, Latin was spoken less and less. In time, only scholars understood it. The vast majority of people no longer spoke it.

Starting about 1080, there were many incidents where the Pope, Church councils, or individual bishops prohibited the translation of the Bible into the language of the common people (the vernacular). Laymen and Laywomen were forbidden to read the Bible in their native language, unless a bishop or an inquisitor gave them permission in writing. (You can read about this online.)[3]

In 1517, seven people were burned at the stake for teaching their children to say the Lord's Prayer in English. In 1536, William Tyndale was burned as a heretic for translating the Bible into English. In 1555, John Rogers and Thomas Cranmer were burned at the stake for translating the Bible. Men and women were also burned for reading the English translation of the Bible.[4]

Laymen were not even allowed to read the Bible in Latin. Reading the Bible was considered to be proof that someone was a heretic. Men and women were burned at the stake for reading the Bible in Latin.[5]

People were so hungry to know what the Bible said that, when an English translation of the Bible was finally made available, crowds of people filled the church where it was kept. Men took turns reading the Bible out loud. As long as there was daylight, men kept reading the Bible out loud, while the crowds listened. (This is online.)[6]

Struggling with Latin

When I became a Catholic, the Mass was still in Latin. I knew some Latin, because I had studied it for three years in college.

At High Mass, portions of the Bible were sung in Latin. The Bible was a large, ornate book. The priest would cover it with incense, bow before it, and sing the Scripture verses in Gregorian chant.

The music was beautiful and the ceremony was impressive. However, I could not understand the Scripture verses that were sung. With my three years of college Latin, I could sometimes understand the meaning of a word or a phrase. However, that did not enable me to understand the Scripture passages.

The end result reminds me of the Andy Warhol painting of a can of Campbell's tomato soup. You can read about it. You can study the picture. If you are an artist, you can paint a copy of it. You can do everything except eat the soup. But why does Campbell's make tomato soup? So that people will eat it. And why did God give us the Bible? So that people will read it, understand it, and be transformed by it.

Translating the Bible

The first English translation of the Bible was made in 1382 by the followers of John Wycliffe, with his help and inspiration. An improved version was completed in 1388. Wycliffe's followers were known as Lollards. They were severely persecuted. Wycliffe's translation of the Bible had to be copied by hand, which is a slow process. Most of the copies of Wycliffe's English Bible were destroyed. (Information is online.)[7]

A century and a half later, the Tyndale-Coverdale Bible was published in 1535. William Tyndale and Bishop Miles Coverdale translated the original Greek and Hebrew texts into English. Their Bible was published in Germany, where Tyndale had taken refuge. The printing press had been invented. This enabled Tyndale and his followers to produce copies of their English Bible faster than they could be found and destroyed. Tyndale was burned at the stake.[8]

Forty-seven years later (1582), the first Catholic translation of the New Testament into English was published. The Catholic translation of the Old

Testament was published in 1609. These translations were not from the original Greek and Hebrew. Rather, they were from a Latin translation of the Bible.[9]

Condemning Bible Societies

In 1846, and again in 1849, Pope Pius IX officially declared that Bible societies are "crafty enemies" of the Catholic Church and of humanity in general. Why? Because they translate the Bible into the language of the common people, and they give Bibles to anybody who wants them. (These encyclicals are online.) On September 3, 2000, Pope Pius IX was beatified. This is the last step before becoming a canonized saint.[10]

In 1864, Pope Pius IX officially declared that the idea that people have a right to freedom of conscience and freedom of worship is "insanity," "evil," "depraved," and "reprobate." He also declared that non-Catholics who live in Catholic countries should not be allowed to publicly practice their religion. In 1888, Pope Leo XIII declared that freedom of thought and freedom of religion are wrong.[11] (Papal encyclicals are online. They are easy to find.)

According to the Catholic doctrine of infallibility, these are infallible statements. (This is online.)[12] Therefore, they cannot be reversed.

This is not ancient history. My great-great-grandparents were alive in 1864.

Adding Tradition to Scripture

The Roman Catholic Church officially states that Catholic tradition is equal in authority to the Bible. (You can see this online.)[13]

Catholic tradition is difficult to define. The *Catechism of the Catholic Church* says that it is the various expressions of worship and belief of the Catholic people. (This is online.)[14] But what does that mean? The religious beliefs and practices of modern Catholics are quite different from those of Catholics in the Middle Ages. (Do you know any modern Catholics who wear relics in order to ward off demons, or who pay money for indulgences to get their loved ones out of Purgatory?) Yet the Catholic definition of tradition encompasses all of these beliefs and practices.

Let's narrow it down to modern Catholics in the United States, which is where I live. I know Catholics who devoutly believe that wearing a Brown Scapular at all times (even in the shower) will get them into Heaven. I know other Catholics who consider that to be superstitious nonsense. Using the pious practices of the Catholic people for a standard is like measuring things with a rubber band.

Jesus rebuked the Pharisees for putting tradition on a level with Scripture. He said that they nullified the Word of God for the sake of their traditions. Jesus said:

> "Howbeit in vain do they worship me, teaching for doctrines the commandments of men. For **laying aside the commandment of God, ye hold the traditions of men,** as the washing of pots and cups: and many other such like things ye do. And he said unto them, Full well **ye reject the commandment of God, that ye may keep your own tradition.**" (Mark 7:7-9, emphasis added)

> "**Making the word of God of none effect through your tradition,** which ye have delivered: and many such like things do ye." (Mark 7:13, emphasis added)

> "This people draweth nigh unto me with their mouth, and honoureth me with their lips; but their heart is far from me. But **in vain they do worship me, teaching for doctrines the commandments of men.**" (Matthew 15:8-9, emphasis added)

The Apostle Paul didn't think much of the traditions of men, either. He warned the Christians of his day:

> "Beware lest any man spoil [ruin] you through philosophy and vain deceit, after the tradition of men, after the rudiments of the world, and not after Christ." (Colossians 2:8)

Forbidding People to Interpret the Bible for Themselves

According to the *Catechism of the Catholic Church,* Catholics are required to find out how the Catholic bishops interpret Scripture passages, and they are to accept what the bishops teach "with docility," as if it came from Jesus Christ Himself. In other words, they are not allowed to believe what they read in the Bible without first checking it out with the Catholic Church. They are not allowed to use their own judgment, or to follow their own conscience. They are required to believe whatever the bishops teach, without questioning it. (You can read this online.)[15]

This attitude is exemplified by a statement that was made by Cardinal Hosius, who presided over the Council of Trent (1545-1564). Hosius wrote that, apart from the authority of the Catholic Church, the Bible would have no more importance than *Aesop's Fables*. (You can read this online.)[16]

The Apocrypha

The Apocrypha are books that occur in Catholic Bibles, but not in Protestant ones. They were never part of the Hebrew Bible. The Jews never considered them to be canonical. In 1548, the Council of Trent declared that the Apocrypha are canonical (part of inspired Scripture) and it anathematized anybody who believes otherwise.[17] (An anathema is a solemn ecclesiastical curse.)

Jesus and the Apostles quoted from the Old Testament hundreds of times, but they never treated any of the apocryphal books as being authoritative. The apocryphal books themselves never claim to be the Word of God. The books of *Tobit* and *Judith* contain serious historical inaccuracies. (Some information is online.)[18, 19]

Following is a summary of the main events in the *Book of Tobit*. (You can read it online.)[20]

My references to chapters and verses are those of the Revised Standard translation of Tobit. There is a wide variation in translations of Tobit, including differences in essential matters. There are also historical and geographical inaccuracies in the *Book of Tobit*. For example, Sennecherib was not the son of Shalmaneser. (Tobit 1:15) He was the son of Sargon the Usurper.[21]

Summary of the Book of Tobit

One night, Tobit slept outdoors, with his face uncovered. He slept by the courtyard wall. There were sparrows on the wall and bird droppings fell into Tobit's eyes. As a result, a white film formed over his eyes and he became blind. The physicians were unable to help him. (Tobit 2:9-10)

A maiden named Sarah was reproached by her maids, who accused her of strangling seven husbands before they consummated their marriage with her. This was attributed to a demon named Asmodeus. (Tobit 3:8)

The angel Raphael was sent to heal Tobit's eyes, to bind the demon Asmodeus, and to give Sarah in marriage to Tobias, the son of Tobit. (Tobit 3:17)

Tobias (Tobit's son) was traveling with the angel Raphael (who appeared in the form of a Jewish man named Azarias). A fish leaped up from the river and tried to swallow Tobias. Then the angel told Tobias to catch this fish. He caught it and threw it on the land. Then the angel told Tobias to cut the fish open, and to keep the heart and liver and gallbladder. He said that smoke from the heart and liver would drive demons and evil spirits away. He also said that, if a man's eyes are covered with white films, then having them be anointed with the fish gall would heal him. (Tobit 6:1-9)

Tobias was afraid to marry Sarah, because seven husbands had died in her bridal chamber. The angel told him to take burning incense, and to put the heart and liver of the fish on it, in order to make a smoke. He said that when the demon smelled the smoke, he would flee and never return. (Tobit 6:11-17)

Tobias married Sarah. He put the heart and liver of the fish upon burning incense. When the demon smelled the odor, he fled, and the angel bound him. Tobias and Sarah went to sleep. Sarah's family was greatly relieved the next morning when both of them were still alive. (Tobit, chapters 7 and 8)

Tobias and his new wife went to Tobit's home. The angel Raphael told Tobias to take the fish gall with him and to rub it on his father's eyes. Tobias followed the angel's instructions, and Tobit's eyes were healed. (Tobit 11:2-16)

Comments on Tobit

Does this sound like inspired Scripture to you? Does it reveal God's nature and character, and His ways of dealing with His people? Does it inspire you to want to know God better? Does it give you strength and courage to be a faithful Christian?

If the *Book of Tobit* was added to the Bible, would that increase your confidence in the rest of the Bible? Would it help you trust the reliability and authority of Scripture? Would it increase your motivation for reading the Bible?

The Catholic Church and the Bible

God gave us the Bible—not the Catholic Church.

The Catholic Church has been double-minded about the Bible. On the one hand, Catholic monks helped preserve it by copying it during the Middle Ages. On the other hand, the Catholic Church kept the Bible in Latin, and it killed scholars who translated the Bible into the language of the common people. In addition, it changed the Bible by adding the Apocrypha to it.

According to the *Catechism of the Catholic Church*, Catholics are not supposed to interpret the Bible for themselves. Rather, they are supposed to accept "with docility" whatever their bishops tell them about it. This is treating the Bible as if it is too dangerous for ordinary men and women to read, unless their understanding of it is constantly filtered through the lens of Catholic doctrine and official explanations.

The Bible is a Priceless Treasure

I live in America, where Bibles are plentiful and inexpensive. It is easy to take them for granted. However, right now, while you are reading this, there are Christians who are risking their lives to give Bibles to people. The ministry Open Doors has couriers who daily risk their lives to smuggle Bibles into countries where Christians are persecuted. I recently read about a man who was sentenced to death, because he gave a Bible to a Muslim.

Courageous men and women paid for the Bible with their blood. William Tyndale was burned at the stake for translating the Bible into English. Men were burned at the stake for teaching their children to say the Lord's Prayer in English. Men and women were burned at the stake for possessing an English translation of the Bible. We cannot comprehend the price that was paid to give us the Bible in our own language, or the great privilege of being able to read it without fear.

Here is what the Psalms say about the Bible. When you read the terms, "the law of the Lord," "the testimony of the Lord," "the statutes of the Lord," and "the judgments of the Lord," remember that these are Old Testament terms for the written Word of God.

May God give us this kind of passion for the Bible! Look at the love and loyalty and gratitude in these Scripture passages:

> "The law of the LORD is perfect, converting the soul: the testimony of the LORD is sure, making wise the simple. The statutes of the LORD are right, rejoicing the heart: the commandment of the LORD is pure, enlightening the eyes. The fear of the LORD is clean, enduring for ever: the judgments of the LORD are true and righteous altogether. More to be desired are they than gold, yea, than much fine gold: sweeter also than honey and the honeycomb. Moreover by them is thy servant warned: and in keeping of them there is great reward." (Psalm 19:7-11)

> "Blessed is the man that walketh not in the counsel of the ungodly, nor standeth in the way of sinners, nor sitteth in the seat of the scornful. But his delight is in the law of the LORD; and in his law doth he meditate day and night. And he shall be like a tree planted by the rivers of water, that bringeth forth his fruit in his season; his leaf also shall not wither; and whatsoever he doeth shall prosper." (Psalm 1:1-3)

"Wherewithal shall a young man cleanse his way? by taking heed thereto according to thy word. With my whole heart have I sought thee: O let me not wander from thy commandments. Thy word have I hid in mine heart, that I might not sin against thee. Blessed art thou, O LORD: teach me thy statutes. With my lips have I declared all the judgments of thy mouth. I have rejoiced in the way of thy testimonies, as much as in all riches. I will meditate in thy precepts, and have respect unto thy ways. I will delight myself in thy statutes: I will not forget thy word." (Psalm 119:9-16)

"For ever, O LORD, thy word is settled in heaven. Thy faithfulness is unto all generations: thou hast established the earth, and it abideth. They continue this day according to thine ordinances: for all are thy servants. Unless thy law had been my delights, I should then have perished in mine affliction. I will never forget thy precepts: for with them thou hast quickened me." (Psalm 119:89-93)

"Great peace have they which love thy law: and nothing shall offend them." (Psalm 119:165)

According to *Strong's Concordance*, the word "offend" in Psalm 119:165 means an enticement, or a stumbling-block. It is something that ruins people, or causes them to fall. So according to this Scripture verse, if we love the Word of God, then it will bring us peace, and it will protect us from temptation and destruction.

The Bible is indeed a priceless treasure!

Doctrine and Credentials

Chapter 12
New Age Catholicism

The "New Age" is actually a resurgence of old paganism that has been "westernized" and dressed up in modern vocabulary. It denies foundational Christian doctrines and basic Christian morality. It also denies Catholic doctrines, such as the authority of the Pope. But in spite of this, some Catholic priests and nuns have been promoting New Age beliefs and practices for many years.

I will give documented information about this from Catholic authors. One of them is a Catholic reporter who spent over 12 years getting first-hand, eye-witness information. Much of this information is available online. (The Notes give information.)

As we will see, there are priests and nuns who promote pagan rituals, occult activities, Hindu religious practices, worship of "the goddess," witchcraft, and "channeling" (having "spirits" speak through you). They deny foundational Christian doctrines, such as the fact that Jesus Christ died to save us from our sins. And they renounce traditional Christian morality.

If you have difficulty with the following information, I understand. So do I. But the facts won't go away just because we don't like them.

Randy England is Catholic. He wrote *The Unicorn in the Sanctuary: The Impact of the New Age on the Catholic Church*. According to England, New Age concepts are taught at Catholic retreats, prayer workshops, and educational conferences.[1]

The theology of Catholic priest Teilhard de Chardin opened the door for New Age concepts to come into the Catholic Church. (*Unicorn*, pages 78-95) These New Age beliefs led to "creation-centered spirituality," which is discussed later in this chapter. (*Unicorn*, pages 118-134)

Thomas Merton was a Trappist monk. He taught that every form of mystical experience is valid, no matter what its source. He praised Hinduism and Buddhism. Merton wanted to see the religions of the world become united. (*Unicorn*, pages 75-77)

Some priests and nuns are teaching trusting Catholics to do Hindu meditation, to use visualization techniques, and to cultivate spirit guides. Randy England says that spirit guides are demons. (*Unicorn*, pages 3 and 77)

Therefore, a person who cultivates spirit guides is actually invoking demons and inviting them to control his or her life.

A Jesuit priest teaches priests, nuns, and lay Catholics to do Eastern meditation, using spirit guides. Priests and nuns teach prayer techniques that are not prayer in the Christian sense at all. Rather, they result in altered states of consciousness, and susceptibility to demonic influence. A Franciscan priest teaches Catholics to "manipulate" reality with the assistance of "spirit beings" (demons). He is especially influential with nuns. Catholics are taught that their "spirituality" will be improved by New Age techniques such as yoga, practices from Eastern religions, and occult meditation. Some Catholic schools no longer teach the Ten Commandments and foundational Christian doctrines, such as the Resurrection. (*Unicorn*, pages 6-9 and 135-146)

Mitch Pacwa is a Jesuit priest who became involved in the New Age when he was in the seminary. He wrote *Catholics and the New Age*. According to Pacwa, some Catholic parishes give workshops on astrology, channeling, and the enneagram (a New Age system of personality analysis). Pacwa had extensive personal experience with the enneagram. He became proficient and he taught it to other priests.[2]

During the period between 1970 and 1980 (when I was still a Catholic), I ran into three New Age things that were promoted by Catholic priests. First, a Catholic priest recommended self-hypnosis and gave me cassette tapes for doing it. Fortunately, I never listened to the tapes. I have since learned that any form of hypnosis is spiritually dangerous.

Second, some Catholic friends enthusiastically recommended that I attend a Catholic workshop on "Centering Prayer," which was given by a priest. Fortunately, I was not able to attend the workshop. I bought the priest's book, but it seemed strange and I didn't read much of it. According to Randy England, "Centering Prayer" is similar to Silva Meditation (Silva Mind Control). It involves altered states of consciousness and spirit guides. (*Unicorn*, pages 143-146)

Third, I went on a Catholic retreat that was led by priests. Much to my surprise, the psychology of Carl Jung was taught throughout the retreat. In addition, they sold books that discussed spirituality in terms that didn't sound Christian. One of the books talked about finding "the goddess within." According to Randy England, Carl Jung was an occultist who had spirit guides.

In each of these situations, I had a genuine desire to become closer to God. I went to Catholic priests, looking for training in how to pray, looking for things to strengthen my spiritual life. But instead of offering me Christian things, those priests offered me New Age things, and they presented it as being normal Catholicism.

New Age Catholicism • 71

According to Randy England, Donna Steichen, and Mitch Pacwa, my experience was not unusual. Similar things have happened to many Catholics.

Radical Catholic Feminists

The following information about radical Catholic feminists comes from the book, *Ungodly Rage*. Some of this information is available in online articles about the book.[3]

Donna Steichen (a Catholic journalist) wrote, *Ungodly Rage: The Hidden Face of Catholic Feminism*. She spent 12 years getting first-hand information. Her book is based on things that she personally saw and heard, plus the writings of Catholic feminists. She is a good reporter, giving names, dates, quotations, and detailed, first-hand, eyewitness accounts of events.

There are some radical Catholic feminist leaders who teach that every kind of sexual expression is good. They say that every act of "love" and pleasure is a ritual that honors the goddess. Their openly stated goal is to redefine sexuality and morality. Donna Steichen asked some feminist nuns about these teachings. The nuns enthusiastically agreed with the teachings and with the morality resulting from them. (*Ungodly Rage*, pages 41-45, 150, and 176-177)

In 1985, Mrs. Steichen attended a conference on "Women and Spirituality." (The following information about this conference is from pages 29 to 63 of *Ungodly Rage*.)

A community of teaching nuns was deeply involved. Some of the nuns gave workshops during the conference. Many of them attended the conference. They helped with preparations and they allowed attendees to stay at their educational center.

The Catholic priest who is the chaplain of a nearby Catholic school announced the conference. He also made arrangements for transportation for women who wanted to attend it. Faculty members and students attended. Donna Steichen interviewed the priest. He had studied the program and he was aware of its nature. He approved of it.

The conference was an ecumenical event. Sixteen of the speakers were Catholics (nuns, former nuns, and laywomen). The majority of the women who attended were Catholics. They included nuns, teachers at parochial schools and Catholic colleges, staff members of Catholic counseling agencies, parish administrators, and laywomen. In other words, many attendees were women in positions of authority and influence.

Speakers promoted goddess worship and the exploration of "sacred" sexuality. A sense of victim mentality was fostered. The idea of sin was mocked.

According to the speakers, the only sin is discriminating against women. Most of the workshops included pagan rituals.

Most speakers ignored Jesus altogether, but one said that some people might want to retain Him as a "symbol." She said that the objective of Catholic feminism is to take over the Catholic church, and in order to do this, it needs to maintain the appearance of legitimate Catholicism.

She told women to establish covens, or Women-Church groups, to celebrate their own rituals. These groups would either replace traditional Christian churches, or else be places of refuge where women who retain church affiliation would be free to share their true feelings. She said that large groups should be subdivided into groups of 13 members, because 13 is the number for a coven. (The term "coven" is usually applied to groups of witches.)

Steichen interviewed many of the attendees. None of the Catholic women saw any conflict between their Catholicism and their attendance at this conference. They even defended the worship of pagan gods, saying that it does not conflict with Catholicism. Mrs. Steichen asked them if the early martyrs were wrong to face death for refusing to worship pagan gods. The women didn't get the point. They usually responded that things are different now.

Mrs. Steichen also interviewed some Protestant women. They were disturbed by the conference. I believe that if the Catholic women had been well grounded in Scripture, they would have been less susceptible to deception.

On Sunday morning, three feminist services were available for conference participants. One of them was a Wiccan ritual, which was attended by about half of the women (including Donna Steichen). As part of the ritual, the participants cast a spell. (Wicca is a pagan religion that is based on witchcraft. It involves goddess worship, rituals, and spells.)

After the ritual was over, Steichen asked one participant if she was a nun. The woman said that she wasn't, but she always sees a lot of nuns at these rituals.

The Catholic feminist movement grew in numbers and in influence. The next year (1986), a "Women in the Church" conference was attended by 2,500 women, 85 percent of whom were nuns. (That is more than 2,000 nuns.) Donna Steichen attended the conference.

One speaker told the women to get rid of the "false god" of Christianity and create a "God-myth" to replace it. She advocated the use of sexuality to empower women. Another speaker said that Scripture should be radically transformed in order to make it support the feminist agenda. An example of this is one speaker's interpretation of what happened in the Garden of Eden. She said that when God banished the snake, it was patriarchy banishing the goddess and banishing Eve's freedom to express herself sexually. (*Ungodly Rage*, pages 123-124 and 145-153)

About 200 of the nuns who attended wore habits. At first, Steichen thought that they must not have realized the nature of the conference when they decided to come. However, every single nun that she interviewed enjoyed the conference and agreed with it. One of them had been orthodox in her beliefs until she took a summer class at the University of Notre Dame. As a result of that class, she became a radical feminist. (*Ungodly Rage*, page 133)

Some Catholic clergymen support the radical Catholic feminists. This conference was given under the auspices of Catholic bishops and priests. Advisors for the conference included nearly 20 bishops and 15 priests. (*Ungodly Rage*, pages 152-153)

In October, 1987, a "Women-Church" Conference was attended by 3,000 women, including Donna Steichen. Most of them were Catholics. Many were nuns and former nuns who were involved in teaching, social service, or pastoral ministry. In other words, they were women in trusted positions of leadership, influence, and authority. (*Ungodly Rage*, page 154)

Speakers identified sexuality with spirituality and with a woman's identity. They said that "sexual empowerment" is the key to empowering women. One speaker said that her lesbianism is a form of goddess religion. Speakers promoted abortion. One speaker openly said that, in order to promote their feminist religion, they need the institutional Catholic Church, because it is a global power with far-reaching influence. Workshops included instruction in animism (worship of nature spirits), and rituals that were a combination of feminism and Native American practices. (*Ungodly Rage*, pages 150-154 and 173-183)

One speaker said that, in order for the Catholic feminist movement to survive, it must influence the next generation. Now this is a practical problem for a movement that is largely founded on nuns and lesbian laywomen, because they usually don't have children. Therefore, they have to influence other people's children. The speaker spoke of the need to create places to influence children, including schools, retreat centers, think tanks, and centers for feminist theology. (*Ungodly Rage*, pages 185-186)

Much of this was already in place when Donna Steichen wrote *Ungodly Rage* in 1991. The conference participants were primarily Catholic teachers, nuns from retreat centers, and women who work with youth. In other words, they were in positions that enable them to influence Catholic children and young people. Conference participants also included women who were administrators in chancery offices and parishes. This position enables them to influence what kinds of programs, retreats, and workshops are given in Catholic parishes.

The problem here is misrepresentation. These women call themselves Catholics, but they are practicing Wicca (or other earth-based religions) in addition to (or instead of) Catholicism. They hold trusted positions of authority as Catholic teachers, counselors, or leaders at retreat centers. To claim to be a Catholic teacher, and then teach Wiccan beliefs and morals to children in Catholic schools, is fraud. (It would be equally fraudulent for a Catholic teacher to pretend to be Wiccan, and teach Catholicism in a Wiccan school.)

One of the speakers was a Carmelite nun who founded the Association of Contemplative Sisters. She said that these contemplative nuns started out with their focus on God, but they changed their focus to feminism and mysticism. They incorporated pagan traditions into their worship and meditation. (*Ungodly Rage*, pages 182-183)

You can see a description of a "Women-Church" conference online, complete with quotations and a description of the pagan ritual. This conference was held on April 20, 1996, at Emmanuel College (a Catholic college in Boston). Starhawk (a witch) led a pagan ritual dedicated to the goddess.[4]

A nun teaches Silva Mind Control, including giving classes on astral projection and "spirit messages." (*Ungodly Rage*, page 342)

There is a conference called, "Womenspirit Rising," that includes workshops on reincarnation, "the goddess within," the use of crystals, and channeling. "Womenspirit Rising" was given at the provincial motherhouse of an order of teaching nuns. (*Ungodly Rage*, page 342)

A Catholic college, that is run by nuns, invited the "Womenspirit Rising" conference to their college twice in the same year. (*Ungodly Rage*, pages 106-107) Catholic parents who sacrificed to send their children to this Catholic college probably did not expect to have them be trained in channeling and goddess worship.

Two people who have had a significant influence on the Catholic feminist movement are Matthew Fox and Rosemary Ruether. Fox will be discussed later.

Ruether is a Catholic feminist theologian who is openly lesbian. She developed a liturgy for the "covenanting" of lesbian couples. Ruether's books include: *Gaia & God: An Ecofeminist Theology of Earth Healing*, and *Religious Feminism and the Future of the Planet: A Christian-Buddhist Conversation*.

Matthew Fox

The following information about Matthew Fox comes from chapter 6 of Randy England's book, *The Unicorn in the Sanctuary*. It is called, "Woman Church, Witchcraft, and the Goddess." (This chapter is online at a Catholic website.)[5]

As a Dominican priest, Matthew Fox promoted Wicca, paganism, and goddess worship in the Catholic Church. For years, he told trusting Catholic priests, nuns, and lay people that the Holy Spirit wants them to adopt these practices.

The Institute for Culture and Creation Spirituality was founded by Fox. It is located at Holy Names College (a Catholic college run by nuns). Staff members of the Institute used to include a practicing witch named Starhawk, a voodoo priestess, a shaman (an animist who worships nature spirits), and a Jungian psychologist. They later moved to the University of Creation Spirituality, which was also founded by Fox. Starhawk is the high priestess of a witches' coven. The Institute has developed a Catholic liturgy that is based on Wiccan sources.

Matthew Fox denies the existence of sin, except for one thing. He says that it is sinful to fail to embrace the New Age.

Fox preaches "sensual" spirituality, hedonism, and "ecstasy." He says that drugs can be used as an aid to prayer. He openly and directly promotes witchcraft.

The following information about Matthew Fox comes from an article by Catholic priest Mitch Pacwa. It is called, *Catholicism for the New Age: Matthew Fox and Creation-Centered Spirituality*. (Pacwa's article and some related information are online. Information about Fox's organizations comes from websites and phone conversations.)[6]

Fox is the founder, president, and editor-in-chief of a magazine called, *Creation*. You can get some idea of what he believes by the pictures in his magazine. The July/August, 1991, issue of *Creation* featured a picture of Jesus Christ, naked, seated in a lotus position, with antlers on his head. The May/June, 1992, issue featured a picture called, "The Qetzalcoatl Christ." It showed the Aztec snake god with the face of Jesus Christ.

Matthew Fox is a popular speaker with great influence. He denies original sin and redemption. He says that, in order to find the "Cosmic Christ," we need to stop seeking the "historical Jesus."

According to Fox, true spirituality is about Eros. He says that Holy Communion should be "intimate" and "erotic." He says that spirituality should be sensual.

Fox teaches that people of all religions should be mystically united. He openly promotes witchcraft, shamanism, astrology, and pagan religions. He praises the writings of the witch, Starhawk, and her vision of a revival of goddess worship.

Fox says that Christianity that focuses on Jesus Christ as personal Savior is "antimystical" and opposed to a "Cosmic Christ" Christianity.

In 1991, Fox was ordered to leave his Institute for Culture and Creation Spirituality, or be dismissed by his religious order. He refused, left the Catholic Church, and became an Anglican priest. He founded the University of Creation Spirituality. Starhawk and the voodoo priestess also left the Institute for Culture and Creation Spirituality. They are now with Matthew Fox at his University of Creation Spirituality. Both organizations are located in Oakland, California.

Although Fox has left the Institute for Culture and Creation Spirituality, it is still at Holy Names College. However, its name has been changed. It is now called the Sophia Center in Culture and Spirituality. It gives graduate degrees in Creation Spirituality. Judging by its courses and faculty members, it teaches shamanism, African religions, and "eco-feminism." Several courses appear to be Wiccan.

Although he is no longer a Catholic, Fox continues to have widespread influence among Catholics. He has influenced priests and nuns, and they influence other Catholics. In addition, Fox's Creation Spirituality is being taught at the Sophia Center in Culture and Spirituality, at Holy Names College.

Fox's books are sold in both Catholic and New Age bookstores. His books are featured at some Catholic retreat houses. They are used by nuns. This not only influences the nuns, it also influences Catholics who come under the influence of those nuns. (For example, other nuns, or students, or Catholics who attend retreats.)

Fox wrote a book called, *Whee! We, Wee All the Way Home: A Guide to a Sensual, Prophetic Spirituality*. [Honest. I'm not kidding. You can check it out for yourself at Amazon.com.] He also wrote, *On Becoming a Musical, Mystical Bear: Spirituality American Style*. Other books by Fox include *One River Many Walls: Wisdom Springing from Global Faiths* and *Exploring the Cosmic Christ Archetype*.

Because of Fox's teachings, some nuns have incorporated Wiccan rituals into their worship. Some nuns are teaching Fox's "creation spirituality" to young children, and are neglecting foundational doctrines such as sin and redemption. (Fox doesn't believe in these doctrines.)

Cultivating Bitterness

Some leaders of the Catholic feminist movement exhort women to cultivate rage and anger against patriarchy. This is contrary to Scripture, which warns us to avoid bitterness. The Bible says:

> "Follow peace with all men, and holiness, without which no man shall see the Lord: Looking diligently lest any man fail of the grace of God; lest any root of bitterness springing up trouble

you, and thereby many be defiled; Lest there be any fornicator, or profane person, as Esau, who for one morsel of meat sold his birthright." (Hebrews 12:14-16)

Strong's Concordance defines the word "profane" as "heathenish." According to *Webster's Dictionary,* "heathen" means "pagan." The Bible connects bitterness with failure to respond to God's grace, defiling other people, sexual immorality, pagan behavior, and forfeiting one's spiritual inheritance. The Catholic feminist movement encourages women to become bitter, and remain bitter, and call it a virtue.

Donna Steichen says that radical feminist nuns tend to be committed to their "careers," and they refuse to leave the Catholic Church, even when they no longer believe its teachings. They stay in their positions, in order to try to destroy the Catholic Church as we know it, and create a new, feminist religion in its place. (*Ungodly Rage,* page 26)

Involuntary New Age Indoctrination

Catholic educators have been exposed to New Age indoctrination, when they didn't expect it, and they weren't prepared for it. This is of strategic importance for the radical Catholic feminist movement. If you indoctrinate an educator, then you influence all of his or her students. If one of those students is a nun, then she is likely to influence other nuns in her convent. In addition, radical feminist educators can influence their colleagues, thus spreading the influence of radical feminism on the educational system.[7]

Jean Houston was the director of the Foundation for Mind Research. She was also the past president of the Association for Humanistic Psychology. She frequently speaks at New Age conferences. In 1982, 1984, and 1989, Jean Houston addressed Catholic educators at the convention of the National Catholic Education Association. (*Ungodly Rage,* pages 242-245)

Between 1985 and 1988, the National Catholic Education Association had a Catholic Education Futures Project. Twenty other Catholic educational organizations participated in it. This conference was attended by leaders in Catholic education. It was billed as being preparation for future needs. However, in actuality, it was New Age indoctrination. (*Ungodly Rage,* pages 244-245)

Some Catholic feminist nuns teach New Age spirituality at parochial schools and Catholic colleges. This betrays the trust of the Catholic parents who send their children to these schools.

Mundelein is a Catholic women's college that is run by nuns. It is affiliated with Loyola University, which is run by Jesuit priests. According to Donna

Steichen, in March, 1985, a conference called "The Goddesses and the Wild Women" was held at Mundelein, and in 1986, the conference was repeated. In addition, a program called, "Her Holiness: Maiden, Mother, Crone" was given. The program honored the "triple goddess" of witchcraft. It included a croning ritual, which is a witchcraft initiation ritual. (*Ungodly Rage*, pages 79-91)

When parents send their daughters to a Catholic college that is run by nuns, they probably think that their daughters will be taught the Catholic doctrines of *The Catechism of the Catholic Church*. Who would ever think that, in such an environment, their daughters would be exposed to goddess worship and a witchcraft initiation ritual.

In the world of business, this would be called "bait and switch." This is the practice of attracting customers by offering them what they want to get, and then switching them to what you want to sell them.

Heythrop College (in London) is run by Jesuit priests. In January, 2002, the college hired a professed witch to teach psychology of religion. This was done with the approval of the Jesuit priest who is the president of the college. (You can read about this online).[8]

Catholic parents who send their children to Heythrop College probably do not expect to have them come under the influence of a teacher who is a practicing witch. Even though her subject matter is not witchcraft, her witchcraft beliefs and values will influence her view of both psychology and religion, and the way in which she presents them. In addition, teachers can have a personal influence on their students.

Again, the problem is false representation. If Catholic parents send their Catholic children to a Catholic school, expecting them to be taught Catholicism, then that is what they should be taught—not something else that the parents didn't expect and don't want. It would be equally wrong to teach Catholicism in a Hindu school or a Wiccan school. When people pay money to have their children be trained in the beliefs of their family's religion, then they should get what they paid for.

Related Issues

Matthew Fox is not the only Catholic priest who teaches New Age spirituality. There are others. One example is George Maloney, who is a Jesuit priest. He wrote, *Mysticism and the New Age: Christic Consciousness in the New Creation*. Several other Catholic priests also teach Fox's creation spirituality.

There is a Benedictine monastery that calls itself a "Christian Ashram." People can study mysticism, comparative religion, and Indian music there. Dom. Bede Griffiths is in charge of it. His books include, *Cosmic Revelation:*

The Hindu Way to God, and *The Other Half of My Soul: Bede Griffiths and the Hindu-Christian Dialogue*.

Griffiths combines Catholicism with Hinduism. Another priest combines Catholicism with Buddhism. Dom. Aelred Graham wrote, *Zen Catholicism*, and *Conversations: Christian and Buddhist*.

Catholic priest Edward Hays runs a Catholic-Hindu "house of prayer" that has statues of Hindu gods. There is also a crucifix. The "house of prayer" is popular and it is usually filled to capacity. (*Unicorn in the Garden*, pages 72-74)

Jesuit priest Anthony de Mello gives workshops that introduce Catholics to Eastern prayer and meditation techniques, including visualization and Transcendental Meditation. He wrote, *Sadhana: A Way to God*. The book's cover shows Jesus on the cross and a person seated in the lotus position, meditating at the foot of the cross. (*Unicorn*, pages 100-114)

Some Catholic theologians teach that it is wrong to insist that Jesus Christ has a unique status in salvation. They say that it hinders unity with people of other religions, such as Buddhists and Hindus. A Catholic "center for spirituality" features readings from the "holy books" of many faiths, celebrates pagan festivals, and includes statues of Buddha and Vishnu in their chapel. In 1998, there was a retreat that was attended by both Catholics and Buddhists. In 1999, a Catholic Advent celebration included Buddhist monks and nuns. There is a website that is devoted to facilitating dialogue between Catholics, Buddhists, and Hindus.[9]

The Ursuline Sophia Center (run by Ursuline nuns) features labyrinth walks, Reiki, and spiritual programs that are inspired by religions that are not Christian. (Reiki involves New Age manipulation of "energy" fields and the transfer of "energy" to other people.) Their store sells items for doing Reiki, Yoga, and T'ai Chi. They have classes for training people to do Reiki. (These are described on their website.)[10]

I know a man who went to a seminary to become a Catholic priest. One of his seminary professors recommended some books written by Wiccan authors. He was influenced by those books, and he became a Wiccan priest instead of a Catholic priest. Eventually, God rescued him, and he became a born-again, Protestant Christian.

New Age Morals

Notre Dame is a well-known Catholic university. It is run by Holy Cross priests. In 2002, some Notre Dame students and faculty members produced a play called *V-Monologues*. ("V-" is my euphemism for the word for female reproductive anatomy. This word, and its slang counterpart, are prominently featured in the play.) (You can read about this at a Catholic website.)[11]

In the play, a 24-year-old woman gets a 13-year-old girl drunk and seduces her. (This is statutory rape.) There is a "chorus" that chants "V–" and its slang counterpart like a mantra. The play is obsessed with female reproductive anatomy. (I apologize. But if it is unpleasant to read an understated summary of the play, what would it be like to have your children watch it, or perform in it—at a Catholic university run by Catholic priests.)

This play was performed with the blessing of Notre Dame's president, a Catholic priest named Edward Malloy. He has publicly stated that the Catholic Church needs to change its approach to alternative forms of sexuality. So this play probably promotes his beliefs.

The play was also performed at Saint Mary's, a Catholic women's college near Notre Dame. Saint Mary's is run by Holy Cross nuns. One of the actresses was a Holy Cross nun, a faculty member of Saint Mary's. The nun wore a tee shirt that said: "Can you say V–?" And she chanted along with the "chorus." (The play is described online.)[12]

I cannot imagine what it would be like to watch a nun do that—a nun who is supposed to embody consecrated purity.

In 2001, this play was performed at Georgetown University, a prestigious Catholic university that is run by Jesuit priests. The editor-in-chief of the university's newspaper (*The Hoya*) wrote an article about the play. He described the audience's rowdy enthusiasm during the raunchiest parts of the play, and he criticized Georgetown University's administration for allowing the play to be performed. He was fired, and his article was never published. (Information is online.)[13]

By March, 2002, six other Catholic colleges and universities had produced V– Monologues. They are: the University of Detroit Mercy, Loyola University, Villanova University, Marist College, Marquette University, and Fordham University.[14]

In 2003, V–Monologues was scheduled to be performed at 42 Catholic colleges and universities. There was a letter-writing campaign against the play, but it failed. The play was performed at 41 of the Catholic colleges.[15]

This play is contrary to traditional Catholic morality. The fact that it was performed at these Catholic universities and colleges demonstrates the wide variety of beliefs and practices among Catholics.

How Could This Happen?

How could this happen? How could priests and nuns become so deeply deceived? How could Catholic laymen and laywomen so easily accept New Age teaching from priests and nuns, when that teaching clearly contradicts traditional Catholic practice and doctrine?

It is easy to deceive people who are used to being told what to think. As we will see, the Catholic Church claims that it has the right to control how Catholics think.

According to Canon Law (the official laws governing the Roman Catholic Church), Catholics are required to **submit their minds and wills** to any declaration concerning faith or morals that is made by the Pope or by a church council. (These laws are online. You can read them for yourself.)[16]

The Catholic Church teaches that only the Magisterium of the Church (the Pope and the bishops in communion with him) has the right to interpret Scripture. According to Catholic doctrine, people like us are not allowed to interpret Scripture for ourselves. Rather, we have to check it out with Church authorities. (This is online.)[17]

In other words, Catholics are required to use authority figures in order to check out Scripture. This is the opposite of the Bible, which tells us that we should use Scripture in order to check out the teachings of authority figures.

The Apostle Paul wrote much of the New Testament. He went to the Third Heaven and was given revelations of things that he was not allowed to tell us about. He was given such great revelations that God sent him a "thorn in the flesh" to keep him humble. (2 Corinthians 12:2-7) Paul was so highly regarded by the Apostles that he was able to publicly rebuke Peter. (Galatians 2:11-14)

Paul was a great apostle, a martyr, and a hero of the faith. Much of our theology is based on his writings. Certainly, the Apostle Paul had more authority than any Pope or bishop. But does the Bible rebuke people who questioned Paul's teachings? Were people expected to submit their minds and wills to whatever the Apostle Paul taught them about faith and morals? Not at all.

On the contrary, the Bible commends the people of Berea because, when the Apostle Paul preached to them, they checked out what he said against Scripture. They "searched the Scriptures daily" in order to "see whether these things were so." (Acts 17:10-11)

God wants His people to check things out for themselves, using Scripture as their yardstick. The Apostle Paul urged Christians to:

> "Prove all things; hold fast that which is good." (1 Thessalonians 5:21).

According to *Strong's Concordance*, the word "prove" means, "to test." We are supposed to test things, to check them out for ourselves, using the Bible for our plumb line. If we are faithful to do that, then it will help us become mature Christians who are not deceived by false doctrines. If we fail to do it, then we will be vulnerable to every "wind of doctrine" that comes along. The Bible says:

> "That we henceforth be no more children, tossed to and fro, and carried about with every wind of doctrine, by the sleight of men, and cunning craftiness, whereby they lie in wait to deceive..." (Ephesians 4:14)

Catholicism and Paganism

Historically, Catholicism has been combined with paganism in various countries and cultures. This was seen with Emperor Constantine, who worshiped both the Roman sun god and Jesus Christ. Many Christians of his day followed his example.

This may be one reason why many Catholics (including priests and nuns) have been vulnerable to New Age beliefs and practices. Following are some modern examples of paganism being mixed with Catholicism. (The following information is all online. See the Notes.)

Voodoo is practiced in Africa, South America, and the West Indies. It is also practiced in some areas of the United States. Haiti and New Orleans are famous for it. Voodoo is a mixture of Catholicism and West African religion. Practitioners invite "spirits" (demons) to "mount" them (possess them). Voodoo involves black magic, curses, and spells. People who practice Voodoo often practice regular Catholicism as well. For example, Marie Leveau was the most famous Voodoo Queen in New Orleans. She went to Mass every day. She considered herself to be a devout Catholic.[18]

In Cuba, there is an annual festival in honor of Saint Lazarus, which combines Catholic and Voodoo rituals. According to *Catholic World News*, celebrations include Catholic Mass, offerings of rum and cigars, and having pilgrims carry crosses or drag heavy weights that are chained to their bodies. In 1996, Cardinal Jaime Ortega of Havana said the Mass.[19]

In South Africa, animals are sacrificed during Roman Catholic Mass. Archbishop Buti Tlhagale of Bloemfontein has actively promoted this practice. Archbishop George Daniel of Pretoria said that animal sacrifice is being done in parishes in his diocese. There is a video showing it. A Catholic priest blessed chickens and goats during Mass. The animals were slaughtered. Their blood was poured into a hole outside of the church.[20]

In Guatemala, Mayan rituals are combined with Catholicism. In Chichicastenango, Guatemala, there is a Mayan-Catholic Mass. Mayan rituals are conducted inside the Catholic church, while the Catholic priest says Mass. One half of the church has pews. The other half has a bare floor, so that people can put candles and flowers and other things on the floor as part of their Mayan rituals. This is so popular that it is featured in Guatemalan tourist guides.[21]

Mexicans celebrate the Day of the Dead. This is a combination of Aztec religion and Catholicism. In modern cities, it can be primarily just a festival. But in rural areas, it is a serious religious ritual. Some Catholic Mexicans actually worship the dead.[22]

Brazil is the largest Catholic country in the world. It has 115 million Catholics, which is 12 percent of the Roman Catholic Church. In other words, one out of nine Catholics lives in Brazil. Ninety-three percent of Brazilians claim to be Catholic. However, at least 60 percent of Brazilians practice spiritism. In other words, more than half of Brazil's Catholics practice spiritism, in addition to Catholicism. Brazilian Catholics are known for having "double affiliations" (being members of two or more different religions at the same time). Religions that are often practiced by Brazilian Catholics include: Candomble, Umbanda, Macumba, and Kardecism. In addition, many Brazilians practice witchcraft or consult witches.[23]

Candomble, Umbanda, and Macumba are all mixtures of Catholicism, various African religions, and the beliefs of Brazilian Indians. Religious practices include inviting "spirits" (demons) to possess the worshipers. Many Brazilians practice both traditional Roman Catholicism and Candomble. Macumba practitioners do black magic. Kardecism is a form of spiritism that includes belief in reincarnation.[24]

Santeria is a Caribbean religion that combines Catholicism with African religions. People who practice Santeria often practice regular Catholicism as well. Cities with large Hispanic populations usually have Santeria.[25]

It is a pagan practice to do painful things in order to try to obtain the favor of the gods. An example of this occurred during the confrontation between Elijah and the prophets of Baal. In their efforts to get Baal to send down fire, the prophets cut themselves with knives "till the blood gushed out upon them." (1 Kings 18:26-28) Some extreme Catholic penitential practices are similar.

In the Philippines, during Holy Week (the week preceding Easter), there are folk rituals. These include penitential processions with hundreds of men who whip themselves until their backs are covered with blood. Some people are literally crucified at the end of a Passion Play on Good Friday (but they are only left on the cross for a short time). The crucifixions first began in 1961, with a "healer" who wanted to be crucified in order to acquire "sacred power" for "esoteric healing." Following his example, many other "healers" were also crucified. The practice spread and was no longer limited to "healers." Some people have come from foreign countries in order to be crucified. Women have been crucified.[26]

Conclusion

When people are used to being told what to believe, then they have little protection against false teaching—especially if it comes from authority figures, such as priests and nuns.

It is far more difficult to deceive people who use the Bible to test things, and who ask God to guide them and correct them. The Bible gives us some beautiful examples of humble prayers for guidance, instruction, and correction. Look at these passages from the Psalms:

> "Who can understand his errors? cleanse thou me from secret faults." (Psalm 19:12)

> "With my whole heart have I sought thee: O let me not wander from thy commandments." (Psalm 119:10)

> "Shew me thy ways, O LORD; teach me thy paths. Lead me in thy truth, and teach me: for thou art the God of my salvation; on thee do I wait all the day." (Psalm 25:4-5)

> "Order my steps in thy word: and let not any iniquity have dominion over me." (Psalm 119:133)

> "Search me, O God, and know my heart: try me, and know my thoughts: And see if there be any wicked way in me, and lead me in the way everlasting." (Psalm 139: 23-24)

Chapter 13

False Credentials

The Roman Catholic Church claims that it goes back to the time of Jesus Christ. However, as we have seen, it only came into being in 314 A.D. when Emperor Constantine and Bishop Silvester made an alliance.

There is evidence that Evangelical Christians, with beliefs similar to those of modern Baptists, were around in the second century, more than a hundred years before the Roman Catholic Church was created. For a fascinating and informative study of early Evangelicals, read Dr. Bill Jackson's recently published book, *The Noble Army of "Heretics."*[1]

Malachi Martin was a Catholic priest, an eminent theologian, and a professor at the Vatican's Pontifical Institute. He describes the wide variety of beliefs and practices within the early Church. He says that there was as much variety back then as there is between different denominations now.[2]

Catholic apologists portray Protestant churches as being unstable, constantly splitting into new denominations, and full of wide-spread disagreement. They contrast this with the Roman Catholic Church, which they portray as being solid and unified. They say that when people interpret the Bible for themselves, it results in chaos and division, as shown by the many Protestant denominations. They conclude that, therefore, Protestantism doesn't work, and interpreting the Bible should only be done by the Catholic hierarchy.[3] In other words, Protestants should become Catholics.

However, the picture of Protestant division, and the picture of Catholic unity, are both greatly exaggerated. The "chaos" is an illusion. And the resulting conclusion is therefore not valid.

Basic Unity Among Protestants

There are some beliefs that define Christianity. These include things such as the Incarnation (Jesus Christ is truly God and truly man), the Atonement (Jesus Christ died for our salvation), the Resurrection of Jesus, the Second Coming of Jesus, and the authority of Scripture. These are not negotiable. Any person who does not believe them is not a Christian.

(There have always been people who claimed to be Christian, but who weren't. The Apostle Paul called them "false brethren" in 2 Corinthians 11:26 and Galatians 2:4.)

Some things are negotiable. These include things such as the form of baptism, the kind of worship music, the form of church structure and organization, defining the relationship between free will and predestination, and beliefs about what will happen during the End Times. These are important issues. They can affect the quality of a person's Christian life, but they do not determine whether or not a person is a Christian. These are areas in which Christians can agree to disagree.

Differences among genuine Protestants (as opposed to "false brethren") occur in the second area, the negotiable things. These differences could be compared to flavors of ice cream. There are many kinds of ice cream, but they are all ice cream. They aren't pie, or cake, or salad. In real life, people know the difference between eating ice cream and eating something else.

Some Catholic apologists say that there are 25,000 different Protestant denominations. Dr. Eric Svendsen has made an in-depth study of this claim. There is no valid foundation for it. His book, *On This Slippery Rock*, has a chapter about it, which you can read online. Dr. Svendsen also has an online article about diversity in Catholic beliefs.[4]

I looked up "churches" in the *Yellow Pages* of my local telephone directory. There were listings for Catholic churches, Orthodox churches, a few cults, and 73 varieties of Protestant churches. Some Protestant listings seemed to be variations of the same thing. For example, there were nine different listings for Baptist churches.

Let's compare this to something in everyday life. There is a huge difference between cats and dogs and horses. Now, if you narrow it down to dogs, there are many different varieties. Within each variety, there are subgroups. For example, there are different kinds of collies and different kinds of poodles.

Catholic apologists act as if the differences in Protestant churches are like the major differences between cats and dogs and horses. In reality, they are like the differences between different kinds of dogs (variations in the same kind of thing.) Often, they are like the differences between different kinds of poodles, or different kinds of collies (small variations in things that are essentially the same).

Wide Diversity Among Catholics

The appearance of unity among Catholics is misleading. There are actually major differences in theology and practice. However, no matter how much they disagree, they call themselves by the same name (Roman Catholic) and they say that the Pope is their leader. This gives a false impression of unity.

In spite of verbally saying that the Pope is their leader, there are Catholic priests and theologians who openly defy the Pope's authority. Malachi Martin wrote about some of them in his book, *The Jesuits: The Society of Jesus and the Betrayal of the Roman Catholic Church*.[5] There are also some radical feminist nuns who openly defy the Pope. (They are discussed later in this chapter.)

There are conservative Catholics who want to go back to the way that things were done before the Second Vatican Council. This includes having Mass said in Latin.

One conservative Catholic group believes that Pope John Paul II is not a valid pope, because he has promoted heresy (things that are contrary to Catholic doctrine that was "infallibly" declared by previous popes).[6]

There are Catholic theologians who teach liberation theology, which equates "salvation" with armed revolution. There are gun-toting Catholic priests who fight alongside communist guerillas, working for communist revolution.[7] I first heard about them from a Latin American friend who personally witnessed the destruction and confusion that they have caused.

As we will see, some Catholic priests and nuns teach things that are clearly contrary to foundational Christian beliefs, such as the Atonement. (Jesus died to save us from our sins). Yet they are still allowed to teach in the name of the Catholic Church, and to hold positions of influence and authority.

Bioethics

The Catholic Church has traditionally been a champion of the sanctity of life. However, some Catholic priests at a prestigious Catholic university are actively working to undermine the sanctity of human life, both theoretically and in practical ways.

Georgetown University is run by Jesuit priests. It is the home of the Kennedy Institute of Ethics, which is headed by a Jesuit priest. Some of its faculty members are also Jesuit priests.

The Kennedy Institute of Ethics actively promotes abortion and euthanasia. It is also working to have "death" be redefined to include people in "irreversible" comas, so that doctors can get better quality organs for transplants. This is documented in the book, *Culture of Death*, by Wesley J. Smith.[8]

The Kennedy Institute of Ethics trains doctors, nurses, lawyers, legislators, teachers, and hospital administrators. Every summer, it gives an Intensive Bioethics Course, which is attended by people from around the world. It has branches in Asia and Europe. According to the woman I spoke with, it has the most comprehensive library of bioethics literature in the world.

New Age Teachings and Practices

The "New Age" is actually a resurgence of old paganism that has been "westernized" and dressed up in modern vocabulary. It denies foundational Christian doctrines and basic Christian morality. It is also contrary to the official teaching of the Catholic Church. However, in spite of this, there are Catholic priests and nuns who openly promote New Age beliefs and practices. This is an area in which there is a wide diversity of beliefs among Catholics.

Thomas Merton is a Catholic contemplative who influenced many people. He himself was strongly influenced by Hindu and Buddhist religious practices. The meditation techniques of Merton and other Catholic contemplatives have influenced some Evangelical pastors.[9]

There are some radical feminist nuns who participate in pagan rituals and worship "the goddess."[10] You can read about them in Donna Steichen's book, *Ungodly Rage: The Hidden Face of Catholic Feminism*. Steichen spent 12 years getting first-hand information. She is an excellent investigative reporter.

There are Catholic contemplatives who embrace pagan mysticism.[11] Some Catholic seminars and retreat centers teach people to use pagan meditation techniques and to cultivate "spirit guides."[12] Some Catholic schools teach New Age beliefs instead of foundational Christian doctrines, such as the fact that Jesus Christ died to save us from our sins.[13] (For more information, see the chapter, "New Age Catholicism.")

Catholic authority figures are teaching beliefs and practices that are opposed to Catholic doctrine. They use the name of the Catholic Church, but they teach things that are opposed to Catholicism. In the world of business, this would be called false advertising, or fraud.

Fire Insurance

Another area of diversity is beliefs about some old-fashioned, Catholic devotional practices. I will illustrate this with one example.

Can Catholics be sure of getting into Heaven if they wear a specific religious item, which shows devotion to Mary? Modern theologians and apologists will probably tell you: "Of course not!" However, as we will see, there are Catholics who believe that Mary will protect them from Hell if they follow her directions. There is an old saying that, if Jesus won't let you into Heaven by the front door, then Mary can get you in through the back door.

According to tradition, on July 16, 1251, the Virgin Mary appeared to Saint Simon Stock, holding a Brown Scapular (two pieces of brown cloth attached by strings). She promised him that any person who dies wearing the scapular will not go to Hell. This promise is for people who belong to the religious order of the Carmelites, or who are associated with them. Catholics can be enrolled into the Carmelites by any Carmelite or authorized Catholic priest. In 1965, Pope Paul VI encouraged all Catholics to wear the Brown Scapular and pray the Rosary.[14]

Catholics who wear the Brown Scapular can also qualify for the "Sabbatine Privilege," if they fulfill certain religious requirements. The "Sabbatine Privilege" is a promise that if they go to Purgatory, Mary will get their Purgatory time shortened.[15]

There are other Catholic devotional practices that have promises attached to them. They often involve the use of medals, rosaries, pictures, different kinds of scapulars, chaplets, and specific prayers. There is a "five-way medal" that consists of a cross, with medals at the end of each of the four arms. This enables people to wear a cross, and four different medals, at the same time, in a neat and orderly way. There are also "four-way medals." (You can see them online.)[16]

I have known Catholics with a wide range of approaches to these devotional practices. Some considered them to be old-fashioned, or even superstitious. Others took them quite seriously. I knew one woman who was so devoted to praying the rosary that, even when she was carrying on a conversation, her rosary beads were going through her fingers.

If you want to know more about Catholic devotional practices, you can go to online Catholic stores. They have pictures of medals, chaplets, scapulars, statues, holy cards, rosary bracelets, prayer rings, bottles for holy water, and other religious objects.[17] You can also search the Internet for specific items such as prayer rings.

Catholic Seminaries

Roman Catholic seminaries have a wide diversity of teaching and practice. Some of them teach traditional Catholic doctrines, morality, and piety. However, many do not.

Michael S. Rose is a devout Catholic and a professional investigative reporter. He wrote the book, *Goodbye, Good Men: How Liberals Brought Corruption into the Catholic Church*. It is a plea for reform in Catholic seminaries.[18]

You can read the book's Introduction online. You can also read book reviews, and feedback from seminarians and priests who read the book.[19] I encourage you to check this out for yourself.

Rose interviewed over 150 people. His book only shows the tip of the iceberg, because many men were afraid to let him write about their experiences. Others allowed him to write about them, but insisted that he change their name to protect them.

Chapter 5 ("The Heterodoxy Downer") tells of seminary faculty members who denied doctrines that are absolutely foundational to Christianity, or taught things that are contrary to basic Christian doctrine and morals. Following are some things that were taught by faculty members in seminaries:

- The death of Jesus was not a sacrifice for our sins.
- The Atonement never happened.
- The Bible should not be taken seriously.
- God is a woman. (A nun taught this.)
- It is OK for celibate priests to have sex with other men.
- It is normal for men to have sex with animals.

One seminary taught Matthew Fox's "creation-centered spirituality," which denies the existence of sin, the Atonement, and other foundational Christian doctrines. It teaches many New Age beliefs. It says that Christianity needs to get rid of any beliefs that hinder it from being united with pagan religions. It promotes a one-world religion. Fox is a priest who works in close association with a witch, a Voodoo priestess, and a shaman.[20]

Some seminarians were required to engage in occult, New Age practices, including using Ouija boards, tarot cards, and crystals.

One seminarian sued his seminary for false advertising. He said that it claimed to be Catholic, but it wasn't.

This kind of doctrine and behavior is contrary to what is taught in the *Catechism of the Catholic Church*. It demonstrates the wide diversity of belief and practice among modern Catholics.

The Problem of Mistakes

Should men and women interpret the Bible for themselves? They might make mistakes. This is a problem, because nobody is immune from making mistakes. But mistakes can be corrected. We serve a living God, who loves us. He is able to correct us if we get off track. Look at these prayers from the Bible:

> "Who can understand his errors? cleanse thou me from secret faults." (Psalm 19:12)

"Order my steps in thy word: and let not any iniquity have dominion over me." (Psalm 119:133)

"Search me, O God, and know my heart: try me, and know my thoughts: And see if there be any wicked way in me, and lead me in the way everlasting." (Psalm 139:23-24)

Men and women who study the Bible and interpret it for themselves may sometimes make mistakes. But if people do not know the Bible well, and they are not used to understanding Scripture for themselves, then they will be easily persuaded by authority figures who teach unbiblical things. In order to test a teaching, people need something solid to compare it to.

Catholics are used to trusting priests and nuns, and accepting whatever they teach them. Catholics have not been taught how to compare teachings with what the Bible says, in order to test whether or not the teachings are Scriptural.

The possibility of making mistakes is something that we have to deal with all the time. For example, there are no perfect parents. Fathers and mothers make mistakes. But that doesn't mean that children should be raised by "experts," in institutions, instead of being raised at home by their parents. "Experts" make mistakes, too.

The learning process always involves the risk of making mistakes. Hebrews 5:14 says that it is "by reason of use" that people "have their senses exercised to discern both good and evil." In other words, it takes time and practice to learn to discern things for ourselves. But God expects us to do it. 1 Thessalonians 5:21 says: "Prove [test] all things; hold fast that which is good." In other words, test everything, and only keep what is good.

Romans 8:28 says that "all things work together for good to them that love God." That includes our mistakes. God is big enough, and powerful enough, and loving enough to make even our mistakes work out for our good. He is able to keep us from falling. (Jude 1:24)

The Catholic approach says: "You might make a mistake. I'll do your thinking for you." This puts people at the mercy of priests and bishops, who make mistakes (as we all do). It becomes especially serious if a Pope makes a mistake and imposes his mistake on the entire Catholic Church.

The Protestant approach says: "Even if you do make a mistake, our God is able to turn it around and use it for good. Do your best, and with the guidance of the Bible and the Holy Spirit, you will be able to grow into a mature Christian." This approach has a self-correcting procedure. Even if a spiritual leader makes a doctrinal mistake, there are others who will check it against

Scripture and point out the error. Therefore, people are not at the mercy of mistakes made by others.

Conclusion

Although Catholics have a common name, and acknowledge a common leader, there is actually a wide variety of beliefs and practices within Roman Catholicism. For a concrete example of this, compare Mother Teresa of Calcutta with radical feminist nuns who worship "the goddess" and participate in pagan rituals.

Although there are variations in Protestant churches, genuine Protestants (as opposed to "false brethren") are in agreement about the foundational doctrines of Christianity. Their differences concern the negotiable areas that are mentioned at the beginning of this chapter, and the practical application of how to nurture, develop, and express our Christian life.

Chapter 14
According to Tradition

We often hear the expression, "according to tradition." But how reliable are these statements? The following illustrates that people's confidence in these traditions can be disproportionate to the evidence supporting them.

According to tradition, around 40 A.D., the Apostle James (the Greater) was in Saragossa, Spain. He was discouraged, because his mission had failed. Mary appeared to him. She gave him a pillar (column) of jasper wood and a small wooden statue of herself. She also told him to build a church in her honor. This is considered to be the first apparition of Mary. (Information about this is online.)[1] However, there are some problems with this story.

In the first place, this seems to be contradicted by Scripture. The Apostle Paul wrote the Book of Romans about 57 A.D.[2] This was about 17 years after Mary supposedly appeared to the Apostle James in Spain. Paul said that he wanted to go to Spain (Romans 15:24, 28). A few verses earlier, Paul said that he made a practice of only preaching the Gospel where it had not been preached before. He told the Roman Christians:

> "Yea, so have I strived to preach the gospel, not where Christ was named, lest I should build upon another man's foundation: But as it is written, To whom he was not spoken of, they shall see: and they that have not heard shall understand." (Romans 15:20-21)

When Paul went to cities, he went to preach the Gospel, or to strengthen churches that he had already established. Why would Paul want to go to Spain, if the Apostle James was already ministering there? Paul said that he did not want to "build upon another man's foundation."

In the second place, in 40 A.D., Mary may well have been alive. (It was only a few years after Jesus was crucified.) If she was alive, then how could she "appear" to anybody?

In the third place, the early Christians didn't have churches. They met in people's homes. (See Acts 2:46; Acts 20:20; Romans 16:5; 1 Corinthians 16:19; Colossians 4:15; and Philemon 1:2. These verses all refer to churches that met in people's homes.) The Book of Acts ends around 60 A.D., when

Paul was in Rome. There is no record of any church buildings. (This is about 20 years after Mary supposedly appeared to James and told him to build a church in her honor.)

Furthermore, starting with the stoning of Stephen, Christians were killed for their faith. It is basic common sense that people who are being killed for their faith do not want to call attention to their religious gatherings. That is not a good time to build church buildings.

According to tradition, in the eighth century, a hermit "discovered" the body of the Apostle James (the Greater) in Saragossa, Spain. (This is online.)[3]

This discovery is questionable in view of the fact that the Catholic Church has a history of fraudulent relics. (Relics are bodies of saints, or portions of saints' bodies. They can also be items that are closely associated with saints, such as clothing. They also include things such as pieces of the cross on which Jesus was crucified.)

Relics were important for raising money. A cathedral without a relic of a saint lacked an important source of revenue.[4] Therefore, cathedrals had a strong motive for finding some way to produce a relic of a well-known saint.

Fraudulent relics were sold. People dug up bodies from graveyards and pretended that the corpses were saints. This enabled them to sell the bodies as relics. Selling relics was a profitable business. They were highly valued, because they were believed to have spiritual power to protect people from demons, to give them victory in war, and to bless them in other ways. People wore small relics on chains around their necks, as charms for protection. Churches were built over the bodies of saints. Important relics drew pilgrims, which brought money. Bodies of saints were stolen, and portions of them were sold for money. Kings and bishops took great risks to steal the bodies of important saints. Towns that had relics prospered and expanded.[5]

A great cathedral was built in Saragossa, in honor of Our Lady of the Pillar. (It is in an area of Saragossa known as Campostella.) It is a major pilgrimage site. The wooden statue of Mary, and the pillar (the column of jasper wood), can be seen on special occasions.[6]

The cathedral in Saragossa has a statue of Mary that wears clothing. It wears a crown of gold and diamonds. It has a wardrobe of clothes that are embroidered with gold and studded with jewels.[7]

According to tradition, the head of the Apostle James (the Greater) is buried in Jerusalem, in the Cathedral of Saint James. This conflicts with the Saragossa tradition.[8] However, it seems to be consistent with Scripture. King Herod had James killed in Jerusalem. (Acts 12:1-2)

Chapter 15

What Is Our Source of Authority?

Ever since Martin Luther's cry of *sola scriptura* (Scripture alone is our authoritative source of spiritual truth), there has been an on-going debate between Catholics and Protestants as to whether our source of authority is the Bible alone, or the Bible plus "Tradition." (I will discuss tradition and the doctrine of infallibility later in this chapter.)

God gave us the Bible to teach us, to guide us, to correct us, and to enable us to lead Godly lives. Through the Bible, God reveals Himself and His ways to us. Scripture says:

> "All scripture is given by inspiration of God, and is profitable for doctrine, for reproof, for correction, for instruction in righteousness; That the man of God may be perfect, thoroughly furnished unto all good works." (2 Timothy 3:16-17)

> "Thy word is a lamp unto my feet, and a light unto my path." (Psalm 119:105)

> "The law of the LORD is perfect, converting the soul: the testimony of the LORD is sure, making wise the simple. The statutes of the LORD are right, rejoicing the heart: the commandment of the LORD is pure, enlightening the eyes." (Psalm 19:7-8)

> "For the word of God is quick, and powerful, and sharper than any two-edged sword, piercing even to the dividing asunder of soul and spirit, and of the joints and marrow, and is a discerner of the thoughts and intents of the heart." (Hebrews 4:12)

> "Sanctify them through thy truth: thy word is truth." (John 17:17)

> "...[R]eceive with meekness the engrafted word, which is able to save your souls." (James 1:21)
>
> "The entrance of thy words giveth light; it giveth understanding unto the simple." (Psalm 119:131)
>
> "...If ye continue in my word, then are ye my disciples indeed: And ye shall know the truth, and the truth shall make you free." (John 8:31-32)
>
> "For whatsoever things were written aforetime were written for our learning, that we through patience and comfort of the scriptures might have hope." (Romans 15:4)
>
> "Heaven and earth shall pass away, but my words shall not pass away." (Matthew 24:35)
>
> "The grass withereth, the flower fadeth: but the word of our God shall stand for ever." (Isaiah 40:8)
>
> "Forever, O LORD, thy word is settled in heaven." (Psalm 119:89)

If Christianity really works, then it has to work under all circumstances. That includes working for new converts who are isolated in prisons, with no Bible and no other Christians to help them. That kind of thing happens today in some Muslim nations. You can read about it in the newsletter of Open Doors (a ministry for persecuted Christians). You can get their newsletter through their website. (Information is in the Notes.)[1]

God has provided for such situations. He sent the Holy Spirit, who helps us remember things (especially Scripture), and enables us to understand the things of God. (See John 14:26 and 1 Corinthians 2:9-13.) It is through prayer, and the guidance of the Holy Spirit, that we are able to understand Scripture. Jesus said:

> "But the Comforter, which is the Holy Ghost, whom the Father will send in my name, he shall teach you all things, and bring all things to your remembrance, whatsoever I have said unto you." (John 14:26)

"Howbeit when he, the Spirit of truth, is come, he will guide you into all truth…" (John 16:13; see John 16:7-15)

"For what man knoweth the things of a man, save the spirit of man which is in him? even so the things of God knoweth no man, but the Spirit of God. Now we have received, not the spirit of the world, but the spirit which is of God; that we might know the things that are freely given to us of God." (1 Corinthians 2:11-12)

If we do not have access to the Bible, God has made provision for us to be able to learn what we need to know directly from Him. He has already provided us with what we need for life and godliness. The Bible says:

"According as his divine power hath given unto us all things that pertain unto life and godliness, through the knowledge of him that hath called us to glory and virtue: Whereby are given unto us exceeding great and precious promises…" (2 Peter 1:3-4)

"But the anointing which ye have received of him abideth in you, and ye need not that any man teach you: but as the same anointing teacheth you of all things, and is truth, and is no lie, and even as it hath taught you, ye shall abide in him." (1 John 2:27)

It is valuable to have Bibles and pastors and teachers. If they are available, then we should be grateful for them and benefit from them as much as possible. But if those things are not available, then God is powerful enough to enable us to live Godly lives without them. God is able to keep us from falling. (Jude 1:24) It does not depend on our circumstances. It depends on God. And He is faithful.

Tradition

The Catholic Church officially states that Catholic tradition is equal in authority to the Bible. (You can read this online.)[2]

According to the *Catechism of the Catholic Church*, "tradition" consists of various expressions of worship and belief of the Catholic people. (The *Catechism* is online.)[3] As a result, tradition keeps changing. It is different at different periods in history, and it varies from place to place. For example, Catholic religious practices that are common in third world countries, such as Latin America, Africa, or the Philippines, may seem strange to Catholics who have a western world view. Some devotional practices that were common during the Middle Ages would seem strange to modern Americans.

Jesus rebuked the scribes and Pharisees, because their traditions nullified the Word of God. He used Scripture to measure the validity of their religious traditions. He was distressed, because the religious leaders of his time considered their traditions to be equal in authority to Scripture. Jesus said:

> "This people draweth nigh unto me with their mouth, and honoureth me with their lips; but their heart is far from me. But in vain they do worship me, teaching for doctrines the commandments of men." (Matthew 15:8-9; see Matthew 15:1-9)

> "Howbeit in vain do they worship me, teaching for doctrines the commandments of men. For **laying aside the commandment of God, ye hold the tradition of men**, as the washing of pots and cups: and many other such like things ye do. And he said unto them, Full well **ye reject the commandment of God, that ye may keep your own tradition**." (Mark 7:7-9, emphasis added; see Mark 7:1-13)

The Bible clearly tells us that we are not to add to Scripture or take away from it. We need to stay with what has been written. It says:

> "What thing soever I command you, observe to do it: thou shalt not add thereto, nor diminish from it." (Deuteronomy 12:32)

> "Ye shall not add unto the word which I command you, neither shall ye diminish ought from it, that ye may keep the commandments of the LORD your God which I command you." (Deuteronomy 4:2)

According to these Scripture passages, if people make additions to Scripture, then they will wind up disobeying God. The Bible says:

"Every word of God is pure: he is a shield unto them that put their trust in him. Add thou not unto his words, lest he reprove thee, and thou be found a liar." (Proverbs 30:5-6)

If we add to God's words, then He will rebuke us and call us liars. We will have misrepresented Him. When we meet God face to face, we will want to hear Him say: "Well done, thou good and faithful servant." But if we add to His words (Scripture), then we may hear Him say something like: "Liar! You misrepresented me!"

If we say that tradition is equal in authority to Scripture, then we can no longer use Scripture to test tradition, as Jesus did. Instead, we are allowing tradition to determine how we interpret Scripture. Either this is "adding to Scripture," or else it is perilously close to it.

Revelation 22:18-19 warns that adding to God's words can cause a person to have his or her name be removed from the "book of life."

Infallibility

Protestants say that the Bible is infallible. Catholics say that the Pope is infallible.

The Catholic doctrine of papal infallibility is based upon Matthew 16:18, in which Jesus told Peter: "And I say unto thee, That thou are Peter, and upon this rock I will build my church; and the gates of hell shall not prevail against it."

A huge doctrine, with immense historical consequences, has been built upon this one short verse. The question is, does the rock on which the church is built represent Peter, or does it represent Jesus?

Peter himself answered this question. He said that the rock is Jesus. In the Book of Acts, the high priest and other Jewish leaders questioned the apostles concerning a man who had been healed. The Bible describes this confrontation:

> "Then Peter, filled with the Holy Ghost, said unto them, Ye rulers of the people, and elders of Israel, If we this day be examined of the good deed done to the impotent man, by what means he is made whole; Be it known unto you all, and to all the people of Israel, that by the name of **Jesus Christ of Nazareth**, whom ye crucified, whom God raised from the dead, even by him doth this man stand here before you whole. **This is the stone which was set at nought of you builders, which is become the head of the corner.** Neither is there salvation in any other: for there is none other name

under heaven given among men, whereby we must be saved."
(Acts 4:8-12, emphasis added)

Peter also referred to Jesus as the cornerstone in his first epistle. He described the church as a building made up of many stones (the individual believers) and founded on Jesus, who is the chief cornerstone. Peter said:

> "If so be ye have tasted that the Lord is gracious. To whom coming, as unto **a living stone, disallowed indeed of men, but chosen of God, and precious**. Ye also, as lively stones, are built up a spiritual house, an holy priesthood, to offer up spiritual sacrifices, acceptable to God by Jesus Christ. Wherefore also it is contained in the scripture, Behold, **I lay in Sion a chief corner stone, elect, precious: and he that believeth on him shall not be confounded**. Unto you therefore which believe he is precious: but **unto them which be disobedient, the stone which the builders disallowed, the same is made the head of the corner, And a stone of stumbling, and a rock of offence**, even to them which stumble at the word, being disobedient: whereunto also they were appointed. But ye are a chosen generation, a royal priesthood, an holy nation, a peculiar people; that ye should shew forth the praises of him who hath called you out of darkness into his marvellous light…" (1 Peter 2:3-9, emphasis added)

So the Catholic Church says that Peter is the rock. But Peter declared that Jesus is the rock.

Jesus Himself said that He is the rock. He told a parable about a vineyard, with tenants who refused to give a portion of their fruit to the owner of the vineyard. The owner sent servants. The tenants beat some servants and killed others. Finally, the owner sent his own son. The tenants killed him. Jesus concluded the parable by quoting Psalm 118:22-23, which says that the cornerstone was rejected by the builders.

This parable describes how God sent prophets to Israel, but the Israelites rejected them. Then God sent His Son, and the Israelites rejected Him and killed Him. They thought that He was worthless. They did not realize that He was of foundational importance to them. In the context of this parable, the stone can only refer to Jesus. It cannot possibly refer to Peter. Jesus said:

"And again he [the lord of the vineyard] sent unto them another servant; and at him they cast stones, and wounded him in the head, and sent him away shamefully handled. And again he sent another; and him they killed, and many others; beating some, and killing some. **Having yet therefore one son, his wellbeloved, he sent him also last unto them, saying, They will reverence my son.** But those husbandmen said among themselves, This is the heir; come, let us kill him, and the inheritance shall be ours. And they took him, and killed him, and cast him out of the vineyard. What shall therefore the lord of the vineyard do? he will come and destroy the husbandmen, and will give the vineyard unto others. And have ye not read this scripture; **The stone which the builders rejected is become the head of the corner:** This was the Lord's doing, and it is marvellous in our eyes?" (Mark 12:4-11; see Mark 12:1-12. Also see Matthew 21:33-46 and Luke 20:9-19)

Look at the context of Jesus' statement. He was on His way to Jerusalem to be crucified. He had already said:

"Behold, we go up to Jerusalem: and the Son of man shall be betrayed unto the chief priests and unto the scribes, and they shall condemn him to death, And shall deliver him to the Gentiles to mock, and to scourge, and to crucify him: and the third day he shall rise again." (Matthew 20:18-19)

In the parable of the vineyard, Jesus was predicting His own death. In that context, Jesus said that the son who was killed by the tenants was the cornerstone.

The Apostle Paul said that the church is built on **all** of the apostles (not just Peter) and that Jesus is the cornerstone. He also said that Jesus Christ is our spiritual rock. Paul wrote:

"Now therefore ye are no more strangers and foreigners, but fellowcitizens with the saints, and of the household of God; And are **built upon the foundation of the apostles and prophets, Jesus Christ himself being the chief corner stone;** In whom all the building fitly framed together groweth unto an holy temple in the Lord: In whom ye also are built together for an habitation of God through the Spirit." (Ephesians 2:19-22, emphasis added)

"...for they drank of that spiritual Rock that followed them: and that Rock was Christ." (1 Corinthians 10:4)

In Romans 9:31-33, Paul said that Jesus was a rock of offense for the Israelites, because they tried to be saved by works of the law, instead of by faith.

In the New Testament, there are three Greek words for "stone." *Lithos* means a stone like a millstone, or a stumbling stone. The other two words are *petra* and *petros*. *Vine's Expository Dictionary* says that *petra* means, "a mass of rock." It says that *petros* means, "a detached stone or boulder." It also says that *petros* means, "a stone that can be thrown or easily moved."

In Matthew 16:18, the word for Peter is *petros*, a detached stone that can easily be moved. The word for the rock on which the church is built is *petra*, a mass of rock. Other examples of the use of *petra* show what a huge mass of rock is meant by the word. They include the man who built his house on rock (as opposed to sand) and the tomb where Jesus' body was placed. (It was carved out of a rock.) (See Matthew 7:24-27 and 27:60.)

Have you ever climbed up a rocky mountain? You are standing on a huge rock (the mountain). This is a *petra*. As you climb up this massive rock, you pass many smaller rocks, varying in size from small stones to large boulders. The smaller rocks are detached. They can be rolled down the mountainside. That kind of rock is a *petros*, which is the name that Jesus gave to Peter.

There is another problem with the doctrine of infallibility. It results in having people act like young children, who accept without question whatever they are told. This is contrary to the Bible, which tells us to test things for ourselves, to discern things, to compare things with Scripture so that we won't be deceived.

The Bible commends the people of Berea, because they "searched the Scriptures daily" in order to "see whether these things were so." (Acts 17:10-11) God wants His people to check everything against Scripture.

Paul's epistles constitute about one-fourth of the New Testament. He was a Scripture scholar. (He had been a prominent Pharisee.) He had been to the Third Heaven, where he had seen mysteries that he was not allowed to tell us about. (2 Corinthians 12:2-4) But the Bible does not criticize the Bereans for questioning what the Apostle Paul taught them. Rather, it commends them for checking it out for themselves by comparing his teaching with Scripture.

The Bible tells us to test everything. It says:

"Prove all things; hold fast that which is good." (1 Thessalonians 5:21)

According to *Strong's Concordance*, the word "prove" means, "to test." God requires that every man and woman test all things. We are responsible for testing things ourselves.

However, the Catholic Church teaches that only the Magisterium of the Church (the Pope, and the bishops in communion with him) has the right to interpret Scripture. It says that people like you and I (and the Bereans) are not supposed to interpret Scripture for ourselves. (You can read this online.)[4]

Where does the Catholic approach leave Christian prisoners in countries where there is persecution? All they have to go on is prayer and their memory of Scripture. They can't read a Bible. They can't consult with a priest or a bishop. They are often doing well if they get to see any Christians at all. Would God set up a system that doesn't take care of His most faithful followers—the people who are willing to pay the highest price to serve Him? Of course not!

Catholicism teaches that Christians are supposed to "receive with docility" any directives given to them by Catholic Church authorities. (You can read this online.)[5]

That doesn't sound like the Berean men who studied the Scriptures, to see whether or not what the Apostle Paul taught them was Biblical. Rather, it sounds like a young child who accepts without question whatever his parents tell him. I believe that is precisely what Jesus warned us against when He told us:

"And call no man your father upon the earth: for one is your Father, which is in heaven." (Matthew 23:9)

In 1854, Pope Pius IX declared the dogma of the Immaculate Conception of Mary. The Pope said that if people "dare" to even think anything contrary to this dogma, then that disagreement will shipwreck their faith, cut them off from the Catholic Church, and make them become "condemned." He said that if people outwardly express disagreement, then they are subject to punishment.[6] (Encyclical are online.)

The Pope's reference to punishment is significant, because a man had been executed for heresy 28 years before this papal bull was issued.[7]

Did Jesus treat people like that for disagreeing in their hearts with something that He or the Apostles told them? When the rich young man turned away from Jesus, He didn't rebuke him or threaten him. He let him go. (Matthew 19:16-22)

Many of Jesus' disciples left Him and no longer followed Him. Jesus asked the Twelve if they also wanted to leave. (John 6:67) He didn't threaten them or rebuke them. He didn't try to force them to believe what He taught them. He didn't try to make them stay with Him. He didn't manipulate them or put emotional pressure on them. Jesus left them free to believe or not believe, to stay or to leave.

If Jesus didn't demand that people believe His teachings, then how can anybody else validly do it? Nobody else has the depth of understanding, or the purity of doctrine, or the purity of heart, that Jesus did.

There was one occasion when James and John wanted to call down fire on some Samaritans who wouldn't listen to them. Jesus rebuked them, saying: "You know not what manner of spirit ye are of." (Luke 9:55-56; see Luke 9:51-56.)

Look at how Jesus responded to "doubting Thomas." All of the Apostles except Thomas had seen Jesus after the Resurrection. Jesus had repeatedly told his Disciples that He would be crucified and then resurrected on the third day. In spite of that, Thomas said that he wouldn't believe unless he put his finger into the holes from the nails and put his hand into the wound in Jesus' side. When Jesus appeared again, did He rebuke Thomas? Did Jesus call down curses and anathemas on Thomas, for not believing what the Apostles had said? No. He invited Thomas to put his finger into the nail holes and to put his hand into the wound in His side. In other words, Jesus invited Thomas to check it out for himself. Then He commended Thomas. (See John 20:24-29)

Look at a theological confrontation that is described in Galatians 2:11-16. Peter made a decision that was theologically incorrect. Paul publicly corrected Peter. We have no record that Paul was rebuked for this. He certainly wasn't embarrassed by it, because he used the incident as a teaching illustration in his Epistle to the Galatians.

According to the Catholic Church, Peter was the first pope. However, if you read Peter's epistles, he did not speak as if he had any special status. Look at how he described himself.

> "Peter, an apostle of Jesus Christ, to the strangers scattered throughout Pontus, Galatia, Cappadocia, Asia, and Bithynia." (1 Peter 1:1)

> "The elders which are among you I exhort, who am also an elder, and a witness of the sufferings of Christ, and also a partaker of the glory that shall be revealed." (1 Peter 5:1)

"Simon Peter, a servant and an apostle of Jesus Christ, to them that have obtained like precious faith with us through the righteousness of God and our Saviour Jesus Christ." (2 Peter 1:1)

This is not the language of a high and mighty Pope, who lords it over the Church. Peter did not set himself apart as being in a higher position of authority than the other apostles. He did not even describe himself as being more important than the average believer. Peter told us that **all** Christians are specially chosen and of great value. He said:

"Ye also, as lively stones, are built up a spiritual house, an holy priesthood, to offer up spiritual sacrifices, acceptable to God by Jesus Christ." (1 Peter 2:5)

Peter said that **every** Christian man and woman is a priest. He said that **our** spiritual sacrifices are acceptable to God.

Dangers of Infallibility

Deception

Jesus warned us against deception. He said:

"…Take heed that no man deceive you." (Matthew 24:4)

Paul warned us against deception. He also warned us that it is dangerous to accept doctrines in the way that children do. He said that it makes people susceptible to deception. Paul said:

"That we henceforth be no more children, tossed to and fro, and carried about with every wind of doctrine, by the sleight of men, and cunning craftiness, whereby they lie in wait to deceive." (Ephesians 4:14)

"Beware lest any man spoil [ruin] you through philosophy and vain deceit, after the tradition of men, after the rudiments of the world, and not after Christ." (Colossians 2:8)

If every Christian reads the Bible, and checks things out against Scripture (as the Bereans did), then the devil has a problem. He and his demon cohorts will have to deceive each and every Christian individually.

However, if people are required to accept whatever the Pope says "with docility," then the devil's job is much easier. If he can just deceive the Pope, and get the Pope to declare something unbiblical to be official doctrine, then the devil will have successfully deceived everybody who is under the Pope's authority.

The Apostle Peter was so deceived by the devil that Jesus rebuked him, saying:

> "...Get thee behind me, Satan: thou art an offense unto me: for thou savourest not the things that be of God, but those that be of men." (Matthew 16:23; also see Mark 8:33 and Luke 4:8)

The devil successfully deceived Peter concerning an important matter of faith (the death and resurrection of Jesus, as prophesied by Jesus Himself). So how can the popes (who claim to be the successors of Peter) say that the devil is incapable of deceiving them?

Corruption

A Catholic historian said: "Power corrupts and absolute power corrupts absolutely." [8] When you give any one man (the Pope) or group of men (the Magisterium) the power to define what people are required to believe in order to be able to go to Heaven, then you invite abuses of power. History is full of examples of this abuse of power. (See the chapters, "Hunting 'Heretics,'" "The Popes," and "Spiritual Coercion.")

There are popes who came to power by murder, by armed conquest, and by buying the papacy. Many popes openly fornicated with women and with boys. Some popes were incredibly cruel. For example, Pope Stephen IV condemned a man to be killed by having little pieces of his body cut off of him every day, until he died. Pope Benedict IX was bisexual, he had sex with animals, and he gave orders for people to be murdered. He also practiced witchcraft and Satanism.[9]

These are extreme cases. Obviously, not all popes are like that. But some were. There is no guarantee that it won't happen again.

David Yallop wrote the book, *In God's Name: An Investigation into the Murder of Pope John Paul I*. Vatican insiders asked Yallop to investigate the death of John Paul I, because they suspected that he was murdered. Yallop did his homework. His information comes from interviews with Vatican insiders and Mafia gangsters. He gives a revealing and disturbing picture of life in the Vatican.[10]

Throughout Church history, there have always been tares among the wheat and wolves among the sheep. I realize that scandals are not limited to the Catholic Church. There have been many scandals in Protestant denominations. But Catholic corruption is more deadly, because the Catholic Church claims to be infallible. That claim makes wolves in sheep's clothing far more dangerous. It gives them great power over the minds and lives of other people.

A Challenge

I have a challenge for you. It will require some work on your part, but it will be worth the effort.

I have discussed the question of our source of authority. Now, I want to demonstrate it to you. You have thought about the issue. Now, I want you to personally taste the difference between Scripture and Roman Catholic tradition.

I can't do this for you. You have to experience it for yourself, in order to understand.

Before reading the rest of this chapter, please ask God to give you wisdom and discernment. (James 1:5)

I want you to read some statements by Pope Pius IX. They are from his encyclical, *Ineffabilis Deus*. I don't have permission to quote the statements, so I can't put them in this book for you. However, you can read them online.

Some Internet addresses are below. If they don't work for you, then you can do an Internet search for "Ineffabilis Deus."

      www.newadvent.org/docs/pi09id.htm
      www.pax-et-veritas.org/Popes/pius_ix/ineffabi.htm
      www.naorc.org/documents/ineffabilis_deus.htm
      www.geocities.com/apologeticacatolica/ineffabilis.html
      www.legacyrus.com/library/Vatican/ImmaculateConcept.htm

Please read the sections, "The Definition" and "Hoped-for Results." They are near the end of the encyclical. You can find them quickly by searching the web page for "The Definition." (Click EDIT. Select FIND. Type "The Definition." Then hit ENTER.) "Hoped-for Results" comes immediately after "The Definition."

We are going to compare what Pope Pius IX said about Mary, with what the Bible says about her. In reading the material, please pay attention to the tone of the writing, as well as to the contents. Please notice how the Pope speaks—his attitude, his bearing, his approach towards his readers, and the general tone of his writing.

Please notice how you feel while you are reading the encyclical. Sometimes we can "sniff" things that our intellects don't pick up. We have expressions reflecting that. For example: "There's something fishy going on." It means that something doesn't smell right—I don't know what's wrong; I can't explain it; but there is something wrong here.

I'll give an example from my own life. When I was a Catholic, I used to recite certain special prayers in order to earn indulgences on behalf of the "poor souls in Purgatory." One day, while I was doing it, something just didn't feel right about it. I stopped doing it. Months later, I realized that reciting prayers is not praying. If my reason for saying the prayers was to earn indulgences (rather than sharing my heart with God), then I wasn't praying. Years later, I realized that Purgatory doesn't even exist. My "sniffer" picked up the problem long before my mind understood it.

I'm asking you to activate your "sniffer" when you read this encyclical. You can ask God to help you do it.

This papal bull is as official as they can get. It is an "infallible" pronouncement of Catholic doctrine. The Pope who wrote it is on his way to becoming a canonized saint. Pope John Paul II beatified him on September 3, 2000. (You can read about it online.)[11] Beatification is the last step before canonization.

* * * * * * *

Have you read the material from the encyclical? If so, then please read what the Bible says about Mary, the mother of Jesus.

The first two chapters of the Gospel of Matthew, and the first two chapters of the Gospel of Luke, have information about the infancy of Jesus, and the time when He was in the Temple, asking questions of the religious leaders. Those Scripture passages are too long to quote here. You can read them in your own Bible. I have quoted all of the other Scripture passages about Mary, the mother of Jesus. (In searching for the word "Mary," I found more references to other women named Mary than I did for Jesus' mother.)

Some women went to the tomb after Jesus was crucified. They included women named Mary, but Jesus' mother is not mentioned as being one of them. (The Gospels refer to her as "Mary the mother of Jesus." Matthew 28:1 refers to "Mary Magdalene and the other Mary." Mark 16:1 says that they are "Mary Magdalene, and Mary the mother of James, and Salome." Luke 24:10 refers to "Mary Magdalene, and Joanna, and Mary the mother of James, and other women that were with them."

Aside from the infancy and childhood of Jesus, the following Scripture passages are the only ones that refer to Mary, the mother of Jesus. Here is what the Bible says about her:

> "While he yet talked to the people, behold, his mother and his brethren stood without, desiring to speak with him. Then one said unto him, Behold, thy mother and thy brethren stand without, desiring to speak with thee. But he answered and said unto him that told him, Who is my mother? and who are my brethren? And he stretched forth his hand toward his disciples, and said, Behold my mother and my brethren! For whosoever shall do the will of my Father which is in heaven, the same is my brother, and sister, and mother." (Matthew 12:46-50) (Also see Mark 3:31-35 and Luke 8:19-21.)

> "Is not this the carpenter's son? is not his mother called Mary? and his brethren, James, and Joses, and Simon, and Judas? And his sisters, are they not all with us? Whence then hath this man all these things? And they were offended in him. But Jesus said unto them, A prophet is not without honour, save in his own country, and in his own house." (Matthew 13:55-57) (Also see Mark 6:1-6 and Luke 4:16-31.)

> "And it came to pass, as he spake these things, a certain woman of the company lifted up her voice, and said unto him, Blessed is the womb that bare thee, and the paps which thou hast sucked. But he said, Yea rather, blessed are they that hear the word of God, and keep it." (Luke 11:27-28)

> "And the third day there was a marriage in Cana of Galilee; and the mother of Jesus was there: And both Jesus was called, and his disciples, to the marriage. And when they wanted wine, the mother of Jesus saith unto him, They have no wine. Jesus saith unto her, Woman, what have I to do with thee? mine hour is not yet come. His mother saith unto the servants, Whatsoever he saith unto you, do it. And there were set there six waterpots of stone, after the manner of the purifying of the Jews, containing two or three firkins apiece. Jesus saith unto them, Fill the waterpots with water. And they filled them up to the brim. And he saith unto them, Draw

out now, and bear unto the governor of the feast. And they bare it. When the ruler of the feast had tasted the water that was made wine, and knew not whence it was: (but the servants which drew the water knew;) the governor of the feast called the bridegroom, And saith unto him, Every man at the beginning doth set forth good wine; and when men have well drunk, then that which is worse: but thou hast kept the good wine until now. This beginning of miracles did Jesus in Cana of Galilee, and manifested forth his glory; and his disciples believed on him." (John 2:1-11)

"Now there stood by the cross of Jesus his mother, and his mother's sister, Mary the wife of Cleophas, and Mary Magdalene. When Jesus therefore saw his mother, and the disciple standing by, whom he loved, he saith unto his mother, Woman, behold thy son! Then saith he to the disciple, Behold thy mother! And from that hour that disciple took her unto his own home." (John 19:25-27)

"Then returned they unto Jerusalem from the mount called Olivet, which is from Jerusalem a sabbath day's journey. And when they were come in, they went up into an upper room, where abode Peter, and James, and John, and Andrew, Phillip, and Thomas, Bartholomew, and Matthew, James the son of Alphaus, and Simon Zelotes, and Judas the brother of James. These all continued with one accord in prayer and supplication, with the women, and Mary the mother of Jesus, and with his brethren." (Acts 1:12-14)

"But when the fulness of the time was come, God sent forth his Son, made of a woman, made unter the law." (Galatians 4:4)

The Scripture passages that I just quoted, plus the first two chapters of the Gospels of Matthew and Luke, are all of the passages that refer to Mary, the mother of Jesus. The Bible doesn't tell us much about her.

Some Questions
I asked you to read two sections from the Pope's encyclical. The first one was, "The Definition." It has two parts: the actual definition of the dogma, and a warning not to doubt or disagree with the dogma. How did you feel when you

read the warning? What was the tone of the warning? What was the Pope's attitude towards his audience?

The second section that I asked you to read was, "Hoped-for Results." How did you feel when you read it? What is the tone of the writing? What is the Pope's attitude towards Mary?

How did you feel when you read the quotations from Scripture? (If you are not used to reading the King James version of the Bible, then you might want to read those passages in your own Bible, in the translation that you are familiar with.)

What is the tone of the Scripture passages? What is the attitude towards Mary? What is the approach towards the readers?

How much prominence does the Bible give to Mary? Compare that with what the Pope said about her.

In the section of the encyclical called, "Hoped-for Results," what did the Pope say about Mary? We know that she was the mother of Jesus. What else did the Pope say about her? Are any of those statements supported by what the Bible says about her?

You may have noticed that the Pope said that Mary would enable the Catholic Church to "reign." He said that, because of Mary, Rome would rule from "the river" all the way to the "ends of the earth"—in other words, throughout the world. ("The river" refers to the Tiber River, which is in Rome. The Vatican is located next to the Tiber River.) Look at Mary, as portrayed in the Bible. Would she want to create a super-power that would rule over the nations?

Some Observations

It is worth noting that, in the Bible, the last thing we hear about Mary, the mother of Jesus, is in the first chapter of the Book of Acts. She was in the upper room, with about 120 people, before the Holy Spirit came upon them on the Day of Pentecost.

Galatians 4:4 does refer to her, but only to say that Jesus was "made of a woman." It is a way of referring to the Incarnation of Jesus, rather than giving new information about Mary.

Scripture tells us about a woman who gave Mary special prominence and praise. It also records what Jesus had to say about it. The Bible says:

> "And it came to pass, as he spake these things, a certain woman of the company lifted up her voice, and said unto him, Blessed is the womb that bare thee, and the paps which thou hast sucked. But he said, Yea **rather, blessed are they**

that hear the word of God, and keep it." (Luke 11:27-28, emphasis added)

Please ask God to give you His perspective about the passages that you read from the papal encyclical.

If you are a Catholic, then you may be so familiar with this kind of writing that you don't notice what it really says. If that is the case, then please read the section, "Hoped-for Results," again. Read it slowly. Think about what it says. There is a lot at stake here. The Apostle Paul said:

> "Beware lest any man spoil [ruin] you through philosophy and vain deceit, after the tradition of men, after the rudiments of the world, and not after Christ." (Colossians 2:8)

Another Challenge

I've got another challenge for you. Get your "sniffer" out and read the Glossary (Appendix C). It gives nitty gritty details of how "tradition" is practiced in the daily lives of real people.

Read this, and see how it compares with Biblical faith in Jesus Christ. It is one thing to talk about "tradition" as an abstract concept. It is quite another thing to see the concrete details of how it is actually applied in real life.

Conclusion

Jesus promised us that the gates of Hell will not prevail against His Church. That requires the supernatural intervention of God. According to the Bible, God has done this by sending us the Holy Spirit to teach us and to guide us. (John 14:26; John 16:13)

According to the Catholic Church, God has done this by miraculously protecting the popes from making mistakes when they make pronouncements about faith or morals.

This idea has a natural appeal. We would all like to have magical protection from error. Also, it is nice to be able to be passive spectators, receiving "with docility" whatever our superiors teach us, without having to face the responsibility of checking it out for ourselves. But, attractive or not, this idea is not supported by Scripture or by Church history. (For a discussion of historical inconsistencies, see the section on "Infallibility" in the chapter, "Was the Early Church Roman Catholic?")

What is our source of authority? God. His primary way of communicating with us is through the Bible. He sent the Holy Spirit to enable us to understand the Bible. If we don't have access to a Bible (as is the case with some persecuted Christians), then God has other ways of teaching us, guiding us, and directing us. No matter what our circumstances are, God is willing and able to keep us from falling. (Jude 1:24)

Chapter 16
Faith Versus Works

The Bible makes it clear that we are only saved by faith. No amount of good works is able to save us. Scripture says:

> "For by grace are ye saved through faith; and that not of yourselves: **it is the gift of God: Not of works**, lest any man should boast." (Ephesians 2:8-9, emphasis added)

> "And if by grace, then is it no more of works: otherwise grace is no more grace. But if it be of works, then is it no more grace: otherwise work is no more work." (Romans 11:6)

> "…according to the power of God, Who hath saved us, and called us with an holy calling, **not according to our works**, but according to his own purpose and grace, which was given us in Christ Jesus before the world began…" (2 Timothy 1:8-9, emphasis added)

Once we have become born-again Christians, our faith should result in a changed heart, which will express itself in good works. Genuine faith will influence our entire life: our thoughts, our desires, and our actions. It should result in love and gratitude towards God, love for our fellow Christians, having a desire to serve and obey the Lord, and wanting nonbelievers to know Jesus Christ. The Apostle James said:

> "Even so faith, if it hath not works, is dead, being alone. Yea, a man may say, Thou hast faith, and I have works: shew me thy faith without thy works, and I will shew thee my faith by my works." (James 2:17-18)

Talk is cheap. It is easy to say a prayer or to say that we have faith. If faith does not result in obeying God, then it may not be genuine faith. Jesus said:

"Not every one that saith unto me, Lord, Lord, shall enter into the kingdom of heaven; but he that doeth the will of my Father which is in heaven." (Matthew 7:21)

"And why call ye me, Lord, Lord, and do not the things which I say?" (Luke 6:46)

Salvation comes through faith. Genuine faith expresses itself in love, obeying God, and doing good works.

Good words do not save us. However, they can be evidence of a faith that saves us. Good works are the fruit of salvation—not the cause of it.

Judaizers

In the Epistle to the Galatians, the Apostle Paul addressed the problem of the "Judaizers." These were Christians who believed that, in addition to faith in Jesus Christ, Christians needed to be circumcised and follow the laws of Moses.[1] Paul said:

"I marvel that ye are so soon removed from him that called you into the grace of Christ unto another gospel: Which is not another; but there be some that trouble you, and would pervert the gospel of Christ." (Galatians 1:6-7)

Paul said that if people rely on good works for their salvation, then the death of Jesus Christ does not benefit them. If we could be saved by following the law, then it would not have been necessary for Christ to die for us. Paul said:

"I do not frustrate the grace of God: for if righteousness come by the law, then Christ is dead in vain." (Galatians 2:21)

The problem with trying to fulfill the law is that it is impossible. Nobody can fulfill all of it all of the time. The Apostle Paul wrote:

"For as many as are of the works of the law are under the curse: for it is written, Cursed is every one that continueth not in all things which are written in the book of the law to do them. But that **no man is justified by the law in the sight of God**, it is evident: for, **The just shall live by faith**. And the law is not of faith: but The man that doeth them shall live in them. **Christ hath redeemed us from the curse of the law**, being made a curse for us: for it is written, Cursed is every one that hangeth on a tree..." (Galatians 3:10-13, emphasis added)

According to the Bible, our righteousness can only come from Jesus Christ—not from our own efforts to make ourselves righteous. If we try to earn our salvation by means of our own good works, then we wind up rejecting the salvation that God wants to freely give us. The righteousness of Christians comes through Jesus Christ. We are not capable of establishing our own righteousness by fulfilling the law, or by doing good works. Paul said:

> "For what saith the scripture? Abraham believed God, and it was counted to him for righteousness. Now to him that worketh is the reward not reckoned of grace, but of debt. **But to him that worketh not, but believeth on him that justifieth the ungodly, his faith is counted for righteousness.** Even as David also describeth the blessedness of the man, unto whom God imputeth righteousness without works, Saying, Blessed are they whose iniquities are forgiven, and whose sins are covered. Blessed is the man to whom the Lord will not impute sin." (Romans 4:3-8, emphasis added)

> "For I bear them record that they have a zeal of God, but not according to knowledge. For they **being ignorant of God's righteousness, and going about to establish their own righteousness, have not submitted themselves unto the righteousness of God.** For Christ is the end of the law for righteousness to every one that believeth. (Romans 10:2-4, emphasis added)

The Apostle Paul discussed the problem of "Judaizers." These men said that circumcision was necessary for salvation, and that Christians should follow the Jewish law. Paul called that slavery. He said that the end result is that people fall from grace, and Christ's death on the cross does not benefit them. Paul exhorted the Christians in Galatia, saying:

> "Stand fast therefore in the liberty wherewith Christ hath made us free, and **be not entangled again with the yoke of bondage.** Behold, I Paul say unto you, that if ye be circumcised,

Christ shall profit you nothing. For I testify again to every man that is circumcised, that he is a debtor to do the whole law. **Christ is become of no effect unto you,** whosoever of you are justified by the law; ye are **fallen from grace.**" (Galatians 5:1-4, emphasis added)

The Catholic Church has some things in common with the Judaizers. It says that, in order for people to be saved, in addition to having faith in Jesus, they must also obey laws (official declarations of popes and church councils) and participate in religious rituals (the sacraments).

Chapter 17

The Good Thief

Jesus was crucified between two thieves. Luke's Gospel gives some very interesting information about one of those thieves. (He is called a "malefactor," which is an old-fashioned word for a criminal.) The Apostle Luke wrote:

> "And one of the malefactors which were hanged railed on him, saying, If thou be Christ, save thyself and us. But the other answering rebuked him, saying, Dost not thou fear God, seeing thou are in the same condemnation? And we indeed justly; for we receive the due reward of our deeds: but this man hath done nothing amiss. And he said unto Jesus, Lord, remember me when thou comest into thy kingdom. And Jesus said unto him, Verily I say unto thee, To day shalt thou be with me in paradise." (Luke 23:39-43)

The thief went to Heaven the day that he died. There was no Purgatory. He went straight to Heaven.

The thief had faith in Jesus. He recognized Jesus' Godly character. He believed in Jesus. Because of that, he believed what Jesus said about Himself. While he and Jesus were both hanging on crosses, in agony, it sure didn't look like Jesus was a King. It sure didn't feel like it. But the thief's faith in Jesus was stronger than his feelings.

The thief asked Jesus to have mercy on him, to help him. And Jesus responded by promising that the thief would go to Heaven with Him—that very day.

The thief wasn't baptized. He didn't receive the "last rites" or the "sacrament of reconciliation" ("confession"). He didn't do any good works to merit salvation. He didn't do any penances. He didn't go see a priest. He didn't obey a Pope.

All he did was have faith in Jesus and ask Him for mercy. And he loved Jesus. That is shown by how he rebuked the other thief for mocking Jesus and speaking against Him.

Faith and love and a plea for mercy—it was as simple as that.

Jesus once called a little child to him and He used that child as a sermon illustration. He said:

> "Verily I say unto you, Except ye be converted, and become as little children, ye shall not enter into the kingdom of heaven. Whosoever therefore shall humble himself as this little child, the same is greatest in the kingdom of heaven." (Matthew 18:3-4)

It takes humility to ask Jesus to save us, instead of trying to earn our own way into Heaven by doing good works. It takes the simplicity and humility of a child to just love Jesus, and trust Him, and ask Him to make it right for us.

In this passage, Jesus warned us about the danger of becoming "adults" who are so sophisticated and so complicated that we are no longer able to receive salvation from Him with the simple faith and trust and love of a little child.

Catholicism is full of rules, and rituals, and complicated theology. It is full of trying to be good enough to earn your way into Heaven by doing things—going to Mass, receiving the sacraments, doing good works, obeying the Catholic Church, being devoted to Mary, praying to saints, etc.[1]

But the Bible talks of simple faith, like a child—and like the thief on the cross. He just believed and asked Jesus to help him. And he went straight to Heaven with Jesus.

Chapter 18
The Numbers Game

People tend to be impressed with size. "Bigger" and "better" often go together in advertising slogans. But is this how God sees things? Can we assume that the Roman Catholic Church must be right, because it is so big?

Goliath was huge, powerful, and a seasoned warrior. He was admired by the Philistines and feared by the Israelites. People were impressed with Goliath, but God wasn't. God used a young shepherd named David to kill the giant. (1 Samuel 17:1-54)

When Gideon fought the Midianites, he started out with 32,000 men. That sounds like an impressive number, until you read that the Midianite soldiers were a multitude that filled the valley like a plague of locusts. But God told Gideon that he had too many men, and he was to send home every man who was afraid. Two-thirds of Gideon's men left (22,000 out of 32,000). Then God disqualified all but 300 of the 10,000 men who remained. That left Gideon with only 300 men, which was only one percent of his original soldiers. (Judges 7:1-9)

In God's eyes, which men were the faithful soldiers through whom He could do miracles? The 31,700? Or the 300 who defeated the Midianites? If you read what happened, you will see that God was with the one percent.

Could the difference be even greater than a hundred to one, and still have God be with the minority? Well, what if the 31,700 had decided that, because the 300 were different, they must be "heretics," and therefore they should be killed?

Jesus spoke about a large crowd of people, who go the wrong way, to their destruction. He compared it with a small group of people, who go the right way, which leads to life. Jesus exhorted His listeners, saying:

> "Enter ye in at the strait gate: for wide is the gate, and broad is the way, that leadeth to destruction, and many there be which go in thereat: Because strait is the gate, and narrow is the way, which leadeth unto life, and few there be that find it." (Matthew 7:13-14)

If you look at the context in which Jesus said this, He was speaking to the multitudes in Israel. These were not pagans who served horrible demon "gods." These were God's chosen people, in covenant with Him, the people who had the Scriptures, the people to whom God had sent the prophets. And Jesus warned **them** that there was a broad, popular way, which most people would choose, that would lead to destruction.

Jesus spoke of Godly people who would be despised, and false people who would be widely accepted. He said:

> "Blessed are ye, when men shall revile you, and persecute you, and shall say all manner of evil against you falsely, for my sake. Rejoice, and be exceeding glad: for great is your reward in heaven: for so persecuted they the prophets which were before you." (Matthew 5:11-12)

> "Woe unto you, when all men shall speak well of you! for so did their fathers to the false prophets." (Luke 6:26)

Obviously, being part of a small minority that is spoken against does not necessarily make people right. Jim Jones claimed to be a Christian leader, but he turned his church into a cult. He was dead wrong. He led his followers to destruction.

My point is that you cannot use numbers to decide whether or not religious leaders are right. We need to see if their teachings agree with Scripture. Our plumb line is the Bible, not the calculator.

Chapter 19

Devotion to Mary

As a faithful Catholic, and later as a nun, I was devoted to Mary. The prayers and practices were so familiar. They were taught to me by sincere people. I prayed the rosary, including rosary novenas. I wore a Brown Scapular and a Miraculous Medal. (You can read about these things in the Glossary, which is Appendix C.) I visited shrines that honor Mary. I had beautiful statues of Mary. I attended special services where we prayed to Mary and recited a litany of titles honoring her. I read books about apparitions of Mary, and dreamed of visiting Lourdes and Fatima. I participated in processions honoring Mary. A statue of Mary was put on a platform that was decorated with flowers. There were poles on the platform, so that men could carry it. The men walked through the streets, carrying the statue on the platform. We walked behind the statue, singing songs in Mary's honor.

Was this worship? At the time, that question never occurred to me. Now, looking back on what I did, I believe that it was.

Priorities

How can you tell what a person's real priorities are? Watch what he or she does when faced with a life-threatening situation.

Pope John Paul II was shot by an assassin on May 13, 1981. While the ambulance was rushing him to the hospital, the Pope did not pray to God or call on the name of Jesus. Instead, he kept saying, over and over: "Mary, my mother!" Polish pilgrims placed a picture of Our Lady of Czestochowa on the throne where the Pope normally sat. People gathered around the picture. Vatican loudspeakers broadcasted the prayers of the rosary. When the Pope recovered, he gave Mary all the glory for saving his life, and he made a pilgrimage to Fatima to publicly thank her.[1]

Another test of a person's priorities is what he or she does with money. Jesus said: "For where your treasure is, there will your heart be also." (Luke 12:34)

Some statues of Mary wear real crowns, which are made of gold. You can see online pictures of statues of Our Lady of Fatima and Our Lady of Lourdes wearing crowns.[2] The statues in the pictures are replicas. Their crowns are ceramic and painted gold. But the crowns on the original statues at Fatima and Lourdes are real crowns, made of real gold.

Vast sums of money are spent on some special statues of Mary. For example, a cathedral in Saragossa, Spain, has a statue of Mary that wears a crown made of 25 pounds of gold and diamonds, with so many diamonds that you can hardly see the gold. In addition, the statue has six other crowns of gold, diamonds, and emeralds. It has 365 mantles that are embroidered with gold, and decorated with diamonds and other jewels. It has 365 necklaces made of pearls and diamonds, and six chains of gold set with diamonds.[3]

Honoring Mary

In Sabana Grande, Puerto Rico, preparations are underway to construct a 305-foot statue of Our Lady of the Rosary. (It will be as large as the Statue of Liberty.) There are also plans for chapels, conference rooms, apartments, a food court, observation decks, and radio and TV stations. The statue will be part of a 500-acre "Mystical City" complex. (This information is online.)[4]

It is traditional to have processions in honor of Mary. They range in size from a few dozen people to multitudes. At Fatima, Portugal, crowds of over a million people gather on the anniversary of the apparition of Our Lady of Fatima. The celebration includes a procession of a million people, who follow a statue of Mary and sing songs praising her.[5]

One traditional prayer in Mary's honor is the "Hail Holy Queen," which is known in Latin as the *"Salve Regina."* It is traditionally included as part of praying the rosary. Please read this prayer and ask yourself: "Does this sound like worship?" It says:

> "Hail, holy Queen, Mother of Mercy! Our life, our sweetness and our hope! To thee do we cry, poor banished children of Eve. To thee do we send up our sighs, mourning and weeping, in this valley of tears. Turn, then, most gracious Advocate, thine eyes of mercy toward us; and after this our exile show unto us the blessed fruit of thy womb, Jesus. O clement, O loving, O sweet Virgin Mary."

Alfonsus de Liguori (1696-1787) was a principal proponent of the Marianist Movement, which glorifies Mary. He wrote a book called, *The Glories of Mary*, which is famous, influential, and widely read. In this book, de Liguori says that Mary was given rulership over one half of the kingdom of God. He said that Mary rules over the kingdom of mercy, and Jesus rules over the kingdom of justice. De Liguori said that people should pray to Mary as a mediator, and look to her as an object of trust for answered prayer. The book says that there is no salvation outside of Mary.

Some people suggest that these views are extreme, and not representative of Catholic Church teaching. However, instead of silencing de Liguori as a heretic, the Catholic Church made him a canonized saint. In addition, he is a "doctor of the Church" (a person whose teachings carry weight and authority). Furthermore, his book is openly and officially promoted by the Catholic Church, and his teachings have influenced popes.[6]

Pope Pius IX reigned from 1846 to 1878. He said that our salvation is based upon Mary.[7] Pope Benedict XV reigned from 1914 to 1922. He said that Mary, with Christ, redeemed mankind.[8] (Encyclicals are online. They are easy to find.)

A lay movement called *Vox Populi* (Voice of the People) gathers signed petitions to send to the Pope, seeking to have him officially declare that Mary is Co-Redemptrix. This doctrine says that Mary and Jesus are Co-Redeemers. (I have seen photographs of crucifixes that show Jesus hanging on one side of the cross, and Mary standing on the other side. She isn't nailed to it, but visually, she looks as essential to our salvation as Jesus does.) Over six million signatures have been sent to the Pope, representing 138 countries and all seven continents. This doctrine is supported by over 40 cardinals and 600 bishops worldwide. (This is online.)[9]

The Catholic Church exalts Mary as an idealized, larger-than-life, perfect mother. However, the Bible shows that, at one point, Mary misunderstood Jesus' ministry. Mary and Jesus' brothers tried to make him stop ministering. This is described in Mark 3:20-35. The first two verses say:

> "And the multitude cometh together again, so that they could not so much as eat bread. And when his friends heard of it, they went out to lay hold on him: for they said, He is beside himself.'" (Mark 3:20-21)

According to *Strong's Concordance*, the Greek word that is translated "friends" has a variety of meanings, including "kinsmen." However, we don't have to depend on the exact meaning of the word here, because it will be made clear in verse 31.

Strong's Concordance defines "lay hold on" as "to use strength, i.e. seize or retain." It defines "beside himself" as "become astounded, insane." In other words, these people thought that Jesus didn't know what he was doing. They intended to take charge of the situation.

Verses 22 through 30 describe a confrontation that occurred between Jesus and the scribes. Then we get back to the people who thought that Jesus was "beside himself" and intended to "lay hold on" Him. The Bible says:

> "There came then his brethren and his mother, and, standing without, sent unto him calling him. And the multitude sat about him, and they said unto him, Behold, thy mother and thy brethren without seek for thee. And he answered them, saying, Who is my mother, or my brethren? And he looked round about on them which sat about him, and said, Behold my mother and my brethren! For whosoever shall do the will of God, the same is my brother, and my sister, and mother." (Mark 3:31-35)

Comparing Scripture with Catholic Doctrines about Mary

My sources for this section are the *Catechism of the Catholic Church* and the Bible. The *Catechism* summarizes the essential and basic teachings of the Roman Catholic Church. It was approved by Pope John Paul II in 1992. It has numbered paragraphs, which makes it easy to find things. It is available online with a search engine. You can search by paragraph numbers or topics. (Information is in the Notes.)[10]

For each doctrinal category, I will indicate the Catholic doctrine, followed by the appropriate references from the *Catechism*. (I will say "*Catechism*" followed by the relevant paragraph numbers.) I will follow this with quotations from the Bible that relate to the doctrine.

The last book in the Bible is called the "Book of Revelation" in Protestant Bibles. It is called the "Apocalypse" in Catholic Bibles. I will refer to it as "Revelation."

Immaculate Conception

Catholic doctrine says that Mary was preserved from all stain of original sin, from the first instant of her conception. (*Catechism* 491, 492, 508). However, according to the Bible, Mary knew that she needed a savior. The Bible records Mary's words to her cousin Elizabeth:

> "And Mary said, My soul doth magnify the Lord, And my spirit hath rejoiced in God **my Saviour**." (Luke 1:46-47, emphasis added)

The doctrine of the Immaculate Conception was first introduced by a heretic (a man whose teachings were officially declared to be contrary to Church doctrine). For centuries, this doctrine was unanimously rejected by popes, Fathers, and theologians of the Catholic Church.[11]

All-Holy

Catholic doctrine says that Mary, "the All-Holy," lived a perfectly sinless life. (*Catechism* 411, 493, 508) However, according to Scripture, **all** people have sinned. The Bible says:

> "For **all have sinned**, and come short of the glory of God…" (Romans 3:23, emphasis added)

> "Who shall not fear thee, O Lord, and glorify thy name? for **thou only art holy**…" (Revelation 15:4, emphasis added)

> "As it is written, There is none righteous, no, not one…" (Romans 3:10)

There is only one exception, one sinless person. Jesus Christ is the only human being who was never soiled by sin. The Bible says:

> "For we have not an high priest which cannot be touched with the feelings of our infirmities; but was in all points tempted like as we are, **yet without sin**." (Hebrews 4:15, emphasis added)

> "For he hath made him to be sin for us, **who knew no sin**; that we might be made the righteousness of God in him." (2 Corinthians 5:21, emphasis added)

> "**Who did no sin**, neither was guile found in his mouth…" (1 Peter 2:22, emphasis added)

The Bible tells us that the parents of John the Baptist were "righteous before God" and that they were "blameless." (Luke 1:6) If Mary was sinless, wouldn't the Bible have told us so? It says that she was "highly favoured" and that God was with her. (Luke 1:28) But it does not say that she was sinless.

Mary herself said that she needed a Savior. If God was her Savior, then Mary was not sinless, because sinless people do not need a Savior. The Bible describes it as follows:

> "And Mary said, My soul doth magnify the Lord, And my spirit hath rejoiced in God my Saviour." (Luke 1:46-47)

In the Book of Revelation, when they were searching for someone who was worthy to break the seals and open the scroll, the only person who was found to be worthy was Jesus. Nobody else in Heaven or on earth (including Mary) was worthy to open the scroll, or even look inside it. (Revelation 5:1-5)

Perpetual Virginity

Catholic doctrine says that Mary was a virgin before, during, and after the birth of Jesus. (*Catechism* 499, 510) However, the Bible says:

> "Then Joseph being raised from sleep did as the angel of the Lord had bidden him, and took unto him his wife: And knew her not **till** she had brought forth her **firstborn** son: and he called his name JESUS." (Matthew 1:24-25, emphasis added)

"Till" (until) means that, after that point, things changed. Joseph did eventually "know" Mary (have sexual relations with her). (See Genesis 4:1, where Adam "knew" Eve, and she conceived, and had a son.) In addition, "firstborn son" implies that there were additional sons.

Mary and Joseph had at least six children. The Bible names four brothers of Jesus. It also says that he had sisters. The Bible says:

> "And when he was come into his own country, he taught them in their synagogue, insomuch that they were astonished, and said, Whence hath this man this wisdom, and these mighty works? Is not this the carpenter's son? is not his mother called Mary? and his brethren, James, and Joses, and Simon, and Judas? And his sisters, are they not all with us?" (Matthew 13:54-56; also see Mark 6:2-3)

When I was a Catholic, I was taught that the word for "brothers" in this passage was a general term that could refer to any kind of kinsman, including cousins. I was taught that Mary was not the mother of these "brothers," and therefore these "brothers" did not interfere with her virginity.

The Hebrew language has a general term that can mean brothers, cousins, or other kinsmen. However, the New Testament was not written in Hebrew. It was written in Greek. The Greek language is very precise. It makes it quite clear whether or not people have the same parents.

According to *Strong's Concordance*, the Greek word used here for the "brothers" of Jesus is *adelphos*. It means, "from the same womb." These are men who have the same mother. *Adelphos* is also used to describe the brothers of Jesus in Matthew 12:46; John 2:12; John 7:3; and Acts 1:14. *Adelphos* is used to describe "James the Lord's brother" in Galatians 1:19. *Adelphos* is also used to describe the brothers Peter and Andrew (Matthew 4:18), and the brothers James and John (Matthew 4:21). *Adelphe* (the feminine form of *adelphos*) is used to describe Jesus' sisters (Matthew 13:56)

The Greek language has another word that is used for relatives who don't come from the same womb. The word *suggenes* is used to describe Mary's cousin, Elizabeth (Luke 1:36). *Suggenes* means, "a blood relative."

Some people who were raised Catholic may wonder why I am talking about Greek and Hebrew words, because they remember hearing the Bible read in Latin during Mass. The Old Testament was written by Israelites who spoke Hebrew and Aramaic. It was written primarily in Hebrew, with some Aramaic. (Jews in modern Israel still speak Hebrew.) The New Testament was written in Greek. This was the common language of the people who lived in the eastern area of the Mediterranean Sea. Greek had been widely spoken since the reign of Alexander the Great. In the fifth century, Saint Jerome translated the Bible into Latin. Until the Second Vatican Council (1962-1965), the Bible was read in Latin during Mass.

Greek is a very precise language. The Greek words used for "brothers" and "sisters" in Matthew 13:54-56 make it clear that Mary was their mother. So why does the Catholic Church insist that she wasn't?

Perhaps it is because of Saint Augustine. His essay, *On Marriage and Concupiscence*, influenced the Catholic Church for 1,500 years. Augustine said that if couples have intercourse in order to have children, without wanting to gratify their sexual desires, that is good. If they want to have children, but they also want to gratify their sexual desires, then that is a forgiveable sin that is allowable within marriage. If they want to gratify their sexual desires, and they don't want to have children, then what they are doing is as bad as adultery or prostitution. (You can read Augustine's treatise online.)[12]

Since the marriage bed was thought to be sinful, it is not surprising that Catholic theologians did not want to think of Mary as being a normal wife.

Mother of God

Catholic doctrine says that, because she is the mother of Jesus, and Jesus is God, Mary is therefore the Mother of God. (*Catechism* 963, 971, 2677). However, this is opposed to Scripture. The Incarnation means that Jesus was both fully God and fully man. Mary was only the mother of Jesus as man. She was not the mother of Jesus as God.

According to the Bible, the world was created through Jesus. This was long before Mary was born. Scripture says:

> "God, who at sundry times and in divers manners spake in time past unto the fathers by the prophets, Hath in these last days spoken unto us by his Son, whom he hath appointed heir of all things, **by whom also he made the worlds**..." (Hebrews 1:1-2, emphasis added)

> "For by him [Jesus] were **all** things created, that are in heaven, and that are in earth, visible and invisible, whether they be thrones, or dominions, or principalities, or powers: **all** things **were created by him, and for him**: And he is **before all things** and by him **all** things consist." (Colossians 1:16-17, emphasis added)

Jesus existed before the world began. He created everything (including Mary). Jesus came first—not Mary. Jesus said:

> "And now O Father, glorify thou me with thine own self with the glory which I had with thee **before the world was**." (John 17:5, emphasis added)

Mother of the Church

According to Catholic doctrine, Mary is the Mother of the Church. (*Catechism* 963, 975). However, this is not seen in the Bible. The Book of Acts gives a picture of a group of people praying together. Mary is mentioned as one of them, but nothing indicates any special prominence. The Bible says:

> "And when they were come in, they went up into an upper room, where abode both Peter, and James, and John, and Andrew, Phillip, and Thomas, Bartholomew, and Matthew, James the son of Alphaeus, and Simon Zelotes, and Judas the brother of James. These all continued with one accord in

prayer and supplication, with the women, and Mary the mother of Jesus, and with his brethren." (Acts 1:13-14)

Mary was probably in the Upper Room when the tongues of fire fell upon the 120 disciples. However, she is never mentioned again in the Book of Acts, which is our only historical record of how the Church was born. She is also not specifically identified in the epistles. Paul did send greetings to "Mary," but that was a common name. The Gospels and the Book of Acts refer to "Mary the mother of Jesus," in order to distinguish her from other women named Mary.

It is notable that John, who took Mary into his home after Jesus was crucified, did not mention her in his epistles. He only mentioned her twice in his Gospel (the wedding at Cana and the crucifixion of Jesus). John mentioned Mary Magdalene more often than he mentioned Jesus' mother.

Assumption

Catholic doctrine says that, at the end of her life, Mary was taken up ("assumed"), body and soul, into Heaven. (*Catechism* 966, 974) However, there is no biblical reference to the assumption of Mary. The Gospel of John is generally believed to have been written around 90 years after Jesus was born. If Mary had been supernaturally assumed into Heaven, wouldn't John (the disciple that Mary lived with) have mentioned it? When Enoch and Elijah were taken up to Heaven, the Bible recorded it. With Elijah, it was recorded in some detail. (See Genesis 5:24 and 2 Kings 2:1-12.)

The Assumption of Mary was officially declared to be a dogma of the Roman Catholic faith in 1950. This means that every Roman Catholic is required to believe this doctrine without questioning it. However, as we will see, the teaching of the Assumption originated with heretical writings that were officially condemned by the early Church.

In 495 A.D., Pope Gelasius declared that men who taught that Mary was assumed into Heaven were heretics. In the sixth century, Pope Hormisdas also condemned men as heretics for teaching it. "Infallible" popes declared the doctrine of the Assumption of Mary to be a heresy. Then, in 1950, Pope Pius XII (another "infallible" Pope) declared it to be official Roman Catholic doctrine.[13]

Mediatrix

Catholic doctrine says that people should invoke Mary as Advocate and Mediatrix, and her prayers contribute to our salvation. (*Catechism* 969). It says that we can trust Mary to take care of our concerns and our petitions. (*Catechism* 2677) However, according to the Bible, Jesus Christ is the only mediator between God and mankind. Scripture says:

> "For there is one God, and **one mediator between God and men, the man Christ Jesus**: Who gave himself a ransom for all, to be testified in due time." (1 Timothy 2:5-6, emphasis added)

> "Wherefore he [Jesus] is able to save them to the uttermost that come unto God by him, seeing he ever liveth to make intercession for them." (Hebrews 7:25)

> "In whom [Jesus] we have boldness and access with confidence by the faith of him." (Ephesians 3:12)

If Jesus is constantly interceding for us, and He is able to save us "to the uttermost" (utterly, completely), then He doesn't need Mary's help. If we can approach God with "boldness" and "confidence," because of our faith in Jesus, then we don't need Mary's help, either.

Queen of Heaven

Catholic doctrine says that God has exalted Mary in heavenly glory as Queen of Heaven and earth, and she should be praised with special devotion. (*Catechism* 966, 971, 2675) However, in the Bible, "Queen of Heaven" is the title of a pagan goddess. God was angry with His people for worshiping her, and He brought judgment on them because of it. (Jeremiah 7:17-20; Jeremiah 44:17-28) The Bible makes it quite clear that only God's name (not Mary's) is to be exalted. It says:

> "Let them praise the name of the LORD: for **his name alone is excellent;** his glory is above the earth and heaven." (Psalm 148:13, emphasis added)

When people tried to give Mary special honor and pre-eminence, because she was His mother, Jesus corrected them. The Bible describes this incident, saying:

> "And it came to pass, as he spake these things, a certain woman of the company lifted up her voice, and said unto him, Blessed is the womb that bare thee, and the paps which thou hast sucked. But he said, Yea rather, blessed are they that hear the word of God, and keep it." (Luke 11:27-28)

Jesus is saying that we should not give special honor to His mother. What matters is that we hear and obey the Word of God. We need to concentrate on that. Jesus' response clearly shows that He did not want people to be distracted by giving undue honor or attention to Mary.

In chapters four and five of the Book of Revelation, we are given a quite detailed picture of Heaven. God is seated on the throne, surrounded by 24 elders and four living creatures. The Lamb (Jesus) is standing in the center of the throne. Thousands upon thousands of angels circle the throne, singing God's praises. And Mary is not in the picture at all. If she is the Queen of Heaven, then why is she not mentioned?

How Did We Get Here?

How did modern Catholic doctrine about Mary wander so far away from what the Bible says? Two reasons are: (1) the importance given to Catholic tradition; and (2) the doctrine of papal infallibility.

The Catholic Church officially states that Catholic tradition is equal in authority to the Bible. (*Catechism* 80, 84, 97) This tradition is based on the religious practices and beliefs of the Catholic people. (*Catechism* 78, 113, 2650, 2661) Therefore, it is constantly subject to change. It is also subject to unchristian cultural influences. Because tradition is difficult to define, Catholic theologians can make it appear to mean whatever suits their purposes at any given moment.

The Early Fathers used Scripture as the standard against which they tested Catholic tradition. The modern Catholic doctrine that Catholic tradition is equal in authority with the Bible is contrary to the writings of the Early Fathers.[14]

According to Jesus, Scripture is the plumb line for measuring everything else. He judged religious traditions by comparing them to Scripture. When religious traditions contradicted Scripture, he condemned them. The Bible says:

> "Then came together unto him the Pharisees, and certain of the scribes, which came from Jerusalem. And when they saw some of his disciples eat bread with defiled, that is to say, with unwashen, hands, they found fault. For the Pharisees, and all the Jews, except they wash their hands oft, eat not, holding the tradition of the elders. And when they come from the market, except they wash, they eat not. And many other things there be, which they have received to hold, as the washing of cups, and pots, brasen vessels, and of tables. Then the Pharisees and scribes asked him, Why walk not thy disciples according to the tradition of the elders, but eat bread

with unwashen hands? He answered and said unto them, Well hath Esaias prophesied of you hypocrites, as it is written, This people honoureth me with their lips, but their heart is far from me. **Howbeit in vain do they worship me, teaching for doctrines the commandments of men**. For laying aside the commandment of God, ye hold the tradition of men, as the washing of pots and cups: and many other such like things ye do. And he said unto them, **Full well ye reject the commandment of God, that ye may keep your own tradition**. For Moses said, Honour thy father and thy mother; and, Whoso curseth father or mother, let him die the death: But ye say, If a man shall say to his father or mother, It is Corban, that is to say, a gift, by whatsoever thou mightest be profited by me; he shall be free. And ye suffer him no more to do ought for his father or his mother; **Making the word of God of none effect through your tradition**, which ye have delivered: and many such like things do ye." (Mark 7:1-13, emphasis added)

This shows clearly that nothing is equal in authority to Scripture. The Bible stands alone as the standard by which all other things are to be judged.

According to the official teaching of the Catholic Church, Catholic men and women are not allowed to believe what they read in the Bible without checking it out with the Catholic Church. They are required to find out how the Catholic bishops interpret a passage, and they are required to accept what the bishops teach, as if it came from Jesus Christ Himself. They are not allowed to use their own judgment, or to follow their own conscience. They are required to believe whatever the bishops tell them, without questioning it. (*Catechism* 85, 87, 100, 862, 891, 2034, 2037)

The Catholic Church teaches that the Pope is infallible whenever he makes an official decree on matters of faith and morals. According to Catholic doctrine, it is impossible for the Pope to teach false doctrine. Catholics are expected to obey the Pope without question, even when he is not making an "infallible" statement about doctrine. They are expected to submit their wills and minds to the Pope without question. (*Catechism* 87, 892, 2037, 2051)

For more information, see the section "Infallibility" in the chapter, "Was the Early Church Roman Catholic?" Also see the chapter, "Mind Control." Some technical information about the doctrine of infallibility is given in Appendix C, which is a Glossary. See the entry, "Infallibility."

Apparitions of "Mary"

Something has been appearing to people. It claims to be the Virgin Mary. Often only one person, or a few people, can see it. In some places, many people can see it. These apparitions are sometimes accompanied by supernatural manifestations, such as physical healings.

Some apparitions (such as the ones in Lourdes and Fatima) have been officially approved by the Catholic Church. Official approval means that Catholic Church hierarchy has decided that an apparition is a valid supernatural event, the thing that is appearing is the Virgin Mary, and nothing that the apparition has said or done is contrary to Catholic doctrine.

If these really are supernatural events, how do we know that they don't come from the devil? The Bible warns us that the devil can appear as an angel of light (2 Corinthians 11:14) and he can cause deceptive supernatural events (2 Thessalonians 2:9).

Millions of Catholics make pilgrimages to places where "Mary" has appeared. Pope John Paul II has encouraged this, by visiting many apparition sites himself. He has a special devotion to Our Lady of Fatima (an apparition that appeared in Fatima, Portugal).

When Pope John Paul II was shot, he prayed to Mary, instead of praying to God. He believed that Mary saved his life. The Pope made a pilgrimage to Fatima to thank her, and to consecrate the entire human race to her.[15] The video, *Catholicism: Crisis of Faith*, shows the Pope bowing down before a statue of Mary and kissing its feet.[16]

Millions of pilgrims go to shrines that honor apparitions of Mary. Every year, fifteen to twenty million pilgrims go to Guadalupe in Mexico, five and a half million go to Lourdes in France, five million go to Czestochowa (Jasna Gora) in Poland, and four and a half million go to Fatima in Portugal. Special dates draw huge crowds. On August 15, half a million pilgrims go to Czestochowa. On October 13, a million people go to Fatima. On December 12, 1999, five million pilgrims went to Mexico, to honor Our Lady of Guadalupe.[17]

Are these pilgrims worshiping Mary? You can observe them and see for yourself, thanks to the video, *Messages from Heaven*.[18]

If you watch the video, you will see the Pope bow in front of a painting of Mary and cover the area with incense. You will see a million pilgrims walking in a procession, following a statue of Our Lady of Fatima, and singing songs in Mary's honor. You will see several million people in a procession following a painting of Our Lady of Guadalupe. You will see the largest assembly of bishops and cardinals since the Second Vatican Council, gathered together to join Pope John Paul II in solemnly consecrating the entire world to the Immaculate Heart of Mary. (You can watch this video online.)[19]

A Question of Vocabulary

Catholic theologians have three Latin words for "worship." *Latria* is for God alone. *Dulia* is for the saints. *Hyperdulia* is for Mary. (It is greater than *dulia*, but less than *latria*.) Catholic theologians say that, because of these verbal distinctions, Catholics do not worship Mary.

However, in real life, how are Catholics supposed to know whether their acts of devotion to Mary are *hyperdulia* or *latria*? How many Catholics have even heard of these words?

When I was a Catholic, sometimes people would ask me about praying to Mary and the saints. I used to say that I was just asking them to pray for me, like I would ask a friend. But there is a difference. When I talk to my friends, I am talking to people who are alive—not people who have died. The Bible tells us that we should not communicate with dead people, that we should not seek the dead on behalf of the living. (Isaiah 8:19; Deuteronomy 18:11-12)

Conclusion

Our minds can be deceived, and so can the minds of bishops and popes. Only the Bible is totally trustworthy. The Bible warns us:

> "Beware lest any man spoil [ruin] you through philosophy and vain deceit, after the tradition of men, after the rudiments of the world, and not after Christ." (Colossians 2:8)

> "There is a way which seemeth right unto a man, but the end thereof are the ways of death." (Proverbs 14:12; also see Proverbs 16:25)

When religious traditions conflict with the plain meaning of Scripture, then we need to discard those traditions. We cannot afford to do otherwise, because our eternal destiny is at stake.

Chapter 20
What Is Idolatry?

Throughout the history of Israel, there was a problem of idolatry. Some of the people would worship "foreign gods" (the gods of foreign nations). At times, idolatry was practiced on a large scale. We first see it with the golden calf that Aaron made, while the Israelites were at Mount Sinai. God warned Moses about idolatry. Wide-spread idolatry is described a number of times in the Book of Judges, and it is a recurring theme of the prophets. Following are some examples:

> "And the LORD said unto Moses, Behold, thou shalt sleep with thy fathers; and this people will rise up, and go a whoring after the gods of the strangers of the land, whither they go to be among them, and will forsake me, and break my covenant which I have made with them." (Deuteronomy 31:16)

> "And yet they would not hearken unto their judges, but they went a whoring after other gods, and bowed themselves unto them: they turned quickly out of the way which their fathers walked in..." (Judges 2:17)

> "And he [King Manasseh] did that which was evil in the sight of the LORD, after the abominations of the heathen, whom the LORD cast out before the children of Israel. For he built up again the high places which Hezekiah his father had destroyed: and he reared up altars for Baal, and made a grove, as did Ahab king of Israel; and worshipped all the host of heaven, and served them." (2 Kings 21:2-3; also see verses 4-9)

> "And they set them up images and groves in every high hill, and under every green tree: And there they burnt incense in all the high places, as did the heathen whom the LORD carried away before them; and wrought wicked things to provoke the LORD to anger: For they served idols, whereof the

LORD had said unto them, Ye shall not do this thing." (2 Kings 17:10-12; see verses 1-23)

Most modern westerners don't overtly worship pagan gods. However, there is more to idolatry than ancient pagan customs. According to *Webster's Dictionary*, idolatry also means, "excessive love or veneration for anything." (Love for God can never be excessive, but love for created things can be.)

Is it idolatry to say that there is no salvation without the Catholic Church? That would mean that the sacrifice of Jesus Christ was not sufficient to save us. Some popes have declared that no person can be saved apart from the Catholic Church. Pope Boniface VIII said that, unless people submit to the Pope, they cannot be saved. Other popes have declared that there is no salvation apart from Mary. Pope Innocent III said that he was the "Foundation of all Christianity." (You can read these statements online.)[1]

Is it idolatry to sing hymns to the Pope? It is traditional to sing papal hymns. You can buy recordings of them online. One hymn says that the Pope rules over "space and time." It also says that all the earth, and Heaven, should sing about the glory of the Pope. (You can read the words of this hymn online.)[2]

Is it idolatry to call the Pope "Holy Father"? In the Bible, that term is only used for God. Jesus used it when praying to His heavenly Father. (John 17:11)

Is it idolatry to say that the Pope is "God on earth"? One Pope openly said it. Others implied it. Pope Innocent III said that every Catholic clergyman must obey the Pope, even if the Pope orders him to do something evil, because nobody can judge the Pope. In 1894, Pope Leo XIII said that, as Pope, he held on the earth the place of God Almighty. Pope Pius X ruled from 1903 to 1914. He said that when the Pope speaks, it is Jesus Christ Himself speaking. He also said that the Pope is the one hope for the world. Pope Pius XI reigned from 1922 to 1939. He said that, because he was the Vicar of Christ, he was "God on earth." (You can read quotations from these popes online.)[3]

Is it idolatry to venerate Mary and the saints? Catholic Canon Law says that all Catholics should cultivate devotion to Mary, including praying the rosary. (The rosary has ten prayers to Mary for every one prayer to God.) Canon Law also says that church altars are required to have a relic of a saint. (A relic is a part of a saint's body, or something closely associated with the saint.) (You can read the Canon Laws online.)[4]

Is it idolatry to venerate "images"? Canon Law says that Catholic churches should have "holy images," such as statues and pictures, and that Catholics should venerate these images. (This is online.)[5] In contrast, the Bible forbids the veneration of statues or other images. It says:

"Thou shalt not make thee any graven image, or any likeness of any thing that is in heaven above, or that is in the earth beneath, or that is in the waters beneath the earth: **Thou shalt not bow down thyself unto them, nor serve them**..."
(Deuteronomy 5:8-9, emphasis added)

The Infant of Prague is an example of the extent to which veneration of images can be taken. A church in Prague, Czechoslovakia, has a statue of Jesus as an infant. Miracles have been attributed to this statue. Pilgrims come from around the world to venerate it. The statue wears expensive clothing and a gold crown set with jewels. It has 70 different sets of ornate clothing. In 1995, the statue was carried in solemn procession through the streets of Prague. The procession was led by two cardinals. Churches in many countries have replicas of this statue. (You can see pictures online.)[6]

Appendix D has Internet addresses of web pages with many pictures, including devotional practices that honor statues. If you go to these websites, you will see pictures of Pope John Paul II, kneeling before a statue of Mary; a candlelight procession in Fatima, Portugal, where millions of pilgrims follow a statue of Mary; and a ceremony in Cuba, where Pope John Paul II put a gold crown on a statue of Mary and declared that Mary is the Queen of Cuba. You will see pictures of statues that wear expensive clothing and gold crowns. (Sometimes the crowns have real jewels on them.) You will see pictures of statues of Mary that are so large that they dominate the church or chapel in which they are placed. In some cases, the crucifix on the altar is underneath the feet of the statue of Mary.

Is it idolatry to worship consecrated bread? The Catholic Church says that, during Mass, the bread and wine literally turn into the body, blood, soul, and divinity of Jesus Christ. Catholics are taught to bow before the bread and to worship it. According to Catholic Canon Law, Catholics are supposed to worship the Eucharist (consecrated bread and wine) with "supreme adoration." (This is online.)[7]

I have discussed a number of Catholic doctrines and devotional practices in this chapter. Do some of them involve forms of idolatry? Please ask God to give you His perspective about it.

Practical Problems

Chapter 21

Mandatory Celibacy

Recently, we have heard a lot about Roman Catholic priests who raped or seduced children and young teenagers (primarily boys). Apparently, these priests were unable to handle mandatory celibacy.

The early Church did not require celibacy. We know that the Apostle Peter was married, because Jesus healed Peter's mother-in-law when she had a fever. (See Matthew 8:14-15 and Mark 1:30-31). We know that bishops were married, because Paul gave them the guideline that they should only have one wife. (1 Timothy 3:2) Paul mentioned that Peter, other apostles, and Jesus' brothers were married. (1 Corinthians 9:5)

The Eastern Rite Church is a branch of the Roman Catholic Church. Eastern Rite priests are allowed to marry.

There are some Roman Catholic priests who are legally married. Over 100 married Protestant ministers converted to Catholicism and were ordained as Roman Catholic priests. (This is online.)[1]

Some priests are secretly married. When I was a Catholic, I had a regular confessor, a priest I met with every week for spiritual guidance. Years later, I was shocked to learn that, while he was my confessor, he was secretly married. (Eventually he left the Catholic Church and openly married his wife. Years later, he left his wife and children, went back to the Catholic Church, and was reinstated as a priest.)

When I was a nun, we were taught that the purpose of celibacy was to enable us to be more totally dedicated to God. The Apostle Paul said:

> "But I would have you without carefulness. He that is unmarried careth for the things that belong to the Lord, how he may please the Lord: But he that is married careth for the things that are of the world, how he may please his wife." (1 Corinthians 7:32-33)

This shows that celibacy is a valid calling, which can help people be more fully devoted to God. When God calls, He equips. I have known precious celibates (both Catholic and Protestant) whose devotion to God is inspiring.

But what about **requiring** people to be celibate? Earlier in the same chapter, Paul said:

> "For I would that all men were even as I myself. But **every man hath his proper gift of God, one after this manner, and another after that.** I say therefore to the unmarried and widows, It is good for them if they abide even as I. But if they cannot contain, let them marry: for it is better to marry than to burn." (1 Corinthians 7:7-9, emphasis added)

While discussing celibacy, Paul said that God has given people different gifts. It is good for a person who has been given the gift of celibacy to be celibate. However, if they do not have that gift, then it is better for them to marry.

In spite of Paul's admonition, the Roman Catholic Church **requires** that priests, nuns, and monks be celibate. How did that happen?

Pope Gregory VII reigned from 1073 to 1085. At the time, many Catholic priests were married. Kings and noblemen donated property to the Roman Catholic Church in exchange for the faithful service of priests. Some priests tried to leave this property to their heirs. In addition, they had loyalty to the noblemen who provided them with homes. In order to protect Church property, and to ensure that the loyalty of the priests went to the Pope, and not to secular rulers, Pope Gregory abolished clerical marriage. He passed laws requiring that priests be celibate, and he got rid of married priests.[2]

In 655 A.D., by passing a decree, the ninth Council of Toledo turned the children of married priests into Church property. They immediately became the permanent slaves of the Catholic Church. In 1089, by passing a decree, the Synod of Melfi under Pope Urban II turned the wives of married priests into Church property. The priests were put into prison and their wives were sold into slavery. Their children were either sold into slavery, or else abandoned. (You can read about this online.)[3]

Married priests were a target of the Inquisition. (This is online.)[4]

There is a website for priests who are struggling with celibacy.[5] There is an online support group for priests and nuns who are involved in "romantic relationships."[6] There are support groups for children who have been fathered by Catholic priests.[7] (You can read about these groups online.)

In the last fifteen years, the Roman Catholic Church in America paid nearly one billion dollars because of Catholic priests who were convicted of sexual abuse. Catholic priests in ten other countries have also been convicted of sexual abuse. There are two support groups for helping women who are sexually involved with Catholic parish priests. Eastern Rite churches (which do not require celibacy) do not have these problems. (Information is online.)[8]

Wherever you have sinful human beings, some people will engage in sexual exploitation. However, the frequency of cases involving celibate Catholic priests is unusual. Because children see priests as representing God, being sexually exploited by them can result in spiritual confusion in addition to emotional trauma.

The sad thing is that all of this could have been avoided. There is a branch of the Catholic Church (the Eastern Rite) where it is normal for priests to be married. If it is OK for them, then why does the Catholic Church require its other priests to be celibate?[9]

Chapter 22

Mind Control

The Catholic Church claims that it has the right to control how Catholics think. Some of its doctrines and practices actually result in a form of mind control.

In discussing this issue, I will pull together some information from other chapters and give it a somewhat different perspective. I also have some additional information.

According to *The Catholic Encyclopedia*, a person's religious beliefs should not be determined by his or her "free private judgment." Rather, they should be determined by the Catholic Church.[1] (*The Catholic Encyclopedia* is online.)

The same attitude is shown in the teachings of Saint Ignatius Loyola, who founded the Jesuits in 1540. He wrote *Spiritual Exercises*, which are rules for the Jesuits. They include rules about how to think. The first rule about thinking says that Jesuits should set their private judgment aside. The thirteenth rule says that it is a virtue to see things the way that the hierarchy of the Catholic Church sees them, even if they are not true. It gives the example of seeing something that is obviously white, but believing that it is really black if the Catholic hierarchy says that it is black. (You can read these rules online.)[2]

According to Canon Law (the official laws governing the Roman Catholic Church), Catholics are required to submit their minds and wills to any declaration concerning faith or morals that is made by the Pope, or by a Catholic Church council. They are also required to avoid anything that disagrees with such declarations. Furthermore, they can be coerced if they don't comply. (You can read these laws online. If you want to buy the book, the Notes give information.)[3]

The Catholic Church teaches that only the Magisterium of the Church (the Pope and the bishops in communion with him) has the right to interpret Scripture. People like us are not allowed to interpret Scripture for ourselves. We are supposed to check it out with Church authorities. (This is online.)[4]

Catholicism teaches that Catholics are supposed to "receive with docility" any directives given to them by Catholic Church authorities. (This is online.)[5]

This sounds like young children, who accept without question whatever their parents tell them. In contrast, the Bible commends the people of Berea, because they "searched the Scriptures daily" in order to "see whether these things were so." (Acts 17:10-11) God wants His people to check things out for themselves, using Scripture as their yardstick.

In 1854, Pope Pius IX declared the dogma of the Immaculate Conception of Mary. The Pope said that if people "dare" to even think anything contrary to this dogma, then that disagreement will shipwreck their faith, cut them off from the Catholic Church, and make them become "condemned." He said that people who outwardly express disagreement could be punished for it.[6] (Encyclicals are online.)

The Pope's reference to legal penalties is significant, because a man had been executed for heresy 28 years before this encyclical was issued.[7]

The Catholic Church has never renounced its past practice of killing people who disagree with Catholic doctrine. On the contrary, the Office of the Inquisition still exists. It is part of the Vatican Curia. In 1965, its name was changed to The Congregation for the Doctrine of the Faith. It is headed by Cardinal Ratzinger.[8]

Some people have paid a high price for disagreeing with the Catholic Church, or acting contrary to the wishes of the Pope. (See the chapter, "Hunting 'Heretics.'")

Mind Control and Politics

Mind control is not limited to Catholic doctrine. Popes and other high-ranking Catholic clergymen have also applied it to politics. Following are two examples. One is from the Middle Ages. The other is quite recent.

Pope Innocent III reigned from 1198 to 1216. In 1215, the *Magna Carta* was signed. This was the beginning of democracy in England. It established the principle that the King is not above the law. The *Magna Carta* is one of the documents that influenced the men who wrote the Constitution of the United States. Innocent said that the *Magna Carta* was immoral. He declared it to be null and void. In addition, he excommunicated everyone who supported it. (You can read about this online.)[9]

In 1962, the island of Malta had an election. The Catholic Church strongly opposed a candidate named Mintoff. It was declared to be a mortal sin to vote for Mintoff. Maltese Catholics who voted for him were placed under interdict. Because they were placed under interdict, they could not go to confession and have their "mortal sin" of voting for Mintoff be absolved by a Catholic priest. They were also denied a Christian burial. (This is online.)[10]

The combination of mind control and spiritual coercion can cause kings to do immoral things, and to require their subjects to do them. For example, Pope Clement V (1305-1314) wanted the King of England (Edward II) to have some men be tortured. The King protested. He said that torture was illegal in England. The Pope said that Church law took priority over the laws of England. In other words, he said that the English law forbidding torture was wrong, because it conflicted with the laws of the Catholic Church. The Pope ordered the King to have the men be tortured, and he threatened to excommunicate him if he refused. The King complied. He made his subjects torture people, in spite of the fact that he believed that torture was wrong. The laws of England were changed in order to allow the torture. (Information is online.)[11]

Required Reverence

According to Canon Law, priests are required to have "reverence" for the Pope. *Webster's Dictionary* defines "reverence" as "profound respect mingled with love and awe."[12]

Moral Confusion

Mind control can result in moral confusion. Catholics are taught to accept, without question, everything that Catholic authority figures teach them about faith and morals. The result is that you put your conscience in the hands of other people. This can cause moral confusion.

The Catholic Church has done various things to make the Bible less accessible to people, and to make it more difficult for people to trust Scripture. (See the chapter, "Undermining the Bible.") Once people lose confidence in the Bible, then they become far more susceptible to mind control and moral confusion. Once Scripture is no longer perceived as being a reliable guide for moral living, then Catholics are dependent on Catholic authority figures to tell them what is right and wrong.

An example of this is Pope Innocent III, who ruled from 1198 to 1216. He said that Catholic clergymen have to obey the Pope, no matter what he tells them to do. He denied their right (and responsibility) to make moral judgments and follow their conscience. He said that, even if the Pope commands them to do something evil, they have to obey him, because nobody can judge the Pope. (This is online.)[13]

The Bible warns us that we need to guard ourselves against deception. It says:

"Take heed that no man deceive you." (Matthew 24:4)

"Beware lest any man spoil [ruin] you through philosophy and vain deceit, after the tradition of men, after the rudiments of the world, and not after Christ." (Colossians 2:8)

We all need to protect ourselves from deception. If we don't stand on the Bible, then we can fall for anything. I will give some examples from the lives of Catholics I know personally.

A Mother

A friend of mine was a devout Catholic. She had a confessor, a priest she went to regularly to confess her sins and to receive moral and spiritual guidance. She had been through a painful divorce, and relied heavily on the priest for guidance.

One day, she found out that her daughter had been sexually molested by a monk. She asked her confessor what to do about it. He advised her to tell the monk's superior, and to let the monastery handle the matter.

My friend never reported the crime to the police, and I doubt if she got any counseling for her daughter. She kept the matter quiet, in order to protect the reputation of the monastery.

There is an appropriate place for expressing anger. That girl needed to see her mother get angry at the man who had molested her. Instead, her mother was quiet about it. When she told me about the incident, she quietly spoke in psychological terms about the emotional problems of the man who had violated her daughter. Not once did she express outrage at what had happened.

A Priest

For several years, I was involved in helping some needy people. One of the people I worked with was a Catholic priest. He had been raised to be a conservative Catholic. At first, he was circumspect in his approach towards women. But one day, his confessor gave him a book. Unfortunately, he had more confidence in his confessor than he did in the Bible, so he never questioned the validity of the book.

The title of the book was, *The Sexual Celibate*. It was written by a Catholic priest. (Information about this book is online.)[14]

According to the book, celibates need to express themselves sexually, in order to be emotionally healthy. The book said that sexual expression is morally right, and not contrary to their vow of celibacy, as long as they don't actually have intercourse.

One of our projects was helping some Vietnamese refugees. They were Buddhists. One of them was a lovely young lady. She converted to Catholicism.

After he baptized her, the priest continued to give her religious instruction. Among other things, he taught her the theology of *The Sexual Celibate*.

The young lady trusted the priest. He was her source of moral authority, her guide for understanding right and wrong. She believed what he told her about celibacy. They became romantically involved.

The priest did not have intercourse with her, but he was passionate with her. She was deeply in love with him. Her family found out about it, and scolded her. The young lady confided in me. She was confused, ashamed, and heartbroken.

Some Religious Communities

I know a religious community whose leader became heavily influenced by Jungian psychology. Monks and nuns depend on their religious superiors for spiritual direction, instead of using the Bible as their primary source of guidance. As a result, every member of that religious community was led into deception. When I visited the community, I heard more about Carl Jung than I did about Jesus Christ. The reference point for their thinking was Jung's writings, rather than the Bible, or even Catholic writings.

I have heard of other religious communities whose superiors were influenced by New Age practices and philosophies. Again, all of the members of the religious community followed their leader into deception.

People can be "sincerely deceived." They can sincerely believe a deception that they have been taught by trusted authority figures. They may teach that deception to other people, and think that they are doing a good thing when they do it. That was the case with these religious communities.

A Foundational Problem

We should never put our conscience in someone else's hands. This is a foundational problem with Catholicism. For obedient Catholics, their primary source of moral guidance is the Catholic hierarchy, rather than the Bible.

No person is good enough, or holy enough, or wise enough, to give our conscience to. We have to discern things for ourselves. We have to get to know the Bible, so that we can have God's perspective about things.

The Bible says that we cannot afford to be like children, whose beliefs are at the mercy of other people. (Ephesians 4:14) We need to grow up and take responsibility for our own beliefs, and for having our consciences be based on Biblical principles. We need to be like the Bereans, and test **everything** against the Bible.

An old hymn says: "On Christ the solid rock I stand. All other ground is sinking sand."

The traditions of the Catholic Church are sinking sand. We need to take our stand on Jesus Christ and the Bible.

Chapter 23

Serving Two Masters

The media has been telling us about Catholic priests who raped boys, priests who sexually molested children. The Catholic Church has treated this situation as an internal Church matter. However, under the American constitutional system, it is not. Sexually molesting a child is a crime, and the offender is subject to criminal prosecution. So why has the rape of children by Catholic priests been treated as an internal Church matter?

Let's go back to the nineteenth century. Pope Pius IX will give us some keys to understanding what is happening now.

Pope Pius IX reigned from 1846 to 1878. This was a time when governments were changing, the power of the Catholic Church was decreasing in some countries, and there was more freedom of religion. In 1864, Pius wrote an encyclical called, *The Syllabus of Errors*, in which he condemned many things.[1] (Encyclicals are online. They are easy to find.)

In this encyclical, Pius said that, whenever there is a conflict between civil law and Catholic Church law, then Church law should prevail. He declared that kings and princes are under the jurisdiction of the Catholic Church. He said that it is right to have Catholicism be a state religion, and it is wrong to allow non-Catholics to worship publicly. He condemned freedom of religion.

The Pope's attitude towards freedom of religion is demonstrated by the case of Edgardo Mortara. The Mortaras were Jews. They had a Catholic servant girl. She secretly baptized their son, Edgardo, when he was a baby. Catholic authorities found out about it. (By then, Edgardo was six years old.) Papal police came to the Mortara home and took Edgardo from his family. They said that, because Edgardo had been baptized, he was a Catholic, and a Catholic child could not be raised in a Jewish home. This became internationally known. Heads of state begged the Pope to return the boy to his family, but the Pope refused. (You can read about this online.)[2]

In 1855, Pope Pius IX signed a concordat (treaty) with the Emperor of Austria. According to this concordat, Catholic clergy were to control Austrian schools and censor literature. If any civil laws contradicted Roman Catholic Canon Law, the civil laws were to be repealed. (This is online.)[3]

In 1866, Austria was defeated in the Austro-Prussian War. One result was the formation of a new government.[4] In 1867, the new Austrian state ratified a Constitution that allowed freedom of religion, freedom of speech, freedom of conscience, and freedom of the press. It allowed non-Catholics to publicly practice their religion. (This Constitution is online. It is short and easy to read.)[5]

Pope Pius officially declared that Austria's new Constitution was "null and void." He threatened Austrian Catholics with "spiritual penalties" if they accepted the Constitution of their own nation.[6] ("Spiritual penalties" would be things such as excommunication or interdict.)

In 1874, Austria passed a "Law on Recognition" of churches. This law allowed Protestants and other non-Catholics to have religious schools, and to import ministers, missionaries, and religious teachers.[7]

Pius wrote an encyclical condemning this law. He condemned freedom of religion. He denounced Austria for allowing Catholics to leave the Catholic Church, and for allowing non-Catholics to have their own schools.[8] (Encyclicals are easy to find online. Directions are given in the beginning of the Notes.)

According to Austria's Constitution, civil law took precedence over the laws of the Catholic Church. Pius declared that Church laws should have priority. In other words, he asserted that the Catholic Church was a higher authority than the national leaders of Austria.

Pius went even further than that. He instructed the Catholic clergy in Austria to do everything within their power to oppose Austrian laws that limited the power of the Catholic Church. He told the Austrian priests and bishops to be willing to go to prison in order to accomplish this. Although these clergymen were Austrian citizens, the Pope expected them to work against their own national government, in order to increase the power of the Catholic Church.

These priests and bishops were under a vow of obedience. They were required to obey the Pope. The Pope's instructions are in his encyclical, in the section, "Role of the Clergy." (See Note 8.)

Austria was not the only case. Pius also condemned the constitutions of France and Belgium, because they allowed freedom of conscience, freedom of religion, and freedom of the press. Because of their loyalty to the Pope, many Catholics in Austria, France, and Belgium supported the Pope instead of their national governments. As a result, Catholics in these countries were considered to be unpatriotic. (You can read about this online.)[9]

These Catholics were torn between two loyalties. They were trying to serve two masters. It was almost like having a dual citizenship. They were citizens of their nations, under the authority of kings or princes or elected officials. But they were also loyal to the Catholic Church, and to the Pope, and they were under the Pope's authority.

Now let's see how this relates to the "Catholic scandals" of the twenty-first century.

We have been hearing about American priests who sexually molested children. This resulted in civil lawsuits against the Catholic Church, most of which were settled out of court.

Why were these civil lawsuits? Ordinarily, when a man rapes or seduces a child, somebody calls the police, and the child molester is prosecuted. According to the laws of America, the normal penalty for sexually abusing children is the imprisonment of the person who did it. Why aren't Catholic priests held accountable like other men? (Recently, a few priests were criminally prosecuted, but this is unusual.)

When bishops and cardinals found out that priests had raped or seduced children, why didn't they call the police? Sexually molesting children is a criminal offense. It is not just a matter for internal Church discipline. It is a crime against American citizens.[10]

If you or I knew that a man had raped a child, and we helped him cover up his crime and escape justice, we would be guilty of aiding and abetting that criminal. If we were caught, we would probably go to prison for it. So why aren't these bishops and cardinals facing criminal charges? They aided and abetted priests who committed the crime of sexually molesting children. They did not report those priests to the civil authorities. They acted as if they and the priests were above the laws of the land.

It looks as if we are right back with Pope Pius IX, who said that the laws of the Catholic Church take priority over the laws of civil governments.

By failing to report these child molesters, the bishops and cardinals acted as if the norms of American society do not apply to them. They behaved like foreign citizens on American soil.

In the case of cardinals, they literally do have a dual citizenship. They are citizens of the Vatican. Some people have questioned whether or not Vatican citizenship would provide cardinals with diplomatic immunity if they are brought to court by civil authorities.[11]

A priest named Ladensack had the courage to report a sexual abuse case. In the 1980s, he was the supervisor of the Catholic schools in Phoenix, Arizona. A 12-year-old boy was sexually molested by a priest. Ladensack told the boy's family to report it to the police. His bishop was furious, and ordered him to have the family withdraw the criminal complaint. The bishop told him that, because he had made a vow of obedience, he had to obey orders and cover up the crime.

That kind of intimidation might work with most priests, but it didn't work with Ladensack. He was a Vietnam war hero. During his training as a military officer, he had been taught that he should never obey an unlawful order. He considered the bishop's order to be unlawful, so he refused to obey it.

Ladensack refused to cover up the crime. In 1986, he left the priesthood. His bishop signed an immunity agreement, and thereby avoided being indicted for obstruction of justice. Seventeen years later (2003), information about this case was published in the newspapers. (You can read about it online.)[12]

On September 3, 2000, we went back to Pope Pius IX again. He was beatified by Pope John Paul II. So the approach of Pius IX to Catholic Church power and authority must still be admired by Catholic hierarchy.[13]

Beatification means that Catholics are allowed to publicly venerate Pope Pius IX, and to publicly ask him to intercede on their behalf. It is the last step before making him a canonized saint. According to *The Catholic Encyclopedia*, when people are beatified, then venerating them is optional. When they are canonized, then venerating them becomes mandatory.[14]

In January, 2002, the Vatican published rules for dealing with pedophile cases. These rules were approved by Pope John Paul II, and published by Cardinal Joseph Ratzinger, through the Vatican's Congregation for the Doctrine of the Faith. According to the Vatican:

- Pedophile cases are subject to "pontifical secrecy."
- Only Catholic priests should handle these cases.
- Judges and lawyers should be Catholic priests.
- Cases should only be handled in Church tribunals.
- Victims must file complaints before age 29.[15]

The world of child molesters is far removed from most of us. Let's see how these rules would apply to something more familiar, such as the world of finance. The Enron Corporation was the center of a major financial scandal. How would we feel if the executives of Enron claimed that their case should only be handled by other Enron executives, and the whole procedure should be subject to "Enron secrecy"? How would we feel if they got away with such a claim?

Enron and the Catholic Church have some things in common. Enron transferred bad debts to off-shore corporations. When cardinals and bishops learned that priests were sexual predators, they transferred those priests from parish to parish. Enron filed for bankruptcy in order to protect itself from its creditors. The Archdiocese of Boston has admitted that it is considering filing for bankruptcy in order to protect itself from lawsuits.[15]

On the issue of child-molesting priests, it looks as if the Roman Catholic Church is still using the approach of Pope Pius IX. Although they are citizens of the United States, American bishops and cardinals are looking out for the interests of Rome, rather than protecting American citizens—the children and young adolescents who became exposed to sexual predators when bishops or cardinals moved pedophile priests to new locations. These bishops and cardinals are serving two masters, and the Vatican takes priority.

Chapter 24
Canon Law and Religious Freedom

During the Middle Ages, the Roman Catholic Church controlled the western world. Popes gave orders to kings and emperors.

Rome is no longer able to rule over secular rulers. However, it does have influence with them. The Vatican has diplomats in most countries. It also has special representatives at the United Nations and the European Union. In addition, Catholic clergy and Catholic citizens influence the countries they live in. (See the chapter, "Serving Two Masters.")

Canon Law provides the legal basis for everything that the Roman Catholic Church does. The *Code of Canon Law* was thoroughly revised in 1983. The English translation was published in 1988. These are contemporary laws that demonstrate the spirit behind Roman Catholicism. (These laws are all contained in one 751-page book that costs $45. If you want to buy it, information is in the Notes.)[1]

The new *Code of Canon Law* was published by the authority of Pope John Paul II. It claims to be inspired by the Second Vatican Council (1962-1965) and to put its reforms into concrete form. It increases the power and authority of the Pope. (An article about this is online.)[2]

The Catholic Church no longer has the kind of power that it used to have. As a result, it can only enforce these laws within the Catholic Church. Even there, its ability to enforce them is somewhat limited, because it does not want to have unfavorable international publicity.

Some provisions of the 1983 *Code of Canon Law* are written in terms that could be interpreted to apply to Protestants as well as to Catholics. (You can read these laws online. The Notes give information.)

The Pope could easily resolve these issues. He could give directives to have some laws reworded, or new laws added. The Pope could also publish an encyclical to clarify these issues. That could be an interim step, while the legal changes are being made. (A reassuring statement by itself would not solve the problem, because it would not have the weight of law.)

Canon 1311 says that the Catholic Church has the right to **coerce** the "**Christian faithful**" if they fail to comply with Canon Law.[3]

Canon 752 says that "**the Christian faithful**" are required to submit their minds and wills to all doctrines declared by the Pope, or the college of bishops, and to be careful to avoid anything that disagrees with those doctrines.

Does the term "the Christian faithful" in these laws refer to Protestants? Or only to Roman Catholics?

Canon 204 defines "the Christian faithful" in terms of baptism. Since Protestants are baptized, the definition could include them. It could also include Orthodox Christians.

Canon 205 gives requirements that "the Christian faithful" must fulfill in order to be members of the Catholic Church. Therefore, the term, "the Christian faithful," is not limited to Catholics.

Section 2 of Canon 825 refers to Catholics who are numbered among "the Christian faithful." This implies that there are "Christian faithful" who are not Catholics.

Canon 750 says that "**a person**" is required to believe all Catholic doctrines. Canon 1371 says that "**a person**" who "obstinately rejects" any Catholic doctrine is to be punished. Does this apply to Protestants and Orthodox Christians? They are people.

Canon 1371 says that "**a person**" who teaches a doctrine that has been condemned by a Catholic Church council is to be punished. The Council of Trent condemned every single doctrine that was proposed by the Protestant Reformers. It also condemned Protestant objections to Catholic doctrines. Does this law apply to Protestants? If it does, then they could be punished for their beliefs.

Canon 1366 says that "**parents**" are to be punished if they allow their children to be educated or baptized in "a non-Catholic religion." The reference to baptism shows that this means Christians. However, the law says "parents," not "Catholic parents." The wording could refer to Protestants and Orthodox Christians as well as to Catholics.

Canon 825 (Section 1) forbids the publication of any Bible that has not been approved by the papacy (Apostolic See) or the conference of bishops. The Catholic Church seems to be claiming the right to control the publication of **all** Bibles (not just Catholic ones).

These laws are worded in such a broad way that they could be interpreted as applying to Protestants or Orthodox Christians. But could Catholic Canon Law actually be applied to people who are not Catholics? It happened during the Protestant Reformation.

If a time ever comes when the Catholic Church interprets and applies these laws as not being limited to Catholics, then the Catholic Church would consider it to be a crime (an act contrary to law) for Protestants or Orthodox Christians to preach or teach or write anything that is contrary to Catholicism. That includes teaching their own children.

These laws say that offenders are to be punished with a "just penalty." The term is so broad that it can be interpreted to mean almost anything. It gives immense discretionary power to whoever is in authority.

During the Protestant Reformation, the Catholic Church considered it to be a crime to be a Protestant. Being burned alive was considered to be a just penalty for the crime of disagreeing with Catholic doctrine. (See the chapter, "Hunting 'Heretics.'")

It would also be considered a crime for Catholics to convert to Protestantism, and then share their new faith with other people (including their own children). Sharing can be considered to be a form of teaching; and their new faith would include things that are contrary to Catholic doctrine.

Most Catholics were baptized when they were babies. In other words, they were made Catholics without their consent. To forbid them to leave the Catholic Church is to treat them like Church property.

It would also be considered a crime to publish Protestant Bibles. That could easily be interpreted to mean that it would be a crime to possess a Protestant Bible. There are historical precedents for this. During the Protestant Reformation, many men and women were burned at the stake for possessing Protestant Bibles.

During the Protestant Reformation, many monks and nuns left their monasteries and convents, and became Protestants. Under modern Canon Law, they would not be allowed to do this. According to Canon 665 (Section 2), monks and nuns who leave their religious community without permission, desiring to get away from the power of their superiors, are to be "sought out" in order to "help" them return and "persevere" in their vocation. In other words, they are to be hunted down, forced to return, and forced to remain.

The Second Vatican Council seemed to approve of freedom of conscience and freedom of religion. However, these laws show a rather different picture.

Chapter 25

The Presence of God

Some Catholics have asked me how I can have peace or joy without the Eucharist (Catholic communion). There are two answers to this question.

First, the Bible says that we can have peace in a way that has nothing to do with taking communion. It is based on relationship, rather than sacraments. Scripture says:

> "Thou wilt keep him in perfect peace, whose mind is stayed on thee: because he trusteth in thee." (Isaiah 26:3)

> "Rejoice in the Lord alway: and again I say, Rejoice. Let your moderation be known unto all men. The Lord is at hand. Be careful for nothing; but in every thing by prayer and supplication with thanksgiving let your requests be made known unto God. And the peace of God, which passeth all understanding, shall keep your hearts and minds through Christ Jesus." (Philippians 4:4-7)

Second, there are some problems with the Catholic doctrine of transubstantiation. According to this doctrine, when a Catholic priest consecrates bread, it literally turns into the body, blood, soul, and divinity of Jesus Christ. The same thing is said to happen when a Catholic priest consecrates wine.

When I was a Catholic, I went to communion as often as possible. I also prayed in front of the Tabernacle (an ornate container where consecrated communion wafers are kept.) I believed that Jesus was in there. I wanted to be with Him.

When I was a Catholic, I sometimes attended special services called Adoration of the Blessed Sacrament. A large, consecrated Host (communion wafer) was put in a Monstrance. (This is a large, ornate, metal container, in the basic shape of a sunburst. It has a stem and a base so that it can stand up.) The Monstrance looked like it was made of gold. It had a circular chamber in the middle, which held a large, round Host. The front of the chamber was glass, so you could see the Host. Visually, it looked like gold rays were coming out of the Host. (You can see pictures of Monstrances online.)[1]

The priest put the Monstrance on the altar. We worshiped the Host, believing that it was Jesus Christ. There were special prayers and special songs in honor of the Host. At the end of the service, we had Benediction. The priest held the Monstrance and made the sign of the cross with it. We believed that Jesus Himself was blessing us.

There are some Biblical reasons for not believing that the bread and wine are literally transformed into Jesus Christ. Many things could be said about that, but I will only mention one of them—Jesus' use of symbolic language. Jesus often used metaphors and symbolism. For example, Jesus said:

> "…Verily, verily, I say unto you, I am the door of the sheep. All that ever came before me are thieves and robbers: but the sheep did not hear them. I am the door: by me if any man enter in, he shall be saved, and shall go in and out, and find pasture." (John 10:7-9)

However, we don't believe that Jesus literally is a door. We don't ritually walk through sacred doors in order to be saved and become part of Jesus' flock.

Even if consecrated bread really did turn into Jesus Christ, it would only bring His presence for a short time. This is what would happen when you took communion. You would eat the consecrated bread. Because of that, Jesus would be inside of you, but only until the bread was digested. Once the bread was gone, then Jesus would also be gone. If you only took communion at Mass on Sundays, then Jesus would be inside of you for a few hours on Sundays. The rest of the time, He would be gone.

This is not what we see in Scripture. Jesus promised to **stay** with us, to be with us **all the time**. He said:

> "…lo, I am with you **alway**, even unto the end of the world." (Matthew 28:20, emphasis added)

Jesus said that a time would come when we would realize that He truly lives in us, and we truly live in Him. He said that He would abide in us (live in us). Jesus said:

> "At that day ye shall know that I am in my Father, and ye in me, and I in you." (John 14:20)

> "Abide in me, and I in you…" (John 15:4)

Jesus expects Christians to dwell in Him, and to have Him dwell in them. Jesus should be our home. We should be His home. This should be a normal part of Christian life.

The Bible tells us that God will be **with** His people and that He will be **in** His people. This does not depend on circumstances, or on consecrated bread. Rather, it depends upon our personal relationship with God. Scripture says:

> "Whosoever shall confess that Jesus is the Son of God, God dwelleth in him, and he in God." (1 John 4:15)

> "That Christ may dwell in your hearts by faith…" (Ephesians 3:17)

> "…He that abideth in the doctrine of Christ, he hath both the Father and the Son." (2 John 1:9)

> "…God is love; and he that dwelleth in love dwelleth in God, and God in him." (1 John 4:16)

> "Know ye not that ye are the temple of God, and that the Spirit of God dwelleth in you?" (1 Corinthians 3:16)

> "For where two or three are gathered together in my name, there am I in the midst of them." (Matthew 18:20)

There are countries where Christians are being persecuted. Some Christians have been killed because of their faith. Others have been put in prison. If Christian prisoners are unable to take communion, does that prevent Jesus from being in them? Would He make His presence depend on circumstances over which persecuted Christians have no control? Would Jesus deny His presence to His most faithful followers—the people who paid the highest price to be faithful to Him—right when they need His presence the most, because of the hardships that they are enduring?

Christianity works everywhere, for all people, regardless of their circumstances. It works for persecuted Christians who are in prison, and who have no access to communion.

Having God's presence in our lives does not depend on our circumstances. It depends on our relationship with God. If we truly love God, then He will be with us. He will abide in us, which means that He will take up permanent residence in us. That is why the Apostle Paul says that we are God's Temple. (1 Corinthians 3:16) God actually dwells in us.

Chapter 26
Catholic Mysticism

I believe that the Catholic mystics were sincere men and women who loved the Lord. However, I also believe that they were deceived. It can be seen in the connection that many of them made between suffering and intimacy with God. They give a distorted picture of the nature and character of God.

The following brief statements are based on my recollection of some Catholic books that I read years ago. (When I was a Catholic, I looked to the mystics to show me how to be close to God. I read their writings, and books written by biographers who admired them.)

Later in this chapter, I will give more detailed information. You can verify it at some Catholic websites that are described in the Notes.

Saint Catherine of Sienna said that Jesus Christ was her novice master. However, supposedly under the direction of Jesus, she regularly whipped herself until the blood ran down her back.

Saint Teresa of Avila recounted an incident when she was sick, in pain, and feeling miserable. According to Teresa, Jesus told her that He deliberately makes His friends suffer.

Saint John of the Cross said that the "dark night of the soul" (intense spiritual and emotional suffering) is necessary for intimacy with God. There is a practical problem with that. If you expect to go through intense suffering, the devil will be delighted to accommodate you. If you welcome the suffering, because you believe that it is a sign that you are becoming closer to God, then the devil has your permission to keep on causing it.

How do we treat our babies? Do they have to prove their devotion by suffering? Is that a requirement for having us hold them and show them love? Of course not. We just love them. Would God the Father do any less for His children?

Suffering is part of life. Jesus said that, in this world, we will have tribulation. (John 16:33) God can use all things (including suffering) for our good. (Romans 8:28) But suffering is not a price that we pay in order to be close to God. God gives His love freely. We cannot earn it.

Saint Francis of Assisi said that it was "perfect joy" to be cold, hungry, rejected, and verbally abused. He glorified pain, suffering, and poverty. At the end of his life, Saint Francis had the stigmata. These are visible, bleeding, painful wounds that occur in the same locations as the wounds that Jesus Christ suffered on the cross. They are wounds in the hands and feet and side. They can also include wounds in the back (from whipping) and head (from the crown of thorns). Francis' disciples considered the stigmata to be a sign of God's great love for Francis.

Other people have also had the stigmata. One modern example is Padre Pio, who regularly whipped himself.

2 Thessalonians 2:9 says that the devil is able to work signs and lying wonders. He would be capable of causing the stigmata, especially if people desire it, because they consider it to be a sign of God's favor. The stigmata are supernatural, and they imitate the wounds of the crucifixion. However, that does **not** mean that they come from God. They could come from the devil.

Moses, Joshua, the prophets, John the Baptist, and the Apostles had an extraordinary level of intimacy with God. Did these men whip themselves? Did they do penances to mortify their flesh? Did any of them have the stigmata?

These men suffered, but they did not glorify suffering, and they did not deliberately seek it. Their suffering was the kind that Jesus told us to expect. Jesus said:

> "…because ye are not of the world, but I have chosen you out of the world, therefore the world hateth you." (John 15:19)

> "…In the world ye shall have tribulation: but be of good cheer; I have overcome the world." (John 16:33)

> "Remember the word that I said unto you, The servant is not greater than his lord. If they have persecuted me, they will also persecute you; if they have kept my saying, they will keep yours also." (John 15:20. Also see Matthew 5:11-12; Matthew 5:44-45; and Matthew 10:22-23)

This is suffering, but it is not sought after, and it is not self-inflicted. It is the natural result of the world's rejection of Jesus Christ and His followers. Jesus described it when He said:

> "And this is the condemnation, that light is come into the world, and men loved darkness rather than light, because their deeds were evil." (John 3:19)

The Bible tells us to rejoice **always** (Philippians 4:4) and to give thanks in **all** circumstances (1 Thessalonians 5:16-18). This is because of our confidence in God, who promised to make **everything** work out for good for people who love Him (Romans 8:28). It has nothing to do with glorifying suffering.

The Bible tells us to rejoice when we endure hardship and suffering, **because it will bear good spiritual fruit in our lives.** (See James 1:2-4; Romans 5:3-5; 1 Peter 1:7.) This is not a glorification of suffering. Rather, it is following in the footsteps of Jesus, who was willing to endure the cross, because of the good that would result from it. Jesus was willing, but He wanted to avoid it if He could. In the Garden of Gesthemane, He asked if there was any other way. (Matthew 26:39)

When Jesus was on earth, He went around healing people. He taught His disciples to heal people. He said that His followers would heal people. Jesus said:

> "And these signs shall follow them that believe: In my name shall they cast out devils; they shall speak with new tongues: They shall take up serpents; and if they drink any deadly thing, it shall not hurt them; they shall lay hands on the sick, and they shall recover." (Mark 16:17-18)

How could Jesus spend his ministry on earth healing people, and teaching His disciples to heal people, and then tell Catherine of Siena to repeatedly whip herself? The whipping is not consistent with the character of Jesus, as shown in the Gospels.

The Gospels say that Jesus was "moved with compassion." (Matthew 9:36; Matthew 14:14; Mark 1:41; Mark 6:34) Compassionate people do not deliberately cause suffering for their friends. The experiences of Catherine of Sienna, Teresa of Avila, and Francis of Assisi are not consistent with the compassion of Jesus.

At the beginning of His ministry, Jesus described His mission. He quoted from Isaiah 61:1. He said:

> "The Spirit of the Lord is upon me, because he hath anointed me to preach the gospel to the poor; he hath sent me to heal the brokenhearted, to preach deliverance to the captives, and recovering of sight to the blind, to set at liberty them that are bruised." (Luke 4:18)

Does this sound like someone who wants people to whip themselves until the blood runs down their back? Does this sound like someone who would make people endure the torment of the stigmata?

It is good to want to be wholehearted and fervent in serving God. We can see examples of this in the Bible.

Read some of Paul's prayers. Look at the way that Paul would be writing about a subject, and mention God, and just have to write about the goodness and glory of God. Logically, it interrupts his discussion of the issue. Emotionally, it shows that Paul was so passionate about God that sometimes he just couldn't help himself—he just had to stop what he was doing (even in the middle of a thought) and speak about the glory of God and His incredible love for us. Now that is a passionate man. That is a man who loves God with everything in him.

Read the Psalms. Look at David's passion for God. We can share in David's rejoicing and his wholehearted worship and praise.

The Apostle Paul

The Apostle Paul had extraordinary visions and revelations. He was caught up into Paradise and he heard things that he was not allowed to reveal to anyone. God gave Paul a "thorn in the flesh," in order to prevent him from becoming proud, because of these amazing revelations. Scripture does not tell us what the "thorn" was, or whether it involved physical pain. Paul begged God to remove it, but instead of getting rid of it, God said: "My grace is sufficient for thee: for my strength is made perfect in weakness." (2 Corinthians 12:9; see 2 Corinthians 12:1-10)

When Paul realized that this was part of God's plan for his life, then he not only accepted it, he demonstrated that he truly had learned to be content no matter what his circumstances were. (Philippians 4:11) He showed that he had learned to rejoice in the Lord **always** and to give thanks in **all** circumstances. (Philippians 4:4; 1 Thessalonians 5:16-18)

God will allow pain if it is necessary for a person's spiritual health. But only God is qualified to judge whether such a thing is necessary, and, if so, what form it should take. This is not even remotely related to self-inflicted pain, penances, and "mortifications" of the flesh. There is a world of difference between rejoicing in spite of pain, and seeking pain.

Paul was a very disciplined man. He had to be, in order to fulfill God's call on his life. Paul said:

> "But I keep under my body, and bring it into subjection: lest that by any means, when I have preached to others, I myself should be a castaway." (1 Corinthians 9:27)

The New International Version says: "I beat my body daily." According to *Strong's Concordance*, the word for "keep under" can mean beat or buffet (either one blow, or many blows). It also has a metaphorical sense of subduing something into compliance. This is reflected in the words "keep under" of the King James Version.

Would Paul have to subdue his body and force it to comply? Let's see what shape his body was in. Paul told the Christians in Corinth:

> "Are they ministers of Christ? (I speak as a fool) I am more; in labours more abundant, in stripes above measure, in prisons more frequent, in deaths oft. Of the Jews five times received I forty stripes save one. Thrice was I beaten with rods, once was I stoned, thrice I suffered shipwreck, a night and a day I have been in the deep; In journeyings often, in perils of waters, in perils of robbers, in perils by mine own countrymen, in perils by the heathen, in perils in the city, in perils in the wilderness, in perils in the sea, in perils among false brethren; In weariness and painfulness, in watchings often, in hunger and thirst, in fastings often, in cold and nakedness." (2 Corinthians 11:23-27)

I asked a chiropractor what Paul's back would be like after it was repeatedly whipped, beaten with rods, and hit with stones. The chiropractor couldn't speak. His face showed horror, and he shuddered visibly. Finally, he said: "I don't want to even think about it."

Have you ever had back pain when you had to do something? You have to force your body to obey, in spite of the pain. Paul probably had to do that many times every day. He must have often had to fight the desire to quit ministering, so that he could minimize the pain, instead of making constant demands on his body.

Paul said: "in weariness and painfulness, in watchings often." He spoke of often being tired, in pain, and sleepless. (According to *Strong's Concordance*, "watchings" means, "sleeplessness.") Some of Paul's sleeplessness may have been the result of praying at night, or working late hours at his trade of tent making. But pain also keeps people awake. Paul spoke of being sleepless immediately after saying that he was often in pain.

So Paul's statement about keeping his body under has nothing to do with whipping himself, or beating himself, as a penance or mortification.

Paul did not glorify being whipped. When he was able to avoid it, he did. When the Romans were about to flog him, Paul said: "Is it lawful for you to scourge a man that is a Roman, and uncondemned?" (Acts 22:25; see verses 24-29) And immediately, the Romans backed off, and they did not harm him.

Mystics and Paganism

Catholics are not the only mystics. There are also Hindu mystics, Buddhist mystics, and Muslim mystics. (Information is online.)[1] Therefore, mystical experiences do not necessarily indicate that a person has encountered the God of the Bible. They don't even indicate that a person is a Christian.

Thomas Merton was Catholic monk. He taught that every form of mystical experience is valid, no matter what its source. He praised Hinduism and Buddhism. Merton wanted to see the religions of the world become united. (You can read about him online.)[2]

Some Catholic priests and nuns teach prayer techniques that are not prayer in the Christian sense at all. Rather, they result in altered states of consciousness, and susceptibility to demonic influence.[3]

A Catholic priest named Anthony de Mello gives workshops that introduce Catholics to Eastern prayer and meditation techniques. He wrote, *Sadhana: A Way to God: Christian Exercises in Eastern Form*. The book's cover shows Jesus on the cross and a person seated in the lotus position, meditating at the foot of the cross.[4]

There are some Evangelical pastors who promote Catholic mysticism. As a result, it is is impacting main-line Protestant denominations. You can read about these men, and their influence, in Ray Yungen's book, *A Time of Departing: How a Universal Spirituality Is Changing the Face of Christianity*. Since Catholic mystics are influenced by pagan mysticism, this is bringing a pagan influence into Protestant churches.

(For more information about mixing Catholic mysticism with pagan mysticism, see the chapter, "New Age Catholicism.")

Some Catholic Mystics

I thought you might like to meet some Catholic mystics. The following information all comes from Internet articles. Most of them are on Catholic websites. Information about these articles is given in the Notes.

I am summarizing the information as the mystics described it. If they say that they talked to Jesus, then that is what I will write. Because there are so many statements of this kind, it would become cumbersome and repetitious if I tried to qualify them.

I use the term "saint" to show that people have been canonized by the Catholic Church. However, in the Bible, **all** Christians are called saints. (See Acts 9:13, 32, 41; 26:10; Romans 1:7; 8:27; 12:13, 25, 26, 31; 1 Corinthians 1:2; 6:1, 2; 14:33; 16:1, 15; 2 Corinthians 1:1; 8:4; 9:1, 12; 13:13; Ephesians 1:1, 15, 18; 6:10; Philemon 4:22; Colossians 1:2, 4, 12, 26; 1 Thessalonians 3:13; 2 Thessalonians 1:10; 1 Timothy 5:10; Philemon 1:5, 7; Hebrews 13:24; Jude 1:3, 14.)

Bernard of Clairvaux

Saint Bernard of Clairvaux was a Cistercian monk and an abbot. He was devoted to the Virgin Mary, and he was influential in spreading devotion to her. Bernard is a "doctor of the Church," which means that the Catholic Church highly values his teachings. In the Middle Ages, he was known as the "cithara of Mary," an instrument that sang her praises. (A cithara is a stringed instrument like a lyre.) He wrote about Mary's supposed role as our mediator.[5]

Bernard promoted veneration of Mary as the Queen of Heaven.[6] Because of his writings, Bernard's devotion to Mary had a profound influence on Catholic spirituality.[7] There is a painting that shows Bernard kneeling in front of Mary, as Queen of Heaven, crowned with stars, floating in Heaven, and accompanied by angels.[8]

Bernard said that, whenever people are in danger, or going through trials, they should call upon Mary. He said that we should walk in Mary's footsteps, and she should be our guide. He claimed that Mary will protect us from deception, and protect us from falling.[9]

There is a "mystical legend" that Saint Bernard was praying in front of a statue of Mary. The statue showed Mary nursing the infant Jesus. Bernard prayed: "Show yourself a mother." Then the statue came to life. Mary pressed her breast and squirted milk into Bernard's mouth. There are 27 works of art commemorating this, including a painting by Murillo.[10]

Catherine of Siena[11]

Saint Catherine of Siena chose to live in a small, dimly-lit room, which was three feet wide and nine feet long. She whipped herself three times a day with an iron chain. She slept on a board. At first, she wore a hair shirt, but then she replaced it with an iron-spiked girdle. She fasted, often living on little food except what she received when she went to communion during Mass. She meditated. She lived in isolation, only leaving her room to go to church. Sometimes she was tormented by visions that she knew to be demonic. For three years, she had "celestial visitations," and conversations with Jesus Christ.

In 1366, Catherine had a mystical experience involving the Virgin Mary and Jesus. They appeared to her. Mary took Catherine's hand. Mary held Catherine's hand up to Jesus. Then Jesus placed a ring upon Catherine's hand and "espoused her to himself." (This is called "spiritual espousals.") Catherine could always see the ring, but it was invisible to other people.

Following a series of mystical experiences, including a "mystical death," Catherine entered public life. She wrote letters to princes and Vatican officials. During the Black Plague, she helped take care of plague victims.

In 1375, Catherine received the stigmata. However, although she felt the pain, other people were not able to see them. This is unusual, because the stigmata are usually visible and gory, and they can usually be verified by doctors. Catherine said that she asked God to prevent them from being outwardly visible, and He granted her prayer.

Saint Catherine of Siena is a "doctor of the Church," which means that the Catholic Church highly values her teachings and revelations. She is a canonized saint, which means that Catholics are encouraged to study her life and be guided by her example, her teachings, and her writings.

Julian of Norwich

Lady Julian (or Juliana) of Norwich was a contemporary of Catherine of Siena. She wanted to have an intense understanding of what Christ suffered during His crucifixion. She also wanted to receive the "last rites" (the sacrament given to Catholics who are in danger of dying). She believed that the "last rites" would enable her soul to be fully cleansed by God, so that she could be more fully consecrated to Him. In order to achieve this, she asked God to give her an illness that would bring her to the point of death, without having her actually die. In 1373, Julian became seriously ill. She received the "last rites." Suddenly, her pain went away. Then she had a series of 16 visions, which she wrote down.[12]

Teresa of Avila and John of the Cross

Saint Teresa of Avila and Saint John of the Cross were Carmelites. This religious order is dedicated to the Virgin Mary. She is considered to be the patron of their order.[13]

According to tradition, in 1251, the Virgin Mary appeared to Saint Simon Stock, holding a Brown Scapular (two pieces of brown cloth attached by strings). She promised him that any person who dies wearing the scapular will not go to Hell. This promise is for people who belong to the religious order of the Carmelites, or who are associated with them.[14]

Teresa and John lived 300 years after the Brown Scapular was given to Simon Stock. Devotion to Mary, and belief in the effectiveness of the Brown Scapular, were a foundational part of their training as Carmelites. Therefore, it influenced their writings and their understanding of their mystical experiences. Teresa said that all of her nuns "belong" to the Virgin Mary. Teresa's love for Mary is scattered throughout her writings.[15] John of the Cross was also known for his devotion to the Virgin Mary.[16]

Teresa of Avila and John of the Cross are studied by a Buddhist/Christian cult that considers them to be a prophet and prophetess. The cult also studies the Kabbala (Cabala).[17] (The Cabala is important to occultists.) Evidently, pagans can identify with the mystical experiences and writings of Teresa and John.

Madame Jeanne Guyon

Madame Guyon advocated "quietism," which involves becoming so passive that you become indifferent to everything, including eternal salvation. The will becomes completely annihilated. The person is supposed to be so totally absorbed in the divine love of God that he or she has no more desire for anything. This passive state of the soul is supposed to enable God to act within it.[18]

This sounds more like Buddhism than Christianity. The New Testament is full of action terms such as "strive," "wrestle," "weapons of our warfare," "resist," and "make every effort."

Madame Guyon said that she had reached the point where she was no longer capable of sinning. She said that sin involves self, and she had become free of self. Therefore, she could no longer sin.[19] However, the Bible says:

> "If we say that we have no sin, we deceive ourselves, and the truth is not in us. If we confess our sins, he is faithful and just to forgive us our sins, and to cleanse us from all unrighteousness. If we say that we have not sinned, we make him a liar, and his word is not in us." (1 John 1:8-10)

Conclusion

The Catholic mystics loved God. They were zealous. They had supernatural experiences. However, because they were Catholics, their understanding of the Bible was distorted by unbiblical Catholic doctrines and pious practices. Therefore, they were poorly equipped to discern whether or not their mystical experiences were from God

For example, Catherine of Sienna believed that Jesus wanted her to whip herself until the blood ran down her back. Jesus, as portrayed in the Gospels, would never have done that. Although Catherine was sincere and devoted, she was mistaken. She had a distorted picture of God's nature and character.

The Bible warns us that the devil can appear as an angel of light (2 Corinthians 11:14) and he can cause deceptive supernatural events (2 Thessalonians 2:9).

How can we know which experiences of the Catholics mystics were from God, and which ones were counterfeits from the devil? All we have are writings from people who trusted those experiences. We weren't there to observe things that might have caused us to interpret them differently.

Some modern Catholic contemplatives, such as Thomas Merton, believe that all mystical experiences are valid, including those of pagan religions. In their search for mystical experiences, these people have abandoned the God of the Bible. The Bible says that pagan gods are really demons. The Apostle Paul said:

> "But I say, that the things which the Gentiles sacrifice, they sacrifice to devils, and not to God: and I would not that ye should have fellowship with devils." (1 Corinthians 10:20)

By embracing mystical experiences from pagan gods, these contemplatives are engaging in "fellowship with devils." This shows that mystical experiences can be dangerous.

It is good to have passion and zeal for God. We can ask God to set our hearts on fire with love for Him. We can ask Him to reveal Himself to us. We can spend time with Him, praying and worshiping and rejoicing in His love for us. We can follow the example of Joshua, who loved to stay in the Tent of Meeting, in the presence of the Lord. We can follow the example of David, who delighted in God and sang songs (psalms) to Him.

God wants us to know Him better and love Him more. He will help us do it. We need to turn directly to God—not to second-hand experiences of people we don't know.

The Spirit of Catholicism

Chapter 27
Mixing Paganism with Christianity

Pope John Paul II mixes paganism with Christianity. In October, 1986, the Pope convened and led a multi-faith service at Assisi, Italy. Leaders of pagan religions participated and publicly prayed to their gods. Muslims, Hindus, Buddhists, animists, and Zoroastrians participated in this service. So did an Orthodox patriarch and some Protestant leaders. (A picture and some articles are online.)[1]

The video, *Catholicism: Crisis of Faith*, has film footage of this service. You can see and hear the Dalai Lama chanting, African shamans calling on their gods, and Muslims chanting from the Koran. (See Appendix H for information about the video.)

The altar that was used for the service had a statue of Buddha on top of the Tabernacle (an ornate container for consecrated bread). Catholics believe that consecrated bread is literally the body, blood, soul, and divinity of Jesus Christ. Putting a statue of Buddha on top of the Tabernacle is, in effect, elevating paganism above Jesus Christ. (A picture is online.)[2]

In 2002, the Pope convened another multi-faith service in Assisi. Leaders of pagan religions participated in the service. (You can read about this online.)[3]

The Pope met with a Buddhist patriarch and told him: "Buddhism is a religion of salvation." (A picture and some quotations from the Pope are online.)[4]

The Pope visited Benin. He apologized for the fact that westerners have rejected African religions, including voodoo. (You can read about this online.)[5]

Some Catholic priests have written books that mix Catholicism with ancient pagan religions or modern New Age paganism. Anthony de Mello wrote *Sadhana, A Way to God: Christian Exercises in Eastern Form*. Bede Griffiths wrote *Cosmic Revelation: The Hindu Way to God*, and *The Other Half of My Soul: Bede Griffiths and the Hindu-Christian Dialogue*. Aelred Graham wrote *Zen Catholicism*, and *Conversations: Christian and Buddhist*. George Maloney wrote *Mysticism and the New Age*. John J. Heaney wrote *The Sacred and the Psychic: Parapsychology & Christian Theology*.[6]

In America, there is a Catholic-Hindu "house of prayer." It has a statue of Shiva (the Hindu god of destruction), a statue of Buddha, and a crucifix. People who come there use mantras and Eastern meditation techniques. The "house of prayer" is popular and is usually filled to capacity. The local archbishop approves of it, and his diocese supports it financially.[7]

In India, there is a Benedictine monastery that is modeled after a Hindu ashram. The members of the community admire Hindu gods and goddesses. The founder (Bede Griffiths) says that Hindu temples are a "sacrament." He teaches that Christians, Hindus, Buddhists, and Muslims are all "brothers in Christ."[8]

Catholic theologian Richard Grigg believes that Americans should replace the God of the Bible with "the Goddess." He wrote the book *When God Becomes Goddess: The Transformation of American Religion*.[9]

This mixture of paganism and Christianity can be seen in the artwork of the Sistine Chapel. It is the Pope's private chapel, but it is as large as a church. Michelangelo painted the ceiling. It has pictures of patriarchs, prophets, apostles, and pagan prophetesses (sybils). Near the entrance of the Sistine Chapel, there is a painting of Greek philosophers. (You can see pictures online.)[10]

This mixture can also be seen in the 22 Vatican museums. Some of them have Christian artwork. Others have statues of pagan gods and goddesses. According to the Bible, these are idols, and they should be destroyed. However, the Vatican has preserved them and put them on public display. (Pictures are online.)[11]

Saint Peter's Basilica is the church of the popes. It is one of the largest churches in the world. There is a circular courtyard in front of it, with an obelisk in the center of the courtyard. (You can see pictures online.)[12]

Obelisks are associated with pagan religions. This particular obelisk is also associated with the slaughter of Christians. It was originally in the Circus of Nero (the Circus Maximus), where Christians were fed to the lions. In 1587, Pope Sixtus V had it moved to the center of the circular courtyard in front of Saint Peter's Basilica. (You can read about this online.)[13]

The Sistine Chapel and Saint Peter's Basilica are much like the Catholic church. They are large, expensive, ornate, and impressive. And they mix paganism with Christinity.

Chapter 28

Behind the Mask

There is an old saying that when the Catholic Church is in the minority, then it is as meek as a lamb. When it has equality, then it is as sly as a fox. When it is in the majority (and therefore in a position of power), then it is as fierce as a tiger.

If you want to know what something really is, then look at how it behaves when it is in a position of power, and it is therefore able to do what it really wants to do.

When the Catholic Church was at the height of its power, popes behaved like Roman Emperors, living in luxury, and exercising great political power. (Pope Innocent III was called the ruler of the world.) Can you imagine Jesus or the Apostles allowing themselves to be dressed in ornate clothing, and carried on a portable throne, on the shoulders of uniformed men? Would they wear jeweled crowns and dress like Roman nobility? Jesus washed the feet of His disciples. Popes required kings and emperors to kiss their feet.

For centuries, the Catholic Church kept the Bible in Latin, even though some scholars wanted to translate it into the language of the common people. As a result, most people were not able to understand the Bible. Men who translated the Bible into English were burned as "heretics." People who read, or owned, even a small portion of an English Bible were burned at the stake. As a result, most people were not able to compare Catholic doctrines with Scripture. This helped maintain the power of the Catholic Church.

According to the Bible, Christians are supposed to use Scripture to test the teachings of authority figures. The Catholic Church reversed this. It requires Catholics to interpret Scripture according to the direction of Catholic authority figures.

Christians who disagreed with Catholic doctrine were often imprisoned, tortured, or killed. There were massacres and persecutions. The Inquisition was established. It killed "heretics" for over 600 years. This was "fierce tiger" Catholicism at its height.

The Inquisition's last execution was in 1826. The Office of the Inquisition still exists, but it changed its name in 1965. According to modern Canon Law (1983), the Catholic Church still claims the right to "coerce" people who fail to comply with it.[1]

The Catholic Church claims the primary allegiance of its members. In 1867, Pope Pius IX declared that Austria's new Constitution was null and void. He ordered Austrian Catholics to try to undermine their constitution. (It allowed freedom of religion and weakened the power of the Catholic Church.) He ordered Catholic clergy in Austria to be willing to go to prison in order to increase the power of the Catholic Church.[2]

The same attitude can be seen in American bishops and cardinals. They violated American law in order to protect the public image of the Catholic Church. They knew that some priests were sexually molesting boys. Instead of reporting the priests to civil authorities, they covered up the crimes and moved the priests to new locations. Cardinals are citizens of the Vatican in addition to being citizens of their homeland. Their primary allegiance is to the Vatican.[3]

The Catholic Church presently engages in ecumenical dialog with Protestants, calling them "separated brethren." But at the same time, it confirms the decrees of the Council of Trent, which condemned all Protestants.

Ecumenism was officially promoted by the Second Vatican Council (1962-1965). According to official documents from that Council, the purpose of ecumenism is to get Protestants to become Catholics. This is "sly fox" Catholicism.

It's working. Since 1993, over 480 Protestant pastors have converted to Catholicism. Hundreds more are seriously considering it. The rate of conversions per year is increasing.[4]

An entire Protestant church converted to Catholicism.[5] In addition, an Evangelical church seems to be heading in that direction. Their last retreat was led by a Catholic priest, and their pastor is going to that priest for "spiritual direction."[6]

What's the bottom line for the Catholic Church?

Rome wants to reverse the Protestant Reformation.

Catholic Myths

The Catholic Church is built on man-made myths. These myths are like the operating system of a computer. The operating system continually works in the background. It determines how everything else functions. However, most people are not aware of it. They just focus on the programs that they are using.

Following are some Catholic Myths that draw people into the Catholic Church and make it difficult for them to leave.

> **MYTH:** All Catholics share the same beliefs. Only the Catholic Church has unity and stability.

MYTH: There is an unbroken chain of apostolic succession. It goes back to the Apostle Peter, upon whom Jesus Christ built the Church.

MYTH: Popes are infallible. It is impossible for them to teach false doctrines.

MYTH: The Pope is called "Holy Father," so he must be a holy man.

MYTH: The Catholic Church is called "Holy Mother Church," so whatever it does must be good and holy.

MYTH: I can't get to Heaven without the priests and the sacraments. I have to depend on the Catholic Church for my salvation.

MYTH: God is so distant and unreachable that I need a bridge to get to Him. Mary and the saints give me that bridge. They understand me. They pray for me.

MYTH: Matters of religion are too deep and too difficult for me to understand. Only Holy Mother Church is capable of dealing with them. If I will just put my mind and my conscience in her faithful and capable hands, then she will get me to Heaven.

MYTH: I cannot understand the Bible. It is too confusing. Only Catholic clergy are qualified to understand it.

MYTH: My prayers aren't good enough. I need to have Mary and the saints pray for me. God will listen to them.

MYTH: I don't have to test things and discern things for myself, because God protects the Catholic Church from error. All I have to do is learn and obey. I am safe in the hands of Holy Mother Church. What a relief!

As I have shown in this book, when you study Scripture and Church history, you discover that these myths have no basis in reality. But it is amazing how much power they have over people.

Doctrine is not the primary thing that draws former Catholics back into the Catholic Church. It is not the main reason why Protestants convert to Catholicism.

The power is in the myths. They give credibility to false doctrines. They make unbiblical practices seem reasonable. They give power to mind control, and make it seem reasonable, or even desirable.

These myths cause fear, confusion, and false guilt in people who have left the Catholic Church. They create a "Catholic undertow," which makes it difficult for people to leave the Catholic Church, and often pulls them back again after they have left.

If you used to be a Catholic, please read Appendix B, "For Former Catholics." It will help break the power of the "Catholic undertow." It will enable you to enter more fully into the abundant life that Jesus came to give you.

Afterword

Some people may face emotional turmoil or difficult decisions as a result of what they have read in this book. Therefore, they will need Scriptural strength to get through some tough times. Jesus told us that tribulation is a normal part of Christian life. He said:

> "These things I have spoken unto you, that in me ye might have peace. In the world ye shall have tribulation: but be of good cheer; I have overcome the world." (John 16:33)

Few people have faced the level of personal hardship that the Apostle Paul endured. He was whipped with 39 stripes on five occasions. He was beaten with rods on three occasions. He was stoned and left for dead. He was shipwrecked three times. He often endured weariness, pain, sleepless nights, hunger, thirst, cold, and inadequate clothing. (2 Corinthians 11:24-27; Acts 14:19) But Paul saw things from the perspective of eternity. Because of his eternal perspective, he described his suffering as being light and temporary. Paul said:

> "For our light affliction, which is but for a moment, worketh for us a far more exceeding and eternal weight of glory; While we look not at the things which are seen, but at the things which are not seen: for the things which are seen are temporal; but the things which are not seen are eternal." (2 Corinthians 4:17-18)

Paul's perspective on suffering, danger, and tribulation was that, because of the love of Jesus Christ, we can overcome it all. Paul's life was a testimony to the fact that we really can do all things, because Jesus Christ gives us strength, and God's grace really is sufficient for us. (See Philippians 4:13 and 2 Corinthians 12:9.)

If we truly love God, and eternity is real to us, then we can draw strength and courage from Paul, who said:

> "Who shall separate us from the love of Christ? shall tribulation, or distress, or persecution, or famine, or nakedness, or

> peril, or sword? As it is written, For thy sake we are killed all the day long; we are accounted as sheep for the slaughter. Nay, in all these things we are more than conquerors through him that loved us. For I am persuaded, that neither death, nor life, nor angels, nor principalities, nor powers, nor things present, nor things to come, Nor height, nor depth, nor any other creature, shall be able to separate us from the love of God, which is in Christ Jesus our Lord." (Romans 8:35-39)

These promises are conditional. They only work if Jesus Christ is your Lord and your Savior. If He isn't, then please read Appendix A, "Eternal Life." If you are not sure about where you stand with God, please read it. This issue is so important that you need to know for sure where you stand.

Some people were baptized as an infant, or confirmed and baptized when they were young. Some people prayed a "sinner's prayer" when they didn't fully understand what they were doing. If you are one of those people, then you can strengthen and renew your commitment to Jesus Christ. Please read Appendix A, "Eternal Life."

If you used to be a Catholic, please read Appendix B, "For Former Catholics."

If you want to know more about Catholicism, this book has appendixes that give the Internet addresses of articles about historical and doctrinal issues, testimonies of former Catholics, and pictures that you can see online. There is a Glossary of some Catholic terms. There is an appendix that recommends books, videos and websites.

Please consider giving a copy of *Unmasking Catholicism* to your pastor. If he reads it, then he will be better equipped to minister to the former Catholics in his church. He will also be more effective in helping church members who have become attracted to Catholicism. And he will realize that Catholics need to be evangelized.

Ecumenism has caused many pastors to lose their awareness of the radical differences between Catholicism and Protestantism. One reason is linguistic confusion. Catholics and Protestants have different understandings of some key words. For example, according to Catholic doctrine, "grace" is something that can be given to inanimate objects, such as water.[1]

If you want to give a book to Catholic friends or family members, I have another one that would be more suitable for them. It avoids some of the difficult issues that are discussed in this book. In addition, it is shorter, which makes it less expensive. The title is *Another Side of Catholicism*.

* * * * * * *

Have you ever ridden on a train or a subway? I've been on many of them. Sometimes waiting in the station has been pleasant. Sometimes it has been tedious, tiresome, and frustrating. The important thing is not what happens in the station. What really matters is getting on the right train, heading for the right destination.

Earth is like a train station. Our time here may be difficult or pleasant. It is often a mixture of the two. The important thing is our eternal destination. Are we heading for Heaven or for Hell?

God has promised that, if we truly love Him, then he will enable us to do whatever is necessary, and endure whatever happens to us. The Bible says:

> "And we know that all things work together for good to them that love God…" (Romans 8:28)

> "I can do all things through Christ which strengtheneth me." (Philippians 4:13)

No matter what happens, we can have joy now and hope for the future. God is faithful, and He loves us.

> *The God who made the earth has always loved us.*
> *Before we drew a breath, our heart was known.*
> *God created us to live with Him forever,*
> *To sing and dance with joy before His throne.*
>
> *Our time on earth is hard, but it is fleeting.*
> *No matter how things seem, God's always there.*
> *He'll guide us and protect us and watch over us,*
> *And take away each tear and fear and care.*
>
> *And when the toil and pain and fear have ended,*
> *When sorrow's gone, and all we know is love,*
> *Then we and God will celebrate forever,*
> *Rejoicing with the saints in Heaven above.*

Appendixes

Appendix A
Eternal Life

Ever since Adam and Eve decided to eat of the fruit of the tree of the Knowledge of Good and Evil, mankind has been plagued with evil. In addition, we have been burdened with the responsibility of constantly having to discern whether things are good or bad.

Today, some people deny the existence of objective good and evil. However, during the terrorist attack of September 11, most people recognized that evil really does exist. If you have been taught that everything is relative, and there is no such thing as sin, please try to remember how you felt when you saw the towers of the World Trade Center being destroyed.

Sinful things put a barrier between us and God. In addition, they have self-destruction built into them. It is obvious in the physical realm. Sexual immorality can result in terrible diseases and unwanted pregnancies. But it is also true in other areas of life. For example, people who habitually tell lies often have difficulty recognizing the truth. They are unable to trust other people, because they themselves can't be trusted. As a result, they never have the kind of rich, beautiful, life-giving personal relationships that God intended for us to have.

The bad news is that we have the problem of sin. The good news is that Jesus Christ is the solution to that problem. He came to destroy the works of the devil and to give us abundant life. (1 John 3:8; John 10:10) He is able to save us. (Hebrews 7:24-25)

Jesus is "the way, the truth, and the life." (John 14:6) He is the One who enables us to come to God. (John 14:6) Because of Jesus, we can become children of God (Galatians 3:26). God the Father sent Jesus into the world so that we could be saved and have everlasting life. (John 3:16)

Jesus became a man. He died to save us from our sins and to reconcile us to God. He was Resurrected from the dead. He ascended into Heaven. He sent His Holy Spirit to help us know Him, and love Him, and live according to Biblical principles. He is interceding for us. Some day, He will come back again, in glory.

Do you believe these things? If not, then please go to www.NewLifeWithChrist.com

If you do believe these things, then you can be saved by declaring your faith, asking God to forgive you for your sins, and choosing to do things God's way. The Bible says:

> "...Believe on the Lord Jesus Christ, and thou shalt be saved." (Acts 16:30-31)

> "...The word is nigh thee, even in thy mouth, and in thy heart: that is, the word of faith, which we preach; That if thou shalt confess with thy mouth the Lord Jesus, and shalt believe in thine heart that God hath raised him from the dead, thou shalt be saved. For with the heart man believeth unto righteousness; and with the mouth confession is made unto salvation. For the scripture saith, Whosoever believeth on him shall not be ashamed." (Romans 10:8-10)

Can it really be that simple? Yes. Remember my chapter about "The Good Thief"? While Jesus was still on the cross, God showed us how simple salvation is.

Our salvation cost Jesus everything. Look at what He went through in order to enable us to be saved. And He did it willingly, because He loves us.

> "Surely he hath borne our griefs, and carried our sorrows: yet we did esteem him stricken, smitten of God, and afflicted. But he was wounded for our transgressions, he was bruised for our iniquities: the chastisement of our peace was upon him; and with his stripes we are healed. All we like sheep have gone astray; we have turned every one to his own way; and the LORD hath laid on him the iniquity of us all." (Isaiah 53:4-6)

Jesus didn't have to go through all that. He could have stopped it at any moment. (John 10:17-18) He could have been rescued by angels. (Matthew 26:53) He could have come down from the cross. But He stayed on that cross because He loves us. He chose to go through all that for us. His love is beyond our comprehension. (Ephesians 3:19)

Do you want to be like the Good Thief, and have your life be transformed by Jesus Christ? Do you want to enter into eternal life, and become part of God's family—a child of God?

If so, then please read the following prayer and see if you agree with it. If you do, then please pray it, or else pray something of your own from your own heart. Prayer is simple. Just talk naturally with God about what is on your heart, as David did in the Psalms.

> **PRAYER:** Jesus, I believe that you became a human being in order to save me. You are God who came in human flesh. You are both God and man. I believe that you died on the cross in order to save me from my sins. Thank you for loving me so much that you were willing to do that for me.
>
> I believe that you were raised from the dead, and you ascended into Heaven. I believe that are interceding for me. I believe that you will come again in glory.
>
> Jesus, I want to know You better. Please reveal Yourself to me. I want to understand the Bible. Please make it come alive for me and help me understand it. I want to be clean and right with you. Please forgive my sins and change my heart. Help me love what You love, and turn away from things that displease You.
>
> Jesus, You know what's best for me. I want to do things Your way. Please give me a willing, obedient, teachable heart. Help me cooperate with Your work in my heart and in my life. Help me be faithful to You. Help me obey You and live according to Biblical principles. Jesus, I want You to be the Lord of every part of my life.
>
> Thank You for being my Lord and my Savior. Amen.

Congratulations! You are now a child of God. You have entered into eternal life. No matter what you go through here on earth, you can look forward to eternity in Heaven with Jesus. And you are now my brother or my sister. God is our father, and we are his children, so we are brothers and sisters. All Heaven is celebrating because of you!

> "…I say unto you, there is joy in the presence of the angels of God over one sinner that repenteth." (Luke 15:10)

There are many things that I want to share with you, but it would make this book too long. Please see the articles on the following website. They will strengthen you and encourage you. They will also give you some practical suggestions.

www.NewLifeWithChrist.com

You can write to me by email. I would be delighted to hear from you.

MaryAnnCollins@juno.com

May the Lord bless you, comfort you, strengthen you, and encourage you. May He increase your love for the Bible and give you greater understanding of it. And may He give you an ever-increasing revelation of how much He loves you.

> *"The LORD bless thee, and keep thee:*
> *The LORD make his face shine upon thee,*
> *and be gracious unto thee:*
> *The LORD lift up his countenance upon thee,*
> *and give thee peace."*
> (Numbers 6:24-26)

Appendix B
For Former Catholics

Leaving the Catholic Church involves more than just understanding doctrinal issues. There are often emotional issues as well. I have had to deal with these issues myself. I also correspond with former Catholics who are currently dealing with them.

Some people see God's truth, simply and suddenly, like a light being turned on inside of them. They walk out of Catholicism and into Biblical Christianity, without emotional turmoil. That is wonderful. It is a precious gift from God.

For many former Catholics, there are difficult emotional issues that we have to deal with. Often our new friends in our new church don't understand them.

Christians often assume that, once Catholics understand doctrinal issues and Biblical principles, then that is the end of the matter. But for many of us, it isn't. There can be a lot more involved than just intellectual understanding.

Catholics are used to having priests tell them how to think and what to do. As a result, it can be difficult for former Catholics to learn to pray for themselves, read the Bible for themselves, and take responsibility for their own life. We can overcome this difficulty, but it requires determination, persistence, and prayer.

Loyalty, Guilt, and Rejection

Some former Catholics are under emotional pressure to return to the Catholic Church, because they don't want to hurt their family members. In addition, the Pope is called "Holy Father," and the Catholic Church is called "Holy Mother Church." As a result, people may feel as if they are betraying their father and their mother if they leave the Catholic Church. Jesus addressed these issues when He said:

> "He that loveth father or mother more than me is not worthy of me: and he that loveth son or daughter more than me is not worthy of me." (Matthew 10:37)

Some former Catholics have had to face control, manipulation, intimidation, rejection, and false accusations. If you are going through something like this, then remember that God is faithful, and His grace really is sufficient. He will get you through it.

In addition, the experience will give you a new appreciation for the rejection and misunderstanding that Jesus endured for our sakes. He left the love and appreciation of Heaven, to come here to earth and be falsely accused, misunderstood, rejected, and mocked, in order to save us. The Apostle Paul said:

> "That I may know him, and the power of his resurrection, and the fellowship of his sufferings…" (Philippians 3:10)

You are sharing in the fellowship of Christ's sufferings. This will give you greater love for Him, and more gratitude for what He has done for you. It will enable you to know His heart in a new way. It will also qualify you to receive the blessing of one of the Beatitudes. Jesus said:

> "Blessed are ye, when men shall revile you, and persecute you, and shall say all manner of evil against you falsely, for my sake. Rejoice, and be exceeding glad: for great is your reward in heaven: for so persecuted they the prophets which were before you." (Matthew 5:11-12)

The process of qualifying for that blessing is no fun at all. But if we see the eternal perspective, then we will be able to endure it, and to trust God while we are going through it. The Apostle Peter said:

> "Beloved, think it not strange concerning the fiery trial which is to try you, as though some strange thing happened unto you: But rejoice, inasmuch as ye are partakers of Christ's sufferings; that, when his glory shall be revealed, ye may be glad also with exceeding joy. If ye be reproached for the name of Christ, happy are ye; for the spirit of glory and of God resteth upon you: on their part he is evil spoken of, but on your part he is glorified." (1 Peter 4:12-14)

Try to find an understanding friend or prayer partner to stand with you, as you go through this. You can pray together. Your friend or prayer partner can help you keep a Biblical perspective when you are under emotional pressure.

If your family is pressuring you to come back to the Catholic Church, then this is probably not a good time to try to share your new-found, Biblical faith with them.

Mind Control

The Catholic Church claims that it has the right to control how Catholics think. We were taught to believe whatever we were told, and to obey the priests. During Mass, we were told when to stand, when to sit, when to reply to what the priest said, and what to say. This attitude of passive compliance was constantly reinforced.

This is more than just our personal experience. It is official Catholic doctrine. For documented information about it, please read the chapter, "Mind Control."

So how do we overcome this? The Bible gives us the answers. Psalm 23 tells us:

> "The LORD is my shepherd: I shall not want. He maketh me to lie down in green pastures: he leadeth me beside the still waters. **He restoreth my soul: he leadeth me in the paths of righteousness for his name's sake.**" (Psalm 23:1-3, emphasis added)

(If you have a Catholic Bible, many of the Psalms are numbered differently. I recommend that you get a Protestant Bible.)

God is able to restore our soul. He can undo the damage that the Catholic Church did to our thinking and our emotions. God is able to change our minds and our emotions, so that they will reflect His truth, and agree with His Word (the Bible). We need to agree with God, instead of agreeing with the Catholic Church.

God tells all Christians to be transformed by the renewing of their minds. (Romans 12:2) And He always enables us to do what He tells us to do. This renewing of our minds is especially necessary for former Catholics, because we have been indoctrinated with unbiblical beliefs, and subjected to mind control. The Apostle Paul tells us to take every thought captive to the obedience of Jesus Christ—not the obedience of the Catholic Church. (2 Corinthians 10:3-5)

God is willing and able to teach us how to lead righteous lives. The Bible and personal prayer are keys to this. We need to ask God to change our hearts. We can pray with Scripture, which says:

> "Search me, O God, and know my heart: try me, and know my thoughts: And see if there be any wicked way in me, and lead me in the way everlasting." (Psalm 139:23-24)

"Let the words of my mouth, and the meditation of my heart, be acceptable in thy sight, O LORD, my strength, and my redeemer." (Psalm 19:14)

The Bible can correct our thinking and instruct us in how to live righteously. It can enable us to understand whether or not doctrines are Biblical. It can equip us to live Godly lives. The Apostle Paul said:

"All scripture is given by inspiration of God, and is profitable for doctrine, for reproof, for correction, for instruction in righteousness: That the man of God may be perfect, thoroughly furnished unto all good works." (2 Timothy 3:16-17)

When reading the Bible, it is important to approach it with a spirit of humility, and to ask God to help us understand it. If we are faithful to do this, then our thoughts (and therefore our actions) will line up more and more with God's thoughts and God's ways of doing things. This is a process. It takes time. God is patient with us. We need to be patient with ourselves.

We not only need to read the Bible, we also need to study it. We need to become so saturated with Scripture that it becomes a living part of us, like a skin graft, or a branch that is grafted onto a tree. The Bible says:

"Study to shew thyself approved unto God, a workman that needeth not to be ashamed, rightly dividing the word of truth." (2 Timothy 2:15)

"...receive with meekness the engrafted word, which is able to save your souls." (James 1:21)

Fear

Catholicism teaches that there is no salvation apart from the Catholic Church, its sacramental system, the priesthood, and the Pope. This is not Biblical, but it can still be deeply ingrained. Once we learn better, then our minds understand, but it may take time for our gut feelings to catch up with our thinking.

There can be other forms of fear. One man told me that when he was a child in parochial school, the nuns terrorized him. For example, they said that the children would burn in Purgatory for every minute that they talked in class. What kind of picture does that give of God?

There are also official curses. When I was confirmed, the ritual (which was in Latin) included a curse that was supposed to come upon me if I ever left the Catholic Church. The anathemas of the Council of Trent still curse anybody who disagrees with any of the doctrinal statements of that Council.

The Blood of Jesus is more powerful than any curse. God is able to protect us and bless us, whether or not the Catholic Church wants Him to. God is in control—not the Catholic Church. The Bible says:

> "No weapon that is formed against thee shall prosper; and every tongue that shall rise against thee in judgment thou shalt condemn. This is the heritage of the servants of the LORD, and their righteousness is of me, saith the LORD." (Isaiah 54:17)

> "And we know that all things work together for good to them that love God, to them who are the called according to his purpose." (Romans 8:28)

> "What shall we then say to these things? If God be for us, who can be against us?" (Romans 8:31)

> "For I am persuaded, that neither death, nor life, nor angels, nor principalities, nor powers, nor things present, nor things to come, Nor height, nor depth, nor any other creature, shall be able to separate us from the love of God, which is in Christ Jesus our Lord." (Romans 8:38-39)

Anger

Many former Catholics go through a period of being angry. One reason is a feeling of betrayal. For some former Catholics, it has taken years before they were able to trust again.

In addition, anger is one way of handling fear, rejection, and the pressure to return to the Catholic Church. It can provide emotional strength, and it can help you stand your ground instead of allowing yourself to be controlled and manipulated. However, long-term anger is not spiritually or emotionally healthy. Jesus told us to forgive people. He said:

> "For if ye forgive men their trespasses, your heavenly Father will also forgive you: But if ye forgive not men their

trespasses, neither will your Father forgive your trespasses." (Matthew 6:14-15)

No matter what has been done to us, we cannot afford to become bitter. Bitterness defiles people, and it spreads like a spiritual cancer. The Bible says:

"Follow peace with all men, and holiness, without which no man shall see the Lord: Looking diligently lest any man fail of the grace of God; lest any root of bitterness springing up trouble you, and thereby many be defiled..." (Hebrews 12:14-15)

It can be difficult to forgive the people who taught us false doctrines and ungodly religious practices. However, you don't have to do it alone. God will help you. Jesus said:

"...The things which are impossible with men are possible with God." (Luke 18:27)

If you are willing to forgive, then God will enable you to do it. Ask God to increase your desire to forgive. Ask Him to change your heart and help you forgive.

Nobody Has All the Answers

When we were Catholics, we mistakenly believed that the Pope is infallible. It is easy to carry this mindset over to other things after we leave the Catholic Church.

Nobody is infallible. The Apostle Paul wrote about a fourth of the New Testament. Much of our theology is based on his writings. He was taken up to the Third Heaven, where he learned things that he was not allowed to tell other people about. (2 Corinthians 12:1-4) But Paul made a point of telling us that even he did not have all the answers, and some things about God are beyond our comprehension. He said:

"For we know in part, and we prophesy in part. But when that which is perfect is come, then that which is in part shall be done away. When I was a child, I spake as a child, I understood as a child, I thought as a child: but when I became a man, I put away childish things. For now we see through a glass, darkly;

> but then face to face: now I know in part; but then I shall know even as also I am known." (1 Corinthians 13:9-12)

> "O the depth of the riches both of the wisdom and knowledge of God! how unsearchable are his judgments, and his ways past finding out!" (Romans 11:33)

Paul said that he only knew "in part" and that his understanding was like looking in a mirror ("glass") that doesn't give a clear reflection. If the Apostle Paul didn't have all the answers, then nobody does—not Luther, not Calvin, not other great men of the Reformation. They loved God and they did the best that they could, but they were not infallible and they did not have all the answers. We should love them and be grateful for them, but we need to be careful not to wind up treating them like infallible popes. The same thing is true of our pastors, our church leaders, and the people who wrote the notes of our Study Bibles. The same thing is true of theologians and seminary professors.

These men base much of their teaching on the writings of the Apostle Paul. But even Paul did not expect people to accept what he said, just because he was the one who said it. The Bible commends the men of Berea, because they used Scripture to test Paul's teachings. The Book of Acts says:

> "And the brethren immediately sent away Paul and Silas by night unto Berea: who coming thither went into the synagogue of the Jews. These were more noble than those in Thessalonica, in that they received the word with all readiness of mind, and **searched the scriptures daily, whether those things were so.**" (Acts 17:10-11, emphasis added)

We need to follow the example of the Bereans. The Bible says that all Christians are supposed to test what they are taught. It says:

> "Prove all things; hold fast that which is good." (1 Thessalonians 5:21)

According to *Strong's Concordance*, the word "prove" means to test or examine. We need to test **everything** against Scripture. This is especially true today, because there is so much deception and false teaching in the world. We need to develop the habit of automatically checking **everything** out against Scripture.

God Is For Us, Not Against Us

Some Catholic traditions give the impression that God enjoys making us suffer. For example, Teresa of Avila told of a time when she was sick, in pain, with a fever, and she fell into the snow. According to Teresa, God told her: "This is how I treat my friends." She replied: "No wonder you have so few." (I'm quoting this from memory, so it may not be completely accurate.)

Another example is some apparitions of "Mary" that portray Mary as loving, and Jesus as a harsh judge. The picture is that of a loving mother, who is trying to protect her children from a child abuser.

Another example is harsh teachers in parochial schools, who taught children that God is out to get them.

These things are totally contrary to the picture of God that is given in the Bible. God the Father loves us so much that He sent Jesus to save us from our sins. Jesus loves us so much that He was willing to die a horribly painful death in order to enable us to become reconciled to God.

Ephesians 3:19 speaks of "the love of Christ, which passeth knowledge." Many Scripture verses speak about the love of God. A few of them follow:

> "For when we were yet without strength, in due time Christ died for the ungodly. For scarcely for a righteous man will one die: yet peradventure for a good man some would even dare to die. But God commendeth his love toward us, in that, while we were yet sinners, Christ died for us." (Romans 5:6-8)

> "He hath not dealt with us after our sins; nor rewarded us according to our iniquities. For as the heaven is high above the earth, so great is his mercy toward them that fear him. As far as the east is from the west, so far hath he removed our transgressions from us." (Psalm 103:10-12)

> "He that loveth not knoweth not God: for God is love. In this was manifested the love of God toward us, because that God sent his only begotten Son into the world, that we might live through him. Herein is love, not that we loved God, but that he loved us, and sent his Son to be the propitiation for our sins. Beloved, if God so loved us, we ought also to love one another." 1 John 4:8-11)

> "We love him, because he first loved us." (1 John 4:19)

"For God so loved the world, that he gave his only begotten Son, that whosoever believeth in him should not perish, but have everlasting life." (John 3:16)

"This is my commandment, That ye love one another, as I have loved you." (John 15:12)

"The LORD is my shepherd; I shall not want. He maketh me to lie down in green pastures: he leadeth me beside the still waters. He restoreth my soul: he leadeth me in the paths of righteousness for his name's sake. Yea, though I walk through the valley of the shadow of death, I will fear no evil: for thou art with me; thy rod and thy staff they comfort me. Thou preparest a table before me in the presence of mine enemies: thou anointest my head with oil; my cup runneth over. Surely goodness and mercy shall follow me all the days of my life: and I will dwell in the house of the LORD for ever." (Psalm 23:1-6)

If your Catholic training gave you reasons to be afraid of God, instead of loving Him and trusting Him, then you need to saturate yourself with Scripture and get to know who God really is. When the negative thoughts and feelings come, you can combat them with the truth of Scripture. The Bible says:

"For though we walk in the flesh, we do not war after the flesh: (For the weapons of our warfare are not carnal, but mighty through God to the pulling down of strong holds;) Casting down imaginations, and every high thing that exalteth itself against the knowledge of God, and bringing into captivity every thought to the obedience of Christ..." (2 Corinthians 10:3-5)

The distorted picture of God that many Catholics were taught is a "high thing" that exalts itself against the knowledge of God. It raises itself up in our minds and our emotions, and it blocks us from seeing who God really is. It hinders us from understanding God. We can pull these things down by taking our thoughts captive to the obedience of Christ. Ask God to show you how to do this.

One way of doing this is to become more aware of the chatter that goes on inside our heads, and to notice when it is talking about God. Then compare what it says with what the Bible says.

There was a time in my life when I became aware of a number of false teachings, false impressions of God. As I read the Bible, I found Scripture verses that told the truth that was the antidote to those false teachings. I memorized those verses. When the false teachings raised their head, I quoted those Scripture verses to myself. I kept doing that, until the false teachings lost their power in my mind and my emotions.

Catholic Condemnation

It is not unusual for people who leave the Catholic Church to have Catholic clergy, family members, or friends tell them that they are apostate, their new church is a cult, and they are going to Hell. Sometimes family members say things like: "You were born Catholic and you will die Catholic." In other words, because you were sprinkled with holy water when you were a baby (without your consent), the Catholic Church owns you and you have no right to leave. This denies the free will that God gave to us.

In the face of such condemnation, some former Catholics are afraid, because they were taught that they cannot get to Heaven without the Catholic Church. The Bible has the antidote to such fears. It says:

> "For I am persuaded, that neither death, nor life, nor angels, nor principalities, nor powers, nor things present, nor things to come, Nor height, nor depth, nor any other creature, shall be able to separate us from the love of God, which is in Christ Jesus our Lord." (Romans 8:38-39)

That includes the Catholic Church. It is not able to separate us from the love of God. Almighty God does not need to get permission from the Catholic Church before He can love us, bless us, and protect us.

Self-condemnation

Some of the Catholic saints seemed to think that self-condemnation is a virtue. For example, Catherine of Sienna saw a vision of Christ. She looked away for a second. When she looked back, the vision was gone. She tormented herself with self-condemnation, because she had looked away from the vision. Another example is Francis of Assisi. He was full of self-condemnation. His biographers interpreted that as a sign of holiness. As Catholics, we were taught to study the lives of the saints and to follow their example. That can easily result in imitating their self-condemnation.

This may not be as much of a problem for younger Catholics, who were raised in a generation that promotes positive self-esteem. But it is a problem for many of us. It used to be a problem for me, until the Bible gave me some understanding of what it really is.

Jesus called the Holy Spirit, "the Comforter." (John 14:16; 14:26; 15:26; 16:7) According to *Strong's Concordance*, the word "comforter" means intercessor, consoler, advocate, comforter. According to *Webster's Dictionary*, the word "comfort" means, "to impart strength and hope to; to relieve of mental distress; console."

The Bible calls the devil, "the accuser of our brethren." (Revelation 12:10) It's the devil's job to accuse us. Why should we do his job for him?

The Holy Spirit comforts, encourages, and strengthens. The devil accuses. We need to follow the example of the Holy Spirit, not the example of the devil. We need to comfort, encourage, and strengthen people. That includes ourselves.

Self-condemnation is a "high thing" that exalts itself against the knowledge of God. It blocks us from realizing that God loves us. It hinders us from recognizing God's love.

According to the Bible, Christians are not under condemnation. The Bible says:

> "There is therefore now no condemnation to them which are in Christ Jesus, who walk not after the flesh, but after the Spirit." (Romans 8:1)

> "Who shall lay any thing to the charge of God's elect? It is God that justifieth. Who is he that condemneth? It is Christ that died, yea rather, that is risen again, who is even at the right hand of God, who also maketh intercession for us." (Romans 8:33-34)

Acts 10:9-16 tells of a vision that Peter had. A sheet came down from Heaven. It was full of all kinds of animals (ones that Jewish law calls clean, and ones that Jewish law calls unclean). A voice told Peter to kill them and eat them. Peter protested, saying that he had never eaten anything unclean. The voice replied:

> "...What God hath cleansed, that call not thou common."
> (Acts 10:15)

According to *Strong's Concordance*, the word "common" means "profane." According to *Webster's Dictionary*, "profane" means "impure, defiled." When self-condemnation hits us, we can remind ourselves that Jesus Christ took away our sins. He paid a horrible price to be able to do that. If God calls us clean, then who are we to disagree with Him?

When we sin, the Holy Spirit convicts us of sin. This is very different from self-condemnation. It is life-giving, rather than destructive. The Bible puts it this way:

> "For godly sorrow worketh repentance to salvation not to be repented of: but the sorrow of the world worketh death." (2 Corinthians 7:10)

The Bible assures us that, because we are children of God, we are not under condemnation. However, we need to remember that our freedom in Christ is not a license to sin. The Bible says:

> "For, brethren, ye have been called unto liberty; only use not liberty for an occasion to the flesh, but by love serve one another." (Galatians 5:13)

> "What shall we say then? Shall we continue in sin, that grace may abound? God forbid. How shall we, that are dead to sin, live any longer therein?" (Romans 6:1-2)

Emotional Isolation

If you studied and imitated the mystics, or if you were in a convent or a monastery, then you may have a problem with emotional isolation.

When I was in the convent, we were told that we should be emotionally detached, that we should only express love in a detached way. We were taught that human attachments interfere with closeness to God.

This is contrary to Scripture. Adam was very close to God. He walked and talked with God every evening. But God said that wasn't enough. God said that Adam needed human companionship. God said: "It is not good that the man should be alone..." (Genesis 2:18)

The Bible says that God spoke to Moses "face to face, as a man speaketh unto his friend." (Exodus 33:11; also see Numbers 12:6-8) That is an unusual level of intimacy with God. Moses was a married man with children. And he was an emotional man. When the people murmured against him, Moses "cried unto the Lord." (Exodus 17:3-4) When God became angry with the people of Israel, Moses pleaded with God to have mercy on them. (Exodus 32:9-14) When his sister Miriam had leprosy, Moses became emotional. The Bible says:

> "Moses cried unto the Lord, saying, Heal her now, O God, I beseech thee." (Numbers 12:10-13)

Emotional detachment is a pagan ideal. It is praised by stoic philosophy and Buddhism. But it is contrary to Scripture. The Bible encourages fervent prayer. It says:

> "...The effectual fervent prayer of a righteous man availeth much." (James 5:16)

You can't do that without feelings. According to *Webster's Dictionary*, the word "fervor" means, "intensity of feeling or expression." Synonyms for "fervent" are, "fiery, vehement, impassioned, passionate, eager, keen." If you are emotionally detached, then how can you pray fervently for someone?

Jesus wasn't emotionally detached, and nobody has ever been closer to God the Father than Jesus was. When Jesus saw that Lazarus was dead, and Mary and Martha were grieving for him, Jesus "groaned in the spirit, and was troubled," and he wept. The people saw this as showing the intensity of Jesus' love for Lazarus. (John 11:33-36)

The Apostle Paul wasn't emotionally detached. He had a fatherly love for Timothy, whom he called his "dearly beloved son." (2 Timothy 1:2; also see 1 Timothy 1:2 and 1:18)

Jesus told us that, in order to enter the Kingdom of Heaven, we need to become like little children. (Mark 10:15). Children are emotional. They have strong feelings and they express them. Their love is personal, emotional, and affectionate.

God designed us for fellowship, not for isolation and detachment. Isolation is spiritually and emotionally unhealthy. That is why prisoners who are kept in solitary confinement for long periods of time often go insane.

If you were taught to be emotionally isolated, the first step towards freedom is to recognize the problem. Then you can pray for God to heal you and give you His perspective. You can also deliberately do things to counteract it.

Animals are safe. Can you have a pet? If not, then you can make a point of being affectionate with other people's pets when you have the opportunity to do so. You can go to petting zoos, or to pet stores that allow you to pet the animals.

Children are safe. You can pick up babies and put your arm around young children. As you show affection for them (both verbally and physically), you will become more comfortable with it, and you will enjoy it, instead of feeling awkward.

It takes time and effort and thought to learn to be affectionate after years of emotional starvation. But it is well worth the effort. It will bring emotional healing, and it will give you a greater understanding of God, and of the men and women in the Bible.

The Catholic Undertow

There is something that I call the "Catholic undertow." Have you ever been swimming in the ocean, and tried to swim back to shore, but the undertow kept pulling you back out to sea? Well, something similar can happen to people who have left the Catholic Church.

Several things contribute to this, including fear, rejection, inappropriate guilt, and the practical consequences of mind control. Some Catholics encounter "culture shock" when attending another church. Also, no church is perfect. No matter where you go to church, sooner or later somebody will disappoint you or hurt you (and they may not even realize it).

People who want you to return to the Catholic Church may add to the difficulty by putting pressure on you, or trying to indoctrinate you with Catholic teachings.

One way to deal with the undertow is to just refuse to give in to it. Stand your ground. Be a bulldog and keep holding on. Pray for God to give you strength and wisdom. Realize that what you are going through is not unusual. There is nothing wrong with you. Many former Catholics go through this kind of thing.

It is not wise to make important decisions when you are under emotional pressure. Applying this principle will give you strength, if you are feeling the pressure of the Catholic undertow. Just refuse to make a decision until the emotional pressure passes.

When people get married, sooner or later they will have bad emotions, and their level of commitment will be tested. The same kind of thing happens when somebody leaves the Catholic Church and joins a Biblical church.

Our emotions change with the weather, with our health, and with our circumstances. But God's truth doesn't change, and our commitment to Him shouldn't change, either.

You didn't leave the Catholic Church because of feelings. You left because it had practices and doctrines that are contrary to Scripture. You left because you wanted the truth. Well, don't let emotions pull you back. The truth hasn't changed just because your emotions have changed. Hang on. In time, your emotions will come around again.

Reinforcing Our Foundations

We former Catholics need to reinforce our Biblical foundations. It is important to read Scripture and to have it become a part of us.

You may want to read *The Gospel According to Rome* by James G. McCarthy (Eugene, Oregon: Harvest House Publishers, 1995). It shows that many Catholic practices and doctrines are contrary to Scripture. McCarthy is a former Catholic. His book is easy to read, thoroughly documented from official Catholic sources, and compassionate in its presentation.

James McCarthy's video, *Catholicism: Crisis of Faith*, was life-changing for me. It ministers on far more than just the intellectual level. You can order it from bookstores by giving them the ISBN number (ISBN 0-962-9152-0-3). You can also order it from D&K Press. They have it in English and Spanish, and they ship all over the world. Their phone number is 800-777-8839. They also have a website.

www.DKPressChristianBooks.com

The video is also available in other languages. (See Appendix H.)

Emotional Attachment

For years after I left the Catholic Church, I still had loyalty to it and an emotional attachment to it. I found it helpful to read David Yallop's book, *In God's Name: An Investigation into the Murder of Pope John Paul I* (London: Transworld Publishers, 1994). This book is well written, gripping, and hard to put down.

Vatican insiders asked Yallop to investigate the death of Pope John Paul I, because they suspected that he was murdered. Yallop did his homework. He interviewed Vatican insiders and Mafia gangsters. He gives a revealing and disturbing picture of life in the Vatican.

Finding a Good Church

Do you have a good church? If not, then you need to find one. The first thing to do is to pray for God to lead you to the right church. Keep on praying until you find it.

A good church is a place where people believe the Bible, have sound doctrine, and are full of love for God and for one another.

Sound doctrine is important. There are some doctrines that are non-negotiable. If a person doesn't believe them, then he or she is not a Christian. These include the Incarnation (Jesus is both God and man), the Atonement (Jesus died for our sins), and the Resurrection of Jesus.

However, there is far more to Christian life than just sound doctrine. Love is essential. In Revelation 2:1-5, Jesus spoke to a church where the people rejected false teaching, did good works, and had patience and courage under adversity. However, He rebuked them, because they let their love fade. This was such a serious problem that Jesus told them to repent and rekindle their love, or else He would deal with their church.

People have different personalities. So do denominations, pastors, and congregations. As a result, individual churches have different personalities. You can find out about a church's doctrine with a phone call to their office, but to get a feel for a church's personality, you will have to visit it a few times.

If you are not comfortable with a church that you try, pray about it. The lack of comfort might indicate that there is a problem. However, it could just be culture shock. Any Protestant church will be different from what we were used to as Catholics.

The primary reason for going to church is to worship God and to learn about His ways and His character, through preaching and Bible studies. Hopefully, you will also make friends who will enrich your life and encourage you to become a more mature Christian. In order to do that, you will probably need to make the effort to get to know people.

You may not be able to find a church that meets all of your needs and desires. Perhaps you want to have activities with other single Christians, or you have children who need good programs for youth, or you find that the pastor isn't as available as you would like him to be. Perhaps the music is not well done, or it is different from what you are used to. Don't let such things discourage you. Be grateful for what you have.

One way to get things into perspective is to remember our persecuted brothers and sisters in other countries. For example, in Indonesia, Christians are grateful to be able to meet together without being attacked by Muslims. In

North Korea, Christians have to meet secretly and quietly. They don't dare worship out loud, for fear of being heard by hostile people.

All of us have strengths and weaknesses. So do pastors. So do churches. There are no perfect churches. It is probably a good thing that there aren't, because knowing human nature, if we found one, we would probably make an idol out of it. Not being able to find a perfect church makes us depend on God. And that's good.

What About Our Families?

For former Catholics, there are two concerns relating to families. The first is how to deal with misunderstanding, condemnation, and pressure to return to the Catholic Church. I have already discussed these issues.

The second is family members who don't know Jesus. We long to have them know Him and love Him. We have found a treasure that is so beautiful, so wonderful, so priceless, that we want to share it.

How do we share Jesus with family members who don't know Him? The first thing to do is to pray for them. The Bible says:

> "…the god of this world hath blinded the minds of them which believe not, lest the light of the glorious gospel of Christ, who is the image of God, should shine unto them." (2 Corinthians 4:4).

We can pray for God to remove the blinders and open their eyes, and enable them to desire and understand the truth.

Jesus told a parable about a man who sowed seed into four kinds of soil. (Matthew 13:3-23; Mark 4:2-20; Luke 8:5-15) The first soil mentioned in the parable was so hard that the seed couldn't get into it. It just stayed on top of the ground, until the birds ate it up. It doesn't do any good to throw good seed (truth about Jesus) onto hard soil that can't receive it.

So pray for God to make your family members hungry for Him and receptive to the truth. You may want to do a lot of praying, before you start sharing with them. Before you talk to them about God, spend time talking to God about them.

When you are walking on a path, there are two ways of getting off it. You can go too far to the right, or too far to the left. Similarly, when it comes to sharing the Good News about Jesus, we can make two mistakes. One is to be afraid of speaking about our faith. The other is to talk about it in a way that turns people off, instead of helping them come closer to Christ.

If you are hesitant to share your new faith with your family, the cause is not necessarily fear. It may be a matter of timing. Perhaps they aren't ready to hear about it yet. Or perhaps you need to become more solidly grounded in your faith before you share it with your family. It's one thing to share your faith with a stranger in a shopping mall. It's quite another thing to share it with your own family.

Sharing your new faith with family members can result in rejection and other forms of emotional pressure. You need to be solidly grounded in your faith first. And you should have a support system—fellow Christians who will pray for you and give you wise counsel, practical advice, and moral support.

Remember that there is much more involved than intellectual understanding of doctrines. We are dealing with living people, not with intellectual abstracts. This is ministry, not a debating club. You can win an argument and lose a relationship.

Jesus told us to speak the truth **in love**. There is more involved than an accurate explanation of doctrinal issues. We need to show love and respect for the people we are talking to. And we need to avoid saying, or doing, anything that might make people feel that we are nagging them, or pressuring them.

Jesus left people free to make their own decisions. When the rich young man turned away from Him, Jesus looked on him with love, but he let him go. He did not try to pressure him or manipulate him. (Mark 10:17-22)

We need to follow Jesus' example. If our friends and family members decide to leave the Catholic Church, it should be based on **their** convictions—not ours.

Jesus said: "…ye shall **be** witnesses unto me…" (Acts 1:8) "Be" refers to what we **are**. What we demonstrate in our lives is more important than what we say. Talk is cheap. It's no good talking about the Good News, if we are living like bad news. People will be watching us to see if we have the fruit of the Spirit—"love, joy, peace, longsuffering [patience], gentleness, goodness, faith, meekness, temperance." (Galatians 5:22-23) Our lives should demonstrate God's love.

Remember that we are dealing with people, not just issues. Having people be open to the Gospel is impacted by the kind of relationship that we have with them. We need to show love for them. We can look for opportunities to show them love, consideration, and understanding

When we do speak with our family members and friends, we can ask God to show us what to say and how to say it—and how much to say. In our zeal, it is easy to overload people with more than they can handle at one time. There are two prayers from the Psalms that I find helpful:

"Let the words of my mouth, and the meditation of my heart, be acceptable in thy sight, O LORD, my strength, and my redeemer." (Psalm 19:14)

"Set a watch, O LORD, before my mouth; keep the door of my lips." (Psalm 141:3)

A "watch" is a watchman, a soldier on guard duty. In this prayer, David asks God to be a sentry on guard duty, a sentry who will not allow the wrong words to come out of David's mouth. We can ask God to do the same thing for us.

This is an area where balance is needed. It is good to pray for God's guidance and protection when sharing our faith, but we should not allow ourselves to be hampered by fear of making mistakes. God promised to make everything work out for good for those who love Him. (Romans 8:28). That includes our mistakes.

If we love God, then our mistakes will work out for our good. If the people we are talking to love God, then God can make our mistakes work out for their good. So we can be spontaneous and natural when sharing our faith. We can trust God to reach people, in spite of our failings.

We need to be careful not to develop false expectations, because they can lead to discouragement or confusion. It took many years for me to realize that some foundational teachings of Catholicism were unscriptural. For me, the light came on slowly and gradually, over a long period of time. In contrast, I have a friend who came to salvation within a few hours. Some Christians came to his door and shared the Gospel with him. He left Catholicism, became a born-again Christian, and never looked back. For him, it was a very quick process, almost instantaneous.

Don't assume that it will be slow and difficult (as it was for me), or that it will be quick and easy (as it was for my friend). Just love the people and pray for them, and ask God to guide you. Be grateful for any progress that you see, even if it seems to be small.

It would be good to give them the *Jesus* video. This will help increase their love for Jesus and their desire to know Him better.

The *Jesus* video is widely known for its excellence. It has been translated into over 700 languages. You can order it from the Jesus Film Project. Their phone number is 949-361-7575. They also have a website.

www.JesusFilm.org

The video ends with a salvation message and a prayer. Personally, I would tell people about that, to give them the option of deciding whether or not to watch that part of the video. You don't want them to feel that you tried to sneak something up on them.

Encourage them to read the Bible and get to know Jesus better. (Encourage them **gently**. Don't nag them. In our zeal, we can become pushy without realizing it.)

If you feel that they are ready to learn that there are some problems with Catholicism, I recommend getting the video *Catholicism: Crisis of Faith*. Watch it yourself several times and get to know it. Pray for them to be receptive. Then offer to watch it with them. If you can afford it, you may want to give copies of the video to family members.

This video deals with unscriptural doctrines and practices in a gentle, respectful way. It reaches people on many levels—not just intellectually. (I told you how to order it earlier in this appendix, in the section "Reinforcing Our Foundations.")

Where do we go from here? Pray. Love them. Ask God to guide us. Share about how much Jesus means to us. There are no cookbook formulas or magic fixes. We have to depend on God every step of the way.

A helpful website is Just For Catholics. It has a series of short, simple articles that explain salvation in ways that are especially appropriate for Catholics. These articles are available in several languages. It also has a Questions and Answers section, with about 150 short articles. You can refer your Catholic family members to this website, or you can print the articles for them.

www.JustForCatholics.org

Should you give *Unmasking Catholicism* to your Catholic friends and family members? My book *Another Side of Catholicism* would be more appropriate for them. It covers much of the material of *Unmasking Catholicism*, but it avoids the more difficult issues. It is also shorter, and therefore less expensive. You can buy it at Amazon.com. You can also read the entire book online at its website. You can refer people to the website.

www.AnotherSideOfCatholicism.com

We need to share our faith with the people we love, but at the same time we need to remember that we are not responsible for their salvation. We should do the best that we can, but if they fail to respond, we should not allow ourselves to become discouraged or depressed because of it. Ultimately, it is between them and God.

God doesn't have any grandchildren. Every man and woman has to decide whether or not to become a child of God. We can't do it for them. But we can pray. And we can be encouraged, because God loves them more than we do.

Renewing Our Minds

We former Catholics have habitual ways of thinking that are contrary to Scripture. We also have emotional responses that are rooted in false teachings. The Bible tells us:

> "And be not conformed to this world: but **be ye transformed by the renewing of your mind**, that ye may prove what is that good, and acceptable, and perfect, will of God." (Romans 12:2, emphasis added)

According to *Strong's Concordance*, the Greek word for "transform" is *metamorphoo*. This is the origin of the word "metamorphosis." It means the kind of radical transformation that occurs when a caterpillar becomes a butterfly.

As former Catholics, we need to have our thinking become radically transformed so that it agrees with Scripture, instead of agreeing with the Catholic Church. In addition, some things in our culture are contrary to Scripture. Where there is a conflict, we need to agree with the Bible, instead of agreeing with our culture.

With God's help, we can overcome all of these things. God has enabled His people to overcome everything that exalts itself against the true knowledge of God. The Apostle Paul said:

> "For though we walk in the flesh, we do not war after the flesh: (For the weapons of our warfare are not carnal, but mighty though God to the pulling down of strong holds;) Casting down imaginations, and every high thing that exalteth itself against the knowledge of God, and bringing into captivity every thought to the obedience of Christ" (2 Corinthians 10:3-5)

Since the Bible is the key to renewing our minds, it is important to become thoroughly familiar with it. Our bodies need food every day, and our souls need Scripture every day. We need to develop the habit of reading the Bible and asking God to help us understand it and apply it in our daily lives.

We may have struggles from time to time. Trials and tribulation are a normal part of life. However, God is able to keep us from falling. (Jude 1:24) We can overcome every obstacle, because God is faithful and He loves us.

Prayers

Some people have found the following prayers to be helpful in breaking any remaining spiritual or emotional attachments to the Roman Catholic Church. Before you read them, I'd like to say a few words about written prayers.

When we were Catholics, we were used to "canned" prayers. We said them during Mass. Many of us prayed rosaries. Some of us recited written prayers, such as novenas, litanies, and prayers which were given to visionaries by apparitions of "Mary." Some written prayers were "indulgenced." If you said them, you were supposed to get indulgences.

I remember being told that certain prayers always "worked"—if you said them, you would get what you wanted. This was treating prayers as if they were magic formulas. God is not a Coke machine. You can't put in the "right" words and have your Coke (the thing you wanted to get) automatically come out.

However, there is nothing wrong with using written prayers, if it is done in the right spirit. We pray the Lord's prayer. Some hymns are prayers.

The following prayers are just examples. You may want to use them as prayers, or you may prefer to look at their content, and then share your heart with God in whatever way is appropriate for you.

Loyalty
Heavenly Father, I renounce every form of false loyalty. My primary loyalty belongs to You alone. I used to give the Catholic Church a degree of love, trust, loyalty, and gratitude that should only have been given to You. Please forgive me for that. I repent for every way in which I have put other things ahead of You. Please help me put You first all of the time. Please help me see things from Your perspective. In the name of Jesus. Amen

The Bible
Heavenly Father, please help me understand the Bible, trust it, and apply it to my life in practical ways. Please help me think biblically and have biblical responses to practical situations. Please remove every hindrance to having my thoughts and my emotions agree with Scripture. Please make me hungry for

Your truth. Please help me know You, love You, and trust You. In the name of Jesus. Amen.

False Doctrines
Heavenly Father, I renounce every false doctrine that I have believed. I repent of having believed these unbiblical doctrines. Please uproot them from my heart and from my mind. Please open my eyes to the truth of the Bible, and set me free from every false teaching. I renounce pagan philosophy and ungodly mystical experiences. I renounce every belief that is based on them. Please give me a renewed mind and a renewed heart. Please enable me to recognize whether or not teachings are consistent with the Bible and with Your nature and character. In the name of Jesus. Amen.

Unbiblical Prayers
Heavenly Father, I renounce the repetition of special verbal formulas. I repent for using them. Please teach me how to trust Your love for me. Please teach me how to share my heart with You, like a trusting child. In the name of Jesus. Amen.

Idolatry
Heavenly Father, I renounce every form of idolatry. I repent for every way in which I have participated in idolatry. Only You are holy. Only You can save me. Only You are worthy of worship. Please remove all idolatry from my heart, my mind, my emotions, my imagination, and my life. If I start to do anything idolatrous, please show me and help me repent. Please help me worship You with all of my heart, with all of my mind, with all of my strength, with all of my soul, and with all of my loyalty. Please teach me to worship You in spirit and in truth. In the name of Jesus. Amen.

Authority
Heavenly Father, I used to give priests and popes a kind of trust that should only be given to You. I put my conscience in their hands, instead of looking to the Bible to show me what is right. I accepted what they taught me, without questioning it, instead of testing it against Scripture. Please forgive me for these things. Please help me trust You directly. Please help me find the moral guidance I need in the Bible. Please help me become a mature Christian who takes responsibility for my own beliefs and my own decisions. In the name of Jesus. Amen.

Rituals
Heavenly Father, I repent of trusting in rituals and objects instead of trusting directly in Your love for me. I repent of attributing power to rituals and objects, instead of believing in Your power, Your love, and Your faithfulness. I repent of praying to dead people (Mary and the saints). I renounce every form of communication with dead people. Please get these things out of my heart and out of my life. Please set me free from any influence of paganism or the occult. Please set me free from any spiritual or emotional harm that was caused by these things. Please increase my faith in You and help me trust You more. In the name of Jesus. Amen.

Objects
Heavenly Father, I am willing to get rid of any object that is associated with idolatry or other false religious practices. Please make me aware of these objects and help me get rid of them. Please set me free from any form of spiritual or emotional bondage. Please set me free from any influence of false religion. Lord God, You are my protector, and my deliverer. Please increase my confidence in Your love for me, and Your ability to take good care of me. In the name of Jesus. Amen.

Saints
Heavenly Father, I repent of asking saints to pray for me. I repent of trying to communicate with dead people (the saints) and asking them to help me. I repent of honoring them and trusting in them. Help me trust You, the living God. In the name of Jesus. Amen.

Mary
Heavenly Father, the Bible says that Mary was an ordinary woman who needed a savior just like the rest of us do. The Bible tells us not to try to communicate with dead people. I repent of praying to Mary, venerating Mary, and singing songs in her honor. I renounce every special title that the Catholic Church has given to Mary. I repent of anything I have said or done because of apparitions of "Mary." I repent of any way in which I have consecrated myself to Mary. Please forgive me for believing Catholic doctrines that exalt Mary above other people. Please get these things out of my heart, out of my mind, and out of my life. In the name of Jesus. Amen.

Forgiving

Heavenly Father, I choose to forgive every person who taught me false doctrines or ungodly religious practices. Please work in my heart so that I will completely forgive these people. In the name of Jesus. Amen.

Giving Thanks

Heavenly Father, thank You for setting me free from every form of bondage to the Catholic Church. Please help me live according to the freedom that You have given me. Please help me grow into a strong, mature Christian. Please increase my faith in You, my trust in You, and my loyalty to You. Help me trust Your goodness, Your faithfulness, Your love, and Your mercy. I want my life to glorify You. I want to demonstrate Your love and Your character. In the name of Jesus. Amen.

Praying Scripture

Many Catholics spend their lives praying written prayers. They have not learned how to pray naturally and spontaneously from their heart.

I have found it helpful to use the Bible as a springboard for personal prayers. That isn't the only way that I pray, but it is something that I often do when reading Scripture. If you are not used to praying spontaneously, Scriptural praying can help you get started.

There are many prayers in the Bible. Have you ever prayed through them, as if they were your own? It is one way of having Scripture become a part of us.

It is also a way of knowing that we are praying according to God's will. For example, if God showed the Apostle Paul that Christians need wisdom and revelation, then we know that praying for those things is according to God's will. We can use Paul's prayer as a springboard for our own prayers.

When we pray the Lord's Prayer, we are praying according to Scripture. But there are many other Biblical prayers that we can pray. We can appropriate them and make them our own. For example, here is one of Paul's prayers for the Christians in Ephesus:

> "For this cause I bow my knees unto the Father of our Lord Jesus Christ, Of whom the whole family in heaven and earth is named, That he would grant you, according to the riches of his glory, to be strengthened with might by his Spirit in the inner man; That Christ may dwell in your hearts by faith; that ye, being rooted and grounded in love, May be able to comprehend with all saints what is the breadth, and length,

> and depth, and height; And to know the love of Christ, which passeth knowledge, that ye might be filled with all the fullness of God. Now unto him that is able to do exceeding abundantly above all that we ask or think, according to the power that worketh in us, Unto him be glory in the church by Christ Jesus throughout all ages, world without end. Amen." (Ephesians 3:14-21)

At first, this may look intimidating. Most of this is one long, complicated sentence. However, we can break it down into bite-sized pieces.

There are many ways that this passage could be approached. I will give an example. This is how I approached that Scripture passage. As you read it, you may see ways that are more appropriate for you. Also, every time you come to this passage, you may find new treasures in it and new ways to pray it. Please take the following as just one possible working example of how this Scripture passage could be prayed.

> Father God, thank You for being my Father in Heaven. Thank you for the riches of your glory. Please give me a revelation of Your goodness and Your glory, and the wonderful treasures that are to be found in You. Lord God, please strengthen me with Your might, by Your Holy Spirit, in my inner man. May Jesus Christ dwell in my heart by faith. Lord, I want to be rooted and grounded in Your love. And I can't do that. I can't make it happen. Please make me like a plant whose roots go down deep into Your love. Make Your love become my source of strength and protection and nourishment. Make the revelation of Your love become a source of vision and motivation for my life. Use me to minister Your love to other people. Lord God, give me a revelation of Your love. Help me comprehend it. Show me how great and how deep Your love is. Enable me to know the love of Christ, which is so great and so pure and so beautiful that it is beyond my understanding. Holy God, thank You that you are able to do far more than anything I can ask or imagine. Thank you for Your great power that is working in me. Lord, may You be glorified. Change my heart, and make me someone whose life glorifies You.

As you read the Bible, you will find many prayers. You will also find many statements that clearly indicate God's will for us, which can be the basis for prayers. Some passages can be prayed directly, word for word. One of my favorites is in Psalm 139:

> "Search me, O God, and know my heart; try me, and know my thoughts: And see if there be any wicked way in me, and lead me in the way everlasting." (Psalm 139:23-24)

I also like to participate in the heavenly worship that was shown to the Apostle John in the Book of Revelation. We can share in the song of the Redeemed:

> "…Worthy is the Lamb that was slain to receive power, and riches, and wisdom, and strength, and honour, and glory, and blessing." (Revelation 5:12)

Isaiah also had a vision of heavenly worship. I like to join in the prayer of the seraphim, who cry out to one another:

> "Holy, holy, holy, is the LORD of hosts: the whole earth is full of his glory." (Isaiah 6:3)

Leaving the Past Behind

Our past experience as Catholics can be useful. We can draw from it to help other people. But in a sense, we need to leave it behind us. Our focus needs to be forward, on the new things that God has for us. The Apostle Paul said:

> "…forgetting those things which are behind, and reaching forth unto those things which are before, I press toward the mark for the prize of the high calling of God in Christ Jesus." (Philippians 3:13-14)

We need to get to know God better. We need to have our minds become transformed by the truth of Scripture. We need to learn to trust God at a deeper level, and commit our lives to Him in a more radical way.

God has good adventures waiting for us. He has things that are "exceeding abundantly above all that we ask or think, according to the power that worketh in us." (Ephesians 3:20)

I'd like to share a poem with you.

> *Following Jesus, my Lord and my Savior.*
> *Leaving the past behind.*
>
> *I press on to the mark of God's high calling.*
> *Leaving the past behind.*
>
> *Forgiving, forgetting, and giving to Jesus.*
> *Leaving the past behind.*
>
> *Replacing old voices with the truth of the Bible.*
> *Leaving the past behind.*

May the Lord bless you, comfort you, strengthen you, and encourage you. May He increase your love for the Bible and give you greater understanding of it. And may He give you an ever-increasing revelation of how much He loves you.

Appendix C

Glossary

ABBOT. The superior of an abbey (a large, independent monastery).

ABSOLUTION. According to Catholic doctrine, during the sacrament of reconciliation (confession), a qualified Catholic priest can absolve Catholics from their sins. (Sacraments are rituals that use objects and actions in order to confer spiritual benefits. When the priest absolves sins, he makes the sign of the cross and recites a precise verbal formula.)

ADORATION OF THE BLESSED SACRAMENT. According to Catholic doctrine, the body, blood, soul, and divinity of Jesus Christ are literally present in every crumb of consecrated bread and every drop of consecrated wine. Therefore, the custom of worshiping consecrated bread is encouraged. A consecrated Host (a large communion wafer) is placed in a monstrance (a special container for displaying the Host). Catholics worship the Host as if it was Jesus Christ Himself, in person, in front of them.

ALTAR. A special table on which the sacrifice of the Mass is offered. Fixed altars (the kind found in churches) contain an altar stone. This is a small, flat stone that is consecrated by a bishop. It has a cavity that contains the relics of two canonized martyrs. It is usually inserted into the center of an altar. During Mass, the ciborium (which contains the Host and smaller communion wafers) and the chalice (which contains the wine) are placed on top of the altar stone.

ANATHEMA. The most severe form of excommunication. It includes a solemn ecclesiastical curse. This can happen automatically. For example, according to the Council of Trent, any person who believes that Christians are saved by faith alone is automatically anathematized. It can also be done using a formal, written ritual, during which the Pope or his representative "sentences" people to be cursed to damnation, unless they "repent" and unconditionally submit their thoughts and actions to the Catholic Church.

ANOINTING OF THE SICK (Last Rites; Extreme Unction). A sacrament in which the priest anoints the hands and forehead of a sick Catholic, using olive oil that has been blessed by a bishop. He says a prayer that is a standard verbal formula. This is traditionally done when Catholics are in danger of dying.

APOSTOLIC. Papal; relating to the Pope. For example, an apostolic delegate is a man who represents the Pope.

APOSTOLIC SEE (Holy See). (1) The official residence of the Pope in Rome. (2) The offices of Vatican officials who assist the Pope. (3) The power and authority of the Pope.

APPARITION. "Mary," "Jesus," angels, or saints appear to people. Some apparitions have been officially approved by the Roman Catholic Church. In other words, Catholic Church officials have formally declared that the apparition is genuine and it has not said or done anything that is contrary to Catholic doctrine. Two well known apparitions that have been officially approved are apparitions of "Mary" at Lourdes, France and Fatima, Portugal.

ASH WEDNESDAY. The first day of Lent. Blessed palms are burned to make ashes. The priests put the ashes on the foreheads of the people. This is a sign of penance.

ATONE. To make amends for an offense; to expiate; to restore harmony between individuals. Jesus atoned for our sins.

ATONEMENT. When Jesus Christ voluntarily died on the cross, He atoned for the sins of mankind. When Jesus was on the cross, He said: "It is finished." However, according to the Catholic Church, when God forgives sins, He may still require that the sinner atone for his or her sins by suffering, either here on earth, or else in Purgatory. According to this doctrine, the death of Jesus Christ was not sufficient to fully pay for our sins. We also have to pay for them.

AVE MARIA (Hail Mary). This traditional prayer to Mary is associated with the rosary, but it is also used for other things. The words are: "Hail Mary, full of grace, the Lord is with thee. Blessed art thou among women and blessed is the fruit of thy womb, Jesus. Holy Mary, mother of God, pray for us sinners, now and at the hour of our death."

BAPTISM. According to Catholic doctrine, the sacrament of baptism cleanses the person who is baptized from all sin. As a result, he or she becomes reborn (born again). It is the sacrament that is said to remove the sin, rather than God's response to the repentance of the person who is baptized. It is the sacrament that is said to cause a person to become born again, rather than the faith of the person who is baptized.

BAPTISMAL GRACES. According to Catholic doctrine, the sacrament of baptism supernaturally accomplishes the following things: (1) It removes all of the guilt of sin. (2) It removes all of the punishment due for past sins. (3) It infuses sanctifying grace into the person. (4) It infuses faith, hope, and charity into the person. (5) It makes the person a member of the Mystical Body of Christ. (See "Mystical Body of Christ.")

BAPTISMAL WATER. A special kind of holy water that is used for the sacrament of baptism. It is ritually blessed on Holy Saturday (the day before Easter Sunday). Baptismal water is a sacramental (an object or action that is supposed to confer spiritual benefits and that has been approved by the Catholic Church).

BEATIFICATION. An official declaration by the Pope that a deceased man or woman is in Heaven. People who have been beatified are given the title "Blessed." Catholics are allowed to publicly pray to them, invoke them, and venerate them.

BENEDICTION. A priest holds up a monstrance containing a consecrated Host (a large communion wafer). He makes the sign of the cross with the monstrance and pronounces a blessing. Catholics perceive this as having been blessed by Jesus Christ Himself. (A monstrance is an ornate container for displaying a consecrated Host.)

BISHOP. According to Catholic doctrine, a bishop is a successor of the Apostles. A bishop has the authority to ordain priests.

BLESSED MOTHER. A term used to honor the Virgin Mary.

BLESSED SACRAMENT (the Eucharist; Holy Communion). Bread and wine that have been consecrated by a priest during Mass. According to Catholic doctrine, the bread and wine literally become the body, blood, soul, and divinity of Jesus Christ. The Catholic Church uses real wine, but it uses communion wafers instead of regular bread.

BLESSED SALT. Salt that has been ritually blessed by a priest. Blessed salt is a sacramental. It is use to protect people from evil. Some people sprinkle blessed salt across thresholds, or in cars, for protection. Some people put it in food or drinking water for physical healing.

BREVIARY. A liturgical book that contains the Divine Office (a collection of hymns, written prayers, Psalms, and readings from Scripture).

BROWN SCAPULAR. According to tradition, in 1251, the Virgin Mary appeared to Saint Simon Stock. She carried a Brown Scapular. She promised that people who are wearing the Brown Scapular when they die will not go to Hell. Wearing the Brown Scapular also enables people to receive the benefits of the Sabbatine Privilege (a promise that Mary will get people out of Purgatory). The use of the Brown Scapular has been strongly recommended by many popes, including Pope Paul VI (1963-1978).

BULL (Papal Bull). A papal encyclical dealing with especially important matters. (An encyclical is a letter written by the Pope to the bishops.)

The term "bull" comes from a special seal (*bulla*) that is put on the encyclical, because of its importance.

CANDLE. (1) A sacramental that is used in the liturgy of the Catholic Church. Candles are blessed on Candlemas (February 2). (2) Objects used in private devotional practices, such as votive candles placed in front of statues, and novena candles that are burned while praying novena prayers.

CANON LAW. The ecclesiastical laws that are used to govern the Roman Catholic Church.

CANONIZATION. An official declaration by the Pope that a deceased man or woman is a saint and is in Heaven. When people have been beatified, Catholics are allowed to pray to them and venerate them. It is optional. When people have been canonized, then Catholics are required to venerate them. Honoring canonized saints is mandatory.

CARDINAL. Apart from the Pope, cardinals hold the highest office in the Catholic Church. They assist the Pope with the government of the Catholic Church. Originally, men could become Pope through various means. Later, popes were (and still are) elected by cardinals. In order to qualify to be elected Pope, a man must first be a cardinal. Cardinals have the honor of being allowed to wear scarlet hats and scarlet cassocks.

CARDINAL'S PURPLE. A term for the color scarlet. Purple used to be a very expensive dye. The color was associated with wealth and power. Purple was worn by Roman Emperors and Roman Catholic popes. In the Middle Ages, scarlet also became associated with wealth and power. It was (and is) worn by Roman Catholic cardinals.

CASSOCK. A long garment that reaches to the feet. It is worn by Catholic clergymen. Cardinals are allowed to wear scarlet cassocks. Depending on the occasion, cardinals wear a cassock that is scarlet, or else they wear a cassock that is black, with scarlet buttons and a wide scarlet sash.

CHALICE. A large goblet used at Mass to contain the wine for consecration. A chalice is consecrated by a bishop, using holy chrism.

CHAPLET. Chaplets are prayers that are said using beads. Some of them, such as the Chaplet of Divine Mercy, use regular rosary beads, but with different prayers. Others, such as the Chaplet of Saint Michael the Archangel and the Chaplet of Saint Joseph, use different beads.

CHRISM. A mixture of olive oil and balsam (an aromatic substance from plants). It is a sacramental that is consecrated by a bishop. Chrism is used in the sacraments of baptism, confirmation, and holy orders (ordination). It is used when blessing baptismal water and church tower bells, and when consecrating churches, altars, chalices, and patens.

CIBORIUM. A covered container that holds communion wafers during Mass. It is similar to a chalice, but larger.

CLERGY. Men who are ordained as deacons, priests or bishops. Clergymen are also called clerics.

CLERICAL. Something that relates to clergy.

CLOISTER. A secluded monastery or convent. In a strictly cloistered convent, the nuns are cut off from the rest of the world. If visitors come to see the nuns, they are separated from them by a grille. This allows conversation and eye contact, but it prevents any kind of physical contact.

COLORS. Colors are used to indicate the rank and importance of Catholic clergy. Priests wear black. Bishops wear purple. Cardinals wear scarlet. There are two special hats that can be worn by bishops and cardinals. One is a skull cap, called a zucchetto. The other is a special kind of cap that is square, with three ridges or peaks on its upper surface. It is called a biretta (or berretta). Bishops are allowed to wear purple zucchettos and birettas, and a purple cassock with crimson trimmings. (A cassock is a long, loose, priestly garment.) Cardinals are allowed to wear scarlet zucchettos, birettas, and cassocks.

COMMUNION (the Eucharist). Bread and wine that have been consecrated by a priest during the sacrament of the Mass. (The priest has performed the ritual of consecration using the correct verbal formula.) According to Catholic doctrine, the bread and wine literally become the body, blood, soul, and divinity of Jesus Christ. The Catholic Church uses real wine, but it uses communion wafers instead of regular bread.

COMMUNION OF SAINTS. According to Catholic doctrine, there is unity among the members of the Catholic Church on earth, in Heaven, and in Purgatory, and they help one another through prayers and good works. Catholics on earth are said to be in communion with the saints in Heaven, because they venerate them, imitate them, pray to them, and invoke their assistance. Catholics on earth are said to be in communion with the souls in Purgatory, because they do things to help them get out of Purgatory (prayers, good works, having masses said for them, and earning indulgences on their behalf).

COMMUNION WAFERS. The Catholic Church uses communion wafers for Mass instead of regular bread. The priest uses a large communion wafer called a Host. People attending Mass eat small communion wafers. They are round, thin, and flat.

CONCLAVE. During an election for a new Pope, the cardinals are kept enclosed in the Sistine Chapel until the new Pope is chosen. The term "conclave" refers to: (1) The temporary living quarters of the cardinals; and (2) The gathering of cardinals who elect the Pope.

CONCORDAT. A treaty between the Holy See (the Vatican) and the ruler of a sovereign nation.

CONFESSION (Sacrament of Penance; Sacrament of Reconciliation). According to Catholic doctrine, Catholics can have their sins be absolved by a qualified Catholic priest. This is done using a ritual that includes the "words of absolution" (a verbal formula that the priest uses to absolve the sins).

CONFESSIONAL. An enclosed place where a priest sits to hear confessions. There is a partition, with the priest sitting on one side of it, and the person confessing his or her sins sitting on the other side of it. There is a small screened window that allows the priest to talk to the penitent.

CONFIRMATION. According to Catholic doctrine, this sacrament causes baptized Catholics to be strengthened by the Holy Spirit. It involves the laying on of hands and anointing with chrism.

CONSECRATE. (1) To declare something to be holy or to make it holy. (2) To set something apart for service to God or worship of God. (3) To make bread and wine turn into the body, blood, soul, and divinity of Jesus Christ.

CONSECRATION. (1) An event that occurs during the sacrament of the Mass. The priest says words of consecration (a verbal formula). According to Catholic doctrine, when those words are said by a validly ordained Catholic priest, then the bread and wine literally become the body, blood, soul and divinity of Jesus Christ. (2) Setting something apart for God, or for liturgical use by the Catholic Church. For example, bishops consecrate chrism. The consecrated chrism is used by bishops when they consecrate chalices and churches.

CONTEMPLATIVE LIFE. Religious life that stresses prayer, self-denial, and meditation on spiritual things.

CONVENT. A nunnery. A community of nuns who are governed by a superior.

CRUCIFIX. An image of Christ on the cross. It can be a carving, a painting, a medal, or any other representation of the crucifixion of Christ.

CRUSADES. Popes raised armies to take the Holy Land (Israel) back from the Muslims. The Albigensian massacre was a crusade against Christians. Hundreds of thousands of French people were killed by the Crusaders, including Catholics who lived in the area inhabited by the Albigensians.

CURIA (Roman Curia). A group of men in the Vatican who assist the Pope in directing the operations of the Catholic Church.

DECADE. A rosary is made of five sets of decades. Each decade has one bead that is separated from a group of ten beads. The "Our Father" (Lord's Prayer) is said on the single bead. The "Hail Mary" is said on the ten beads. (There are ten prayers to Mary for every one prayer to God.) The words of the "Hail Mary" are: "Hail Mary, full of grace, the Lord is with thee. Blessed art thou among women and blessed is the fruit of thy womb, Jesus. Holy Mary, mother of God, pray for us sinners, now and at the hour of our death."

DIVINE MERCY. Saint Faustina had an apparition of "Jesus" who showed her a picture. He said that souls who venerate that image will not perish. The picture shows Jesus with rays of light coming out of His chest. It has an inscription: "Jesus I trust in you." The apparition taught Sister Faustina some devotional practices based on the Divine Mercy of Jesus. There is a chaplet of Divine Mercy, which he said would be especially effective if it is prayed at 3:00 o'clock (the "hour of divine mercy"). There is a Novena of Mercy which is prayed from Good Friday until the Sunday after Easter.

DIVINE OFFICE. A liturgical book that contains written prayers, hymns, and readings from Scripture. All 150 Psalms are read every week. However, the longer psalms are not read in their entirety. Only portions of them are read. The Divine Office is read by priests, monks, and nuns. In some religious communities, it is sung publicly. It is traditional to use Gregorian chant when singing it.

ECCLESIASTICAL. Something that relates to the church.

ENCYCLICAL. A document that the Pope sends to the bishops, dealing with matters related to the general welfare of the Catholic Church. They often contain pronouncements about matters of faith and morals. Encyclicals that deal with especially important matters are called "papal bulls."

EUCHARIST (the Blessed Sacrament; Holy Communion). Bread and wine that have been consecrated by a priest during Mass.

EXCOMMUNICATION. Cutting a person, or group of people, off from the Roman Catholic Church and its sacraments. The most severe form of excommunication is the anathema, which can be accompanied by a solemn, written ritual, with ecclesiastical curses.

EXTREME UNCTION (Anointing of the Sick; Last Rites). A sacrament in which a priest anoints the hands and forehead of a sick person, using olive oil that has been blessed by a bishop. The priest says a prayer that is a standard verbal formula. This is traditionally done when a Catholic is in danger of dying.

FASTING. A form of penance that involves abstaining from particular foods, or limiting the quantity of foods eaten. Fasting requirements are determined by local Catholic bishops. The rules change from time to time. At present (2003), American Catholics are required to abstain from eating the meat of birds or land animals on Ash Wednesday and Fridays during Lent. However, they are allowed to eat fish. In 1997, the American bishops met to decide whether or not to again require Catholics to abstain from eating meat on all Fridays. According to Canon Law, abstaining from eating meat on all Fridays is mandatory, unless the bishops substitute other forms of penance for it. (See "Lent.")

FEAST DAYS. Days on which Mary, angels, saints, or sacred events are honored.

FINAL PENITENCE. Having a person's sins be absolved by a priest before the person dies.

FINAL PERSEVERANCE. Having a person be in a state of grace when he or she dies.

FINGER ROSARY. A small pocket rosary with one decade of beads that touch each other. It looks like a ring with bumps on it and a cross attached to it. People can put it on their index finger and move through the beads with their thumb. When they come to the cross, then they know that they have completed the decade. One variation of the finger rosary is the rosary ring.

FIRST FRIDAYS. According to tradition, Jesus appeared to Saint Margaret Mary Alacoque in 1699. He asked her to observe the "Devotion of First Fridays" (receiving Communion on the first Friday of nine consecutive months). He also asked that people keep a picture of the Sacred Heart of Jesus in their homes and honor it. He promised that if people do these things, then their names will be written in Jesus' Heart and will never be blotted out, and the Sacred Heart of Jesus will be their refuge when they die.

FIRST SATURDAYS. Our Lady of Fatima (the apparition of "Mary" at Fatima, Portugal) gave promises of things she would do for Catholics who observe the "Devotion of First Saturdays." In order to fulfill the conditions for receiving the promises, Catholics have to do the following things on the first Saturday of five consecutive months: (1) Go to confession (the sacrament of reconciliation); (2) Receive communion (this requires them to attend Mass); (3) Pray the rosary; (4) Spend 15 minutes "keeping Mary company"; (5) Consecrate themselves to the Immaculate Heart of Mary; and (6) Do these things with the intention of making reparation to Mary for sin. The apparitions at Fatima were officially approved by the Roman Catholic Church. Therefore, the observation of First Saturdays (including making reparation to **Mary** for sin) does not conflict with Catholic doctrine.

FLAGELLATE. To flog, whip, scourge. Flagellation has traditionally been used as a form of penance, to mortify the body and to atone for sin. Padre Pio is a modern example of a Catholic priest who was known for whipping himself.

After the Second Vatican Council (1962-1965), flagellation became less common.

FLAGELLANTS. People who whip or scourge themselves, or one another, as an act of penance or atonement for sin. On Good Friday (the Friday before Easter), some countries have processions of flagellants who whip themselves or one another.

GENUFLECT. A gesture of reverence or worship. One knee goes down to the floor and the other knee remains bent. It is traditional to genuflect in front of the Blessed Sacrament (bread that has been consecrated during Mass) and before entering a church pew. It is also traditional to genuflect before the Pope, a cardinal, or a bishop, and to kiss his ring.

GOOD FRIDAY. The Friday before Easter. Traditionally, there are services in honor of the crucifixion of Jesus.

GRACE. Catholic perception of grace is different from that of Protestants. This can be illustrated by the following two examples. (1) According to Catholic liturgy, grace can be given to inanimate objects. The Catholic ritual for baptizing infants includes a prayer asking God to give grace to the water that will be used. (2) Grace is said to be automatically given to people as a result of the sacraments. (One example is "baptismal graces.")

GREEN SCAPULAR. According to tradition, the Virgin Mary appeared to Sister Justine Bisqueyburu in 1840. Mary was carrying the Green Scapular. It had a picture of Mary's heart, pierced with a sword, with drops of blood coming out of it. On the scapular was written the following prayer: "Immaculate Heart of Mary, pray for us now and at the hour of our death." Healings have been attributed to the Green Scapular.

HABIT. Special clothing that is worn by monks and nuns. Each religious order has its own distinctive habit.

HAIL MARY. This prayer to Mary is associated with the rosary, but it is also used for other things. The words are: "Hail Mary, full of grace, the Lord is with thee. Blessed art thou among women and blessed is the fruit of thy womb, Jesus. Holy Mary, mother of God, pray for us sinners, now and at the hour of our death."

HERESY. If a person claims to be a Christian, and he or she believes something that is contrary to Catholic doctrine, then the Catholic Church calls that belief a heresy.

HERETIC. A person who teaches or believes a heresy. According to the Catholic Church, in order to be considered heretics, people must have been baptized, they must claim to be Christians, and they must doubt or deny a Catholic doctrine. In addition, the Catholic Church must consider their disbelief to be "morally culpable." However, in Spain, the

Inquisition killed Jews and Muslims as heretics, in spite of the fact that they were not baptized and they did not claim to be Christians. During the Protestant Reformation, men and women who had been born and raised as Protestants were killed as heretics.

HOLY CARDS. Cards that have religious pictures related to Catholicism. These include pictures of Jesus, Mary, saints, popes, or shrines. There is often a prayer written on the back of the card. Sometimes holy cards commemorate special events, such as a child's first communion.

HOLY CHRISM. A mixture of olive oil and balsam (an aromatic substance from plants). It is a sacramental that is consecrated by a bishop. Chrism is used in the sacraments of baptism, confirmation, and holy orders (ordination). It is used when blessing baptismal water, and when consecrating churches, altars, chalices, and patens.

HOLY COMMUNION (the Eucharist; the Blessed Sacrament). Bread and wine that have been consecrated by a priest during Mass.

HOLY DAYS OF OBLIGATION. Special days on which Catholics are required to attend Mass. Attendance at Mass is mandatory for Catholics on Sundays and on holy days of obligation.

HOLY FATHER. A term used by Jesus to address God, and by Catholics to address the Pope.

HOLY MOTHER CHURCH. A term used for the Roman Catholic Church. This is why writers sometimes refer to the Catholic Church as "she" rather than "it."

HOLY OFFICE. Another name for the Office of the Inquisition. In 1965, its name was changed to The Congregation for the Doctrine of the Faith.

HOLY OILS. (1) Holy oils for liturgical use are sacramentals. They are blessed by a bishop. There are three kinds of holy oil: oil of catechumens (used for baptism), chrism, and oil of the sick (for anointing the sick). Oil of catechumens and oil of the sick are pure olive oil. Chrism is a mixture of olive oil with balm or balsam (an aromatic substance). Holy oils are used for the sacraments of baptism, confirmation, and the anointing of the sick. The blessing of the holy oils is done by a bishop on Holy Thursday (the Thursday before Easter). The oils are distributed to local churches, where they are kept in locked boxes. Any oil that is not used within a year is burned in the sanctuary lamp. (2) There are holy oils for personal use. They are usually taken from oil lamps burning at shrines. Some examples are: Saint Anne's Oil, Saint Joseph's Oil, and Saint Philomena's Oil. Healings have been attributed to Saint Anne's Oil.

HOLY ORDERS. The sacrament of ordination. Deacons, priests, and bishops are ordained.

HOLY SEE (Apostolic See). (1) The official residence of the Pope in Rome. (2) The offices of Vatican officials who assist the Pope. (3) The power and authority of the Pope.

HOLY WATER. Holy water is a sacramental. It is blessed by a priest, using chrism. When Catholics enter a Catholic Church, they often dip their fingers in holy water and make the sign of the cross. Priests use holy water when blessing people or objects. In addition to ordinary holy water, there are also some special kinds of holy water. Baptismal holy water is used in the sacrament of baptism. Easter holy water is used during the Paschal Season (the period of time from the Saturday before Easter to the Saturday after Pentecost). Some Catholics keep holy water in their homes and use it during times of physical or spiritual danger. Some people sprinkle it around their home, sprinkle it on themselves or other people, or drink it.

HOST. A large communion wafer, which is used by the priest when saying Mass.

IMMACULATE CONCEPTION. The doctrine that Mary was conceived without sin, that she did not have "original sin" (the sin inherited from Adam).

IMMACULATE HEART OF MARY. There is a picture that represents the Immaculate Heart of Mary. It shows Mary with her chest open, her heart exposed, flames above it, light coming out of it, and a sword piercing it. The apparition of "Mary" at Fatima, Portugal, told people to consecrate themselves to the Immaculate Heart of Mary, using a special prayer.

INCENSE. Incense is an aromatic gum or resin, that is in the form of powder or grains, so that it can readily be burned. It gives off a fragrant smoke. Priests carry burning incense in a censer (a special container that releases the fragrance and protects the priest from the heat of the burning material). Incense that has been blessed is a sacramental. It is used during Mass, at Benediction, and during processions. Five large grains of incense are placed in the Paschal Candle, symbolizing the five wounds of Christ. The Paschal Candle is used during the Paschal Season (the period of time from the Saturday before Easter to the Saturday following Pentecost).

INDULGENCED. Prayers and pious acts for which the Catholic Church grants indulgences. In addition to praying the indulgenced prayers or doing the indulgenced acts, the Catholic must also: (1) Go to confession (the sacrament of reconciliation); (2) Take communion (which means going to Mass); and (3) Pray for the Pope's "intentions." ("Intentions" mean prayer requests that have not been specifically identified by the person who wants prayer for them.) Indulgenced prayers and indulgenced pious practices are listed in *The Enchiridion of Indulgences*, which is published by the Vatican.

INDULGENCES. According to Catholic doctrine, when God forgives sins, He may still require that the sinner pay for his or her sins by suffering. When good Catholics die, if they are not saintly enough to go directly to Heaven, then they have to spend time suffering in Purgatory, in order to atone for their sins. However, the suffering of the souls in Purgatory can be shortened by means of indulgences. According to the Catholic Church, there is a "treasury" of merits that have been won by Christ and the saints. The Catholic Church claims that it is able to draw from this "treasury," in order to remit the temporal punishments that are required for sins that have already been forgiven by God. This is done by means of indulgences, which the Catholic Church gives to people who do certain good works. In modern times, earning indulgences is done primarily by means of praying indulgenced prayers (such as the rosary), or participating in indulgenced pious practices (such as adoration of the Blessed Sacrament). During the Middle Ages, indulgences were sold for money. Indulgences can be applied to the person earning them, or to loved ones who are in Purgatory.

INFALLIBILITY. According to Catholic doctrine, God protects the Pope from making errors whenever he teaches the Catholic Church in matters of faith or morals. In order to speak infallibly, the Pope must speak *ex cathedra* (with the weight of his apostolic authority, as opposed to speaking as a private theologian.) However, according to Canon Law, Catholics are required to submit their minds and wills to **any** declaration concerning faith or morals that is made by the Pope. They are also required to avoid anything that disagrees with such declarations, and they can be coerced if they don't comply. In other words, they must respond as if the statement is infallible, whether or not the Pope has spoken *ex cathedra*. This gives the Catholic Church the power over people that comes from infallibility, without requiring the accountability that is associated with infallibility. If one infallible papal pronouncement contradicts another infallible papal pronouncement, then the theologians and apologists can attempt to avoid the dilemma by saying that one (or both) of the popes was just speaking as a private theologian. In the meantime, the Catholic people were required to obey both papal pronouncements as if they were infallible.

INFANT OF PRAGUE. A statue of Jesus as an infant. Miracles have been attributed to this statue. It is kept in Prague, Czechoslovakia, where nuns care for it and change its clothing. Pilgrims travel to Prague to venerate this statue. It wears a gold crown set with jewels. It also has over 70 sets of ornate clothes. Replicas of the statue are found in Catholic churches around the world.

INQUISITION. The Office of the Inquisition was established to suppress heresy. Inquisitors sought out "heretics." They tortured the "heretics" to get confessions. They had trials in which the Inquisitors were the judges and the "heretics" had no one to defend them. In addition, the "heretics" were never told what the charges against them were. The Inquisitors passed sentences on the "heretics" and then required the local civil authorities to carry out the sentences. The last execution for heresy was in 1826. However, the Office of the Inquisition still exists. In 1965, its name was changed to The Congregation for the Doctrine of the Faith.

INTERDICT. Catholics under interdict are not allowed to have a Christian burial. Most of the sacraments are denied to them. However, dying Catholics are allowed to receive the Last Rites. For centuries, popes used the interdict, and the threat of interdict, to force secular rulers to submit to them.

KISSING THE SACRED PURPLE. In formal correspondence with high-ranking clergy, it used to be proper protocol to say "kissing the Sacred Purple," or "kissing the Sacred Ring." In 1969, the rules were changed and this was no longer required.

LAST RITES (Sacrament of the Sick; Extreme Unction). A sacrament in which a priest anoints the hands and forehead of the sick person, using olive oil that has been blessed by a bishop. The priest says a prayer that is a standard verbal formula. This is traditionally done when Catholics are in danger of dying.

LATIN. (1) The language of ancient Rome. (2) The language of the Roman Catholic Church. Until the Second Vatican Council (1962-1965), Mass was said in Latin and the Divine Office was said or sung in Latin. Official Roman Catholic Church documents are still written in Latin, including papal encyclicals and Canon Law. Latin is still the language of the Vatican.

LENT. A 40-day period of prayer and penance before Easter. It begins on Ash Wednesday and ends on Easter Sunday. During Lent, Catholics are required to fast. The fasting requirements are determined by the local Catholic bishops. Therefore, the rules change from time to time, and they vary from place to place. At present (2003), fasting for American Catholics means abstaining from the meat of birds and land animals on Ash Wednesday and on all Fridays during Lent. However, eating fish is allowed. During the Middle Ages, Catholics were not allowed to eat meat or drink wine during the entire 40 days of Lent. In some countries, they were not allowed to eat any animal products at all, including butter, milk, eggs, and cheese.

LIMBO. According to the Catholic Church, if a baby is not baptized, then he or she cannot go to Heaven, because of original sin (sin inherited from Adam). However, because the baby has not actually committed any sins, he or she does not go to Hell. Therefore, unbaptized babies go to Limbo. This is a place of happiness, but it does not have the joy of Heaven.

LITANY. A structured form of prayer that includes petitions and responses. Litanies to Mary address her by a series of titles, including the following: Queen of Heaven, Star of the Sea, Mystical Rose, Tower of David, Ark of the Covenant, Mother of God, Mother of our Creator, Mother of the Church, Mirror of Justice, Gate of Heaven, Morning Star, Health of the Sick, Refuge of Sinners, Queen of Angels, Queen of the Most Holy Rosary, Queen of Peace, and Comforter of the Afflicted.

LITURGY. Official public worship, such as the Mass, or public recitation of the Divine Office.

MASS. According to Catholic doctrine, the sacrament of the Mass is a propitiatory sacrifice, in which Jesus Christ is sacrificed on the altar, in order to appease God. When Jesus was on the cross, He said: "It is finished." The doctrine that Jesus has to be sacrificed over and over says that it is **not** finished.

MEATLESS DAYS. Days on which Catholics are required to abstain from meat. The fasting requirements for meatless days are determined by the local bishops. At present (2003), American Catholics are not allowed to eat the flesh of birds or land animals on meatless days. However, they are allowed to eat fish.

MEDAL. A metal disk with a religious image on it (Jesus, Mary, saints, popes, shrines, etc.) Sometimes medals have prayers inscribed on them. Medals are sacramentals. Some of them are indulgenced (Catholics are given indulgences if they wear them).

MENTAL RESERVATION. Using words that have a generally recognized meaning, but mentally limiting their meaning while speaking them. The result is that the listeners understand the words to mean something different than the meaning intended by the speaker. In other words, the speaker says something that can be said to be technically correct, but the intent is to have it be misunderstood.

MERIT. According to Catholic doctrine, if a man or woman does good works while in a state of grace, then he or she is entitled to receive a reward from God. There are conditions that must be met in order to merit a reward. The work must be morally good. It must be done freely, without coercion. It must be supernaturally motivated and accompanied by grace.

MERITORIOUS WORKS. Good works that merit a reward from God.

MERITS OF THE SAINTS. According to the Catholic Church, there is a "treasury" of merits that have been won by Christ and the saints. This "treasury" is the basis for the practice of indulgences. The Catholic Church says that it is able to draw from this "treasury," in order to give indulgences to Catholics who meet certain specified requirements.

MIRACULOUS MEDAL (Medal of the Immaculate Conception). According to tradition, Saint Catherine Labouré had an apparition of Mary in 1830. Mary carried a medal with a picture of herself on it. The medal had an inscription that said: "O Mary, conceived without sin, pray for us who have recourse to thee." Mary showed Saint Catherine both sides of the medal and instructed her to have medals made according to the design shown to her. The medal became known as the Miraculous Medal, because some people who wore it attributed miracles to it.

MITER. A tall clerical hat worn by bishops, cardinals, abbots, and popes.

MONASTERY. A community of monks who are governed by a superior. The term applies primarily to religious who live a contemplative life and recite or sing the Divine Office together. Convents of contemplative nuns are sometimes referred to as monasteries. Monasteries are known for asceticism, self-denial, and seclusion from the world. (See "Religious.")

MONK. A member of a religious community of men. The most strict use of the term means men who have taken solemn perpetual vows (vows until death). The broad sense of the term includes new monks (novices) and monks who have made temporary vows.

MONSTRANCE. An ornate container for displaying a consecrated Host (a large communion wafer). It is used during Adoration of the Blessed Sacrament, Benediction, and in processions. It looks like a sunburst on top of a pedestal. The monstrance is gold or gold-plated. A large, round, consecrated Host goes into a round compartment in the center of the sunburst. It is covered by a glass door. This protects the Host, while at the same time enabling people to see it. The shiny gold and the sunburst pattern make it look as if rays of light are coming out of the Host. The sunburst pattern is traditional, but some monstrances use other decorative patterns.

MORTAL SIN. According to Catholic doctrine, sins are categorized as being mortal or venial. Mortal sins are the most serious. They are said to destroy the supernatural life of the soul, resulting in spiritual death. When a person is baptized, his or her soul receives spiritual life. If the person commits a mortal sin, the result is spiritual death. Confession (the sacrament of penance) restores spiritual life to the soul when the sin is absolved by a priest. Another mortal sin would cause spiritual death. Having the sin be absolved by a priest during the sacrament of penance would restore spiritual life to the soul. This cycle can continue indefinitely. A person who commits a mortal sin, and dies before having it be absolved, goes to Hell. Some examples of mortal sins are: murder, rape, adultery, and missing Mass on Sunday.

MYSTICAL BODY OF CHRIST. The Church militant (the Roman Catholic Church on earth), the Church suffering (the souls in Purgatory), and the Church triumphant (the saints in Heaven).

NOVENA. Nine consecutive days of prayer for a special request from Jesus, Mary, or a saint. It can be nine days in a row, the same day of the week for nine consecutive weeks, the first Friday or first Saturday of nine consecutive months, etc. There are many standard novena prayers. They can be prayed publicly or privately. Some people use novena candles when praying novena prayers for nine days in a row.

NOVENA CANDLES. Large candles that are burned while praying novena prayers. Traditional novena candles burn for nine days, but some novena candles don't burn that long. Novena candles are inside glass containers. The containers often have a picture of Mary or a saint on one side and a written prayer on the opposite side.

NOVICE. The term comes from *novicius*, a Latin word that means "new." In religious life, a novice is a new monk or a new nun. If a novice has been accepted into a religious order, and has been given a religious habit, then he or she is a monk or a nun in the broad sense of the term. Novices undergo training and "spiritual formation" in preparation for making vows. Before making solemn perpetual vows (vows until death), they make temporary vows.

NUN. A member of a religious community of women, living under the authority of a superior. The most strict use of the term means women who live a cloistered, contemplative life, and have taken solemn perpetual vows (vows until death). The broad sense of the term includes new nuns (novices), and nuns who have made temporary vows.

OFFICE OF THE INQUISITION (Holy Office). An office in the Vatican. It is responsible for repressing heresy. Presently, this is done by means of written statements and by disciplining Catholic clergy whose teachings are heretical. In the past, repressing heresy was done by means of torture, imprisonment, and death. In 1965, the Office of the Inquisition changed its name to The Congregation for the Doctrine of the Faith.

OIL OF CATECHUMENS. A special kind of holy oil that is used in the sacrament of baptism. It is a sacramental.

OIL OF THE SICK. A special kind of holy oil that is used in the sacrament of the anointing of the sick (extreme unction). The oil is a sacramental.

ORDINATION. The sacrament of holy orders. Deacons, priests, and bishops are ordained.

ORIGINAL SIN. The sin that the human race inherited as a result of Adam's sin. According to Catholic doctrine, babies have original sin. However, the Virgin Mary did not.

OUR FATHER (Pater Noster). The Lord's Prayer.

OUR LADY OF. (1) An apparition of the Virgin Mary. For example, Our Lady of Fatima, Our Lady of Lourdes, Our Lady of Guadalupe. (2) An attribute or title of Mary. For example, Our Lady of the Rosary, Our Lady of Good Counsel.

PALM SUNDAY. The Sunday before Easter. During Mass, blessed palms are given to the people to commemorate Jesus' triumphal entry into Jerusalem, when the crowds waved palm branches to honor Him. It is traditional for people to take the palms home and keep them. The priests keep some of the palms. The next year, the palms are burned to provide the ashes to be used on Ash Wednesday (the day when Lent begins).

PAPAL BULL. A papal encyclical dealing with important subject matter. The term "bull" comes from a special seal (*bulla*) that is put on the encyclical, because of its importance.

PAPAL THRONE. The Pope is a sovereign monarch in the Vatican. He sits on an ornate throne. The Pope also has a portable throne (*sedia gestatoria*), which is carried on the shoulders of uniformed footmen. This is used in solemn processions.

PASCHAL CANDLE. A large candle containing five grains of incense that represent the five wounds of Christ. It is blessed on Holy Saturday (the day before Easter). It is used in the liturgical blessing of baptismal water. During the Paschal season, it is kept in the sanctuary and lit during Mass. (Paschal season is the period of time from the Saturday before Easter to the Saturday following Pentecost.)

PATEN. The paten is similar to a saucer and it is used to cover the chalice. It is consecrated by a bishop or his delegate, using chrism.

PATRON SAINT. A saint who is invoked by a particular group of people. There are patron saints for countries, states of life, and specific circumstances. For example, Saint Joseph is the patron saint of carpenters; Saint Christopher is the patron saint of travelers; and Saint Jude is the patron saint of people whose circumstances seem to be hopeless.

PENANCE. (1) The sacrament of penance (confession; the sacrament of reconciliation). (2) Voluntary suffering to atone for sins.

PENITENT. (1) A person who seeks absolution for sins from a Catholic priest during the sacrament of penance (confession). (2) A person who repents for sins and does something to expiate guilt. Penitents may subject themselves to voluntary suffering now, in order to avoid having to suffer in Purgatory later.

PERPETUAL ADORATION OF THE BLESSED SACRAMENT. Continual adoration of a large, consecrated Host that is displayed in a monstrance. People take turns, so that somebody is always in the chapel or church, worshiping the Host. The Catholic Church grants indulgences for Adoration of the Blessed Sacrament.

PERPETUAL VOW. A solemn vow that is binding until the death of the person who made the vow.

PILGRIMAGE. A journey to a place that is considered to be sacred. Pilgrimages are often made to the Holy Land, the Vatican, famous shrines, and sites where there have been apparitions.

POCKET ROSARY. A small rosary that people can keep in their pocket and use with only one hand. It is circular, consisting of one decade, a medal of Mary, and a crucifix. People can count the rosary beads using just one hand. When they feel the medal or the crucifix, then they know that they have completed the decade.

POSTULANT. A man or woman who is taking the first steps towards becoming a monk or a nun. Postulants have not yet been accepted as members of a religious community.

PRAYER RING. Religious jewelry. These rings have brief prayers inscribed on them, such as "Lord have mercy." They can also have "Mary" or "Jesus" inscribed on them.

PRIEST. Priests are ordained by bishops. According to Catholic doctrine, a Catholic priest is a mediator between the people and God, and he offers true sacrifices to God.

PROPITIATION. (1) To appease a person who has been offended by wrongdoing. (2) To atone for sin. (3) To appease God, who has been offended by our sins.

PROPITIATORY. Something that propitiates. According to Catholic doctrine, the Mass is a propitiatory sacrifice. It appeases God and atones for the sins of the people.

PURGATORY. According to Catholic doctrine, when God forgives sins, He may still require that the sinner pay for his or her sins by suffering. When good Catholics die, if they are not saintly enough to go directly to Heaven, then they have to spend time in Purgatory, where they atone for their sins by suffering. After they have been sufficiently purified, then they can go to Heaven. However, the suffering of the souls in Purgatory can be shortened by means of good works done on their behalf, such as earning indulgences for them, or having priests say masses for them. In modern times, earning indulgences is done primarily by praying indulgenced prayers, or engaging in indulgenced pious practices. During the Middle Ages, indulgences were sold for money.

RECONCILIATION (Confession; Sacrament of Penance). A sacrament during which Catholic priests absolve Catholics of their sins. According to Catholic doctrine, people who commit mortal sins after they are baptized are required to confess their sins to a qualified priest in order to receive absolution from their sins.

RELICS. Relics are an attempt to make physical contact with saints. A first-class relic is part of a saint's body. A second-class relic is something worn by a saint or used by a saint. A third-class relic is any other kind of object that is related to a saint. It can be a piece of cloth that has touched a saint's bone. When an altar is consecrated, a relic of a martyr is placed in the altar stone.

RELIGIOUS. A monk (brother), or nun (sister), who is a member of a religious order.

RELIQUARY. A special container for holding relics. They can be ornate and expensive.

REMISSION OF SIN. Having a sin be absolved; forgiveness of sin.

REPARATION FOR SIN. Atonement for sin. When Jesus Christ died on the cross, He paid for our sins.

ROMAN CURIA. A group of men in the Vatican who assist the Pope in directing the operations of the Catholic Church.

ROME. (1) A city in Italy. (2) The Vatican (which is located in the city of Rome). (3) The Roman Catholic Church (which is governed by the Vatican, which is located in Rome).

ROSARY. (1) Traditional prayers that are said in honor of the Virgin Mary. (2) A string of beads that is used to keep track of the prayers. There are five sets of decades. Each decade consists of one bead that is separated from a group of ten beads. The "Our Father" (Lord's Prayer) is said on the single beads. The "Hail Mary" is said on each bead in the groups of ten beads. (There are ten prayers to Mary for every one prayer to God.) The five decades are joined together to form a circle. A medal of Mary connects a short string of beads to the circle of five decades of beads. At the end of the short string of beads is a crucifix. The Catholic Church gives indulgences to people who pray the rosary. Some people hang rosaries from their car mirrors, or wear them like a necklace (under their clothes, where the rosary doesn't show). Some people claim that the rosary is powerful for protection from demons.

ROSARY BRACELET. A small, one-decade rosary that can be worn like a bracelet. It is a circle of beads with a crucifix attached to it.

ROSARY NOVENA. Using the rosary as a novena prayer. This means praying the full rosary on nine consecutive occasions.

ROSARY PROMISES. An apparition of "Mary" at Fatima, Portugal, gave 15 promises to people who recite the rosary. She said that they will not die without receiving the sacraments; that they will share in the merits of the saints at the moment of their death; and if they go to Purgatory, then Mary will get them out. The apparitions of "Mary" at Fatima have been officially approved by the Roman Catholic Church. This means that the Rosary Promises do not conflict with Catholic doctrine. The Catholic Church gives indulgences to Catholics who pray the rosary.

SABBATINE PRIVILEGE. According to tradition, an apparition of Mary promised to get people out of Purgatory on the Saturday after their death, if they fulfilled certain conditions during their lifetime. These include wearing the Brown Scapular and reciting the rosary.

SACRAMENT. Sacraments are rituals that use objects and actions to confer spiritual benefits. Objects include bread, wine, oil, chrism, water, and incense. Actions include the sign of the cross, gestures made by the priest, and precise verbal formulas. The Catholic Church has seven sacraments: baptism, confirmation, the Eucharist (Mass), penance (confession, or sacrament of reconciliation), holy orders (ordination), matrimony (marriage), and anointing of the sick (extreme unction, or the last rites). According to the Catholic Church, the effectiveness of the sacraments is due to the rituals that are performed.

SACRAMENT OF RECONCILIATION (Confession; Sacrament of Penance). During this sacrament, Catholic priests absolve Catholics from their sins. If people commit mortal sins after they are baptized, then they are required to confess their sins to a qualified priest in order to receive absolution from their sins.

SACRAMENTALS. Religious objects or actions that have the official approval of the Catholic Church. They include things such as holy water, medals, and scapulars. They include pious practices, such as praying rosaries, reciting litanies, and adoration of the Blessed Sacrament. Sacramentals are similar to sacraments, because they use physical objects and physical actions in order to confer spiritual benefits. However, their effectiveness depends on the influence of the prayers of the participants. According to Catholic teaching, people who use sacramentals benefit from the merits and prayers of the "Mystical Body of Christ."

SACRED HEART OF JESUS. Devotion to the Sacred Heart of Jesus was promoted by several mystics. A picture associated with this devotion portrays Jesus with His chest open, His heart exposed, flames above His heart, and light coming out of His heart. It is traditional to honor and venerate this picture.

SACRED HEART PROMISES. According to tradition, Jesus appeared to Saint Margaret Mary Alacoque in the seventeenth century. He gave her 12 promises for people who are devoted to His Sacred Heart. They include promises for people who observe the "Devotion of First Fridays" (receiving Communion on the First Friday of nine consecutive months). "Jesus" said that these people will not die without receiving the sacraments; they will not be displeasing to Jesus when they die; and the Sacred Heart of Jesus will be their refuge.

SAINT. In the New Testament, the term "saint" applies to all Christians. The Catholic Church has restricted the use of the word to mean canonized saints and people who have traditionally been recognized as saints. The Catholic Church encourages people to publicly pray to saints, to publicly honor them, and to publicly invoke their assistance.

SAINT ANNE'S OIL. According to tradition, Saint Anne is the mother of the Virgin Mary. In Canada, there is a shrine in honor of Saint Anne. Healings are attributed to oil from this shrine. Bottles of Saint Anne's oil can be purchased.

SAINT BENEDICT MEDAL. The Catholic Church gives indulgences to Catholics who wear this medal. It has a picture of Saint Benedict, a cross, and a prayer of exorcism. The medal is said to protect people from evil. Some people put Saint Benedict Medals over their doorways to protect their homes. The Saint Benedict Medal is used for a special blessing that is said to heal people.

SAINT BLAISE BLESSING. On the feast day of Saint Blaise, there is a special blessing of throats. Two candles are consecrated by a prayer. A priest holds the candles in a crossed position, touches the throats of the people with them, and repeats a written prayer. In some places, it is traditional for the priest to only use one candle instead of two crossed candles. He touches the wick of a small candle with consecrated oil, and then uses the wick of the candle to touch the throats of the people.

SAINT CHRISTOPHER MEDAL. According to tradition, Saint Christopher was a large young man who carried people across a dangerous river. One day he carried a child across the river. It turned out to be Jesus Christ in the form of a child. Saint Christopher is the patron saint for travelers. His medal is very popular.

SAINT PETER'S BASILICA. A special church adjoining the Pope's palace. It is famous for its architecture and art work.

SAINT MICHAEL'S CHAPLET. According to tradition, Saint Michael the Archangel appeared to Antonia d'Astonac. He told her that he wanted to be honored by nine salutations, one for each of the nine angelic choirs of angels. He promised that any person who honored him with the daily recital of these nine salutations would receive his help, and the help of all of the heavenly angels, during his or her lifetime, and would be delivered from Purgatory after death. In addition, his or her relatives would also be delivered from Purgatory.

SCAPULAR. (1) Part of the habit of a monk or nun. (2) Two small pieces of cloth that are joined by strings. They are worn around the neck, under the clothing. Two of the most popular scapulars are the Brown Scapular and the Green Scapular.

SEDIA GESTATORIA. A portable throne used by the Pope. It is a richly adorned chair that is covered with silk. Long rods go through gold-covered rings. The throne is carried by twelve uniformed footmen. When the Pope celebrates solemn pontifical Mass in Saint Peter's Basilica, he arrives in state, preceded by a procession of cardinals, bishops, and prelates. The Pope is carried on the sedia gestatoria, with a canopy over him and special fans made of white feathers on either side of him.

SEVEN SACRAMENTS. The Catholic Church officially recognizes seven sacraments: baptism, confirmation, Eucharist (the Mass), penance (confession, or sacrament of reconciliation), holy orders (ordination), matrimony (marriage), and anointing of the sick (extreme unction, or the last rites).

SIGN OF THE CROSS. Tracing the pattern of a cross. People can make the sign of the cross over themselves, by having their hand go to the forehead, then to the breast, then to the left and right shoulders. It is traditional to make the sign of the cross, using holy water, when entering a Catholic Church. Before praying the rosary, it is traditional to kiss the crucifix of the rosary and make the sign of the cross while holding the crucifix. During Benediction, priests make the sign of the cross with a monstrance that contains a consecrated Host. Priests can also make the sign of the cross with a censer (a vessel that contains burning incense).

SISTINE CHAPEL. This is the Pope's private chapel, but it is as large as a church. The altar is inlaid with mother of pearl. Only the Pope is allowed to use it. The chapel is filled with paintings by famous artists. When a new Pope is to be elected, the cardinals are kept enclosed in the Sistine Chapel until the Pope is chosen.

STATE OF GRACE. If a person is free from mortal sin, then he or she is said to be in a state of grace. According to Catholic doctrine, in order for people to go to Heaven, they must be in a state of grace when they die. In order to perform meritorious works, they must be in a state of grace when they perform them.

STIGMATA. Bleeding, painful wounds that occur in the places where Jesus Christ was wounded during the crucifixion. The wounds usually occur in the hands, feet and side. They can also occur in the back (where Jesus was whipped) or the head (where He was wounded by the crown of thorns). Saint Francis of Assisi and Padre Pio are well known stigmatics (people who had the stigmata). There have been more than 300 cases of stigmatization, including more than 60 canonized saints.

TEMPORAL PUNISHMENT. According to Catholic doctrine, when God forgives sins He may still require that the sinner atone for his or her sins by suffering, either here on earth or else in Purgatory. If we have to pay for our own sins by suffering, then the death of Jesus Christ was not sufficient to pay for them. This Catholic doctrine denies the sufficiency of the death of Jesus. It also negates the statement of Jesus on the cross, when He said: "It is finished."

TIARA. The Pope's crown. It is made of gold and covered with precious jewels.

TRADITION. According to Catholic doctrine, tradition is divine revelation that was not written in the Bible. It has been passed down through the Catholic Church. Tradition and Scripture are said to be equally authoritative. However, in the real world, that is not possible. When Catholic tradition and the Bible are not in agreement, then one of them has to be used to judge the validity of the other. For example, the Bible says that Jesus had brothers and sisters. This conflicts with the doctrine that Mary remained a virgin throughout her lifetime. Protestants rely on the Bible first, so they say that Mary must have had normal sexual relations with Joseph after Jesus was born. Catholics rely on tradition first, so they say that the brothers and sisters must have been cousins instead of real brothers and sisters. (The New Testament was written in Greek, which has different words for "brothers" and "cousins." The Greek word used for these people means "brothers.")

VATICAN. (1) The Pope's palace, Saint Peter's Basilica, and the administrative offices of the Catholic Church. (2) The power structure of the Catholic Church.

VATICAN CITY. Territory in Rome that is under the jurisdiction of the Pope. The Pope is its ruling monarch. Its government is based on Catholic Canon Law. It is a state that enjoys all of the privileges of a sovereign nation. It has diplomatic relations with other nations and makes treaties (concordats) with them. It has representatives at the United Nations and the European Union. Cardinals are citizens of Vatican City, in addition to being citizens of their own countries.

VENERATION. Special honor given to Mary and the saints. It can take many forms, including the following: (1) Publicly praying to Mary and the saints, and invoking their assistance. (This can be accompanied by kneeling in front of statues, or placing lit votive candles in front of statues.) (2) Carrying statues of Mary or saints in solemn processions. (3) The liturgical crowning of statues of Mary. (4) Having pictures of Mary or saints. (5) Wearing medals or scapulars associated with Mary or saints. (6) Praying novenas, litanies, rosaries, and chaplets that honor Mary or saints. (7) Doing things requested by apparitions of "Mary."

VENERATION OF IMAGES. Reverence given to images of Jesus, Mary, and the saints. Canon Law requires Catholic Churches to have sacred images, such as crucifixes, statues, paintings, and mosaics. Catholics are supposed to venerate these images. They are also encouraged to have sacred images in their homes. Images for personal use include statues, pictures, medals, crucifixes, jewelry, scapulars that have pictures on them, and rosaries. (A rosary has a crucifix and a medal of Mary.)

VENIAL SIN. A sin that is not serious enough to be a mortal sin.

VESTMENTS. Special garments worn by Catholic clergy when saying Mass or participating in other public religious functions.

VICTIM SOUL. A person who willingly endures suffering in order to atone for the sins of other people. Some apparitions of "Mary" have asked people to be victim souls.

VOTIVE CANDLES. Candles that are burned before a statue or a shrine in order to honor Jesus, Mary, or a saint. It is traditional to light candles when praying to Mary and the saints. After the Second Vatican Council (1962-1965), there was less emphasis on votive candles.

VOTIVE OFFERING. An offering associated with prayers for something, or given in gratitude for prayers that have been answered. Common forms of votive offerings are votive candles and newspaper advertisements. It is traditional for people to pay to put an advertisement in a Catholic newspaper, publicly thanking a saint for "favors granted."

WORDS OF ABSOLUTION. A verbal formula that is used by a Catholic priest to absolve the sins of a Catholic during the sacrament of penance (confession).

YOUR EMINENCE. The correct form of address that Catholics are supposed to use when writing to, or speaking with, a cardinal.

YOUR EXCELLENCY. The correct form of address for a bishop. In Canada and the United States, it is also used for archbishops.

YOUR GRACE. In Australia and the United Kingdom, this is the correct form of address for an archbishop. In Canada and the United States, an archbishop is addressed as "Your Excellency."

YOUR HOLINESS. The correct form of address when writing to, or speaking with, the Pope. Proper protocol also requires Catholics to refer to the Pope as "His Holiness" in formal correspondence that refers to him.

Appendix D
Pictures

There are some excellent photographs on the Internet. I have given you the addresses of web pages which have the pictures. They are grouped into categories.

At the end of this appendix, there are Internet addresses of web pages that have hundreds of pictures of the Vatican. For example, the heading "Saint Peter's Basilica, the Pope's Palace, and the Vatican Gardens" has 14 web pages, containing a total of 254 pictures. (They are small pictures that will be enlarged if you click on them.)

Sometimes web pages get moved, discontinued, or replaced. If you can't get through to a picture that is important to you, please try again. Sometimes websites go down temporarily.

If you can't find a picture that you want, then go to the home page and look for it. To find the home page, copy the Internet address of the article. Then delete everything in the address that comes after "com," "net," or "org." You can get hints from the Internet address. For example, if you are looking for the pictures which are at first address that is listed below, you can go to www.sspxasia.com, then look for Newsletters, then look for 2001, then look for October-November, then look for pictures of the procession.

You can also do an Internet search. For example, I found some good pictures by doing searches for "procession + Mary" and "statue + Mary." You can get hints for how to find things from the internet addresses of the articles. For example, if you are looking for the first address that is listed below, you can do searches for "procession + Our Lady of the Rosary" or "picture + procession + Our Lady of the Rosary" or "statue + Our Lady of the Rosary."

Some Internet addresses are too wide for the pages of this book. In those cases, I have divided them into two sections. If you type both sections into your browser (with no spaces in between them), then the addresses should work. I will always tell you when I have divided an Internet address.

Statues of Mary Wearing Real Crowns and Elaborate Clothing
Statues of Mary wearing crowns and clothing. I have divided this address into two sections, because of its width.
www.sspxasia.com/Newsletters/2001/Oct-Dec/

Procession_in_honour_of_Our_Lady_of_the_Rosary.htm
   A statue of Mary with baby Jesus. Both wear crowns and clothing.
www.aloha.net/~mikesch/crown.htm

Venerating Statues
Nuns venerating a statue of Mary
www.op-stjoseph.org/nuns/angels/picpages/procession.htm

Large Statues that Dominate Chapels
NOTE: If you have difficulty getting any of these pictures, then go to the website of the Basilica of the National Shrine of the Immaculate Conception and take their "virtual tour." The Internet address is below. If it doesn't work for you, then do a search for the name of the shrine.
www.nationalshrine.com
   Chapel of Our Lady of Siluva
www.nationalshrine.com/NAT_SHRINE/tour_u32.htm
   Chapel of Our Lady of the Miraculous Medal
www.nationalshrine.com/NAT_SHRINE/tour_u04.htm
   Statue of Mary, Mother of Mankind (many candles are in front of the statue)
www.nationalshrine.com/NAT_SHRINE/tour_c37.htm
   Chapel honoring the apparition of Mary to Saint Catherine Laboure
www.cammonline.org/pagesShrineTour/shrine05En.html

The Pope Wearing His Crown
Six pictures of popes with the papal crown (tiara). Most of these pictures are black and white. However, there is a colored picture of the papal tiara on the head of a statue of the Apostle Peter. The color enables you to see the jewels on the gold crown. (Once a year, the Pope's crown is put on a statue of Saint Peter.) Two of these pictures show Popes Pius XII and John XXIII seated on an ornate papal throne.
www.geocities.com/rexstupormundi/papalcrown.html
   "The Papal Monarchy." An article with two pictures of popes wearing the tiara (papal crown).
www.geocities.com/rexstupormundi/papalmonarchy.html
   Pope John XXIII, seated on his throne, wearing his crown.
www.traditio.com/papal/john23.htm

Crowning Statues of Mary
NOTE: The liturgy of the Catholic Church includes an official ritual for crowning statues of Mary. Following are addresses of web pages that show

pictures of this. It is done at all levels, ranging from the Pope to classes in Catholic schools.

The Pope crowning a statue of Mary in Cuba. There are seven pictures, accompanied by descriptions of what is going on.
www.aloha.net/~mikesch/crown.htm

Crowning ceremony at a cathedral. The pictures are small. If you click on them you will see large ones.
www.cathedralcarmel55.org/mary-crowning1/

Crowning ceremony at a fifth grade class of a Catholic school
www.stfrancisvernon.org/Crowning5th.htm

The Infant of Prague

NOTE: The Infant of Prague is a statue of Jesus as an infant. It is kept in a church in Prague, Chezchoslovakia. It has 70 sets of elaborate clothes and a crown made out of real gold with real jewels. Nuns dress the statue and take care of it. Miracles are attributed to this statue. Replicas of the statue can be found in Catholic churches around the world. If you have difficulty getting any of these pictures, you can do a search for "Infant of Prague," or for "Infant of Prague + picture."

Article with pictures showing nuns changing the clothes of the statue
http://karmel.at/prag-jesu/english/eng/saticken.htm

Article with a picture of a cardinal carrying the statue
www.medjugorjecenter.org/prague/page2.htm

Article with pictures showing details of the crown and some of the clothes
http://karmel.at/prag-jesu/english/eng/muzejen.htm

Article with pictures of the statue (clothed and unclothed)
http://religion-cults.com/childjesus/prague.htm

Article with several pictures and history of the statue
http://karmel.at/prag-jesu/english/eng/jezuleen.htm

Processions with Statues

A processions in the United States in honor of Our Lady of Guadalupe. I have divided the address into two sections, because of its width.
http://hemi.ps.tsoa.nyu.edu/archive/
studentwork/colony/reed/procession.htm

Another procession in honor of Our Lady of Guadalupe. I have divided the address into two sections, because of its width.
www.laprensa-sandiego.org/archieve/
december14/PARADE.HTM

A procession honoring Our Lady of Mount Carmel
www.fcsn.k12.nd.us/Shanley/broanth/carmel.htm

A procession with a statue of Mary
www.catholic-doc.org/miscellany/1998/0598-may.html

A church procession honoring Mary. (Click on the pictures to enlarge them.)
www.olphparish.org/mayprocession2000.htm

A procession honoring Our Lady of Mount Carmel. (These pictures take time to load.)
http://users.rcn.com/olmckey/feast2.htm

Monstrances

NOTE: Monstrances are ornate containers that are used to display Hosts (large, consecrated communion wafers). They are used in "eucharist adoration" (worship of the Host).

A gold-plated monstrance with 18 rubies
www.monstrans-de-kel.nl/monst6.html

An ornate monstrance containing a Host
www.lightofmary.org/coadorermonpic.htm

Two web pages, each having 12 small pictures of monstrances. (If you click on them you will see large pictures.)
www.monstrans-de-kel.nl/foto_index1.html
www.monstrans-de-kel.nl/foto_index2.html

A monstrance with a Host, on an altar
www.gachaska.org/monstrancesunburstaltar.htm

A gothic monstrance that is on sale for $3,250
pages.tias.com/1056/PictPage/523111.html

A website where people come to look at a picture of a consecrated Host, which is inside a monstrance. People look at the Host and worship it. A schedule is established so that there will be "perpetual adoration." People take turns worshiping the Host, so that there is coverage 24 hours a day, every day.
www.lightofmary.org/Sisters_of_Charity/peac/coadorer.htm

Perpetual Online Rosaries

People go to these websites to join others is praying a perpetual rosary. The vision is to have somebody be praying the rosary at all times. The pictures at the top of the first website represent the Immaculate Heart of Mary and the Sacred Heart of Jesus. These are interactive websites that are java based.
www.fatima.org/perpetual.html
www.mich.com/~buffalo/rosary.html

A website with audio clips of rosary prayers. People can listen and pray along with the recording. This creates the feeling of praying the rosary with other people.
www.donabate.irishchurch.net/rosary/frame1.html

Saint Peter's Basilica and the Pope's Palace
A series of 14 web pages, with color pictures of Saint Peter's Basilica, the Pontifical Palace, and the Vatican Gardens. Each page has a number of small pictures. If you click on them you will see large pictures.
www.christusrex.org/www1/citta/0-Citta.html

If this address doesn't work for you, then go to the home page and click on "The Vatican City." (In October, 2003, it was near the bottom of the page. If you don't find it there, then search the page.) The home page is below. If the address doesn't work, then do an Internet search for "Christus Rex."
www.christusrex.org

The Sistine Chapel
A series of 27 web pages, with color pictures of the Sistine Chapel. Three of these web pages have pictures of prophets and sybils. A sybil is a pagan prophetess. Each page has a number of small pictures. If you click on them you will see large pictures.
www.christusrex.org/www1/sistine/0-Tour.html

If this address doesn't work for you, then go to the home page and click on "The Sistine Chapel." (In October, 2003, it was near the bottom of the page. If you don't find it there, then search the page.) The home page is below. If the address doesn't work, then do an Internet search for "Christus Rex."
www.christusrex.org

Three web pages with pictures of the fresco, *The School of Athens*, by Raphael. This is near the entrance to the Sistine Chapel. It features a number of Greek philosophers. Some of these pictures will be enlarged if you click on them.
www.artchive.com/artchive/R/raphael/school_athens.jpg.html
www.christusrex.org/www1/stanzas/S2-Segnatura.html
http://un2sg4.unige.ch/athena/raphael/raf_ath4.html

The School of Athens. I have divided the address into two sections, because of its width.
www.vatican.va/museums/patrons/documents/
vm_pat_doc_12101999_raphael_en.html

22 Vatican Museums

A series of 22 web pages with color pictures of the Vatican museums. A number of them have statues of Greek, Roman, and Egyptian gods and goddesses. Each page has a number of small pictures. If you click on them you will see large pictures.

www.christusrex.org/www1/vaticano/0-Musei.html

If this address doesn't work for you, then go to the home page and click on "The Vatican Museums." (In October, 2003, it was near the bottom of the page. If you don't find it there, then search the page.) The home page is below. If the address doesn't work, then do an Internet search for "Christus Rex."

www.christusrex.org

Appendix E
Testimonies of Former Catholics

Stan Weber
www.stanweber.com/_wsn/page4.html

Oliver McAllister
www.angelfire.com/ky/dodone/Oliver.html

Mary Hertel (a former Roman Catholic nun)
www.bereanbeacon.org/test2.htm

Doreen Sawchak
www.angelfire.com/ky/dodone/sawchak2.html

Bill Casey
www.angelfire.com/ky/dodone/Casey.html

Peggy O'Neill (a former Roman Catholic nun)
www.bereanbeacon.org/Peggy_ONeill.html

Jacqueline (a former Roman Catholic nun)
www.arabicbible.com/testimonies/Jacqueline.html

Mary Ann Pakiz (a former Roman Catholic nun)
www.christiananswers.net/q-eden/edn-r010.html

Richard Bennett (a former Roman Catholic priest)
www.bereanbeacon.org/testimony.html

Joseph Cherucheril (a former Roman Catholic priest)
www.bereanbeacon.org/Tesimony_Joseph_C.html

Joseph Tremblay (a former Roman Catholic priest)
www.bereanbeacon.org/JosephTremblay.htm

Mary Ann Collins (a longer version of my testimony)
www.CatholicConcerns.com/Bio.html

Convent Life (my experience in the convent)
www.CatholicConcerns.com/Convent.html

Appendix F
History and the Catholic Church

I recommend the book, *The Church of Rome at the Bar of History*, by William Webster (Carlisle, Pennsylvania: The Banner of Truth Trust, 1995). Webster is a former Catholic. His book shows that many modern Catholic practices and doctrines contradict the teachings of the early Church.

There are some excellent articles on the Internet about historical issues relating to Catholicism. I have grouped them into categories.

Sometimes Internet articles get moved, discontinued, or replaced. I have often provided several articles about the same subject. That way, if you can't get through to one article, others will be available for you. If you can't get through to an article that is important to you, please try again. Sometimes websites go down temporarily. You can also do a search for the information yourself. The descriptions of the articles give key words that can be used for doing searches.

Some Internet addresses are too wide for the pages of this book. In those cases, I have divided them into two sections. If you type both sections into your browser (with no spaces in between them), then the addresses should work. I will always tell you when I have divided an Internet address

Overview of Church History
Two Millennia of Church History
www.foigm.org/IMG/millhist.htm

Two Millenia of Church History. This is another address for the same article. I have divided the address into two sections, because of its width.
www.christianity.com/CC/article/
0,,PTID306608 | CHID556136 | CIID1397350,00.html

Forged Church Documents
Thomas Aquinas relied on forged documents, but he thought that they were genuine
www.christiantruth.com/forgeries.html

An article about the Medieval Papacy. It includes a good summary of information about forged documents and their use to increase papal power.
www.christianchronicler.com/history1/medieval_papacy.html

An article about the use of forged documents in developing papal power. The author is a former Jesuit priest.
www.remnantofgod.org/x-jesuit.htm
www.crusadeforcatholics.com/newpage63.htm
    Canon Law and forged decretals
http://jmgainor.homestead.com/files/PU/PF/cld.htm
    Liber Pontificalis (Book of the Popes). These biographies of popes contain forged material.
http://jmgainor.homestead.com/files/PU/PF/lp.htm
    The *Donation of Constantine*. This is a famous forgery
http://jmgainor.homestead.com/files/PU/PF/doco.htm
    A forged document which was attributed to the Council of Nicaea
http://jmgainor.homestead.com/files/PU/PF/6c.htm
    More forged documents
http://jmgainor.homestead.com/files/PU/PF/sf.htm
    Articles about false Decretals
www.britannica.com/eb/article?eu=34257
www.bartleby.com/65/fa/FalseDec.html
www.encyclopedia.com/html/F/FalseD1ec.asp
www.slider.com/enc/18000/False_Decretals.htm
http://concise.britannica.com/ebc/article?eu=389494

The Papacy
Information about some corrupt popes
members.aol.com/jasonte/papacy.htm
    An article about the papacy. It includes historical information about some corrupt popes. This starts about half-way down the page.
http://origin.island.lk/2002/07/16/featur04.html
    An article about the Medieval Papacy. It includes information about corrupt popes and ways in which they increased their power.
www.christianchronicler.com/history1/medieval_papacy.html
    An article written by a skeptic. He uses corrupt popes to try to discredit Christianity. He is wrong about Christianity, but he has some good historical information.
www.geocities.com/paulntobin/papacy.html
    Pope Alexander VI: his personal faults and his political skills
http://itrs.scu.edu/students/winter03/bukestead/pope.html
http://history.boisestate.edu/hy309/papacy/alexandervi.html

A long article with some detailed information about Pope Alexander VI (the Borgia Pope). I have divided the address into two sections, because of its width.
www.goacom.com/overseas-digest/Religion/
Church%20History/history11.html
An article about Pope Alexander VI, the Borgia Pope. I have divided the address into two sections, because of its width.
www.crimelibrary.com/serial_killers/
history/borgias/2.html?sect=6
An article about Cardinal Cesare Borgia, the son of the Borgia Pope. I have divided the address into two sections, because of its width.
www.crimelibrary.com/serial_killers/
history/borgias/3.html?sect=6
If those addresses didn't work for you, then go to the address below. It has a search engine. Do a search for "Borgia."
www.CrimeLibrary.com
Two articles about Pope John XII
www.infoplease.com/ce6/people/A0826379.html
www.slider.com/enc/28000/John_XII_pope.htm
The Development of Papal Power
www.geocities.com/Athens/Parthenon/2104/papal_power.html
Popes said that there is no salvation apart from the Pope
www.reachingcatholics.org/pastpopes.html

The Sale of Indulgences
Official Instructions for the Sale of Indulgences
www.aloha.net/~mikesch/instruc.htm
Tetzel's Sale of Indulgences
www.aloha.net/~mikesch/tetzel.htm

The Inquisition
Text of the Fourth Lateran Council's decree regarding treatment of heretics
www.fordham.edu/halsall/source/lat4-c3.html
www.historyguide.org/ancient/3canon_b.html
The Medieval Inquisition
http://jmgainor.homestead.com/files/PU/Inq/mi.htm
The Spanish Inquisition
http://jmgainor.homestead.com/files/PU/Inq/si.htm
The Roman Inquisition
http://jmgainor.homestead.com/files/PU/Inq/ri.htm

A study of the history, theology, and methods of the Inquisition
www.sundayschoolcourses.com/inq/inqcont.htm
"The Inquisition: A Study in Absolute Catholic Power"
www.mtc.org/inquis.html
http://la.znet.com/~bart/inquis.htm
www.crusadeforcatholics.com/bart.htm

The Crusades
The Crusades
http://gbgm-umc.org/umw/bible/crusades.stm
    The First Crusade and the bloodbath in Jerusalem
http://crusades.boisestate.edu/1st/28.htm
http://gbgm-umc.org/umw/bible/crusades.stm#first
http://jmgainor.homestead.com/files/PU/Cru/1cr.htm
    The Fourth Crusade and the pillaging of Constantinople
http://gbgm-umc.org/umw/bible/sack.stm
http://crusades.boisestate.edu/4th/12.htm
http://jmgainor.homestead.com/files/PU/Cru/4cr.htm
    The Albigensian Crusade (the Albigensian Massacre)
http://jmgainor.homestead.com/files/PU/Cru/albcr.htm
http://militaryhistory.about.com/cs/albigenscrusade/
    The Reconciliation Walk. Some Christians walked the route of the Crusades and repented for the atrocities that were committed by the Crusaders.
www.soon.org.uk/page15.htm
www.reconciliationwalk.org/crusades.htm
www.reconciliationwalk.org/jpost970626.htm

Opposing the Bible
Rules issued by the Council of Trent regarding forbidden books. The general public was forbidden to read the Bible. Only certain special people were allowed to read it.
www.fordham.edu/halsall/mod/trent-booksrules.html
    Protestant Bibles, and Bibles which were translated into the language of the common people without permission from the Catholic hierarchy, were banned by the Inquisition. They were on their Index of Forbidden Books. I have divided the address into two sections, because of its width.
palimpsest.stanford.edu/byform/mailing-lists/
bookarts/1998/01/msg00284.html
    The Catholic Church's historical and theological approach to the Bible
www.angelfire.com/ky/dodone/Bible.html

William Tyndale translated the Bible into English. His Bibles were burned. Tyndale was burned at the stake. Between 1400 and 1557, over a thousand English men and women were burned at the stake for reading, or possessing, English Bibles.
www.williamtyndale.com/0crimesofwilliamtyndale.htm

More information about Tyndale and the Bible. When the King of England authorized an English translation of the Bible, it was kept in a church. All day long that church was crowded with people. Men took turns reading the Bible out loud while the people listened.
justus.anglican.org/resources/bio/260.html

Information about Tyndale and Wycliffe
www.prca.org/books/portraits/tyndale.htm

The burning of John Hus and his books. (Hus believed the Bible. He influenced Tyndale.) I have divided the address into two sections, because of its width.
www.lawbuzz.com/cherished_rights/
freedom_speech/hus_burns.htm

The martyrdom of John Hus
www.johnhus.org/martyrdom/index.html

Saint Peter's Basilica and the Circus Maximus

This travel narrative describes Saint Peter's Basilica and the Circus Maximus (the Circus of Nero). A picture of Saint Peter's shows the obelisk from the Circus Maximus, in the center of a great circular courtyard, in front of Saint Peter's.
www.aerenlund.dk/rom/rome_day3.html

Gladiators, the Roman Circus, and Christians. I have divided the address into two sections, because of its width.
www.christianity.com/partner/Article_Display_Page/
0,,PTID4859%7CCHID45%7CCIID142387,00.html

"Tacitus on the Christians." This historical document describes how Christians were killed in the Circus Maximus.
www.livius.org/cg-cm/christianity/tacitus.html

An article about the Obelisk from the Circus Maximus. In 1587, Pope Sixtus V had it dug up and placed in the center of the circular courtyard in front of Saint Peter's Basilica. I have divided the address into two sections, because of its width.
http://itsa.ucsf.edu/~snlrc/encyclopaedia_romana/
circusmaximus/obelisk.html

Pictures of the Obelisk in front of Saint Peter's Basilica. (If you click on the small pictures you will see large ones.)
www.christusrex.org/www1/citta/B-Exterior.html

Saint Peter's Basilica and the Sistine Chapel

A series of 14 web pages, with color pictures of Saint Peter's Basilica, the Pontifical Palace, and the Vatican Gardens. Each page has a number of small pictures that give different perspectives and details. If you click on them you will see large pictures.
www.christusrex.org/www1/citta/0-Citta.html

If this address doesn't work for you, then go to the home page and click on "Vatican City." (In October, 2003, it was near the bottom of the page. If you don't find it there, then search the page.) The home page is below. If the address doesn't work, then do an Internet search for "Christus Rex."
www.christusrex.org

A series of 27 web pages, with color pictures of the Sistine Chapel. Three of these web pages have pictures of prophets and sybils. A sybil is a pagan prophetess.
www.christusrex.org/www1/sistine/0-Tour.html

If this address doesn't work for you, then go to the home page and click on "The Sistine Chapel." (In October, 2003, it was near the bottom of the page. If you don't find it there, then search the page.) The home page is below. If the address doesn't work, then do an Internet search for "Christus Rex."
www.christusrex.org

Three pictures of *The School of Athens*, by Raphael. It shows a number of Greek philosophers. The painting is near the entrance of the Sistine Chapel.
www.artchive.com/artchive/R/raphael/school_athens.jpg.html
www.christusrex.org/www1/stanzas/S2-Segnatura.html
http://un2sg4.unige.ch/athena/raphael/raf_ath4.html

Another picture of *The School of Athens*. I have divided the address into two sections, because of its width.
www.vatican.va/museums/patrons/documents/
vm_pat_doc_12101999_raphael_en.html

A series of 22 web pages, with color pictures of the Vatican museums. A number of them have statues of Greek, Roman, and Egyptian gods and goddesses.
www.christusrex.org/www1/vaticano/0-Musei.html

If this address doesn't work for you, then go to the home page and click on "The Vatican Museums." (In October, 2003, it was near the bottom of the page. If you don't find it there, then search the page.) The home page is below. If the address doesn't work, then do an Internet search for "Christus Rex."
www.christusrex.org

Priests Have Raped Nuns

NOTE: This is happening today. It demonstrates the credibility of statements by Protestant historians that similar events occurred throughout much of the history of the Catholic Church. A former Catholic priest has also written about this problem. Peter de Rosa is a practicing Catholic. He did research in the Vatican Archives while he was a priest. His book, *Vicars of Christ*, gives extensive quotations from official church documents that describe the sexual immorality of Catholic clergy. One documents tell how a group of priests went into a convent and raped the nuns. It was brutal. The quotation comes from an official report that was written for the Pope.

Nuns who were raped by priests are filing official complaints (August 2002) www2.bostonherald.com/news/local_regional/nun08202002.htm

Some priests have been raping nuns (*National Catholic Reporter*, March 2001) www.natcath.com/NCR_Online/archives/031601/031601a.htm

Some priests and bishops have been sexually exploiting nuns. I have divided the address into two sections, because of its width.
www.guardian.co.uk/Distribution/Redirect_Artifact/
0,4678,0-460287,00.html

The Vatican was given a report about priests who were sexually abusing nuns. Nothing was done about it for seven years. Finally, in 2001, the report was leaked to the press. One of the cases involved a priest who got a nun pregnant and then forced her to have an abortion. She died as a result of the abortion.
news.bbc.co.uk/1/hi/world/europe/1234268.stm

The Vatican acknowledged that some priests have raped nuns. This happened after the report was leaked to the press, so it had already become public knowledge.
www.cnn.com/2001/WORLD/europe/11/22/pope.apology/

A statement by the National Coalition of American Nuns. This focuses on the problem in Africa (where it is especially severe), but it also says that priests have raped nuns in 23 countries, including the United States, Italy, Brazil, India, Ireland, and the Philippines.
www.calltoaccountability.org/coalition.htm

Demonstrations demanding that the Vatican stop priests from raping nuns www.calltoaccountability.org/071401Advisory.htm
www.calltoaccountability.org/071001Advisory.htm

A history of how celibacy became mandatory for priests. It includes information about married priests who were put in prison. Their wives and children were sold into slavery.
www.rentapriest.com/thirtynine_popes.htm

A ministry to help children whose fathers are priests
www.marriedpriests.org/HOLYINNOCENTS.htm
Legal guidelines for women whose children were fathered by priests
www.marriedpriests.org/Alegalguide.htm

Bishops Allowed Pedophile Priests to Stay in Office

NOTE: Modern bishops allowed child-molesting priests to remain in office. They protected the priests and covered up their crimes. This demonstrates the credibility of statements by Protestant historians who say that sexual abuse by priests occurred throughout much of the history of the Catholic Church.

Bishops covered up sexual crimes of priests
www.washingtonpost.com/wp-dyn/articles/A9255-2002Jun6.html

"Vatican Sets Rules on Sex Abuse Cases." According to the Vatican: (1) Pedophile cases are subject to "pontifical secrecy." (2) Only Catholic priests should handle them. (3) Only priests should be judges, prosecutors, or defense advocates. (4) The cases should only be handled in Catholic church tribunals.
www.boston.com/globe/spotlight/geoghan/010902_vatican.htm

As of December, 2002, the Archdiocese of Boston was considering filing for bankruptcy, in order to protect itself from lawsuits. The editorial was published in *The Boston Globe* on December 8, 2002, with the title "A New Chapter in Church Tale." I have divided the address into two sections, because of its width.
www.boston.com/dailyglobe2/342/oped/
A_new_chapter_in_church_tale+.shtml

The same article was published in *The Washington Post* on December 9, 2002, with the title "The Catholic Church."
www.postwritersgroup.com/archives/good1205.htm

A summary of some key priest rape cases involving boys and girls
www.angelfire.com/de/knowledgeoftruth/celibacy.html

"Vatican Stance on Gay Clergy Criticized." According to this article in *The Boston Globe*, the Catholic priesthood is becoming a gay profession. Eliminating gay clergy would mean getting rid of about half of the priests and seminarians, and about a third of the bishops. I have divided the address into two sections, because of its width.
www.boston.com/globe/spotlight/
sexabuse/related/030402_vatican.htm

A web page with links to many articles about priest sex-abuse cases. It has links to some websites that have extensive coverage of such cases. I have divided the address into two sections, because of its width.
www.vawnet.org/VNL/library/res_room/
Clergy-SA2.html?where=library

Articles about priests who sexually molested children and adolescents in the confessional (a place where Catholics go to confess their sins to a priest)
http://news.bbc.co.uk/1/hi/uk/52884.stm
www.sexcriminals.com/news/11868/
www.freep.com/news/religion/priest22_20020622.htm

Another article about pedophile priests. I have divided the address into two sections, because of its width.
www.boston.com/globe/spotlight/abuse
/stories/030602_xaverian.htm

Appendix G
Doctrinal Issues

I recommend the book, *The Gospel According to Rome*, by James G. McCarthy (Eugene, Oregon: Harvest House Publishers, 1995). McCarthy is a former Catholic. His book is easy to read. It is thoroughly documented from Catholic sources. The presentation is gentle and compassionate.

There are some excellent articles on the Internet about doctrinal issues relating to Catholicism. I have grouped them into categories.

If you have difficulty getting one of these articles, then go to the home page and look for it. To find the home page, copy the Internet address of the article. Then delete everything in the address that comes after "com," "net," or "org."

Some Internet addresses are too wide for the pages of this book. In those cases, I have divided them into two sections. If you type both sections into your browser (with no spaces in between them), then the addresses should work. I will always tell you when I have divided an Internet address

The Bible
"The Bible is a Unique Book"
www.justforcatholics.org/a18.htm
   "The Bible is the Word of God"
www.justforcatholics.org/a45.htm
   "Did the Early Christians Have the Bible?"
www.justforcatholics.org/a126.htm
   "What Is *Sola Scriptura?*"
www.justforcatholics.org/a74.htm
   "Why the Bible Alone?"
www.justforcatholics.org/a54.htm
   "2 Timothy 3 and *Sola Scriptura*"
www.justforcatholics.org/a151.htm
   "Disagreement among Protestants and *Sola Scriptura*"
www.justforcatholics.org/a87.htm
   "Does the Church Give Authority to the Bible?"
www.justforcatholics.org/a24.htm
   "Private Interpretation of the Bible"
www.justforcatholics.org/a79.htm

"The Bible about Mary"
www.justforcatholics.org/a20.htm
"Infallible Interpreter of the Bible"
www.justforcatholics.org/a148.htm
"The Apocrypha Contradicts Scripture"
www.justforcatholics.org/a109.htm
The Catholic Church's historical and theological approach to the Bible
www.angelfire.com/ky/dodone/Bible.html
"Sola Scriptura"
www.pro-gospel.org/articles/solascriptura.php
"The Certainty of the Written Word of Truth"
www.bereanbeacon.org/CertaintyWrittenWordTruth.html
"Are the Apocrypha Quoted in the New Testament?"
www.justforcatholics.org/a63.htm

Salvation

"Jesus Christ Is Sufficient to Save Sinners Completely"
www.reachingcatholics.org/save_sinners.html
"Crucial Questions for Catholics"
www.catholicconcerns.com/Crucial.html
"No One Can Merit the Unmerited Favor of God"
www.reachingcatholics.org/unmerited.html
"Are Works Necessary for Salvation?"
www.justforcatholics.org/salvation_works.htm
The Sacrifice of Christ"
www.justforcatholics.org/cross.htm
"Justified by Faith Alone"
www.justforcatholics.org/faithalone.htm
"Justification"
www.pro-gospel.org/articles/justification.php
"It Is Finished"
www.pro-gospel.org/articles/finish.php
"Salvation: God's Graciousness in Christ"
www.bereanbeacon.org/Justification.html
"The Biblical Teaching of Justification"
www.christiantruth.com/gospeljustification.html
"The Roman Catholic Teaching on Salvation and Justification"
www.christiantruth.com/gospelrcsalvation.html
"Salvation, God's Graciousness in Christ"
www.bereanbeacon.org/Justification.html

"Salvation, Not in the Sacramental System, But in Christ Alone"
www.bereanbeacon.org/sacramentalsystem.htm

The Papacy
"Was Peter a Pope?"
www.justforcatholics.org/a89.htm
  "Five Historical Realities That Are Against an Early Papacy"
http://members.aol.com/jasonte2/five.htm
  "The Corrupt Papacy"
http://members.aol.com/jasonte/papacy.htm
  "The New Testament's Denial of the Papacy"
http://members.aol.com/jasonte2/newtest.htm
  "Early Post-Apostolic Denials of a Papacy"
http://members.aol.com/jasonte2/denials.htm
  "No Papacy in the Early Church"
http://members.aol.com/jasonte2/nopapacy.htm
  "Who Holds the Keys?"
www.pro-gospel.org/articles/key.php
  "The Patristic Exegesis of the Rock of Matthew 16:18"
www.christiantruth.com/fathersmt16.html
  "The Claim and Boast to Have the Keys of the Apostle Peter"
www.bereanbeacon.org/Popedom_II.html

The Mass
"The Sacrifice of the Mass"
www.justforcatholics.org/a102.htm
  "The Eucharist"
www.justforcatholics.org/a04.htm
  "A Present Sacrifice for Sin?"
www.justforcatholics.org/a13.htm
  "The Eucharist in the Early Church"
www.justforcatholics.org/a34.htm
  "I Am the Bread of Life"
www.justforcatholics.org/a11.htm
  "The Mass: From Mystery to Meaning"
www.gnfc.org/mass.html
  "Eucharistic Adoration: Worship or Idolatry?"
www.reachingcatholics.org/eucharistic_adoration.html
  "The Priesthood"
www.bereanbeacon.org/priesthood.htm

"The Eucharist: A Biblical Review"
www.catholicconcerns.com/Eucharist.html

Baptism
"Baptism"
www.justforcatholics.org/a62.htm
    "Born Again By Baptism?"
www.justforcatholics.org/a70.htm
    "Baptism and Original Sin"
www.justforcatholics.org/a25.htm

Confession
"Confession of Sin"
www.justforcatholics.org/a39.htm
    "Forgiveness Through a Priest"
www.bereanbeacon.org/Forgiveness_through_a_Priest.html

Purgatory
"Purgatory or Christ?"
www.justforcatholics.org/a93.htm
    "Suffering in Purgatory"
www.justforcatholics.org/a12.htm

Tradition
"Sacred Tradition"
www.justforcatholics.org/a77.htm
    "Tradition and the Magician's Hat"
www.justforcatholics.org/a169.htm
    "Traditions"
www.pro-gospel.org/articles/traditions.php
    "Rome's New and Novel Concept of Tradition"
www.christiantruth.com/livingtradition.html

Mary
"The Bible about the Virgin Mary"
www.justforcatholics.org/a20.htm
    "Christian Attitude toward Mary"
www.justforcatholics.org/a05.htm
    "The Rosary"
www.justforcatholics.org/a07.htm

"The Immaculate Conception"
www.justforcatholics.org/a69.htm
"Is Mary Our Mother?"
www.justforcatholics.org/a47.htm
"Is Mary a Mediator?"
www.justforcatholics.org/a78.htm
"Mary Worship"
www.justforcatholics.org/a64.htm
"The Doctrine of the Assumption"
www.justforcatholics.org/assumption.htm
"Mary around the World." This is a series of articles about how Mary is venerated in various countries.
www.angelfire.com/ky/dodone/MaryLawson.html
"The Assumption of Mary"
www.christiantruth.com/assumption.html
"Past Popes Taught Destructive Heresies" (no salvation without Mary)
www.reachingcatholics.org/pastpopes.html
"Do You Know Mary?"
www.reachingcatholics.org/knowmary.html
"Mary Who?"
www.reachingcatholics.org/marywho.html
"Hail Mary?"
www.reachingcatholics.org/hailmarymd.html
"Mary and Catholicism"
http://members.aol.com/jasonte/mary.htm
"Mary in Roman Catholicism"
http://members.aol.com/jasonte2/mary2.htm
"Apparitions Exposed"
www.pro-gospel.org/articles/apparitions.php

The Brown Scapular
The Brown Scapular of Our Lady of Mount Carmel
www.rc.net/lansing/ctk/cc/ocds1.html
The Brown Scapular
www.cin.org/saints/brownsca.html
The Rosary, Brown Scapular, and the Sabbatine Privilege
http://olrl.org/pray/rosary.html

Rosary Promises
Fifteen Promises made by an apparition of "Mary" to Catholics who recite the Rosary. Indulgences promised by the Catholic Church for praying the rosary.
rosarycreations.com/rosarypromises.htm
    Fifteen promises of the Rosary and twelve promises of the Sacred Heart
www.memorare.com/devotions/promises.html

The Miraculous Medal
The Miraculous Medal (picture and description of the apparition)
www.cammonline.org/pages/miraculousMedal.html
    Apparition Chapel in Paris. Two million pilgrims come every year.
www.cammonline.org/pages/appritionChapel.html
    Novena Prayers to Our Lady of the Miraculous Medal
www.cammonline.org/pages/novena.html

Veneration of Statues
"Venerating Statues" (article with links to pictures)
www.catholicconcerns.com/Statues.html
    Nuns venerating a statue of Mary (picture)
www.op-stjoseph.org/nuns/angels/picpages/procession.htm

Statues that Dominate Chapels
NOTE: If you have difficulty getting any of these pictures, then go to the website of the Basilica of the National Shrine of the Immaculate Conception and take their "virtual tour." The Internet address is below. If it doesn't work for you, then do a search for the shrine's name. Some of these have prayers to Mary in addition to showing the picture.
www.nationalshrine.com
    Chapel of Our Lady of Siluva
www.nationalshrine.com/NAT_SHRINE/tour_u32.htm
    Chapel of Our Lady of the Miraculous Medal
www.nationalshrine.com/NAT_SHRINE/tour_u04.htm
    Statue of Mary, Mother of Mankind (many candles are in front of the statue)
www.nationalshrine.com/NAT_SHRINE/tour_c37.htm
    Chapel honoring the apparition of Mary to Saint Catherine Laboure
www.cammonline.org/pagesShrineTour/shrine05En.html

Infant of Prague

NOTE: The Infant of Prague is a statue of Jesus as an infant. It is kept in a church in Prague, Chezchoslovakia. It has 70 sets of elaborate clothes and a crown made out of real gold with real jewels. Nuns dress the statue and take care of it. Miracles are attributed to this statue. Replicas of the statue can be found in Catholic churches around the world. If you have difficulty getting any of these pictures, you can do a search for "Infant of Prague," or for "Infant of Prague + picture."

Article with pictures showing nuns changing the clothes of the statue
http://karmel.at/prag-jesu/english/eng/saticken.htm

Article with a picture of a cardinal carrying the statue
www.medjugorjecenter.org/prague/page2.htm

Article with pictures showing details of the crown and some of the clothes
http://karmel.at/prag-jesu/english/eng/muzejen.htm

Article with several pictures and history of the statue
http://karmel.at/prag-jesu/english/eng/jezuleen.htm

History of the Infant Jesus of Prague
www.cwo.com/~pentrack/catholic/infhist.html

Statues with Gold Crowns

This article has four pictures of statues wearing gold crowns. Three of them are wearing expensive and elaborate clothing. It also has pictures of two processions with statues. One of them is the candlelight procession in Fatima, Portugal, with a million people.
www.aloha.net/~mikesch/baruch.htm

Statues of Mary wearing crowns and clothing. I have divided the address into two sections, because of its width.
www.sspxasia.com/Newsletters/2001/Oct-Dec/
Procession_in_honour_of_Our_Lady_of_the_Rosary.htm

A statue of Mary with baby Jesus. Both wear crowns and clothing.
www.aloha.net/~mikesch/crown.htm

Crowning Statues of Mary

NOTE: The liturgy of the Catholic Church includes an official ritual for crowning statues of Mary. Following are addresses of web pages that show pictures of this. It is done at all levels, ranging from the Pope to classes in Catholic schools.

Pope John Paul II crowning a statue of Mary. (There are seven pictures with descriptions.)
www.aloha.net/~mikesch/crown.htm

Crowing ceremony at a cathedral. (Click on small pictures and you will see large ones.) I have divided the address into two sections, because of its width.
www.cathedralcarmel55.org/mary-crowning1/
pages/reaux-grandaughter.htm

Crowning ceremony at a fifth grade class of a Catholic school
www.stfrancisvernon.org/Crowning5th.htm

Processions with Statues
"Millions in Mexico Gather for Marian Feast" (2.5 million people, October 1999)
www.cwnews.com/news/viewrec.cfm?RefNum=11317

Our Lady of Guadalupe (8 million people in Mexico City, December 2001)
www.e3mil.com/vm/index.asp?vm_id=1&art_id=930

A procession in the United States honoring Our Lady of Guadalupe. I have divided the address into two sections, because of its width.
http://hemi.ps.tsoa.nyu.edu/archive/studentwork/
colony/reed/procession.htm

Another procession in honor of Our Lady of Guadalupe
www.laprensa-sandiego.org/archieve/december14/PARADE.HTM

A church procession honoring Mary. (Click on the pictures to enlarge them.)
www.olphparish.org/mayprocession2000.htm

Overview of Recent Canon Law
"Has Roman Catholicism Changed? An Overview of Recent Canon Law"
www.gnfc.org/ant_v1n2_canon.html
www.reachingcatholics.org/rcchanged.html

Required Fasting
According to Canon Law, Catholics are still required to abstain from eating meat every Friday
www.catholic-pages.com/life/fridaymeat.asp

In 1997, American bishops met to discuss whether or not to again require Catholics to abstain from eating meat on all fridays. (The term "abstinence" in these articles refers to abstaining from eating meat.)
www.news-star.com/stories/111297/lfe_bishop.html
www.cin.org/archives/al-bushra/199711/0069.html
www.ncregister.com/Register_News/060103_3.htm
www.geocities.com/Heartland/Estates/4152/meatless.htm
www.geocities.com/Heartland/2964/meatless.html
www.cwnews.com/news/viewstory.cfm?recnum=6264

www.cwnews.com/news/viewstory.cfm?recnum=6281
www.hollandsentinel.com/stories/111497/rel_meat.html
 Rules about eating meat on "meatless days" if Catholics have dinner with non-Catholics
www.cmri.org/adsum02-1a.html
 Eating fish on Fridays.
www.cin.org/users/james/questions/q034.htm
 Information about days when fasting is required, and what Catholics are allowed to eat on those days
www.traditio.com/cal.htm

Appendix H
Books, Videos, and Websites

The following books and videos are appropriate for Catholics, former Catholics, and Protestants who want to understand Catholicism. I have also included two books about the credibility and authority of the Bible.

Books

James G. McCarthy used to be a Catholic. He wrote, *The Gospel According to Rome: Comparing Catholic Tradition and the Word of God.* This book was life-changing for me. It deals with foundational issues in a clear and compassionate manner. It is easy to read and it is thoroughly documented from official Catholic sources. This book helps people understand doctrinal issues. It also gives an inside picture of how Catholicism affects the daily lives of people. It is available at Amazon.com and at regular bookstores. You can also order it by phone from D&K Press. Their phone number is (800) 777-8839. A Spanish version of the book is available from Kregel Publications. Their phone number is (616) 451-4775.

William Webster wrote, *The Church of Rome at the Bar of History.* He has some valuable insights into Church history. He demonstrates that some Catholic doctrines are contrary to the beliefs of early Christians. Webster is also a former Catholic. I found this book to be quite helpful.

Richard Bennett (a former priest) and Mary Hertel (a former nun) compiled and edited, *The Truth Set Us Free: Twenty Former Nuns Tell Their Stories.* If you are interested in behind-the-scenes information about convent life, this is a good book to read. These testimonies are "inside stories," intensely personal, and down-to-earth. The book should be available at Amazon.com. If you live in the United States, you can also order it through Richard Bennett's website. (It is listed later in this appendix.) When you go to the website, click on "Catalog." As of October, 2003, the book was the second item listed. There is an order form at the end of the catalog.

Josh McDowell wrote two books that helped me recover from the way that my Catholic training undermined my confidence in Scripture. You can order these books at Amazon.com or through regular bookstores. Amazon.com has a special deal if you order both books.

More Than A Carpenter (Tyndale House, 1987) is a short book that thoroughly establishes the credibility of the Biblical account of the Resurrection. In the process, it increases the reader's confidence in all of Scripture.

The New Evidence That Demands a Verdict (Nelson Reference, 1999) has excellent information about the reliability and authority of Scripture, including evidence from modern archeology. It is a revised and updated version of a previous two-volume work (*Evidence That Demands a Verdict*, Volumes 1 and 2). It has been fully updated to answer the questions challenging Christians today. I read the earlier two-volume work. I look forward to reading this one.

Videos

The *Jesus* video is beautifully done. It is well acted, in a spirit of making the Bible come alive and helping people relate to Jesus more directly. The text of the dialogue comes from the Gospel of Luke. At the end of the video, there is a presentation of the salvation message, with a prayer. This video has been translated into 700 languages. You can order it from the Jesus Film Project. Their phone number is (949) 361-7575. Their website is www.JesusFilm.org.

James McCarthy produced an excellent video called, *Catholicism: Crisis of Faith*. The video was life-changing for me. A friend of mine, who is a missionary in Guatemala, said that this video gave him a better understanding of Catholicism than a college course that he had taken on the subject. The video is a valuable resource for people with Catholic friends and family members, for Catholics, and for former Catholics. You can order it from bookstores by giving them the ISBN number (ISBN 0-962-9152-0-3).

D&K Press has the video in English and Spanish. They ship all over the world. Their phone number is (800) 777-8839. Their website is www.DKPressChristianBooks.com.

A Polish version is available from Gober Multimedia. Their phone number is (216) 447-9067. A German version of the video is available in Munich, Germany. You can contact Uwe Brinkman. His email address is bfc_muenchen@t-online.de. His phone number is 011-49-89-184221. A Korean version is available from the Korea Video Mission Center (47 Sam John-Dong, Song Pa-Gu, Seoul, Korea). Their phone number is 011-822-420-2992. Their fax number is 011-822-420-2994.

The video, *Messages from Heaven*, deals primarily with apparitions of Mary. The producer is Jim Tetlow, a former Catholic. He and his partner have read hundreds of Catholic books about apparitions of Mary. The video is available from D&K Press. Their phone number is (800) 777-8839. You can watch the video online at the website below.
www.harpazo.net/EternalProductions/ApparitionsofMary/

Websites

I have published four books about Catholicism. They are custom-tailored for different audiences. You can read the books online. Information about the books and their websites is given at the end of the Bibliography.

Unmasking Catholicism
You can read the book online at this website. Please tell your friends about this website.
www.UnmaskingCatholicism.com

Just For Catholics (Dr. Joe Mizzi, a former Catholic)
This website has articles in eight languages.
www.JustForCatholics.org

New Life with Christ (my website)
www.NewLifeWithChrist.com

Christians Evangelizing Catholics (Dr. Bill Jackson)
This website has a "Glossary of Catholic Doctrine and Biblical Rebuttal." There is a search engine. In addition, you can look up subjects alphabetically. There are a number of testimonies of former Catholics. Dr. Jackson does public speaking. You can contact him through his website.
www.DoDone.org
www.angelfire.com/ky/DoDone

Proclaiming the Gospel (Mike Gendron, a former Catholic)
This website has articles, testimonies, online audio tapes, and a store with books and tapes. It also has a chat room. Mike Gendron does public speaking. So does Rich Kris, who is associated with him. You can contact them through the website.
www.pro-gospel.org

Good News for Catholics (James McCarthy, a former Catholic)
This website has articles, booklets, and excerpts from books. It also tells where to get some good resource materials.
www.gnfc.org

Mission to Catholics (Bart Brewer, a former Roman Catholic priest)
This website has online tracts (articles and testimonies), and a bookstore.
www.mtc.org

Berean Beacon (Richard Bennett, a former Roman Catholic priest)
This website has articles, testimonies, and a bookstore (catalog). There are some Spanish articles. It has an online video and numerous online audio tapes. Richard Bennett does public speaking. You can contact him through his website.
www.BereanBeacon.org

Reaching Catholics for Christ
This website has articles and audio tapes.
www.ReachingCatholics.org/mainpage.html

Crusade for Catholics (Anthony Ruiz, a former Catholic)
This website has articles, tracts, and a store with books and videos. Anthony Ruiz does public speaking.
www.CrusadeForCatholics.com

Catholic Concerns (my website)
This website has numerous articles.
www.CatholicConcerns.com

Bibliography and Notes

Bibliography

Audisio, Gabriel (translated by Claire Davison), *The Waldensian Dissent: Persecution and Survival*, Cambridge, England: Cambridge University Press, 1999.

Bloesch, Donald G., *Essentials of Evangelical Theology*, Volume 1, San Francisco, California: Harper & Row, Publishers, 1982.

Catechism of the Catholic Church, Washington, DC: U.S. Catholic Conference, 2000.

Code of Canon Law, Latin-English edition, New English Translation, Washington, DC: Canon Law Society of America, 1999.

De Rosa, Peter, *Vicars of Christ: The Dark Side of the Papacy*, Dublin, Ireland: Poolbeg Press, 1988, 2000. The author used to be a priest. He is still a practicing Catholic. While he was a priest, he did research in the Vatican archives.

Edwards, Brian H., *God's Outlaw: The Story of William Tyndale and the English Bible*, Darlington, England, Evangelical Press, 1976, 1999.

Elwell, Walter A. (editor), *Evangelical Dictionary of Theology*, Grand Rapids, Michigan: Baker Book House, 1984.

England, Randy, *The Unicorn in the Sanctuary: The Impact of the New Age on the Catholic Church*, Rockford, Illinois: TAN Books and Publishers, 1990. The author is Catholic.

Flannery, Austin (editor), *Vatican Council II, The Conciliar and Post Conciliar Documents*, New Revised Edition, Volume 1, Northport, New York: Costello Publishing Company, 1975, 1996.

Hardon, John A., *Pocket Catholic Dictionary*, New York: Doubleday, Image Books, 1980, 1985. The author is a Catholic priest with a doctorate in theology.

Hunt, Dave, *A Woman Rides the Beast*, Eugene, Oregon: Harvest House Publishers, 1994.

Jackson, Bill, *The Noble Army of "Heretics."* The author personally visited the Martyrs Monuments in England, and the valleys where the Waldensians lived. He studied original documents in addition to doing research in books. You can read the entire book online at the following website. www.NobleArmy.com

Johnson, Paul, *A History of Christianity*, New York: Touchstone, Simon & Schuster, 1995. The author is a Catholic and a prominent historian.

Jones, Peter, *Pagans in the Pews: How the New Spirituality Is Invading Your Home, Church and Community*, New York: Continuum, 1995.

Küng, Hans, *The Catholic Church: A Short History* (translated by John Bowden), New York: Modern Library, 2001, 2003. The author is a Catholic theologian.

Martin, Malachi, *The Decline and Fall of the Roman Church*, New York: G.P. Putnam's Sons, 1981. The author recently died. He was a Catholic priest, a theologian, a professor at the Vatican's Pontifical University, and a Vatican insider. He was also the personal confessor of Pope John XXIII. His books are a plea for reform.

Martin, Malachi, *The Jesuits: The Society of Jesus and the Betrayal of the Roman Catholic Church*, New York: Simon & Schuster, 1987.

McBirnie, William Steuart, *The Search for the Twelve Apostles*, Wheaton, Illinois: Living Books, Tyndale House Publishers, 1973, 1982.

McCarthy, James G., *The Gospel According to Rome: Comparing Catholic Tradition and the Word of God*, Eugene, Oregon: Harvest House Publishers, 1995. The author is a former Catholic.

Rose, Michael S., *Goodbye, Good Men: How Liberals Brought Corruption into the Catholic Church*, Washington, DC: Regnery Publishing, 2002. The author is Catholic.

Shelley, Bruce, *Church History in Plain Language*, Nashville, Tennessee: Thomas Nelson Publishers, 1982, 1995.

Smith, Wesley J., *Culture of Death: The Assault on Medical Ethics in America*, San Francisco, California: Encounter Books, 2000.

Steichen, Donna, *Ungodly Rage: The Hidden Face of Catholic Feminism*, San Francisco: Ignatius Press, 1991, 1992. The author is Catholic.

Svendsen, Eric, *On This Slippery Rock*, Calvary Press, 2002.

Tetlow, Jim, *Messages from Heaven* (self published). You can order it from D&K Press (800-777-8839).

Webster, William, *The Church of Rome at the Bar of History*, Carlisle, Pennsylvania: The Banner of Truth Trust, 1995. The author is a former Catholic.

Yallop, David, *In God's Name: An Investigation into the Murder of Pope John Paul I*, London, England: Transworld Publishers, 1994.

Yungen, Ray, *A Time of Departing: How a Universal Spirituality Is Changing the Face of Christianity*, Silverton, Oregon: Lighthouse Trails Publishing Company, 2002.

Videos

James G., *Catholicism: Crisis of Faith*. You can buy this video from D&K Press (800-777-8839).

Tetlow, Jim, *Messages from Heaven*. You can buy this video from D&K Press (800-777-8839).

My Books and Websites

I've written a cluster of books relating to Catholicism. They have much of the same information, but each one is custom-tailored for a specific audience. All of them were published by iUniverse in 2003 or 2004. You can buy them at Amazon.com. You can also read them online. The books and websites are listed below.

I also have a website called New Life With Christ. It is appropriate for new believers, people who are considering becoming Christians, and mature Christians who would appreciate some encouragement. It has information that I wanted to include in the books, but I couldn't because it would have made the books too long.

Please tell your friends about the websites.

Another Side of Catholicism (for Catholics)
www.AnotherSideOfCatholicism.com

Catholicism Unveiled (for Protestants)
www.CatholicismUnveiled.com

The Catholic Undertow (a manual for former Catholics)
www.CatholicUndertow.com

Unmasking Catholicism (a longer book with more information, for serious students of Catholicism)
www.UnmaskingCatholicism.com

New Life With Christ
www.NewLifeWithChrist.com

Notes

The first time that I list an author, I give his name and the title of his book. After that, I just give his name. If you want information about his book, then look for the author in the Bibliography. Authors are listed alphabetically.

Many of the Notes give addresses of Internet articles. Sometimes articles get moved, discontinued, or replaced. I have often provided addresses for several articles about the same subject. That way, if one Internet address doesn't work any more, you can still read the other articles.

Finding Valuable Resources Online—Some things, such as papal encyclicals, are easy to find online. Therefore, I usually don't give Internet addresses for them. (At first I gave several addresses for each encyclical, but that made the book too long, so I deleted them. I thought that you would rather search for a few encyclicals than have to pay more for the book.)

You can read papal encyclicals online. To find them, do an Internet search for the Latin title of the encyclical plus the name of the Pope who wrote it. Be sure that you spell the Latin words correctly. (You may be able to find the encyclical using only one or two key Latin words instead of the entire title. It's worth trying, because you are less likely make typing errors.)

The documents of the Second Vatican Council are online. Search for "Vatican Council II" or "Second Vatican Council."

Declarations (canons) of the Council of Trent are online. Search for "Council of Trent." You might want to search for "Council of Trent" plus "justification" or "justified."

The *Catholic Encyclopedia* is online. To find articles, search for the title of the article plus "Catholic Encyclopedia." (For example, "scapulars + Catholic Encyclopedia.")

The *Catechism of the Catholic Church* is online with a search engine. You can search for words or paragraph numbers. To find it, search for "Catechism of the Catholic Church."

You can find the *Code of Canon Law* online by searching for its title. You can use the FIND function to search for the numbers of the laws that you want to see.

The FIND Function—You can quickly locate things within Internet articles by using the FIND function. Click on EDIT. When you get the drop-down menu, click on FIND. You will get a dialog box with a place where you can type the word or phrase that you are searching for. Type it and then hit ENTER.

Hyphen Problems—There have been times when I was online, and copied the address of the document, and put it into something that I was writing. Later, I copied the address from my article, pasted it into my browser, and got an error message instead of the article. I discovered that sometimes hyphens disappear or get replaced by question marks or other characters. If that happens to you, check the original address carefully, and then make sure that there is no missing hyphen or additional character in your browser.

Good Pictures—There is a website for the Basilica of the National Shrine of the Immaculate Conception. It has a "virtual tour" that shows numerous chapels that honor Mary. The pictures of the statues and mosaics, and the accompanying prayers, novenas, and information, will give you some insight into devotional practices relating to Mary. If the following address doesn't work for you, then do a search for "National Shrine of the Immaculate Conception."
www.NationalShrine.com

Chapter 1—Hiding Behing Words

1. John A. Hardon, *Pocket Catholic Dictionary*, page 295 ("merit"). Hardon is a Catholic priest with a doctorate in theology.
2. *The Rites of the Catholic Church*, Volume 1, pages 394-407. Quoted in James G. McCarthy, *The Gospel According to Rome: Comparing Catholic Tradition and the Word of God*, page 22.
3. John A. Hardon, pages 166-167 ("grace").
4. Pope Boniface VIII, *Unam Sanctam*, November 18, 1302. (See the very last sentence.) Pope Eugene IV, *Cantate Domino*, 1441. Pope Pius IX, *Quanto Conficiamur Moerore*, August 10, 1863. (See paragraph 8.) Pope Leo XIII, *Super Quibusdam*, June 29, 1896. (See paragraph 16.) Pope Pius XII, *Mystici Corporis Christi*, June 29, 1943. (See paragraph 41.) Pope Pius XII, *Ad Apostolorum Principis*, June 29, 1958. (See paragraphs 45 and 46.)

    A conservative Catholic website has an article with quotations from popes and saints who say that there is no salvation apart from the Pope.
    www.romancatholicism.org/digest/ad5-1.html

    "Outside the Catholic Church There Is Absolutely No Salvation," *A Voice Crying in the Wilderness*, No. 6. You can read this newsletter at the website of a Catholic monastery. Look for the article on the home page.
    www.mostholyfamilymonastery.com
5. Pope Pius IX, *Ineffabilis Deus*, December 8, 1854. (See the last paragraph of the encyclical.) Pope Pius IX, *Ubi Primum*, February 2, 1849. (See paragraph 5.) Pope Pius X, *Ad Diem Illum Laetissium*, February 2, 1904. (See paragraphs 12 through 15.) Pope Benedict XV, *Inter Sodalicia*, March 22, 1918. (Quoted in *The Church Teaches*, published by the Jesuit fathers of St. Mary's College, pages 210-211. Pope Pius XI, *Miserentissimus Redemptor*, May 8, 1928. You can see some quotations from popes at the following website.
    www.reachingcatholics.org/pastpopes.html
6. The Catechism of the Catholic Church, paragraph 969.
7. Pope John Paul II, *Veritatis Splendor* (*Splendor of the Truth*), August 6, 1993. (See paragraph 120.)
8. Brian H. Edwards, *God's Outlaw: The Story of William Tyndale and the English Bible*, pages 168-170.

    A biography of William Tyndale. This has information about men reading the Bible out loud in English so that crowds of people could hear it.
    http://elvis.rowan.edu/~kilroy/JEK/10/06.html
    http://justus.anglican.org/resources/bio/260.html

Chapter 2—Ecclesiastical Curses

1. "Anathema," *The Catholic Encyclopedia*, Volume I, 1907. The ritual is described in detail, with a lengthy quotation. If this address doesn't work for you, then do an Internet search for "anathema + Catholic Encyclopedia."
    www.newadvent.org/cathen/01455e.htm
2. "Inquisition," *The Catholic Encyclopedia*, Volume VIII, 1910. The quotation is from the second paragraph of the article. The Office of the Inquisition is an ecclesiastical institution for suppressing heresy. It is a permanent office with headquarters in Rome.

    The article says that, according to the Law of Moses, heretics were to be tortured or killed. That is not Biblical. People who tried to get the Israelites to worship "foreign gods" were stoned to death. Stoning was the normal method of execution in those days. Having a mob of people throw large rocks at a person would kill him quickly—it was not torture.

Worshiping "foreign gods" was not at all comparable to heresy. An example of heresy is Martin Luther, who said that we are saved by faith alone. An example of worshiping "foreign gods" is abandoning Christianity in order to become a Hindu.
www.newadvent.org/cathen/08026a.htm
> For a Protestant perspective on the Inquisition, please see the following two articles.
> A study of the history, theology, and methods of the Inquisition
www.sundayschoolcourses.com/inq/inqcont.htm
> "The Inquisition: A Study in Absolute Catholic Power"
www.mtc.org/inquis.html
http://la.znet.com/~bart/inquis.htm
www.crusadeforcatholics.com/bart.htm

3. *Code of Canon Law*, page 247, Canon 752. The 1983 *Code of Canon Law* was translated into English in 1988. You can read it online. You can use the FIND feature to locate laws by number.
www.intratext.com/X/ENG0017.htm
www.ourladyswarriors.org/canon/
www.deacons.net/Canon_Law/Frame_Index.htm
www.smolchicago.com/Canon/cic_en.htm
> You can buy the *Code of Canon Law* from the Canon Law Society of America. Information is given in Note 1 of Chapter 24 ("Canon Law and Religious Freedom")

4. *Code of Canon Law*, page 409, Canons 1311-1312.

5. I saw a video about John Hus. You can read about his martyrdom online.
www.johnhus.org/martyrdom/index.html

6. The Congregation for the Doctrine of the Faith (formerly known as the Office of the Inquisition). This article is on the Vatican's website. [Click on "Profile."]
www.vatican.va/roman_curia/congregations/cfaith/index.htm
> The Vatican website is slow and it doesn't always come up. You can also find information about the change of name of the Office of the Inquisition at the following websites.
www.geocities.com/iberianinquisition/office.html
http://es.rice.edu/ES/humsoc/Galileo/Student_Work/Trial96/breu/timeline.html
http://news.bbc.co.uk/hi/english/world/europe/newsid_1251000/1251677.stm

7. *Ineffabilis Deus* (*Apostolic Constitution on the Immaculate Conception*). Encyclical of Pope Pius IX, issued December 8, 1854. Near the end of this papal bull there is a section called "The Definition." The statements that I described are in the last paragraph of that section. If these addresses don't work for you, then do a search for "Ineffabilis Deus."
www.newadvent.org/docs/pi09id.htm
www.pax-et-veritas.org/Popes/pius_ix/ineffabi.htm
www.geocities.com/apologeticacatolica/ineffabilis.html

8. Paul Johnson, *A History of Christianity*, page 308. Paul Johnson is a Catholic and a prominent historian.

9. *Munificentissimus Deus* (*Defining the Dogma of the Assumption*). Encyclical of Pope Pius XII, issued November 1, 1950. See paragraph 47. If these addresses don't work for you, then do a search for "Munificentissimus Deus."
www.geocities.com/papalencyclicals/Pius12/P12MUNIF.HTM
www.ewtn.com/library/PAPALDOC/P12MUNIF.HTM
www.papalencyclicals.net/Pius12/P12MUNIF.HTM

10. Paul Johnson, page 199.

11. "Anathema," *The Catholic Encyclopedia*, Volume I, 1907. The article says that the ritual was developed by Pope Zachary, who reigned from 741 to 752. You can use the FIND function to search for "Zachary." (Click on EDIT. Click on FIND. Type in "Zachary" and hit ENTER.)
www.newadvent.org/cathen/01455e.htm
    "Pope St. Zachary," *The Catholic Encyclopedia*, Volume XV, 1912. The title of the article indicates that Pope Zachary is a canonized saint. The article does not mention the anathema ritual.
www.newadvent.org/cathen/15743b.htm

Chapter 3—The Council of Trent

1. This article from a Baptist website gives general information about the Council of Trent. It quotes a number of decrees relating to Evangelical doctrines.
www.wayoflife.org/fbns/trent.htm
www.biblebc.com/Roman%20Catholicism/summary_of_trent.htm
    Canons of the Council of Trent that deal with justification, the eucharist (communion), and the mass.
www.biblebc.com/Roman%20Catholicism/council_of_trent_full.htm
    Canons of the Council of Trent that deal with communion (the eucharist)
http://codesign.scu.edu/arth12/text_counciloftrent.html
    The entire text of the Council of Trent is available online. If these addresses don't work for you, then do a search for "Council of Trent."
http://history.hanover.edu/early/trent.htm
http://history.hanover.edu/texts/trent/ctbull.html
www.pax-et-veritas.org/Councils/trent/trent.htm
    The Council of Trent covered a lot of material, including many things that are probably not of interest to most people. If you read the book (either as a book or online), I suggest that you look for the following:
    - 4th session, decree concerning the canonical scriptures (This says that Bibles must include the apocryphal books.) ("Tobias" is "Tobit.")
    - 6th session, canons on justification (especially canons 12, 24, and 33)
    - 7th session, canons on baptism (especially canons 3, 5, 13)
    - 13th session, canons on the eucharist (communion) (especially canons 1 and 8)
    - 14th session, canons on the sacrament of penance (especially canons 1, 7, 8)
    - 22nd session, canons on the mass (especially canons 1, 2, 3, 5)
    - 23rd session, canons on the sacrament of order (priesthood) (especially canons 1 and 8)
    - 25th session, the decree on Purgatory, and the decree on the invocation and veneration of saints, relics of saints, and "sacred images"
2. *Lumen Gentium* (*Dogmatic Constitution on the Church*), paragraph 51. In Austin Flannery (Editor), *Vatican Council II: The Conciliar and Post Conciliar Documents*, Volume 1, page 412. The documents produced by the Second Vatican Council are available online. If the following addresses don't work for you, then do an Internet Search for "Vatican Council II" or "Second Vatican Council."
www.stjosef.at/council/
www.stjosef.at/council/search/
www.cin.org/vatiidoc.html
www.rc.net/rcchurch/vatican2/

www.christusrex.org/www1/CDHN/v1.html
www.vatican.va/archive/hist_councils/ii_vatican_council/
3. *Optatum Totius (Decree on Priestly Training)*, Conclusion. In Austin Flannery, Volume 1, page 724.
4. Pope John XXIII said that he accepts what the Council of Trent declares about justification. (It declares that any person who believes that we are saved by faith alone is anathema.) He also confirmed all past anathemas against "false doctrine"—in other words, the Protestant doctrines that were condemned by the Council of Trent.
www.angelfire.com/ky/dodone/J23.html
   All Catholic clergymen who participated in the Second Vatican Council signed a document stating that they accepted the declarations of the Council of Trent. (This is in the opening paragraph of the article.)
www.biblebc.com/Roman%20Catholicism/summary_of_trent.htm
www.wayoflife.org/fbns/trent.htm
5. You can check this out for yourself. *The Catechism of the Catholic Church* is available online with a search engine. You can search for words or paragraph numbers. Do a search for "Council of Trent." If these addresses don't work, search for "Catechism of the Catholic Church."
www.scborromeo.org/ccc.htm
www.christusrex.org/www2/kerygma/ccc/searchcat.html
6. *The Catechism of the Catholic Church*, Paragraph 891.

Chapter 4—Ecumenism

1. *Unitatis Redintegratio (Decree on Ecumenism)*, Paragraph 24. In Austin Flannery (Editor), *Vatican Council II: The Conciliar and Post Conciliar Documents*, Volume 1, page 470.
   The documents produced by the Second Vatican Council are available online. If these addresses don't work, search for "Vatican Council II" or "Second Vatican Council."
www.stjosef.at/council/
www.stjosef.at/council/search/
www.cin.org/vatiidoc.html
www.rc.net/rcchurch/vatican2/
www.christusrex.org/www1/CDHN/v1.html
2. *Reflections and Suggestions Concerning Ecumenical Dialogue* (Post Conciliar Document No. 42). In Austin Flannery, pages 540-541. The quotation is on page 541.
3. Pope Boniface VIII, *Unam Sanctam*, November 18, 1302. See the very last sentence. (Papal encyclicals are online. You can find this one by searching for "Unam Sanctam.")
4. Pope Pius IX, *Quanto Conficiamur Moerore (On Promotion of False Doctrines)*, August 10, 1863, paragraph 8.
   Pope Pius IX, *Nostis et Nobiscum (On the Church in the Pontifical States)*, December 8, 1849. See paragraph 10.
5. *Catechism of the Catholic Church*, paragraph 891.
6. *Code of Canon Law*, page 427, Canon 1366. Canon Laws provide the legal basis for everything that the Roman Catholic Church does. Even the Inquisition and the persecution of Protestants were based on Canon Law.
7. Opening Speech of Pope John XXIII to the Second Vatican Council. Use the FIND function to search for the section, "How to Repress Errors."
www.christusrex.org/www1/CDHN/v2.html

www.ourladyswarriors.org/teach/v2open.htm
www.rc.net/rcchurch/vatican2/j23open.txt
www.catholic-forum.com/saints/pope0261i.htm

If these addresses don't work, then search for "opening speech + Vatican II + John XXIII." You can also search for "Second Vatican Council" or "Vatican Council II." You should find documents from the Council. Some of these websites should have the speech.

8. Mike Gendron, "Protestant Pastors Converting to Rome," *Proclaiming the Gospel* (March/April 2004, Vol. 13, No. 2), page 3. The author is a former Catholic. You can read his newsletter online. These statistics only include pastors who contacted the Coming Home Network, which was founded in 1993. They do not include pastors who converted before 1993, or who converted without contacting the network. They also do not include pastors who are considering converting to Catholicism, but have not contacted the network.
www.pro-gospel.org

9. I read an Internet article about an entire church that converted to Catholicism. At the time, I didn't know that I would be writing this book, and I didn't keep the website address. I've searched for that article, but I haven't been able to find it again.

10. A member of that church contacted me several times, asking for advice. He was very distressed by the situation.

Chapter 5—Spiritual Coercion

1. Paul Johnson, *A History of Christianity*, page 199. Johnson is a Catholic and a prominent historian.
2. Bruce Shelley, *Church History in Plain Language*, page 185.
   "Excommunication," *The Catholic Encyclopedia*, Volume V, 1909.
   www.newadvent.org/cathen/05678a.htm
   "Interdict," *The Catholic Encyclopedia*, Volume VIII, 1910.
   www.newadvent.org/cathen/08073a.htm
3. Malachi Martin, *The Decline and Fall of the Roman Church*, pages 133-134. Malachi Martin recently died. He was a Catholic priest, a Vatican insider, and the personal confessor of Pope John XXIII. He did research in the Vatican Archives. His books are a plea for reform.
   This summarizes the differences between the Orthodox Church and the Roman Catholic Church. Information about the excommunication is in the beginning of the article.
   www.ipfw.edu/ipfwhist/syllabi/h201/orthodoxy.htm
   An article from an Orthodox website. You can find information about the excommunication quickly by doing a search for "1054" (the date when it occurred).
   www.goannunciation.org/main/what_is.htm
   www.orthodoxusa.org/uao/abouttheuao/west1054.htm
   Quotations from popes who said that there is no salvation apart from the Pope.
   www.reachingcatholics.org/pastpopes.html
   A papal encyclical that says that there is no salvation apart from the Pope. The statement is in the very last sentence of the encyclical. Pope Boniface VIII, *Unam Sanctam*, November 18, 1302.
   Pope Innocent III said that he was the "Foundation of all Christianity." This article has information about many popes. Use the FIND function to search for Innocent III.
   www.whiterobedmonks.org/netsor1a.html
4. Bruce Shelley, page 185.

5. Peter de Rosa, *Vicars of Christ: The Dark Side of the Papacy*, pages 66-73. This includes information about Pope Innocent III's excommunication of people who supported the *Magna Carta*. De Rosa is a practicing Catholic and a former priest.
   Bruce Shelley, pages 185-186.
   This article has a lot of information about Pope Innocent III, including his excommunication of anybody who supported the *Magna Carta*. Click on the time period 1200-1300.
   www.goacom.com/overseas-digest/god.html
   This article tells how Pope Innocent III condemned the *Magna Carta* as immoral. However, it does not mention the excommunication of people who supported it. It has brief summaries of information about Innocent, including the fact that he placed the nations of England and France under interdict. I recommend that you read the entire section about him. This article has information about many popes. Search for Innocent III.
   www.whiterobedmonks.org/netsor1a.html
   Articles about the influence of the *Magna Carta* on democracy in England and America. It was one of the foundational documents that influenced the American Constitution.
   www.archives.gov/exhibit_hall/featured_documents/magna_carta/
   www.blupete.com/Law/ConstitutionDocs/MagnaCarta.htm
   www.crf-usa.org/Foundation_docs/Foundation_home.html
   www.bl.uk/collections/treasures/magna.html
   The *Magna Carta* is called the Great Charter of English Liberty. The text is online.
   www.constitution.org/eng/magnacar.htm
   www.britannia.com/history/magna2.html
   www.cs.indiana.edu/statecraft/magna-carta.html
   www.fordham.edu/halsall/source/mcarta.html
6. Clifford Pereira, "Glimpses of Church History, 1200-1300 CE" [A.D.]. Click on the time period 1200-1300.
   www.goacom.com/overseas-digest/god.html
7. Paul Johnson, page 199.
8. Pope Boniface VIII, *Unam Sanctam*, November 18, 1302. The very last sentence says that nobody can be saved without submitting to the Pope.
9. Malachi Martin, pages 137-145.
   Articles about Pope Gregory VII's excommunication of Emperor Henry IV.
   www.saburchill.com/history/biblio/006.html
   http://en.wikipedia.org/wiki/Henry_IV,_Holy_Roman_Emperor
   www.bartleby.com/65/he/Henry4HRE.html
10. Paul Johnson, pages 196-197. Malachi Martin, page 140.
11. *Code of Canon Law*, Canons 1331-1332 (page 416) and 1364-1399 (pages 427-435).
12. Dr. Mark F. Montebello, "Civil Rights in Malta's Post-Colonial Age," Part III, "Independence According to the British," first subheading, "The Most Shameful Episode." Dr. Montebello is a Catholic priest from Malta.
    www.maltamag.com/features/civil_rights3.html
13. E.C. Schembri, "The Making of a Statesman." This is an article about Mintoff, the Labor Party candidate in Malta's 1962 election.
    http://members.tripod.com/~bezzul/mintoff2.html
14. Joe Mizzi, "Liberty of Conscience." An article by a citizen of Malta whose parents personally experienced the interdict of 1962.
    www.justforcatholics.org/a76.htm
15. *The Catechism of the Catholic Church*, paragraphs 1854, 1855, 1856, 1863.

16. *The Catechism of the Catholic Church*, paragraphs 1033, 1874.
17. *The Catechism of the Catholic Church*, paragraphs 1484, 1497, 1395, 1424, 1449.

Chapter 6—Hunting "Heretics"

1. Paul Johnson, *A History of Christianity*, pages 112-119. Bruce Shelley, *Church History in Plain Language*, page 128.

    Saint Augustine laid the theological groundwork for the Inquisition. To find the information in the following articles, do a search for "inquisition."
    www.gospelcom.net/chi/GLIMPSEF/Glimpses/glmps115.shtml
    www.thenazareneway.com/inquisition.htm
    www.wayoflife.org/fbns/augustinefather.htm

    Some quotations from Saint Augustine.
    www.angelfire.com/ky/dodone/Augustine.html
    "Inquisition," *The Catholic Encyclopedia*, Volume VIII, 1910.
    www.newadvent.org/cathen/08026a.htm
2. *Code of Canon Law*, page 247, Canon 751.
3. Paul Johnson, page 273.
4. Tyndale, William," *World Book Encyclopedia 2000* (on CD-Rom).

    Articles about William Tyndale
    www.hertford.ox.ac.uk/alumni/tyndale.htm
    www.loc.gov/loc/lcib/9707/web/tyndale.html
    www.cantonbaptist.org/halloffame/tyndale.htm
    www.llano.net/baptist/tyndale.htm
    www.williamtyndale.com/0welcomewilliamtyndale.htm
5. If you want to get a feel for the times, then read the book *God's Outlaw* by Brian H. Edwards.
6. Paul Johnson, pages 254-255; 273.
7. Paul Johnson, pages 119-120.
8. Gabriel Audisio, *The Waldensian Dissent: Persecution and Survival*, pages 11-12.

    "Francis, Saint," *Encyclopedia.com*
    www.encyclopedia.com/articles/04681.html
    "Francis, Saint, Conversion," *Encyclopedia.com*
    www.encyclopedia.com/articles/04681Conversion.html
9. Bill Jackson, "Waldenses," *The Noble Army of "Heretics."* Dr. Jackson combines excellent scholarship with touching portraits of heroic people. You can read this chapter online.
    www.NobleArmy.com
    www.angelfire.com/ky/dodone/NA5.html
10. Paul Johnson, page 251.
11. Clifford Pereira, "Glimpses of Church History, 1200-1300 CE" [A.D.]. Click on the time period 1200-1300.
    www.goacom.com/overseas-digest/god.html
12. Bruce Shelley, page 185.
13. Bruce Shelley, page 215.
14. Pope Boniface VIII, *Unam Sanctam*, November 18, 1302.
15. Gabriel Audisio, page 11.

    "Heritage of the Waldensians"
    www.wrs.edu/journals/jour896/waldensians.html

16. Bruce Shelley, pages 206-209.
17. "Waldenses," *Encyclopedia.com*
    www.encyclopedia.com/articles/13592.html
    "Heritage of the Waldensians"
    www.wrs.edu/journals/jour896/waldensians.html
18. Gabriel Audisio, summary from the back cover of the book
    "Heritage of the Waldensians"
    www.wrs.edu/journals/jour896/waldensians.html
19. Gabriel Audisio, pages 189-190.
    "Waldenses," *Encyclopedia.com*
    www.encyclopedia.com/articles/13592.html
    "Heritage of the Waldensians"
    www.wrs.edu/journals/jour896/waldensians.html
    Dr. Bill Jackson, Waldenses"
    www.NobleArmy.com
    www.angelfire.com/ky/dodone/NA5.html
20. Paul Johnson, pages 253-255. Bruce Shelley, pages 211-212.
21. Bruce Shelley, page 231.
22. Peter de Rosa, pages 166-172.
23. Dave Hunt, *A Woman Rides the Beast*, page 246.
    This begins by talking about Islam, but it has good information about popes coercing kings. It quotes the order that Pope Clement V gave to King Edward II., requiring the King to torture some men. (Search for "torture.")
    www.thechristianexpositor.org/page94.html
    The methods of the Inquisition. (Use the FIND function to search for "torture.")
    www.mosquitonet.com/~prewett/amer147.html
    Pope Clement V ordered King Edward II to torture the Templars. (Search for "torture.")
    templarium.tripod.com/end.htm
    I apologize for the tone and attitude of this article. However, the quotation from Pope Clement V is accurate. It is what I have in my source book. I don't have permission to quote it, so I'm making it available to you online. The quotation is at the very end of the first entry.
    www.livejournal.com/users/dmsherwood53/278.html
    The Inquisitors complained to Pope Clement V that torture was not allowed in England. The Pope intervened by putting pressure on King Edward II. As a result, special laws were passed in order to allow the torture.
    www.pharo.com/history/templars/articles/mhte_13_trial.asp
    Text of the Fourth Lateran Council's decree regarding treatment of heretics. This includes information about forcing secular rulers to cooperate with the Inquisitors.
    www.fordham.edu/halsall/source/lat4-c3.html
    www.historyguide.org/ancient/3canon_b.html
    A study of the history, theology, and methods of the Inquisition
    www.sundayschoolcourses.com/inq/inqcont.htm
    "The Inquisition: A Study in Absolute Catholic Power"
    www.mtc.org/inquis.html
    http://la.znet.com/~bart/inquis.htm
    www.crusadeforcatholics.com/bart.htm
24. Paul Johnson, page 308.

25. Dave Hunt, page 253.
26. Paul Johnson, page 353.
27. Bruce Shelley, page 274.
28. Paul Johnson, page 308.
29. The Congregation for the Doctrine of the Faith (formerly known as the Office of the Inquisition). This article is on the Vatican's website. [Click on "Profile."]
www.vatican.va/roman_curia/congregations/cfaith/index.htm
    The Vatican website is slow and it doesn't always come up. You can also find information about the change of name of the Office of the Inquisition at the following websites.
www.geocities.com/iberianinquisition/office.html
http://es.rice.edu/ES/humsoc/Galileo/Student_Work/Trial96/breu/timeline.html
http://news.bbc.co.uk/hi/english/world/europe/newsid_1251000/1251677.stm
30. Bruce Shelley, pages 225-231.
    "Lolladry," *Encyclopedia.com*
www.encyclopedia.com/articles/07588.html
31. Paul Johnson, page 318.

Chapter 7—Was the Early Church Roman Catholic?

1. Malachi Martin, *The Decline and Fall of the Roman Church*, pages 31-33. A major theme of this book is the radical change that occurred in the Church as a result of Constantine. The author recently died. He was a Catholic priest, a theologian, and a Vatican insider. He was the personal confessor of Pope John XXIII. He did research in the Vatican Archives.
2. Paul Johnson, *A History of Christianity*, pages 67-68. Johnson is a Catholic and a prominent historian.
3. Malachi Martin, page 33. Paul Johnson, page 67.
4. Paul Johnson, pages 68-69.
5. Paul Johnson, page 69.
6. Malachi Martin, pages 33-34.
7. Malachi Martin, pages 34-35.
8. James G. McCarthy, *The Gospel According to Rome*, pages 231-232. McCarthy is a former Catholic.
9. Paul Johnson, page 69.
10. Theodosius was forbidden to go into the Cathedral of Milan or to take the sacraments. This is excommunication, being cut off from the Church. Theodosius had to repent in order to be restored to the Church. Articles about this event are online at the following addresses.
    "Ambrose, Saint," *The Columbia Electronic Encyclopedia*, Sixth Edition, copyright 2000
www.encyclopedia.com/articlesnew/00413.html
    "Theodosius," *The Catholic Encyclopedia*, Volume XIV, 1912.
www.newadvent.org/cathen/14577d.htm
    "St. Ambrose Humiliates Theodosius the Great"
www.fordham.edu/halsall/ancient/theodoret-ambrose1.html
    Christopher S. Mackay, "Theodosius." See the section, "Theodosius in the Thrall of Ambrose"
www.ualberta.ca/~csmackay/CLASS_379/Theodosius.html
11. Paul Johnson, pages 113-119.
12. Vatican finances are a major theme of David Yallop's book, *In God's Name: An Investigation into the Murder of Pope John Paul I*. This book is well written, thoroughly

researched, and gripping. Vatican insiders asked Yallop to investigate the Pope's death because they believed that he had been murdered. Yallop did his homework. He interviewed Mafia gangsters and Vatican insiders.
13. Articles about Weems and the cherry tree story.
http://xroads.virginia.edu/~CAP/gw/gwmoral.html
www.virginia.edu/gwpapers/lesson/life/life1.html
www.law.umkc.edu/faculty/projects/ftrials/trialheroes/HEROSEARCH2.html
14. Malachi Martin, pages 11-28. Martin was an eminent theologian and a professor at the Vatican's Pontifical Institute. He describes the wide variety of beliefs and practices within the early Church. He says that there was as much variety back then as there is between different denominations now.
15. Malachi Martin, page 132.
16. *Catechism of the Catholic Church*, paragraph 891.
17. *Catechism of the Catholic Church*, paragraph 891.
18. William Webster, *The Church of Rome at the Bar of History*, pages 63-71.
19. William Webster, pages 81-85.
20. Pope Pius IX, *Quanta Cura (Condemning Current Errors)*, December 8, 1864.

    Pope Pius IX, *The Syllabus of Errors*, December 8, 1864, paragraphs 15, 77, and 78. *The Syllabus of Errors* accompanied the encyclical *Quanta Cura*. In reading it, remember that Pius condemned every statement that you are reading.

    Pope Leo XIII, *Libertas Praestantissimum (On the Nature of Human Liberty)*, June 20, 1888, paragraph 42.
21. *Dignitatis Humanae (Declaration on Religious Liberty)*. In Austin Flannery (editor), *Vatican Council II, The Conciliar and Post Conciliar Documents*, pages 799-812.

    The documents produced by the Second Vatican Council are available online. If the following addresses don't work for you, then do an Internet Search for "Vatican Council II" or "Second Vatican Council."
    www.stjosef.at/council/
    www.stjosef.at/council/search/
    www.cin.org/vatiidoc.html
    www.rc.net/rcchurch/vatican2/
    www.christusrex.org/www1/CDHN/v1.html
22. *Code of Canon Law*, page 427, Canon 1366. Canon Law provides the legal basis for everything that the Roman Catholic Church does. Even the Inquisition and the persecution of Protestants were based on Canon Law.
23. Articles by Catholic liberals and Catholic conservatives who have documented numerous discrepancies between the Second Vatican Council, Pope John Paul II, and the decrees of previous popes and councils.

    The Errors of Pope Pius IX. This article has extensive quotations, with references to encyclicals of Pope Pius IX, and documents from the Second Vatican Council. This is from a very liberal Catholic website.
    www.womenpriests.org/teaching/piusix.htm

    Summary of the Principal Errors of Vatican II Ecclesiology. From the website of True Catholic, an extremely conservative Catholic website.
    www.truecatholic.org/v2ecclesio.htm

    Lucian Pulvermacher, "Vatican II Council—Accepts Freedom of Religion, Teaches Heresy," *Caritas Newsletter*, August 19, 1989.
    www.truecatholic.org/car8908.htm

24. Patrick John Pollock, "101 Heresies of Anti-Pope John Paul II"
    www.truecatholic.org/heresiesjp2.htm
25. Lucian Pulvermacher, "Papal Election," *Caritas Election News #1*
    www.truecatholic.org/electionnews1.htm

Chapter 8—Forged Documents and Papal Power

1. Hans Küng, *The Catholic Church: A Short History* (translated by John Bowden), page 61. The author is a Catholic theologian and a priest. Pope John XXIII appointed him to be a theological consultant during the Second Vatican Council. In 1979, the Vatican disciplined him because he opposed the doctrine of papal infallibility.
2. William Webster, *The Church of Rome at the Bar of History*, pages 62-63. (Webster is a former Catholic.) Paul Johnson, *A History of Christianity*, page 195. (Johnson is a Catholic.) Peter de Rosa, *Vicars of Christ*, pages 58-61, 174, 208. De Rosa is a practicing Catholic and a former Catholic priest. While he was a priest, he did research in the Vatican Archives.
3. "Benedict Levita," *The Catholic Encyclopedia*, Volume II, 1907. Benedict Levita is the pseudonym of the author of the *Pseudo-Isidorian Decretals*.
   www.newadvent.org/cathen/02466a.htm
4. Peter de Rosa, page 59.
   An article about the use of forged documents in developing papal power. The author is a former Jesuit priest.
   www.crusadeforcatholics.com/newpage63.htm
   www.remnantofgod.org/x-jesuit.htm
5. Peter de Rosa, page 166.
6. Paul Johnson, pages 170-172.
7. Peter de Rosa, page 59.
8. "The False Decretals of Isidore." This is an excerpt from *The Papacy* by Abbee Guette, who was a devout Catholic and a historian. As a result of his historical research about the papacy, he eventually joined the Orthodox Church.
   www.orthodoxinfo.com/inquirers/decretals.htm
   "The Great Schism of 1054" (a sermon given at a Russian Orthodox Cathedral)
   www.stjohndc.org/Homilies/9606a.htm
9. William Webster, pages 62-63. Peter de Rosa, page 60.
10. William Webster, page 63. Peter de Rosa, page 60.
11. William Webster, "Forgeries and the papacy: The Historical Influence and Use of Forgeries in Promotion of the Doctrine of the Papacy." This article gives detailed accounts of Aquinas' use of forged documents. Aquinas mistakenly believed them to be genuine.
    www.christiantruth.com/forgeries.html
12. Pius X, *Pieni l'animo* (*On the Clergy in Italy*), July 28, 1906.
13. William Webster, "Forgeries and the Papacy: The Historical Influence and Use of Forgeries in Promotion of the Doctrine of the Papacy"
    www.christiantruth.com/forgeries.html
    An article about the use of forged documents in developing papal power. The author is a former Jesuit priest.
    www.crusadeforcatholics.com/newpage63.htm
    www.remnantofgod.org/x-jesuit.htm
14. An article about the Medieval Papacy. It includes a good summary of information about forged documents and their use to increase papal power.
    www.christianchronicler.com/history1/medieval_papacy.html

An article about the use of forged documents in developing papal power. The author is a former Jesuit priest.
www.crusadeforcatholics.com/newpage63.htm
www.remnantofgod.org/x-jesuit.htm
  Articles about various forged Church documents
http://jmgainor.homestead.com/files/PU/PF/cld.htm
http://jmgainor.homestead.com/files/PU/PF/lp.htm
http://jmgainor.homestead.com/files/PU/PF/6c.htm
http://jmgainor.homestead.com/files/PU/PF/sf.htm
http://jmgainor.homestead.com/files/PU/PF/doco.htm
15. "The Great Schism of 1054"
www.stjohndc.org/Homilies/9606a.htm

Chapter 9—The Popes

NOTE: The following articles give historical information about a number of popes. You can find the particular pope by searching for him by name. (Click EDIT. Click FIND. Type the pope's name and hit ENTER.) (The second article is written by a skeptic who seems to be anti-Christian, but it has valuable historical information.)
www.whiterobedmonks.org/netsor1a.html
www.geocities.com/paulntobin/papacy.html
http://members.aol.com/jasonte/papacy.htm
http://origin.island.lk/2002/07/16/featur04.html
www.christianchronicler.com/history1/medieval_papacy.html

POPES AND CHURCH HISTORY: This website has some valuable historical information about popes. There are 16 articles, according to time periods.
www.goacom.com/overseas-digest/god.html

1. William Webster, *The Church of Rome at the Bar of History*, pages 63-71. Peter de Rosa, *Vicars of Christ*, 208-209. (De Rosa is a practicing Catholic and a former Catholic priest. While he was a priest, he did research in the Vatican Archives.) Hans Küng, *The Catholic Church: A Short History*, page 60. The author is a Catholic theologian.
   You can search for information about Honorius in this article.
   www.whiterobedmonks.org/netsor1a.html
2. Malachi Martin, *The Decline and Fall of the Roman Church*, pages 85-89. Martin was a Catholic priest and a Vatican insider. He did research in the Vatican Archives. His books are a plea for reform within the Catholic Church.
   You can search for "Stephen IV" in this article.
   www.geocities.com/paulntobin/papacy.html
3. Malachi Martin, page 123.
4. Peter de Rosa, pages 211-215. Hans Küng, page 79.
   Pope John XII
   www.infoplease.com/ce6/people/A0826379.html
   www.slider.com/enc/28000/John_XII_pope.htm
5. Malachi Martin, page 119. Hans Küng, page 79.
   You can search for "Marozia" in these articles.
   http://members.aol.com/jasonte/papacy.htm
   www.geocities.com/paulntobin/papacy.html
   www.christianchronicler.com/history1/medieval_papacy.html

6. Malachi Martin, page 131.
7. Malachi Martin, pages 130-131.
8. Malachi Martin, pages 131-132.
9. Malachi Martin, page 132. Peter de Rosa, pages 54-56.
10. Paul Johnson, *A History of Christianity*, pages 191, 218-219. Malachi Martin, page 175.
11. Peter de Rosa, pages 84-88.
12. Paul Johnson, pages 280, 363. Peter de Rosa, pages 103-110. Hans Küng, pages 119-120.

    You can search for information about Alexander VI in this article. It tells how he appointed men to be cardinals if they paid him. Then he poisoned them so that he could sell their cardinal's office again. He also freed murderers from prison if they paid him.
    www.whiterobedmonks.org/netsor1a.html

    This website has two articles about Pope Alexander VI (the Borgia Pope). Go to the website below and use the FIND function to search for "Borgia."
    www.crimelibrary.com

    This has a lot of information about Alexander VI. Go to the following website and click on the time prior 1492-1550. (It begins with the reign of Alexander VI.) I recommend that you read about the other popes in this article. (If you have difficulty getting this article, see the information about "Hyphen Problems" at the beginning of the Notes.)
    www.goacom.com/overseas-digest/god.html
13. Paul Johnson, pages 274, 280. Hans Küng, pages 125-126.
14. Malachi Martin, pages 202-203.
15. Paul Johnson, pages 194-198, 161. Peter de Rosa, pages 57-66. Hans Küng, pages 85-92.

    William Webster, "Forgeries and the Papacy: The Historical Influence and Use of Forgeries in Promotion of the Doctrine of the Papacy." The author is a former Catholic.
    www.christiantruth.com/forgeries.html

    The Development of Papal Power
    www.geocities.com/Athens/Parthenon/2104/papal_power.html

    An article about the Medieval Papacy. It includes a good summary of information about forged documents and their use to increase papal power.
    www.christianchronicler.com/history1/medieval_papacy.html

    The use of forged documents in developing papal power. The author is a former Jesuit priest.
    www.crusadeforcatholics.com/newpage63.htm
    www.remnantofgod.org/x-jesuit.htm

    Articles about various forged Church documents
    http://jmgainor.homestead.com/files/PU/PF/cld.htm
    http://jmgainor.homestead.com/files/PU/PF/lp.htm
    http://jmgainor.homestead.com/files/PU/PF/6c.htm
    http://jmgainor.homestead.com/files/PU/PF/sf.htm
    http://jmgainor.homestead.com/files/PU/PF/doco.htm

    Articles about false Decretals
    concise.britannica.com/ebc/article?eu=389494
    www.britannica.com/eb/article?eu=34257
    www.encyclopedia.com/html/F/FalseD1ec.asp
    www.bartleby.com/65/fa/FalseDec.html
    www.slider.com/enc/18000/False_Decretals.htm
16. Malachi Martin, pages 141-142.

17. Paul Johnson, pages 199-201, 252. Peter de Rosa, pages 66-74, 152-155. Hans Küng, pages 87-103.
    You can search for "Innocent III" in these articles. The first one has a lot of information.
    www.whiterobedmonks.org/netsor1a.html
    http://origin.island.lk/2002/07/16/featur04.html
    www.geocities.com/paulntobin/papacy.html
    The Albigensian Crusade (Massacre)
    http://militaryhistory.about.com/cs/albigenscrusade/
    http://jmgainor.homestead.com/files/PU/Cru/albcr.htm
    A lengthy article about Innocent III. Click on the time period 1200-1300.
    www.goacom.com/overseas-digest/god.html
18. "Antipopes"
    www.angelfire.com/ky/dodone/Antipopes.html
    "Antipope," *The Catholic Encyclopedia*, Volume I, 1907 (online edition 1999). If this address doesn't work for you, then do an Internet search for "antipope + Catholic Encyclopedia" and you should find the article. This article may take a while to load. At first you will see a white page. Then the text will suddenly come in.
    www.newadvent.org/cathen/01582a.htm
19. Malachi Martin, *The Decline and Fall of the Roman Church*, pages 141-142.
    John Shuster, "A Concise History of the Married Priesthood in Our Roman Catholic Tradition"
    www.rentapriest.com/history.htm

Chapter 10—Imperial Popes

1. James G. McCarthy, *The Gospel According to Rome*, pages 231-232.
2. Malachi Martin, *The Decline and Fall of the Roman Church*, pages 19-38. (Martin was a Catholic priest and He did research in the Vatican Archives.) Peter de Rosa, *Vicars of Christ*, page 45. (De Rosa is a practicing Catholic and a former Catholic priest. While he was a priest, he did research in the Vatican Archives.)
3. Paul Johnson, *A History of Christianity*, pages 194-197. (Johnson is a Catholic.) Peter de Rosa, pages 62-64. Malachi Martin, pages 137-146.
    Pope Gregory VII and Henry IV
    www.saburchill.com/history/biblio/006.html
    Declaration made by Pope Gregory VII when he deposed Henry IV
    www.uoregon.edu/~klio/tx/med/g7-ban1.html
4. Malachi Martin, page 140.
5. Peter de Rosa, pages 66-73. Paul Johnson, page 199.
    "Glimpses of Church History, 1200-1300 CE" [A.D.].Cclick on the time period 1200-1300. It has a lot of information about Pope Innocent III.
    www.goacom.com/overseas-digest/god.html
    Pope Innocent III said that he was the "Foundation of all Christianity." He also said that every Catholic clergyman must obey the Pope, even if the Pope orders him to do something evil, because nobody can judge the Pope. (Search for "Innocent III.")
    www.whiterobedmonks.org/netsor1a.html
6. Bruce Shelley, *Church History in Plain Language*, page 215.
7. Pope Boniface VIII, *Unam Sanctam*, November 18, 1302. See the very last sentence.

8. Paloma Pajares Ayuela, *Cosmatesque Ornament: Flat Polychrome Geometric Patterns in Architecture* (New York: W.W. Norton & Company, 2002). Chapter 2 (*Rome*) tells how wealthy medieval popes used purple and gems in papal architecture in order to show their imperial power. The purple came from porphyry (a rock that has crystals embedded in a purple groundmass). Excerpts from this chapter are online.
www.wwnorton.com/NPB/nparch/cosmornexpt.htm
9. "History, Shellfish, Royalty, and the Color Purple"
http://pffc-online.com/ar/paper_history_shellfish_royalty
10. Six pictures of popes with the papal crown (tiara).
www.geocities.com/rexstupormundi/papalcrown.html
www.geocities.com/rexstupormundi/papalmonarchy.html
www.traditio.com/papal/john23.htm
www.ewtn.com/jp2/papal3/tiara.htm
www.nationalshrine.com/NAT_SHRINE/tour_c06.htm
11. The papal throne. There are six pictures of popes wearing the papal crown (tiara). Two pictures show Popes Pius XII and John XXIII seated on an ornate papal throne.
www.geocities.com/rexstupormundi/papalcrown.html
12. Eric Convey and Tom Mashberg, "Law Grilled in Deposition," *Boston Herald*. The third and fourth paragraphs discuss Cardinal Law's dual citizenship.
www2.bostonherald.com/news/local_regional/blaw05082002.htm
13. Pictures of pectoral crosses
www.exquisitevestments.com/crosses.html
    Pictures of bishops' rings
www.exquisitevestments.com/rings.html
    Pictures of bishops' chairs and staffs
www.exquisitevestments.com/church.htm
    "Rings," *The Catholic Encyclopedia*, Volume XIII, 1912.
www.newadvent.org/cathen/13059a.htm
    "Pectorale," *The Catholic Encyclopedia*, Volume XI, 1911. This is the pectoral cross that is worn by popes, cardinals, bishops, and abbots. It is made of precious metal (gold, silver, or platinum) and ornamented with jewels (diamonds, pearls, etc.). It contains a relic of a saint.
www.newadvent.org/cathen/11601a.htm
14. A diocesan newsletter with a story about some people who had an audience with the Pope. There are two pictures of people kneeling and kissing the Pope's ring.
www.ecclesia-ottawa.org/dio-news/dn240502.html
    A story from *Catholic World News* that mentions kneeling and kissing the Pope's ring
www.cwnews.com/Browse/1999/01/9465.htm
    News stories about the President of Mexico kissing the Pope's ring. He bowed rather than kneeling, but even that caused a political controversy.
www.signonsandiego.com/news/mexico/20020802-0124-pope.html
www.arabia.com/afp/news/int/article/print/english/0,11868,256871,00.html
www.signonsandiego.com/news/mexico/20020731-1917-pope-fox.html
15. Pictures of gold vestments and miters
www.gordonfabrics.com/TTWEB/threads/fx130010.htm
www.floscarmeliliturgicalarts.com/
www.exquisitevestments.com/bishops.htm
www.stalbanswestcliff.pwp.blueyonder.co.uk/Chasible%20Gold%20R.jpg
www.stalbanswestcliff.pwp.blueyonder.co.uk/Casible%20gold%20f.jpg

Pictures of the liturgical dress of popes and bishops in the sixteenth and seventeenth century. They show gold vestments and gold miters.
www.siue.edu/COSTUMES/PLATE51DX.HTML
www.siue.edu/COSTUMES/PLATE51CX.HTML

A doll of Pope John Paul II. It shows him wearing a gold miter and red vestments with gold embroidery.
http://ashtondrake.collectiblestoday.com/ct/product/prdid-327665001.jsp

16. "Mozzetta" (cape), *The Catholic Encyclopedia*, Volume X, 1911. This is a special red cape worn by the Pope. In the six winter months, he wears a mozzetta trimmed with white ermine. In the six summer months, he wears a lighter mozzetta without ermine.
www.newadvent.org/cathen/10624b.htm

17. "Sedia Gestatoria," *The Catholic Encyclopedia*, Volume XIII, 1912. This is the portable papal throne that is carried on the shoulders of men.
www.newadvent.org/cathen/13679a.htm

"Pontifical Mass," *The Catholic Encyclopedia*, Volume XII, 1911. This describes the use of the sedia gestatoria (portable papal throne) during the procession.
www.newadvent.org/cathen/12232a.htm

18. Paul Johnson, page 503

19. A series of 14 web pages with color pictures of Saint Peter's Basilica, the Pontifical Palace, and the Vatican Gardens. Each page has a number of small pictures that give different perspectives and details. If you click on them, you will see larger pictures.
www.christusrex.org/www1/citta/0-Citta.html

If this address doesn't work for you, then go to the home page and click on "Vatican City." If that doesn't work, then do an Internet search for "Christus Rex."
www.christusrex.org

A series of 27 web pages with color pictures of the Sistine Chapel. Three of these web pages have pictures of prophets and sybils. A sybil is a pagan prophetess.
www.christusrex.org/www1/sistine/0-Tour.html

If this address doesn't work for you, then go to the home page and click on "The Sistine Chapel."
www.christusrex.org

A series of 22 web pages with color pictures of the Vatican museums. A number of them have statues of Greek, Roman, and Egyptian gods and goddesses.
www.christusrex.org/www1/vaticano/0-Musei.html

If this address doesn't work for you, then go to the home page and click on "The Vatican Museums."
www.christusrex.org

Chapter 11—Undermining the Bible

1. William Webster, *The Church of Rome at the Bar of History*, page 8.
"The Canon of the New Testament: A Brief Introduction"
www.tmch.net/ntcanon.htm

2. Walter A. Elwell (editor), *Evangelical Dictionary of Theology*, page 141.

3. Paul Johnson, *A History of Christianity*, page 273.
Laymen and laywomen were forbidden to read the Bible in their native language, unless a bishop or an inquisitor gave them permission in writing.

www.justforcatholics.org/a79.htm
4. "Tyndale, William," *World Book Encyclopedia 2000* (on CD-Rom)
    "English Bible History." In 1517, seven people were burned at the stake for teaching their children to say the Lord's Prayer in English.
    http://www.greatsite.com/timeline-english-bible-history/
    "The History of the English Bible"
    www.williamtyndale.com/0biblehistory.htm
    Articles about William Tyndale
    www.hertford.ox.ac.uk/alumni/tyndale.htm
    www.loc.gov/loc/lcib/9707/web/tyndale.html
    www.cantonbaptist.org/halloffame/tyndale.htm
    www.llano.net/baptist/tyndale.htm
    www.prca.org/books/portraits/tyndale.htm
    www.williamtyndale.com/0welcomewilliamtyndale.htm
5. Paul Johnson, page 273.
6. Brian H. Edwards, *God's Outlaw: The Story of William Tyndale and the English Bible*, pages 168-170.
    Men read the Bible out loud in English, while crowds of people listened.
    http://elvis.rowan.edu/~kilroy/JEK/10/06.html
    http:///justus.anglican.org/resources/bio/260.html
    William Tyndale translated the Bible into English. His Bibles were burned. Tyndale was burned at the stake. Between 1400 and 1557 over 1,000 English men and women were burned at the stake for the sake of the Gospel.
    www.williamtyndale.com/0crimesofwilliamtyndale.htm
7. "Wycliffe, John," "Lollards," and "Bible," *World Book Encyclopedia 2000* (on CD-Rom).
    Articles about John Wycliffe and the Lollards.
    http://justus.anglican.org/resources/bio/27.html
    www.wycliffe.org/history/JWycliff.htm
    www.epc.org.au/literature/bb/wycliffe.html
    An article about the Lollards
    http://icg.harvard.edu/~chaucer/special/varia/lollards/lollards.html
    An article about Wycliffe
    www.island-of-freedom.com/WYCLIFFE.HTM
8. "Tyndale, William" and "Bible," *World Book Encyclopedia 2000* (on CD-Rom). See Notes 4 and 6 for online articles about Tyndale.
9. "Bible," *World Book Encyclopedia 2000* (on CD-Rom)
10. Pope Pius IX, *Qui Pluribus* (*On Faith and Religion*), November 9, 1846. See paragraph 14.
    Pope Pius IX, *Nostis et Nobiscum* (*On the Church in the Pontifical States*), December 8, 1849. See paragraph 14.
    Articles about the beatification of Pope Pius IX.
    www.concilium.org/english/PiusIX.htm
    www.abc.net.au/am/s171619.htm
    www.us-israel.org/jsource/anti-semitism/piusix.html
    www.americapress.org/articles/Omalley-pius9.htm
    http://members.tripod.com/~dabz_2/updates/protest/protest.htm
11. Pope Pius IX, *Quanta Cura* (*Condemning Current Errors*), December 8, 1864. The "error" is given in Section 3, second paragraph. The condemnation of all of the "errors" described in the encyclical is given in paragraph 6.

Pope Pius IX, *The Syllabus of Errors*, December 8, 1864. See paragraphs 15, 77, and 78. *The Syllabus of Errors* accompanied the encyclical *Quanta Cura*. In reading it, remember that Pius condemned every statement that you are reading.

Pope Leo XIII, *Libertas Praestantissimum* (*On the Nature of Human Liberty*), June 20, 1888. See paragraph 42.

12. *Catechism of the Catholic Church*, paragraph 891. It is available online with a search engine. If these addresses don't work for you, then do an Internet search for "Catechism of the Catholic Church" and you should find some links for it.
www.scborromeo.org/ccc.htm
www.christusrex.org/www2/kerygma/ccc/searchcat.html
13. *Catechism of the Catholic Church*, paragraphs 80, 84 and 97.
14. *Catechism of the Catholic Church*, paragraphs 78, 113, 2650, and 2661.
15. *Catechism of the Catholic Church*, paragraphs 85, 87, 100, 113, 862, 891, 2037.
16. J.A. Wylie, *The Papacy: Its History, Dogmas, Genius, and Prospects*; Volume II, *Dogmas of the Papacy*, Chapter 2, "Scripture and Tradition" (London: Hamilton, Adams, & Co., 1888). You can read this chapter online.
www.fbinstitute.com/papacy/b2c2.html
www.wayoflife.org/papacy/02-02.htm
www.historicist.com/papacy/b2c2.html
www.freepres.org/papacy/pap02-02.htm
www.bpc.org/resources/books/wylie/papa0202.html
17. Walter A. Elwell (editor), *Evangelical Dictionary of Theology*, pages 66-67.
18. Gregory Koukl, "The Apocrypha," 1998. This website has a search engine. Search for "apocrypha."
www.str.org
19. The Epistle of Jude refers to an event that is described in the *Book of Enoch*, a work that was familiar to Jude's readers. However, Jude does not state or imply that *The Book of Enoch* is inspired Scripture. Rather, he uses it in a manner that is similar to modern pastors who use well-known books or movies as sermon illustrations. The *Book of Enoch* is not one of the Apocrypha. It is not part of the Catholic Bible.
20. The *Book of Tobit* is available online. Do a search for "Book of Tobit."
21. *International Standard Bible Encyclopedia*, Electronic Database, 1996, by Biblesoft (a Bible study program).

Chapter 12—New Age Catholicism

1. Randy England, *The Unicorn in the Sanctuary: The Impact of the New Age on the Catholic Church*. The author is Catholic. Amazon.com has nine pages of the book online.
Online reviews and summaries of *The Unicorn in the Sanctuary*
www.tanbooks.com/books/unic1156.htm
www.marianland.com/errors024.html
2. Mitch Pacwa, *Catholics and the New Age*. Pacwa is a Catholic priest.
Online reviews and summaries of *Catholics and the New Age*
www.catholicmart.com/catnewage.html
www.tiberriver.com/covers/089283756xz2.jpg
Byron Snapp, "New Age and Old Rome," *Contra Mundum*, No. 11, Spring 1994
www.visi.com/~contra_m/cm/reviews/cm11_rev_newage.html

3. Donna Steichen, *Ungodly Rage: The Hidden Face of Catholic Feminism.* Steichen presents carefully documented facts, and she lets the facts speak for themselves. Amazon.com has 25 pages of the book online.

    Ungodly Rage (a short summary by the publisher, with quotations from reviewers) www.catholic-pages.com/dir/link.asp?ref=17711

    John F. McCarthy, "The Whole Truth about Catholic Feminism." This is a six-page article based on the book, *Ungodly Rage*. McCarthy is a Catholic priest. He is angered by some things that Catholic feminists have done, and his anger shows in his article. www.rtforum.org/lt/lt53.html

4. Kathleen Howley, "Catholic College Welcomes Feminists, Bans Rosary," *Catholic World News*, April 24, 1996.
    www.cwnews.com/Browse/1996/04/383.htm

5. Randy England,*Unicorn in the Sanctuary*, chapter 6, "Woman Church, Witchcraft, and the Goddess." This chapter is on a Catholic website.
    www.ewtn.com/library/ANSWERS/FOX.HTM

6. Mitch Pacwa, "Catholicism for the New Age: Matthew Fox and Creation-Centered Spirituality"
    www.equip.org/free/DF105.htm

    Transcript of an interview with Matthew Fox
    www.wisdomtalk.org/b-5-32.html

    Sophia Center in Culture and Spirituality (located at Holy Names College in Oakland, California)
    www.hnc.edu/programs/gradcs.html
    www.hnc.edu/~sophia/courses.html
    www.hnc.edu/~sophia/faculty.html

    University of Creation Spirituality (located in Oakland, California)
    www.creationspirituality.com/matthew.html
    www.creationspirituality.com/faculty.html

7. If the educators are nuns, then they are in double jeopardy. (1) They did not expect to receive New Age teaching and therefore they were not prepared to deal with it. (2) As nuns, they have been taught to accept what they are told by people in authority. In an instructional setting, a speaker or teacher is a person in authority.

8. News stories about a witch teaching at Heythrop College
    www.unsolvedmysteries.com/usm214051.html
    www.ananova.com/yournews/story/sm_503171.html

9. Bernard D. Green, "Catholicism Confronts New Age Syncretism." Green is a Catholic priest.
    www.ewtn.com/library/NEWAGE/SYNCRET.TXT

    Hans Hallundbaek, "A Year of Dialogue Culminates in Buddhist Participation in Maryknoll Advent Celebration," *BAUS Newsletter*, Issue 58. (Maryknoll is a Catholic religious order.)
    www.baus.org/baus/newsletter/1999/nl58_dialog.html

    "The Los Angeles Buddhist-Catholic Dialogue"
    www.kusala.org/bccontent1.html

    A Buddhist-Catholic Retreat
    www.kusala.org/buddhistcatholic/bcmalibu.html

    "East-West Contemplative Dialogue: Where Christian Mysticism and Metaphysics Enters into Dialogue with Buddhism and Hinduism"
    www.innerexplorations.com/ewtext/east-wes.htm

"Inner Explorations: Where Christian Metaphysics and Mysticism Meet Eastern Religions, Jungian Psychology, and a New Sense of the Earth"
www.innerexplorations.com/
10. The Ursuline Sophia Center. (If this address doesn't work, then search for the name.).
http://ursulinesophiacenter.com
11. Bud Macfarlane, "Our Lady Weeps: V-Monogues Comes to Notre Dame."
www.catholicity.com/commentary/macfarlane/vmonologues.html
12. E. Michael Jones, "V-Day at St. Mary's College," *Culture Wars*. This article contains some raunchy quotations from the play. It will give you a feel for the nature of the play.
www.culturewars.com/CultureWars/2000/April/stmarys.html
13. Michele Malkin, "Columnist Dropped for Exposing Feminism," March 31, 2000
www.spiritone.com/~law/dropped.html
  Wendy McElroy, "Feminists Who Celebrate Rape," April 2, 2000
www.spiritone.com/~law/celebrate.html
www.lewrockwell.com/orig/mcelroy2.html
www.gabnet.com/lit/theatre.htm
  The February 16, 2001 edition of Georgetown University's newspaper, *The Hoya*, has a favorable review of the play. It is called "'V–': A True, Moving Drama."
www.thehoya.com/guide/021601/guide3.htm
  Another positive review of the play in *The Hoya*
www.thehoya.com/guide/101901/guide3.cfm
  The editor-in-chief of *The Hoya* wrote an article condemning the play. He was fired and *The Hoya* didn't publish his article. However, *Accuracy in Academia* published it. Here is the article.
www.academia.org/campus_reports/2000/may_2000_4.html
14. Information about six Catholic colleges that showed the play by March, 2002:
  Promotional notice from the University of Detroit Mercy
http://eng-sci.udmercy.edu/womres/
  News Briefs from Loyola World (February 7, 2001), "Women's Studies Spring Events." (Search for "monologues.")
www.luc.edu/publications/loyolaworld/nb-020701.html
  Philly.burbs.com, "Halloween Guide." (Events in the area). (Search for "monologues." This is the second listing.)
www.phillyburbs.com/halloween2000/courier.shtml
  Beth Levy, "The V– Monologues," *Westchester NOW Newsletter*, Spring 2000
www.westchesternow.org/sp00vaginamonologues.html
  Article from *The Truth*, dated Winter, 2000. This is a newsletter of conservative Catholics. To find the article, search for "Catholic Universities Could Use a Little Judgment."
www.lesfemmes-thetruth.org/5twilightwin.htm
  Article from *The Truth*, dated Spring, 2000. They awarded the "Millstone Award" to Catholic colleges that scandalized people by showing the play.
www.lesfemmes-thetruth.org/v52award.htm
  "Was V-Day Celebrated on Your Campus?" Clare Boothe Luce Policy Institute.
www.cblpolicyinstitute.org/vday.htm
15. "42 Catholic Colleges to Present Vulgar V– Monologues," *Lifesite*, February 3, 2003. According to this article, 42 Catholic colleges planned to show the play. There was a

letter-writing campaign, protesting the play. It did not succeed. As you will see from the next article, 41 of the colleges performed the play.
www.lifesite.net/ldn/2003/feb/03020306.html
    According to this article, 41 of the Catholic colleges did perform the play.
www.vday.org/contents/vday/press/releases/0304301

16. *Code of Canon Law*, pages 247 and 409, Canons 75 and 1311-1312.
17. *The Catechism of the Catholic Church*, paragraphs 85, 100, 113, 891, and 2051.
18. Articles about Voodoo and Marie Leveau
www.brnet.com/vopage.html
www.prairieghosts.com/laveau.html
www.culturalorientation.net/haiti/hrelig.html
19. "Cubans Flock to Saint Festival Combining Catholic, Voodoo Beliefs," *Catholic World News*, News Brief, 12/18/1996
www.cwnews.com/Browse/1996/12/3279.htm
20. Articles about animal sacrifices during Mass in South Africa.
www.christianitytoday.com/ct/2000/115/46.0.html
www.christianitytoday.com/ct/2000/143/34.0.html
www.goodnews.org.uk/Articles/wnr0003.htm
www.raidersnewsupdate.com/animalsac2.htm
www.worthynews.com/news-features/animal-sacrifice-catholic-mass.html
21. Articles about combining Catholicism with Mayan religion
www.atitlan.com/catholic/
www.uwec.edu/academic/curric/greidebe/hos/Spirit/bgcathol.htm
www.journalstar.com/gua_stories?page=Mon06.html
    Tourist Guides of Guatemala that Feature Mayan/Catholic Rituals
www.abstravel.com/guatemala/
www.enjoyguatemala.com/guateinfo.htm
www.lonelyplanet.com/destinations/central_america/guatemala/
http://travel.discovery.com/dest/lpdb/cenam/guat/intro.html
22. Articles about the Mexican "Day of the Dead"
www.public.iastate.edu/~rjsalvad/scmfaq/muertos.html
www.nacnet.org/assunta/dead.htm
www.mexweb.com/muertos.htm
23. Articles about mixing Catholicism with native religions in Brazil. For the last article, look for the subheading, "Roman Catholicism."
www.ob.org/brazil/aboutbrazil.asp
www.gospelcom.net/lcwe/dufe/Papers/Brazil.htm
www.wcc-coe.org/wcc/what/interreligious/cd36-03.html
www.wholesomewords.org/missions/msnews5.html
www.brazzil.com/cvrsep97.htm
www.geocities.com/Athens/Acropolis/2960/brazil/rel-history.html
24. Articles about Brazilian religions including Candomble, Umbanda, Macumba, spiritism, and Kardecism.
www.fmpsd.ab.ca/schools/df/Brazil/mreligion.htm
www.africana.com/Articles/tt_497.htm
www.geocities.com/arrudax/umbanda.htm
http://philtar.ucsm.ac.uk/encyclopedia/latam/kardec.html

25. Articles about Santeria
    www.themystica.com/mystica/articles/s/santeria.html
    www.religioustolerance.org/santeri.htm
26. Articles about extreme penances (including crucifixion) in the Philippines
    www.wildcat.co.uk/text/crucifixion_txt.htm
    www.oneworld.org/ips2/apr98/04_45_007.html
    www.filipinoheritage.com/religious/Cuaresma.htm

Chapter 13—False Credentials

1. Bill Jackson, *The Noble Army of "Heretics"*. See chapter 1 ("Montanus and Tertullian") and chapter 2 ("Martyrs before Roman Catholicism Started"). You can read these online.
   www.NobleArmy.com
   www.angelfire.com/ky/dodone/NA1.html
   www.angelfire.com/ky/dodone/NA2.html
2. Malachi Martin, pages 11-28. Martin was a Catholic priest, an eminent theologian, and a professor at the Vatican's Pontifical Institute. He describes the wide variety of beliefs and practices within the early Church. He says that there was as much variety back then as there is between different denominations now.
3. This is the subject of the book *On This Slippery Rock* by Dr. Eric Svendsen (Calvary Press, 2002). I have personally corresponded with people who have been told these things. You can order Dr. Svendsen's book at Amazon.com or on his website.
   www.ntrmin.org
4. Dr. Eric Svendsen, "30,000 Protestant Denominations?" This is chapter 5 of *On This Slippery Rock*. You can read it online.
   www.ntrmin.org/30000denominations.htm

   Dr. Eric Svendsen, "The Roman Catholic Challenge." Dr. Svendsen posed 18 questions and offered a $100,000 prize to any person who could give him the official Catholic answer (an answer that Catholics officially agree on) to any of his questions. If they could answer just one, they would win the money. Nobody was able to do it, not even professional Catholic apologists. The questions and a summary of responses are online at the following address.
   www.ntrmin.org/rcchallenge.htm
5. Malachi Martin, *The Jesuits: The Society of Jesus and the Betrayal of the Roman Catholic Church* (New York: Simon & Schuster, 1987). Martin was a Jesuit priest.
6. True Catholic's website has articles about the state of the papacy
   www.truecatholic.org
7. Malachi Martin, *The Jesuits*.
8. Wesley J. Smith, *Culture of Death: The Assault on Medical Ethics in America*. The Introduction is online.
   www.encounterbooks.com/mainstory/mainstoryCUDE.html
9. Ray Yungen gives documented, detailed information, with numerous quotations, in his book, *A Time of Departing: How a Universal Spirituality Is Changing the Face of Christianity*.
10. See the sections "Catholic Feminists" and "New Age Morals" in the chapter, "New Age Catholicism."
11. With one exception, these articles come from Catholic websites. I put the Protestant one first because it is a good, short overview with quotations from Catholic sources.
    Bill Jackson, "Scapulars"
    www.angelfire.com/ky/dodone/Scapulars.html

"The Brown Scapular of Our Lady of Mt. Carmel" (Blue Army of Our Lady of Fatima) members.aol.com/ccmail/scapular.html

"Brown Scapular" (Catholic Information Network)
www.cin.org/saints/brownsca.html

"St. Simon Stock," *The Catholic Encyclopedia*, Volume XIII, 1912.
www.newadvent.org/cathen/13800a.htm

"Scapular," *The Catholic Encyclopedia*, Volume XIII, 1912.
www.newadvent.org/cathen/13508b.htm

12. "The Rosary, Brown Scapular, and the Sabbatine Privilege" (Our Lady of the Rosary Library) olrl.org/pray/rosary.html

"Sabbatine Privilege," *The Catholic Encyclopedia*, Volume XIII, 1912.
www.newadvent.org/cathen/13289b.htm

13. Pictures of four-way medals and five-way medals. These are sold at online Catholic stores. If the Internet addresses don't work, then do searches for "four way medal" and "five way medal."

www.discountcatholicstore.com/four_way.htm
www.zieglers.com/seasonal.asp
www.sacredheart.com/Medals_Five_Way_Medal_Round_Style.htm
www.sacredheart.com/Medals_Four_Way_Cross_Medal.htm
www.sacredheart.com/CR-SS4444_Maltese_Cross.htm

14. Websites of online Catholic stores. You can see pictures of medals, rosaries, chaplets, scapulars, statues, bottles for holy water, religious jewelry, and other religious objects.

Discount Catholic Store. This has a wide variety of religious items, including water from Lourdes, holy water bottles, and "special devotions."
www.DiscountCatholicStore.com

Your Catholic Store. If you look under "church goods" you can see monstrances (which hold consecrated Hosts) and reliquaries (which hold the relics of saints). (You can use the FIND function to search for "church goods.")
www.YourCatholicStore.com

In His Name. This has palms, ashes, paschal candles, rosaries, scapulars, and statues. "Church supplies and clerical apparel" has monstrances and censer stands. (Censers hold burning incense.) The jewelry section has medals, including four-way medals and scapular medals.
www.InHisName.com

Catholic Mart is also called My Catholic Store. If you click on "Catholic Gifts," you will find statues, rosaries, scapulars, holy water bottles, chaplets, holy cards, pictures, and candles. You might want to see the picture called "Sacred Heart."
www.CatholicMart.com
www.MyCatholicStore.com

Catholic Family Catalog. If you click on "Church Goods," you will see monstrances and large statues. If you click on "Jewelry," you will see medals, monstrance pins, rosary rings (they have one decade of the rosary on them), a Saint Benedict crucifix (a combination of a crucifix and a Saint Benedict medal), rosaries, and "heavenly watches" (watches with pictures of Mary or saints on them). If you click on "Religious Articles," you will see Brown Scapulars, medals, monstrance pins, and rosaries. (A monstrance pin looks like a monstrance with a Host in it. A Host is a consecrated communion wafer.)
www.CatholicFamilyCatalog.com

Catholic Shopper. The "Automobile Witness Center" has medals that clip onto the sun visor of your car. One medal shows an angel, and has the inscription: "Guardian Angel Protect Us."
www.CatholicShopper.com

Everything Catholic. If you click on "Shrines," you will go to a web page that has links to various Catholic shrines. These shrines have pictures, or "tours." Seeing these shrines is an education in itself.
www.EverythingCatholic.com/800
www.EverythingCatholic.com

Basilica of the National Shrine of the Immaculate Conception. This has a "virtual tour" that shows numerous chapels that honor Mary. It has statues, mosaics, prayers, novenas, and information.
www.NationalShrine.com

15. Michael S. Rose, *Goodbye, Good Men: How Liberals Brought Corruption into the Catholic Church*. The author is Catholic. You can find information about the book online by doing an Internet search for "Michael Rose Goodbye Good Men."
16. The Introduction to *Goodbye, Good Men* is available online. So are feedback testimonials of seminarians and priests who have read the book. There is a collection of excerpts from reviews. At the end of each excerpt, there is a place that you can click if you want to read the entire review.
www.goodbyegoodmen.com

An online summary and review provided by a book service
www.thbookservice.com/BookPage.asp?prod_cd=C5976
17. *Goodbye, Good Men* only briefly discussed Fox's "creation-centered spirituality." I have added additional information about it based on the following sources:

Randy England, *The Unicorn in the Sanctuary: The Impact of the New Age on the Catholic Church*, chapter 6 (pages 118-134). This chapter is called, "Woman Church, Witchcraft, and the Goddess." It is available on a Catholic website. The author is Catholic.
www.ewtn.com/library/ANSWERS/FOX.HTM

Mitch Pacwa, "Catholicism for the New Age: Matthew Fox and Creation-Centered Spirituality." The author is a Catholic priest.
www.equip.org/free/DF105.htm

Chapter 14—According to Tradition

1. "Some Important Marian Apparitions." (The information is on pages 1 to 2 of my print-out.)
http://members.aol.com/bjw1106/marian5.htm
2. *Life Application Study Bible*, notes on the Book of Romans
3. "Some Important Marian Apparitions"
http://members.aol.com/bjw1106/marian5.htm
4. Paul Johnson, *A History of Christianity*, page 226.
5. Paul Johnson, pages 105-107 and 161-166.
6. "Some Important Marian Apparitions"
http://members.aol.com/bjw1106/marian5.htm
7. Dave Hunt, *A Woman Rides the Beast*, pages 239-240.
8. William Steuart McBirnie, *The Search for the Twelve Apostles*, page 103.

Chapter 15—What Is Our Source of Authority?

1. Open Doors has been smuggling Bibles and other Christian materials into Communist and Muslim nations for over 40 years. Their website gives information about the persecution of Christians in various countries.
www.opendoorsusa.org
2. *Catechism of the Catholic Church*, paragraphs 80, 84, 97. It is available online with a search engine. If these addresses don't work for you, then do an Internet search for "Catechism of the Catholic Church."
www.scborromeo.org/ccc.htm
www.christusrex.org/www2/kerygma/ccc/searchcat.html
3. *Catechism of the Catholic Church*, paragraphs 78, 98, 113, 2650, and 2661.
"Tradition and the Magician's Hat." This article shows how tradition keeps shifting, is unwritten, and cannot be pinned down. Therefore, it is like the magician's hat. Theologians can pull anything they want to out of it. They can also ignore anything that is inconvenient.
www.justforcatholics.org/a169.htm
4. *Catechism of the Catholic Church*, paragraphs 85, 100, 113, 891, and 2051.
5. *Catechism of the Catholic Church*, paragraphs 87, 2037.
6. *Ineffabilis Deus* (*Apostolic Constitution on the Immaculate Conception*). Encyclical of Pope Pius IX, issued December 8, 1854. Near the end of this papal bull there is a section called "The Definition." The statements that I described are in the last paragraph of that section. If these addresses don't work for you, then do a search for "Ineffabilis Deus."
www.newadvent.org/docs/pi09id.htm
www.pax-et-veritas.org/Popes/pius_ix/ineffabi.htm
www.geocities.com/apologeticacatolica/ineffabilis.html
www.naorc.org/documents/ineffabilis_deus.htm
www.legacyrus.com/library/Vatican/ImmaculateConcept.htm
7. Paul Johnson, *A History of Christianity*, page 308.
8. Lord Acton (a nineteenth century Catholic historian)
9. Malachi Martin, The Decline and Fall of the Roman Church, pages 85-89, 132. The author is a Catholic priest who was devoted to Our Lady of Fatima. Martin's books are a plea for reform within the Catholic Church.
10. David Yallop, *In God's Name: An Investigation into the Murder of Pope John Paul I*.
11. Articles about the beatification of Pope Pius IX. The author of the first one is a Catholic priest.
www.americapress.org/articles/Omalley-pius9.htm
www.concilium.org/english/PiusIX.htm
www.abc.net.au/am/s171619.htm
www.us-israel.org/jsource/anti-semitism/piusix.html
http://members.tripod.com/~dabz_2/updates/protest/protest.htm

Chapter 16—Faith Versus Works

1. *Life Application Study Bible*, notes on the Epistle to the Galatians.

Chapter 17—The Good Thief

1. For a good, well documented presentation of the difference between Biblical simplicity and Catholic complexity, see Mike Gendron's article, "Jesus Christ Is Sufficient to Save Sinners Completely."
www.reachingcatholics.org/save_sinners.html

Chapter 18—The Numbers Game

There are no notes for this chapter.

Chapter 19—Devotion to Mary

1. James G. McCarthy, *The Gospel According to Rome: Comparing Catholic Tradition and the Word of God*, pages 181-184 and 199-200.
2. Pictures of Pope John Paul II putting a gold crown on a statue of Mary
www.aloha.net/~mikesch/crown.htm
   Pictures of statues of Mary that wear crowns. I have divided the address into two sections, because of its width.
www.sspxasia.com/Newsletters/2001/Oct-Dec/
Procession_in_honour_of_Our_Lady_of_the_Rosary.htm
   Pictures of a crowned statue of Mary. The statue is carried in a procession. I have divided the address into two sections, because of its width.
www.sspxasia.com/Newsletters/2001/Oct-Dec/
Procession_in_honour_of_Our_Lady_of_the_Rosary_page_5.htm
   Pictures of replicas of statues of Our Lady of Lourdes and Our Lady of Fatima. The crowns on these replicas are made of porcelain that is painted gold. The original statues at Lourdes and Fatima wear real crowns made of real gold.
www.pacificheritage.com/images/Products/fatimachild22.JPG
www.pacificheritage.com/images/Products/fatimag45.JPG
www.pacificheritage.com/images/Products/Lo90.JPG
3. Dave Hunt, *A Woman Rides the Beast*, pages 239-240
4. James Anderson (Associated Press), "Giant Statue of Mary Part of Shrine Plan," *Lexington Herald-Leader*, July 17, 1999.
www.kentuckyconnect.com/heraldleader/news/071799/faithdocs/shrine17.htm
5. Jim Tetlow, *Messages from Heaven*, Chapter 1. This is privately published. You can buy it from D&K Press (800-777-8839).
6. William Webster, *The Church of Rome at the Bar of History*, page 87.
7. Pope Pius IX, *Ubi Primum* (On The Immaculate Conception), February 2, 1849. The paragraphs are numbered. Paragraph 5 says that salvation comes through Mary. If these addresses don't work for you, then do a search for "Ubi Primum."
www.ewtn.com/library/ENCYC/P9UBIPR2.HTM
www.catholic-forum.com/saints/pope0255a.htm
papal-library.saint-mike.org/PiusIX/Encyclicals/Ubi_Primum2.html
8. Pope Benedict XV, *Inter Sodalicia* (1918). Quoted in Donald G. Bloesch, *Essentials of Evangelical Theology*, Volume 1, page 196.
   These articles give reasons why Mary is Co-Redemptrix. It gives quotations from a number of popes, including Pope Benedict XV. You can search the page for "Benedict."
www.christendom-awake.org/pages/marian/5thdogma/voxpopbk1.htm
www.christendom-awake.org/pages/marian/5thdogma/co-redemptrix2.htm

9. The Queenship Marian Center for World Peace promotes the doctrine that Mary is Advocate, Mediator, and Co-Redemptrix. It sells books glorifying Mary and promoting this doctrine. It promotes a petition asking the Pope to officially declare the doctrine. Their online catalog gives information about the petition's progress, and about church leaders who support the doctrine. Look for Vox Populi at the home page below.
www.queenship.org
10. *Catechism of the Catholic Church*. It comes in numerous editions and languages. Because it has numbered paragraphs, statements can be accurately located in spite of the variety of editions. It is available online with a search engine. You can search by topic or paragraph number. If these addresses don't work for you, then do an Internet search for "Catechism of the Catholic Church."
www.scborromeo.org/ccc.htm
www.christusrex.org/www2/kerygma/ccc/searchcat.html

If you read the *Catechism*, remember that the authors are not only giving instructions to Catholics, they are also trying to keep them from being persuaded by a Protestant perspective. For example, the book says that Catholics should be devoted to Mary, but then it turns around and says that this does not constitute worship.
11. William Webster, pages 72-77.
12. Paul Johnson, *A History of Christianity*, pages 511-512. Peter de Rosa, *Vicars of Christ*, pages 318-319.

Saint Augustine's treatise, *On Marriage and Concupiscence*, is online.
www.newadvent.org/fathers/15071.htm
http://ccel.org/fathers2/NPNF1-05/npnf1-05-27.htm#P3826_1451208
13. William Webster, pages 81-85.
14. William Webster, pages 22-33. For a description of how pious practices can become official Catholic doctrine, and how this conflicts with both Scripture and the writings of the Early Fathers, see James G. McCarthy, pages 281-309. You can see some of these pious practices for yourself. Appendix D ("Pictures") gives Internet addresses of online photographs.
15. James G. McCarthy, pages 181-184 and 199-200.
16. James McCarthy, *Catholicism: Crisis of Faith* (video). You can order it from D&K Press (800-777-8839).
17. Jim Tetlow, *Messages from Heaven*, Chapter 1. (He also produced a video with the same title.) Tetlow is a former Catholic.
18. Jim Tetlow, *Messages from Heaven* (video). The main subject of the video is apparitions of Mary, but it also deals with other things. You can order it from D&K Press (800-777-8839). You can watch the video online.
www.harpazo.net/EternalProductions/ApparitionsofMary/
19. Jim Tetlow, *Messages from Heaven* (video). You can watch it online.
www.harpazo.net/EternalProductions/ApparitionsofMary/

Chapter 20—What Is Idolatry?

1. "Past Popes Taught Descructive Heresies." This article has quotations from popes who said that there is no salvation apart from the Catholic Church, or Mary, or the Pope.
www.reachingcatholics.org/pastpopes.html

Pope Boniface VIII, *Unam Sanctam*, November 18, 1302. This encyclical says that no person can be saved unless he or she submits to the Pope. (If these addresses don't work for you, then do a search for "Unam Sanctam.")

http://faculty.juniata.edu/tuten/unam.html
www.catholicism.org/pages/unam.htm
www.newadvent.org/docs/bo08us.htm
www.fordham.edu/halsall/source/b8-unam.html
www.geocities.com/papalencyclicals/Bon08/B8unam.htm

    Pope Innocent III said that he was the "Foundation of all Christianity." He also said that every Catholic clergyman must obey the Pope, even if the Pope orders him to do something evil, because nobody can judge the Pope. (This article has information about many popes. Use the FIND function to search for Innocent III.)
www.whiterobedmonks.org/netsor1a.html

    Pope Pius IX, *Ubi Primum* (*On The Immaculate Conception*), February 2, 1849. This encyclical says that salvation comes from Mary. (See Paragraph 5._ If these addresses don't work for you, then do an Internet search for "Ubi Primum."
www.ewtn.com/library/ENCYC/P9UBIPR2.HTM
www.catholic-forum.com/saints/pope0255a.htm
http://papal-library.saint-mike.org/PiusIX/Encyclicals/Ubi_Primum2.html

    Pope Pius IX, *Quanto Conficiamur Moerore* (*On Promotion of False Doctrines*), August 10, 1863. This encyclical says that there is no salvation apart from the Catholic Church. (See paragraph 8.) If these addresses don't work for you, then do a search for "Quanto + Pius IX."
www.geocities.com/papalencyclicals/Pius09/p9quanto.htm
www.petersnet.net/browse/3115.htm
www.ewtn.com/library/ENCYC/P9QUANTO.HTM
www.catholic-forum.com/saints/pope0255d.htm

    Pope Pius IX, *Nostis et Nobiscum* (*On the Church in the Pontifical States*), December 8, 1849. This encyclical says that there is no salvation apart from the Catholic Church. (See paragraph 10.) If these addresses don't work for you, then do a search for "Nostis + Pius IX."
www.geocities.com/papalencyclicals/Pius09/p9nostis.htm
www.catholic-forum.com/saints/pope0255z.htm
www.ewtn.com/library/ENCYC/P9NOSTIS.HTM

2.   This music CD can be purchased online. It includes three papal hymns written by Liszt.
www.mondodellamusica.com/rome.html

    Music for a solemn Papal Mass that was held in Saint Louis in 1999. During the "Entrance of Holy Father," a papal hymn was sung by the choir. The hymn is, *Tu Es Petrus* (*You Are Peter*).
www.archstl.org/worship/papalmusic.htm

    The words of a papal hymn are online. The hymn is on a Catholic website and is part of a section honoring the Pope. If these addresses don't work for you, then do a search for "Long Live the Pope + hymn." You can also search for "hymn for the Pope."
www.ewtn.com/jp2/papal3/long_live.htm
www.cedarnet.org/bles_sac/pope2.html

    An alternative Internet address for the papal hymn is below. It gives the words of the hymn, followed by a strong criticism of it.
www.cultlink.com/CathAnswers/EWTNwatch.htm

    Jesuit missionary imprints. Items 15 and 16 are "The Universal Papal Hymn"
www.serendipitybooks.com/jesuit.htm

3.   Peter de Rosa, *Vicars of Christ*, pages 73 and 259. Page 73 tells how Pope Innocent III demanded that all Catholic clergymen obey the Pope, even if he commanded them to do

something evil. Page 259 quotes Pope Pius X's statement that the Pope is the one hope of the world.

Claims made for the Pope
www.patmospapers.com/daniel/claims.htm

Pope Leo XIII, *Præclara Gratulationis Publicæ*, June 20, 1894. The first sentence of the fifth paragraph says that the Pope holds the place of God Almighty on earth. (If these addresses don't work for you, then do a search for "Leo XIII + Praeclara." Note that "Praeclara" has "AE." This spelling is unfamiliar for most Americans.)
www.aloha.net/~mikesch/l13-pgp.htm
www.users.qwest.net/~slrorer/ReunionOfChristendom.htm

Pope Innocent III said that he was the "Foundation of all Christianity." He also said that every Catholic clergyman must obey the Pope, even if the Pope orders him to do something evil, because nobody can judge the Pope. This article has information about many popes. Do a search for "Innocent III."

4. Code of Canon Law, pages 218 and 381, Canons 663 (Section 4) and 1237 (Section 2).
5. Code of Canon Law, pages 370-371, Canons 1186-1190. These are in Book IV, Part II, Title IV.
6. Article with pictures showing nuns changing the clothes of the statue
http://karmel.at/prag-jesu/english/eng/saticken.htm
Article with picture of a cardinal carrying the statue
www.medjugorjecenter.org/prague/page2.htm
Article with pictures showing details of the crown and some of the clothes
http://karmel.at/prag-jesu/english/eng/muzejen.htm
Article with pictures of the statue of the Infant of Prague (clothed and unclothed)
http://religion-cults.com/childjesus/prague.htm
Article with several pictures and history of the statue
http://karmel.at/prag-jesu/english/eng/jezuleen.htm
History of the Infant Jesus of Prague
www.cwo.com/~pentrack/catholic/infhist.html
7. Code of Canon Law, page 294, Canon 898.

Chapter 21—Mandatory Celibary

1. "Current Statistics and Facts." This article is on a Catholic website.
www.rentapriest.com/statistics.htm
2. Malachi Martin, *The Decline and Fall of the Roman Church*, pages 141-142.
John Shuster, "A Concise History of the Married Priesthood in Our Roman Catholic Tradition"
www.rentapriest.com/thirtynine_popes.htm
3. Philip S. Kaufman, *Why You Can Disagree—And Remain a Faithful Catholic* (New Expanded and Revised Edition) (New York: Crossroad, 1995), page 46. Kaufman is a Catholic priest. This chapter is online at a Catholic website. Some details come from the following articles. They are all on Catholic websites.
www.sja.osb.org/kaufman/chapter3.html
"Mating and Dating Among Eastern Rite Priests," *The National Catholic Reporter*, April 16, 2004. This article shows that early priests (and even popes) were allowed to marry. Four married popes are canonized saints. The Eastern Rite branch of the Catholic Church has married priests.
www.natcath.com/NCR_Online/archives2/2004b/041604/041604r.htm

"A Concise History of the Married Priesthood in Our Roman Catholic Tradition."
www.rentapriest.com/thirtynine_popes.htm
"Birth Control and the Catholic Church."
http://members.aol.com/revising/history.html
John Shuster, "39 Popes Were Married–Part IV," subtitle "Infallibility: A Man-Made Concept."
www.ffbcorpus.com/001204h.asp

4. Raymond A. Grosswirth, "Celibacy." The author is Catholic.
www.angelfire.com/ga2/religious/celibacy.html
5. Married Priests Website
www.marriedpriests.org
6. Good Tidings Ministry
www.marriedpriests.org/GoodTidings.htm
7. Ministries and Groups
www.marriedpriests.org/MinistriesAndGroups.htm
8. "Current Statistics and Facts." The is on a Catholic website.
www.rentapriest.com/statistics.htm
9. "Mating and Dating Among Eastern Rite Priests," *The National Catholic Reporter*, April 16, 2004. This article shows that early priests (and even popes) were allowed to marry. Four married popes are canonized saints. The Eastern Rite branch of the Catholic Church has married priests.
www.natcath.com/NCR_Online/archives2/2004b/041604/041604r.htm

Chapter 22—Mind Control

1. "Inquisition," *The Catholic Encyclopedia*, Volume VIII, 1910.
www.newadvent.org/cathen/08026a.htm
2. Ignatius Loyola, *The Spiritual Exercises* (1521-1535). These rules are quoted in Marvin Perry, Joseph R. Peden and Theodore H. Von Laue, *Sources of the Western Tradition: From Ancient Times to the Enlightenment*, Volume I, 4th edition (Boston, MA: Houghton Mifflin, 1999), pages 330-332. You can read these rules online. The addresses below have the "spiritual exercises" that are called, "Rules to Have the True Sentiment in the Church."
www.fordham.edu/halsall/source/loyola-spirex.html
http://faculty.wm.edu/rbsche/loyola.html
http://faculty.juniata.edu/tuten/loyola.html
http://departments.ozarks.edu/hfa/jwalden/worldciv2/loyola.htm

More addresses for the rules. These web pages have all of Loyola's "spiritual exercises." The one you want is called, "Rules to Have the True Sentiment in the Church." It is the last item on the list, at the bottom of the page. Click on it.
www.ccel.org/i/ignatius/exercises/exercises.html
www.intratext.com/X/ENG0036.htm

Another addresses for the rules. Search for "True Sentiment."
www.yale.edu/adhoc/etexts/ignatius_exercises.html

If these addresses don't work for you, then you can search for "Ignatius Loyola + Rules for Thinking with the Church," or for "Ignatius Loyola + Rules to Have the True Sentiment of the Church," or for "Ignatius Loyola + the True Sentiment which we Ought to have in the Church." You can also search for "Ignatius Loyola + Spiritual Exercises."

However, that is a more indirect route, because he has many spiritual exercises besides the "Rules for Thinking with the Church."

3. *Code of Canon Law*, pages 247 and 409, Canons 752-753, and 1311-1312. The 1983 *Code of Canon Law* was translated into English in 1988. It is available online. The following web pages have the Index of the book. The Index has links to the laws. Canons 752-753 are near the beginning of Book III. Canons 1311-1312 are in the beginning of Book VI. When you find the right place in the Index, you can search for the laws by canon number.

    Addresses of websites that have the *Code of Canon Law* are below. Some of them take a while to load after you click on the links. If you can't get through to the web page, then go to the home page and try to find it from there. If these addresses don't work, then do a search for "Code of Canon Law."
    www.intratext.com/X/ENG0017.htm
    www.ourladyswarriors.org/canon/
    www.deacons.net/Canon_Law/Frame_Index.htm
    www.smolchicago.com/Canon/cic_en.htm
    www.ung.com/Catholic_Resources.htm

    You can buy the *Code of Canon Law* from the Canon Law Society of America. For information, see Note 1 of Chapter 24 ("Canon Law and Religious Freedom").

4. *The Catechism of the Catholic Church*, paragraphs 85, 100, 113, 891, 2051. The *Catechism* is available online with a search engine. If these addresses don't work for you, then do an Internet search for "Catechism of the Catholic Church."
    www.scborromeo.org/ccc.htm
    www.christusrex.org/www2/kerygma/ccc/searchcat.html

5. *Catechism of the Catholic Church*, paragraphs 87, 2037.

6. *Ineffabilis Deus* (*Apostolic Constitution on the Immaculate Conception*). Encyclical of Pope Pius IX, issued December 8, 1854. Near the end of this papal bull there is a section called "The Definition." The statements that I described are in the last paragraph of that section. If these addresses don't work for you, then do a search for "Ineffabilis Deus."
    www.newadvent.org/docs/pi09id.htm
    www.pax-et-veritas.org/Popes/pius_ix/ineffabi.htm
    www.geocities.com/apologeticacatolica/ineffabilis.html
    www.naorc.org/documents/ineffabilis_deus.htm
    www.legacyrus.com/library/Vatican/ImmaculateConcept.htm

7. Paul Johnson, *A History of Christianity*, page 308.

8. The Congregation for the Doctrine of the Faith (formerly known as the Office of the Inquisition). This article is on the Vatican's website. [Click on "Profile."]
    www.vatican.va/roman_curia/congregations/cfaith/index.htm

    The Vatican website is slow and it doesn't always come up. You can also find information about the change of name of the Office of the Inquisition at the following websites.
    www.geocities.com/iberianinquisition/office.html
    http://es.rice.edu/ES/humsoc/Galileo/Student_Work/Trial96/breu/timeline.html
    http://news.bbc.co.uk/hi/english/world/europe/newsid_1251000/1251677.stm

9. Peter de Rosa, *Vicars of Christ*, page 72. This tells about Pope Innocent III's excommunication of people who supported the *Magna Carta*. De Rosa is a practicing Catholic and a former priest.

    This article has a lot of information about Pope Innocent III, including his excommunication of anybody who supported the *Magna Carta*. Go to the following web page and click on the time period 1200-1300. Do a search for Innocent III.
    www.goacom.com/overseas-digest/god.html

This article tells how Pope Innocent III condemned the *Magna Carta* as immoral. However, it does not mention the excommunication of people who supported it. The article has information about many popes. Do a search for "Innocent III."
www.whiterobedmonks.org/netsor1a.html

Articles about the influence of the *Magna Carta* on democracy in England and America. It was one of the foundational documents that influenced the American Constitution.
www.archives.gov/exhibit_hall/featured_documents/magna_carta/
www.blupete.com/Law/ConstitutionDocs/MagnaCarta.htm
www.crf-usa.org/Foundation_docs/Foundation_home.html
www.bl.uk/collections/treasures/magna.html

The *Magna Carta* is called the Great Charter of English Liberty. The text is online.
www.constitution.org/eng/magnacar.htm
www.britannia.com/history/magna2.html
www.cs.indiana.edu/statecraft/magna-carta.html
www.fordham.edu/halsall/source/mcarta.html

10. Joe Mizzi, "Liberty of Conscience." This is written by a citizen of Malta whose parents were subjected to the interdict.
www.justforcatholics.org/a76.htm

Dr. Mark F. Montebello, "Civil Rights in Malta's Post-Colonial Age," Part III, "Independence According to the British," first subheading, "The Most Shameful Episode." The author is a Catholic priest in Malta.
www.maltamag.com/features/civil_rights3.html

11. Dave Hunt, *A Woman Rides the Beast*, page 246.

This article begins by talking about Islam, but it has good information about popes coercing kings. It quotes the order that Pope Clement V gave to King Edward II, requiring the King to torture some men. (Use the FIND function to search for "torture.")
www.thechristianexpositor.org/page94.html

This article describes the methods of the Inquisition, including the pressure put on Edward II to torture some men. (Search for "torture.")
www.mosquitonet.com/~prewett/amer147.html

The men who were tortured were Knights Templar. This Templar website gives information about how Pope Clement V ordered King Edward II to torture the Templars. (Search for the word "torture.")
http://templarium.tripod.com/end.htm

I apologize for the tone and attitude of this article. However, the quotation from Pope Clement V is accurate. It is what I have in my source book. I don't have permission to quote it, so I'm making it available to you online. The quotation is at the very end of the first entry.
www.livejournal.com/users/dmsherwood53/278.html

Some Knights Templar were tortured in England under the reign of King Edward II. The Inquisitors complained to Pope Clement V that torture was not allowed. The Pope intervened by putting pressure on the King. As a result, special laws were passed in order to allow the torture.
www.pharo.com/history/templars/articles/mhte_13_trial.asp

12. *The Code of Canon Law*, page 86, Canon 273. This is in Book II, Chapter III.
13. Peter de Rosa, page 73. Pope Innocent III said that Catholic clergymen must obey the Pope, even if the Pope orders him to do something evil, because nobody can judge the Pope.

Information about this is in the following article. It has information about many popes. Use the FIND function to search for "Innocent III."
www.whiterobedmonks.org/netsor1a.html

14. Donald Goergen, *The Sexual Celibate* (New York: Seabury Press, 1975). This book is out of print, but you can buy it online. Amazon.com sometimes has used copies.

This web page has the table of contents, an excerpt from the Preface, and an excerpt from the book.
www.jknirp.com/goergen.htm

"They Didn't Think It Was Any Big Deal," *Mission*, July/August 2002. An article about sexuality at a Catholic seminary. It describes the book, *The Sexual Celibate*. To find the reference to the book in the article, search for "Sexual Celibate."
www.losangelesmission.com/ed/articles/2002/0702rk.htm

Some seminary lectures are based on the book. Modern seminarians read the book.
http://groups.yahoo.com/group/MonasticLife/message/3085

There is a modern book that deals with the theme of *The Sexual Celibate*. Keith Clark wrote, *Being Sexual...and Celibate* (Ave Maria Press, 1995). It is out of print, but Amazon.com sometimes has used copies.

A description of the book. Many books are described in this article. Do a search for "Keith Clark + Being Sexual."
www.bible.claret.org/new_2001.htm

An article by a nun. She tells of the influence that *Being Sexual...and Celibate* had on her. She includes some quotations from the book. (Search for "Keith Clark.")
http://sacred-quest.com/Articles/vows.htm

Books such as these, and classes based on them, contribute to moral corruption in modern Catholic seminaries. Michael S. Rose tells about it in his book, *Goodbye, Good Men: How Liberals Brought Corruption into the Catholic Church*. There is some detailed information about Rose's book in my chapter, "False Credentials."

Chapter 23—Serving Two Masters

1. Pope Pius IX, *The Syllabus of Errors*, December 8, 1864. In reading this, remember that Pius condemned every statement that you are reading. See the items numbered 15, 18, 24, 42, 54, 55, 77, 78, and 79. If these addresses don't work for you, then do an Internet search for "Syllabus of Errors."
www.reformation.org/syllabus_of_pius.html
www.geocities.com/papalencyclicals/Pius09/p9syll.htm
www.stthomasaquinas.net/encyclicals/Pius09/P9SYLL.HTM
www.catholic-pages.com/documents/pius_9/syllabus.htm

2. David I. Kertzer, *The Kidnapping of Edgardo Mortara*. The author has a website with a synopsis of the book and four book reviews.
www.davidkertzer.com/books_edgardo_a.htm [synopsis]
www.davidkertzer.com/books_edgardo_b.htm [book reviews]

Carole D. Bos, J.D. "The Kidnapping of Edgardo Mortara." This is a detailed discussion of the incident, with quotations from Canon Laws that were used to justify it. (Canon Laws provide the legal foundation for administering the Catholic Church.) The author has a doctorate in law.
www.lawbuzz.com/tyranny/mortara/mortara.htm

3. "Pius (Popes)," online edition of the 1911 Edition of the *Encyclopedia Britannica*. Most of the article deals with Pius IX. At the very end, there is a short paragraph about Pius X. Search for "concordat."
http://3.1911encyclopedia.org/P/PI/PIVOT.htm

   H. Wickham Steed, Walter Alison Phillips, and David Hannay, *A Short History of Austria-Hungary*. Chapter X, "Party Government in Austria." This book is reproduced from the eleventh edition of the *Encyclopaedia Britannica* by permission of the Publishers, The Cambridge University Press. (London: The Encyclopaedia Britannica Company, Ltd., 1914). The online edition reproduced by permission of the publishers, 1995. (Search for "concordat.")
http://historicaltextarchive.com/austria/chap10.htm

4. "Austro-Hungarian Monarchy," *Encyclopedia.com*. I have divided the address into two sections, because of its width.
www.encyclopedia.com/html/section/austrohu_thenatureofaustria-hungary.asp

5. "The Austrian Constitution of 1867"
www2.h-net.msu.edu/~habsweb/sourcetexts/auscon.htm

6. Peter de Rosa, *Vicars of Christ*, page 247. The author was a Catholic priest who did extensive research in the Vatican Archives. He left the priesthood in order to marry. He is a practicing Catholic. His book is a plea for reform within the Catholic Church.

7. Some articles that describe the 1874 Austrian *Law on Recognition* of churches.
http://atheism.about.com/library/irf/irf99/bl_irf_austria99.htm
www.usis.usemb.se/human/human1998/austria.html
http://religiousfreedom.lib.virginia.edu/nationprofiles/Austria/status.html

8. Pius IX, *Vix Dum a Nobis* (*On the Church in Austria*), March 7, 1874. If these addresses don't work for you, then do a search for "Vix Dum a Nobis."
www.catholic-forum.com/saints/pope0255jj.htm
www.ewtn.com/library/encyc/p9vixdum.htm

9. Peter de Rosa, page 247.

   Pius IX. (The information is in the last paragraph of the article.)
www.brooklyn.cuny.edu/bc/ahp/MBG/MBG4/PiusIX.html

10. Charles Krauthammer, "Why Didn't the Church Call the Cops?," *The Washington Post*, Friday, June 7, 2002, page A27.
www.washingtonpost.com/wp-dyn/articles/A9255-2002Jun6.html

11. Eric Convey and Tom Mashberg, "Law Grilled in Deposition," *Boston Herald*. Paragraphs 3 and 4 discuss Cardinal Law's dual citizenship and possible diplomatic immunity.
www2.bostonherald.com/news/local_regional/blaw05082002.htm

12. "Records: Ex-Bishop Ordered Stonewall of Abuse Investigation," *The Arizona Republic*, September 15, 2003.
www.azcentral.com/news/articles/0915priest-ON.html

    "Documents: Bishop Told Priest Not to Report Abuse to Police," *USA Today*, September 16, 2003.
www.usatoday.com/news/nation/2003-09-16-church-abuse_x.htm

    "Priest: Bishop Wanted Abuse Cases Hidden." This story by the Associated Press appeared in several online newspapers on September 16, 2003.
www.dfw.com/mld/dfw/news/nation/6786021.htm
www.guardian.co.uk/uslatest/story/0,1282,-3154968,00.html
www.centredaily.com/mld/centredaily/news/6786021.htm
www.fortwayne.com/mld/newssentinel/6786021.htm

www.ohio.com/mld/ohio/news/6786021.htm
www.macon.com/mld/macon/news/6786021.htm
www.kansas.com/mld/kansas/news/6786021.htm
www.belleville.com/mld/newsdemocrat/6786021.htm
www.grandforks.com/mld/grandforks/news/6786021.htm
www.grandforks.com/mld/grandforks/news/6786021.htm
www.phillyburbs.com/pb-dyn/news/1-09162003-160633.html

13. Articles about the beatification of Pope Pius IX. The author of the first article is a Catholic priest.
www.americapress.org/articles/Omalley-pius9.htm
www.concilium.org/english/PiusIX.htm
www.abc.net.au/am/s171619.htm
www.us-israel.org/jsource/anti-semitism/piusix.html
http://members.tripod.com/~dabz_2/updates/protest/protest.htm

14. "Beatification and Canonization," *The Catholic Encyclopedia*, Volume II, 1907.
www.newadvent.org/cathen/02364b.htm

15. "Vatican Sets Rules on Sex Abuse Cases." According to the Vatican: (1) Pedophile cases are subject to "pontifical secrecy." (2) Only Catholic priests should handle them. (3) Only priests should be judges, prosecutors, or defense advocates. (4) The cases should only be handled in church tribunals. (5) Once victims reach the age of 18, they only have 10 years to file complaints. In other words, they have to file a complaint before they reach age 29.
www.boston.com/globe/spotlight/geoghan/010902_vatican.htm

16. A columnist with *The Boston Globe* wrote an editorial saying that the Archdiocese of Boston was considering filing for bankruptcy in order to protect itself from lawsuits. It was published in *The Boston Globe* on December 8, 2002, with the title, "A New Chapter in Church Tale."
www.boston.com/dailyglobe2/342/oped/A_new_chapter_in_church_tale+.shtml

The same article was published in *The Washington Post* on December 9, 2002, with the title, "The Catholic Church."
www.postwritersgroup.com/archives/good1205.htm

Chapter 24—Canon Law and Religious Freedom

1. *Code of Canon Law*. Canon Laws provide the legal basis for what the Catholic Church does. Even the Inquisition and the persecution of Protestants were based on Canon Law. These are short laws, often consisting of only one sentence. All of them are contained in one 751-page book that costs $45.

    You can buy the *Code of Canon Law* from the Canon Law Society of America. Their phone number is (301) 362-8197. Ask for the Latin-English edition, New English Translation (text only). This edition was printed in 1999. If they no longer have it, then ask if there is a more recent edition. Be sure to get it in **English**. The Latin-English edition has both English and Latin. Some editions are only in Latin. Their website address is below. If it doesn't work, then do an Internet search for "Canon Law Society of America."
www.clsa.org

    You can order the book by phone from Newman Book Store in Washington, DC. (It is located near a number of seminaries.) They have two phone numbers (202-526-1036 and 202-526-1037).

Notes • 317

The ISBN number for the book is ISBN 0-943616-79-4. It used to be possible to order it through regular bookstores. However, in October, 2003, my local bookstores were no longer able to get it. If you want to try ordering it through a regular bookstore, you will need to give them the ISBN number.

2. "Has Roman Catholicism Changed? An Overview of Recent Canon Law"
www.gnfc.org/ant_v1n2_canon.html
www.reachingcatholics.org/rcchanged.html

3. The 1983 *Code of Canon Law* is available online. The following web pages have the Index of the book. The Index has links to the laws. Information is given below to help you locate the canons that are discussed in this chapter. If these addresses don't work for you, then do an Internet search for "Code of Canon Law."

Canons 204 and 205 are in the beginning of Book II. Canon 665 is in Book II, Part III, Section I, Title II, Chapter IV. Canons 750 and 752 are in the beginning of Book III. Canon 825 is in Book III, Title IV. Canon 1311 is in the beginning of Book VI. Canon 1366 is in Book VI, Part II, Title I. Canon 1371 is in Book VI, Part II, Title II.

When you find the right place in the Index, you can search for the laws by canon number. (Click on EDIT. Click on FIND. Type the number of the law and hit ENTER.)

Addresses of websites that have the *Code of Canon Law* are below. Some of them take a while to load after you click on the links. If you can't get through to the web page, then go to the home page and try to find it from there. [To find the home page, delete everything that comes after "com," "org," or "net."]
www.intratext.com/X/ENG0017.htm
www.ourladyswarriors.org/canon/
www.deacons.net/Canon_Law/Frame_Index.htm
www.smolchicago.com/Canon/cic_en.htm

This website will not allow you to go directly to the *Code of Canon Law*. You have to go through their home page. Look for "Code of Canon Law" on the home page, and click on it.
www.ung.com/Catholic_Resources.htm

Chapter 25—The Presence of God

1. Monstrances are ornate containers that are used to display Hosts (large, consecrated communion wafers) so that people can worship the Hosts. Websites with color pictures are given below. Following are pictures of monstrances. Some have Hosts in them.
www.monstrans-de-kel.nl/monst6.html
www.lightofmary.org/coadorermonpic.htm
www.gachaska.org/monstrancesunburstaltar.htm
http://pages.tias.com/1056/PictPage/523111.html

Two web pages, each having 12 small pictures of monstrances. If you click on them, you will see larger pictures.
www.monstrans-de-kel.nl/foto_index1.html

Websites where people come to look at a picture of a consecrated Host that is inside a monstrance. They look at the Host and worship it.
www.monksofadoration.org/chapel.html
www.savior.org
http://members.core.com/~orcat27/tour0.htm

Chapter 26—Catholic Mysticism

1. Following are some Internet articles with information about pagan mysticism
    Mysticism in the World's Religions
    www.unityarts.com/mysticisminworldreligions.html
    Hindu and Muslim Mysticism
    www.unityarts.com/hinduandmuslimmysticism.html
    Sufi/Islami mysticism
    www.digiserve.com/mystic/Muslim/
    Hindu mysticism
    www.digiserve.com/mystic/Hindu/
    Buddhist mysticism
    www.digiserve.com/mystic/Buddhist/
    www.hindutva.org/AnwarShaikh/Mysticism/BuddhistMysticism.html
2. Randy England, *The Unicorn in the Sanctuary: The Impact of the New Age on the Catholic Church*, pages 75-77. The author is Catholic.

    Ray Yungen, *A Time of Departing: How a Universal Spirituality Is Changing the Face of Christianity*, pages 60-63. According to Yungen, Thomas Merton was heavily involved in the mysticism of the Sufis (Islamic mystics). He promoted Buddhist and Hindu mystical traditions. He has been a strong New Age influence on Catholicism. His influence is now spreading to mainline Protestant denominations.

    An article about Thomas Merton's appreciation for Eastern mysticism
    www.angelfire.com/ky/dodone/Merton.html
3. Randy England, pages 6-9 and 135-146.
4. Randy England, pages 101-107.
5. Abbot M. Basil Pennington, "Saint Bernard of Clairvaux, 1090-1153"
    www.osb.org/cist/bern.html
6. "St. Bernard of Clairvaux," *The Catholic Encyclopedia*, Volume II, 1907.
    www.newadvent.org/cathen/02498d.htm
7. "Bernard of Clairvaux, Saint," online edition of the *Columbia Encyclopedia*
    www.bartleby.com/65/be/BernardCSt.html
8. Painting of Bernard of Clarivaux kneeling before Mary as Queen of Heaven
    www.kfki.hu/keptar/english/p/pesce/muvek/szbernat.html
9. There is a quotation under the heading "Readings" that is attributed to Saint Bernard of Clairvaux
    www.catholic-forum.com/saints/saintb08.htm
10. "A Mystical Legend on Canvas" (from a Franciscan website)
    www.americancatholic.org/Messenger/Dec1997/Wiseman.asp
11. "Saint Catherine of Siena Virgin"
    www.ewtn.com/library/MARY/CATSIENA.htm
    "St. Catherine of Siena," *The Catholic Encyclopedia*, Volume III, 1908.
    www.newadvent.org/cathen/03447a.htm
12. Julian of Norwich
    www.saintnicholas.contactbox.co.uk/archive/julian.htm
13. "Mary and the Holy Spirit in the Writings of John of the Cross"
    www.icspublications.org/archives/others/cs6_10.html
14. The Brown Scapular
    www.rc.net/lansing/ctk/cc/ocds1.html
    www.cin.org/saints/brownsca.html

15. "Saint Teresa of Jesus and the Virgin Mary"
    www.helpfellowship.org/Info/st_teresa%20and%20mary.htm
16. "Mary and the Holy Spirit in the Writings of John of the Cross"
    www.icspublications.org/archives/others/cs6_10.html
17. Order of Nazorean Essenes
    http://essenes.crosswinds.net/bnei7.htm
18. "Madame Jeanne Guyon, Method of Prayer, 1648-1717"
    homechurch.org/spirituality/guyon_prayer.html
    "Quietism," *The Catholic Encyclopedia*, Volume XII, 1911.
    www.newadvent.org/cathen/12608c.htm
19. "Quietism," online edition of the *Columbia Encyclopedia*, sixth edition, 2001.
    www.bartleby.com/65/qu/quietism.html

Chapter 27—Mixing Paganism with Christianity

1. A picture of Pope John Paul II, at the multi-faith service in Assisi, Italy, which he convened and led In October, 1986. Leaders of pagan religions participated, praying to their gods. I apologize for the harsh tone of the text that accompanies this picture. It is on an ultra-conservative Catholic website called True Catholic. They believe that the Pope is a heretic, because he has said and done things that are contrary to Catholic doctrine, as declared by previous popes and Catholic Church councils.
   www.truecatholic.org/nop/jp2assisi.htm

   "October 1986: The Day Assisi Became the 'Peace Capitol' of the World," *American Catholic*, January 1987. This takes a while to load because it has some pictures.
   www.americancatholic.org/Features/Assisi/PeaceCapital.asp

   John Cotter, "Assisi Assessed," Saint Benedict Center. The author is a Catholic who is an expert on syncretism (combining Christianity with pagan religions).
   www.catholicism.org/PAGES/Assisi.htm

   This article appears to be written by a conservative Catholic. It has a number of pictures. One of them shows Pope John Paul II at the multi-faith service at Assisi in 1986. This web page takes a while to load, because of the pictures.
   www.geocities.com/Vienna/Strasse/5816/jp2.html

2. A picture of the altar that was used for the religious service in Assisi. There is a statue of Buddha on top of the Tabernacle (an ornate container for consecrated bread).
   www.truecatholic.org/nop/jp2buddha.htm

3. An article about the multi-faith service that Pope John Paul II convened at Assisi, in 2002. Leaders of pagan religions participated in the service.
   www.catholic-ew.org.uk/CN/02/020123.htm

   An article from CNN. It includes descriptions of the multi-faith services at Assisi in both 1986 and 2002.
   www.cnn.com/2002/WORLD/europe/01/24/pope.assisi0825/

4. A picture of the Pope with a Buddhist patriarch. The text gives quotations from the Pope, including his statement that salvation can be found through Buddhism.
   www.truecatholic.org/nop/jp2buddhist.htm

5. The Pope visited Benin. He apologized because westerners have rejected African religions, including voodoo. This article is written by an African who endorses African religions and approves of what the Pope did.
   www.mamiwata.com/pope.html

http://afgen.com/afr_pope.html
www.secularhumanism.org/ahal/ReligionCult.html#ANewLook
6. These books are available at Amazon.com.
7. Randy England, *Unicorn in the Sanctuary: The Impact of the New Age on the Catholic Church*, pages 72-74.
8. Randy England, pages 70-72.
9. Peter Jones, *Pagans in the Pews: How the New Spirituality Is Invading Your Home, Church and Community*, page 127.
10. A series of 27 web pages with color pictures of the Sistine Chapel. Three of these web pages have pictures of prophets and sybils. A sybil is a pagan prophetess.
www.christusrex.org/www1/sistine/0-Tour.html

    If this address doesn't work for you, then go to the home page and click on "The Sistine Chapel." If that doesn't work, then do an Internet search for "Christus Rex." You can also search for "Sistine Chapel + picture," or "Christus Rex + Sistine Chapel."
www.christusrex.org

    Pictures of Raphael's painting, *The School of Athens*. Some of these pictures will be enlarged if you click on them. This is a fresco, which means that it is painted on plaster.
www.artchive.com/artchive/R/raphael/school_athens.jpg.html
http://un2sg4.unige.ch/athena/raphael/raf_ath4.html
www.christusrex.org/www1/stanzas/S2-Segnatura.html
11. A series of 22 web pages with color pictures of the Vatican museums. A number of them have statues of Greek, Roman, and Egyptian gods and goddesses.
www.christusrex.org/www1/vaticano/0-Musei.html

    If this address doesn't work for you, then go to the home page and click on "The Vatican Museums." If that doesn't work, then do an Internet search for "Christus Rex." You can also search for "Vatican Museums + picture" or "Christus Rex + Vatican Museums."
www.christusrex.org
12. A series of 14 web pages with color pictures of Saint Peter's Basilica, the Pontifical Palace, and the Vatican Gardens. Each page has a number of small pictures that give different perspectives and details. If you click on them, you will see larger pictures.
www.christusrex.org/www1/citta/0-Citta.html

    If this address doesn't work for you, then go to the home page and click on "The Vatican City." If that doesn't work, search for "Christus Rex." You can also search for "St. Peter's + picture," or "Christus Rex + Saint Peter's," or "Christus Rex + St. Peter's."
www.christusrex.org
13. "Tacitus on the Christians." This historical document describes the martyrdom of Christians in the Circus Maximus.
www.livius.org/cg-cm/christianity/tacitus.html

    Description and picture of the Circus Maximus. It mentions the obelisk.
www.crystalinks.com/romearchitecture.html

    The Circus Maximus (Circus of Nero, where Christians were slaughtered)
www.romeguide.it/MONUM/ARCHEOL/ccircus_maximus/circus.htm

    An article about the Obelisk from the Circus Maximus. In 1587, Pope Sixtus V had it dug up and placed in the center of the circular courtyard in front of Saint Peter's Basilica.
http://itsa.ucsf.edu/~snlrc/encyclopaedia_romana/circusmaximus/obelisk.html

    This travel narrative describes Saint Peter's Basilica and the Circus Maximus. A picture of Saint Peter's shows the obelisk from the Circus Maximus in the center of a great circular courtyard in front of Saint Peter's.
www.aerenlund.dk/rom/rome_day3.html

Pictures of the Obelisk in front of Saint Peter's Basilica. (If you click on the small pictures, you will see larger ones.)
www.christusrex.org/www1/citta/B-Exterior.html
If this address doesn't work, then go to the address below and click on "Basilica di San Pietro: Exterior."
www.christusrex.org/www1/citta/0-Citta.html
If that doesn't work, then go to the home page. The address is below. If that doesn't work, then do an Internet search for "Christus Rex."
www.christusrex.org

Chapter 28—Behind the Mask

1. *The Code of Canon Law*, Canon 1311.
2. "Pius (Popes)," online edition of the 1911 Edition of the *Encyclopedia Britannica*. Most of the article deals with Pius IX. At the very end, there is a short paragraph about Pius X. Use the FIND function to search for "concordat."
http://3.1911encyclopedia.org/P/PI/PIVOT.htm
H. Wickham Steed, Walter Alison Phillips, and David Hannay, *A Short History of Austria-Hungary*. Chapter X, "Party Government in Austria." This book is reproduced from the eleventh edition of the *Encyclopaedia Britannica* by permission of the Publishers. To find the information about the 1855 concordat, use the FIND function to search for "concordat."
http://historicaltextarchive.com/austria/chap10.htm
3. Charles Krauthammer, "Why Didn't the Church Call the Cops?," *The Washington Post*, Friday, June 7, 2002, page A27.
www.washingtonpost.com/wp-dyn/articles/A9255-2002Jun6.html
Eric Convey and Tom Mashberg, "Law Grilled in Deposition," *Boston Herald*. Paragraphs 3 and 4 discuss Cardinal Law's dual citizenship and possible diplomatic immunity.
www2.bostonherald.com/news/local_regional/blaw05082002.htm
4. Mike Gendron, "Protestant Pastors Converting to Rome," *Proclaiming the Gospel* (March/April 2004, Vol. 13, No. 2), page 3. The author is a former Catholic. You can read his newsletter online. These statistics only include pastors who contacted the Coming Home Network, which was founded in 1993. They do not include pastors who converted before 1993, or who converted without contacting the network. They also do not include pastors who are considering converting to Catholicism, but have not contacted the network.
www.pro-gospel.org
5. I read an Internet article about an entire church that converted to Catholicism. At the time, I didn't know that I would be writing this book, and I didn't keep the website address. I've searched for that article, but I haven't been able to find it again.
6. A member of that church contacted me several times, asking for advice. He was very distressed by the situation.

Afterword

1. *The Rites of the Catholic Church* (New York: Pueblo Publishing Co., 1990), Volume 1, pages 394-407. Quoted in James G. McCarthy, *The Gospel According to Rome: Comparing Catholic Tradition and the Word of God*, page 22.

0-595-31678-6

Printed in the United States
99133LV00005B/146/A